Beautiful Waters

An Urgent Message from Mother Waters to Her Children

By Omileye Achikeobi - Lewis

A Naked Truth Book

UK, United States

A Naked Truth Book
P. O. Box 461
South Carolina, SC 29720
www.yeyeosun.com

This book is printed in the United States of America
August 2012

0-9542066-6-5

978-0-9542066-6-6

Library of Congress Control Number: 2013900012

I would like to dedicate this book to my son Kem Ra, baby daughter Omololu and all the children of the world

You've been walking in circles, searching. Don't drink by the water's edge. Throw yourself in. Become the water. Only then will your thirst end.

-Jeanette Berson

CONTENTS

With each chapter may the original Wisdoms be ignited

Acknowledgements

I would like to thank the Divine Mother, Divine Father, All the Holy Ones, the Ancestors, My Mother Remah, my brother Jeff, husband Derrick, son Kem Ra, daughter Omololu, Chief Popoola, Chief Agboola, Beckee Garris, Ann Rosencranz, Bob Boyll, Ellen Whiteside, Chief Holy Eagle, Chief Randall, USCL Library staff who encouraged me on this journey, and all those who made it possible. Thank You

In one drop of water are found all the secrets of all the oceans; in one aspect of you are found all the aspects of existence.

— Khalil Gibran

Introduction

*Since almost all archaeological work today is carried out on land, we are probably missing
the artifacts that are hidden in water*
-Spencer Wells

Recently, as I was finishing this book, I was warned by an elder from Africa,

"the oracle says you must share your messages from the mother and ancient ones with the world before it is too late. If you don't your health, along with that of the worlds will suffer."

What does one say to that? So I hesitate no longer and invite you to take a swim with me into this journey. I suppose the first thing to know about it is that I have written more introductions for this book than you would care to know about. Including one that I thought sounded very clever, and would impress clever people such as academics. However, that small voice that has guided me for my whole life clearly stated, "write from the heart". Writing from the heart (in fact living from it) can be very scary, but now I believe doing so is fully necessary for living courageously in these times.

This journey started in a strange way and called me to live life from a different perspective. It asked me to suspend all belief, and everything I thought was real to walk an ancient road that would take me deep into the Belly of the Whale and a sort of Dreamtime Awakening. That place and time from which all ancient wisdom arises.

My calling started with a series of three dreams where a beautiful woman asked me to help her save the world. As serendipity would have it, a few weeks later a well-respected

African Priest and theologian turned up in the Caribbean where I had relocated to with my mom. Unfortunately, for me (it felt highly unfortunate at the time) when he consulted the oracle he confirmed my dream was indeed a calling and one that I had contracted to fulfill before I had even left heaven. It was at that point my whole world turned upside down, and all reality (as I understood it) began to slip away. For the oracle told me that I had no choice but to take this mission on.

The whole thing sounded totally bizarre, and a little Harry Potterish. I mean how does an ordinary person end up with a life mission to help an Old World Mother Goddess save the Earth? The priest told me with all the aura of seriousness that wrapped around him like a blanket,

"the answer will be revealed to you".

He was right, it was. But it made no sense. The only answer I received was to "go to water", and to document everything.

Bewildered, I did not know what else to do but to take the instruction quite literally. I religiously journaled everything that happened along the way. What was strange was how everything that unfolded seemed to have a logical order to it. This book is merely a documentation of all that happened, exactly as it happened and in the way it was revealed to me. It was not written after the fact, but with every footstep taken. I also gathered a small group of people together, and we went to the waterways to pray. In those early days I felt a little, no a lot, foolish. For what was going to the waterways to pray going to do for the world? At the time, I was quite a hardnosed journalist, and a very analytical person. So praying at the waterways to help save our world just didn't seem to cut it for me.

However, as the journey went on, and each time I visited a waterways an amazing thing started to happen. I began to develop the ability (at first without realizing it) to hear the messages from the waters. The energy of water began to lead me. Mystical experiences such as books falling into my hands (I mean that literally), instructional dreams, people bringing me important information, began to happen more often than not in my life. I was in a place and space where the reality we see with our eyes open, and the one we see with our eyes closed began to meld into each other like an exquisite painting.

What was more amazing was how the waters seemed to magically throw jigsaw pieces into my life which appeared to contain some kind of spiritual DNA encoding of humanity. As well as ancient wisdom detailing cosmic laws on living in balance with the all. As I rose, albeit reluctantly, to the challenge of the decoding I was taken on a fascinating white knuckle (and quite exhausting) boat ride across continents, cultures, languages, waterways, mystical sites and the ancient ruins of old civilizations.

As I unraveled the strings of spiritual DNA code that began to appear before me - a monumental story started to unfold itself. It was our story, and the tale of our Earth from the beginnings of time. One that was cleverly secreted away in the symbols, stories, songs and iconographies of the Old World Water Mother Goddesses of various cultures. Who rose and sung themselves and us back to an interwoven cloth of oneness again. They even solved mysteries that have puzzled Anthropologists for eons, as they song the primordial Songlines back awake again. Those tracks, that contain the laws of existence, and help us to trace our origins back to the First Times. For according to the Aborigine they were left behind by the first Creator Beings of the Dreamtime. They say that the Songlines must be sung in order for the Earth not to die.

14

During the course of being swept away by the rushing currents of time I discovered an overwhelming message from the waters - we are in trouble, big trouble. The polluted waterways are dying and we with them. This is something the scientist can see clearly. However, there is something more subtle that they don't see. That warns us of the danger of the choices we have and are making. These are the disappearing and even re-appearing symbols that are traditionally associated with Mother Earth, as Goddess. They include her honey bees, birth of the White Lions of South Africa, and the birth of the White buffaloes. Of course, water itself is a symbol of Mother Earth, and as stated, it is dying rapidly.

It is now agreed that clean available drinking water is becoming even rarer than it already is (There's only one percent of fresh drinking water available to the whole plant). In fact, nowadays water is referred to as Blue Gold. It is becoming more and more of a commodity, which is being more and more abused. However, as we abuse the waters, we abuse ourselves, and the worse we make our future. We become like a frog that dares to drink its own home. Scientist say we are swiftly heading towards a sixth extinction caused by one species, and one species only - us.

Ancient Cultures did not believe that water is a commodity. They have always believed that it is sacred, and the ancient holding pot of a deep compassionate consciousness. Their belief about water and its sentience is encoded within their stories, songs, and laws. In the Egyptian Book of the Dead the 42nd Negative Confession states, "I have not polluted the waters".

When I travelled to Osogbo, Nigeria I witnessed the sentience of water honored in a very real way. Epitomized as the Mother Osun (who is seen as the Universal Mother of all) she is treated with the highest regard (even by the succession

15

of Muslim Kings who have ruled the region). In fact, the locals believe that the day Mother Osun is not treated like the Queen she is - poverty, pestilence and all the bad things of life would befall the place.

After this long journey I too cannot help but believe (and by now I definitely cannot deny it) that water is indeed a sacred force to be reckoned with. It definitely does appear to hold this astounding consciousness and ability to raise our own to a higher level. As all things on Earth contain water, and as we are 70% water I believe we have an ancient and special resonates with it. When it holds its mirror up to our hearts it affords us the ability to see a deeper truth. This function of water is represented by the Goddess iconography of her upheld mirror.

Where am I now with this journey? I bow my head deeply to our Mother Earth and Mother Waters. I bow deeply to all the ancient ones who came to make this journey and the decoding possible. I thank them for showing that alone we can go fast, but together we can go far. So we must go together. I thank them for making this easier for us to embrace, by helping us to understand that we are truly part of one unbroken river of Maat, now called the Dharma. The river that emphasizes the interconnection of all living things, and upholding of cosmic law for the benefit of Seven Generations. The Navajo call this river Hozho, "to walk in beauty".

Mother Earth and Waters has this way of helping one find and accept the magic of life. I no longer fight how this information came about. Nor do gawk in disbelief at how it emerged from deep within the primordial watery womb of Mother Earth and my dreams. I now accept there is another way of research and finding things, especially since reading Tenzin Wangyal Rinpoche's "The Tibetan Yogas of Dream and Sleep" where he states,

16

"volumes of teachings have been "discovered" this way (through dreams), including many of the practices of the practices that Tibetans have been doing for centuries. This is what we call "mind treasures" (gong-ter). Imagine entering a cave and finding a volume of teachings hidden inside. This is finding in a physical space. Mind treasures are found in the consciousness rather than in the physical world. Masters have been known to find these treasures both in dreams of clarity and when awake."

I found it interesting that my son calls this written documentation of my five year journey "The Thousand Year Old Book". It seemed like an appropriate title since this book never did seem to stop writing itself. It is divided into 16 Lamps which in Africa represent the first 16 Wisdoms/Prophets who came and gave the Earth its wisdom, and divine laws. As each chapter is read, so too is the lamp of each Wisdom lit. The stories that open the chapters are from the 16 Wisdom's original oracle corpus. They are there for you to drink deeply from. The honoring of these 16 Wisdoms happens at the annual Osun sacred festival where 16 Lamps are lit. The four Ashe's at the end of the book is the way in which the Yoruba culture of West Africa seal their prayers.

My main hope is that the powerful messages and revelations from our great Mother Waters, Earth, and those wise ones gone by reaches all our ears. That we each hear their song calling us back to the ceaseless river of oneness, love, compassion and togetherness. That we all understand that returning back to this nourishing river will help us to mend our broken world. It may be well worth noting that Spencer Wells who wrote "The Journey of Man" stated many of the answers to our history may well lie under the waters.

Is it a coincidence that our Mother Waters and Earth has chosen this time to deliver her poignant message and guidance to her children? I don't think so. We have just entered what is being heralded as the New Dawn. The old one of 5000 years has now ended, as I conclude this book. Now we are in a New Era which will be governed by the choices we chose to continue to make. It is also governed by the two potent astrological energies of Aquarius (the celestial Water Messenger), and Leo. In fact, an ancient South African prophecy reveals that it was the Rain Queen and the Lion Queen who had worked together to protect the Love and balance on Earth.

Now it's time to meander with Mother Waters, and catch the Golden Ball.

BOOK I

CATCHING THE GOLDEN BALL

Ogbe Meji

Double Blessings

*Once upon a time there was a man and a woman. The man really
wanted a baby who he could love and care for. The woman, his wife
was not really bothered about this. The man prayed every day to
make his wish come true. One day God seemed to answer this wish
because he had a beautiful baby boy. Now this baby boy was born in
very ancient times. In times when people had taboos and stuck to
them. The man's taboo was drinking palm wine and the woman's
was having salt. The man's wife was known to be quite mean
spirited. One day he went to get her some food from the market and
he was a little late coming home. The woman who was angry decided
to put palm wine in his food. On seeing this the child told the father
when he came home. "father do not eat that food you will die." The
father looked around the house and saw no one. The small voice said
again, "father do not eat that food you will die, Mama put palm wine
in your food." Soon the father realized it was the child who was
talking. He was astonished and took the child's advice. Out of his
anger he decided to put salt in his wife's food. When he left the house
the wife came home. She went to eat the food but the son said,
"Mama don't eat that food father put salt in the food." The mother
looked around, could not see where the voice was coming from and
proceeded to begin her meal. But a small voice said, "Mama don't eat
that food father put salt in the food." This time the woman saw it was*

her son and she did not eat the food. The woman was so upset that she went and told the whole village. A court was held and when it came to hear who warned the parents they were shocked to hear it was the baby. "Babies of that age don't talk," said the father of justice Ogun. "This one does," said the baby's father. They tested the baby and found he could talk. Everyone was astonished and said the baby was very special. Because of that and the fact the baby had saved both parents he was called, "Ogbe Meji" "double blessings"

"This place is cold and I just want to leave." It was 2005, and mum was shivering and making her way to the car almost sliding on the ice. I was shivering too, and almost had tears in my eyes. London was almost minus something degrees and we both were not happy. Especially since the Traffic Officer had given us a ticket for not having a parking ticket displayed on our dash board. When we in fact did. Even showed him the ticket, but he really wasn't interested in the facts. He just wanted to "do his job". It was like talking to a robot and that was London. Sometimes talking to people in positions of "power" was a bit like that. If they had a bad day, you sure as bet you were going to have a bad day too. He was obviously having a bad day with the ice and freezing weather beating up against his face. So he was going to give us a bad one. He succeeded in all his intents.

"We are leaving this place," mum said gritting her teeth against the icy cool and getting into the car.

The car would not start up immediately because it was so cold. Mum's face never lost that look of determination until approximately one year latter we were in the Islands. Now we did not go to beautiful white sanded beach Jamaica. The land of her birth. No, we ended up in Trinidad the land of my father's birth.

There is something about destiny you just can't run away from it. Now what determines destiny I am not quite sure. Some people say you write a contract before you leave heaven. I am sure there's a lot of truth in that. I also think destiny is written in the ancient stones of one's family lineage. The ancient stones of my family's lineage had written on them our gift to "See" and dream. In the Islands we were known as a family of dreamers and seers.

22

I remembered the first time I moved to Trinidad from London. I was ten years old and I stayed there for three years with Tanti (that was the name we called my paternal Great Aunt). Every weekend I remembered people of all ages, shapes, colors and sizes coming to her house to have their dreams interpreted.

I also remembered Mrs. Jackson's daughter who lived opposite Tanti's house coming home one day and acting like she was possessed, ripping her clothes off and calling down the devil. Her mother took her to their local priest, but after he finished with her she was still calling out the devil's name.

After over a week of this, her family realized the preacher had not cured her. They got scared and fed up of her screaming all the time, and came over to Tanti's old wooden house. I can't remember totally what she did. But I know she did a whole lot of praying and within a few days that girl's spirit calmed right down, and she became as right as rain.

According to my family one woman from every generation became the chief carrier of the lineage gift of dreaming and seeing. It was many many years latter in my mid 30's that I was told I was that woman. It surprised me and not. Since a teenager I was very aware that I had the family gift. Unfortunately for me I could see everyone's lives. I remember one day how a family relative came to visit us. She was telling my mom how happy her relationship was, but all I saw was misery.

Then there were the dreams. The ones that told me what was going to happen long before things happened, and gave me odd directions. One dream, in particular I had when I was doing my undergraduate degree at London University's School of Oriental and African Studies (SOAS). It rose from the mist of my life in all its vibrant blues, joyful yellows, and edible orange. I still remember that dream to this day. It seemed to seal my fate.

In it I rode on a London tube with white collared workers looking all smart and ready for their desk jobs. It appeared to be a normal London working day. That was until these very poor African women boarded. I remember how I shamefully turned away from their screeching poverty, dark skins and tattered clothes. I sunk down in my seat trying to slide out of my ancestral connection with them all together. As I sat on the train all brown red faced I remember the tube driver shouting over his mic,

"next stop is Africa! Get prepared to get off!"

Suddenly I seemed engulfed in this dilemma, should I get off or should I stay on, and continue onward towards the heart of London? I was acutely aware that to get off would mean leaving all that I knew behind, including my family. I was torn in pieces.

Then the train stopped. I felt myself float of my seat, heard myself say goodbye to my mother who was present, and made contact with warm white sand. When I looked around I was on a beautiful beach with vibrant blue waters. The water was so beautiful. No breathtaking. As I took in the scene about five children ran up to me. They spoke a strange language.

They tried their hardest to communicate with me, but neither of us had any success in understanding the other. So they led me by the hand until we reached the soft peaks of a small sand dune. Then they pointed to the bottom. At the bottom were ten women dressed from head to toe in deep blue. They appeared to have their heads pressed together. Their backs were facing me. I was transfixed by their presence. Then they turned around, very slowly, as if they had sensed me standing there staring at them. When our eyes met, their arms stretched out towards me. My body lifted off the ground and literally floated down to them, landed in the midst of their presence, and became wet by the force of their tear drops. I cried, and as I did so a warm feeling overcame me and I felt as though I had arrived home.

When I woke up I strangely thought of my great great paternal grandmother, Grannil Rosalie. My birth name is for her. Even though I had never met her and she died at a 128 (when I was five), I felt as though I knew her very well. I always sensed her presence. Apparently I look like her too (only Grannil Rosalie was much darker than me). When I woke up from the dream I could feel her presence. She wanted me to do something. She wanted me to change my name to an African one.

"If I could have chosen my own name I would have given myself an African name," I could hear her say to me.

I felt different after that dream. I can't really explain how or what was different, but I just felt different. I had this strong sense of my lineage, of all the age old wisdom that had gone before, and that I must never forget it. In fact, somehow it was as though I was to seek it out.

Straight after the dream I frantically began to look for an African name. I felt driven. I borrowed several African name books from the college library, but nothing grabbed me. If I was going to change my name to honor Grannil Rosalie it had to be a name that grabbed me. It was three weeks into my search when I had almost given up on finding a suitable one when I collided into Ogonna, as we both left the student bar (we first met right there in the student bar that night where a student meeting was going ahead). Fate had it that both he and I were heading to the campus library for some late night revision. We chatted easily on our way to our destination, as if we had known each other for years.

When we reached the library we chatted some more. I found out that he was an Igbo priest doing a PHD in Igbo Religion and Language. At some point in our conversation, and for some reason I didn't quite understand I blurted out,

"do you know the name Achikeobi?"

Ogonna looked at me for a little while all strange, and eventually replied,

"that name is from my region. It is from the Niger region of Nigeria. It's an Igbo name, and it means - One Who Gathers and Rules the People. In fact there is a famous family with that name called the Chikeobi family. They became famous because they have a famous world renown mathematician in the family called professor Chikeobi. In fact, the family has had quite a few outstanding achievements throughout history. Chikeobi would really be traditionally spelt Achikeobi, but in Igboland many times we do not pronounce the first letter of a name."

My heart thumped wildly. It felt as though a piece of destiny had landed on my doorstep. It was actually Grannil Rosalie's father African John Achikeobi who had insisted on the family always remembering their name. They, (my dad, aunts and great aunts) say that African John Achikeobi arrived in Trinidad as a free man. He was a diplomat and was given a lot of land. I know this story must be true, because I remember when I grew up for those few years I spent in Trinidad how my father use to bring home bags of mangos and cashews from Tanti's lands. I didn't like the cashews but I would munch on at least a whole sack of mangos. Dad would often say to me,

"Girl the family's not rich in money but it is rich in land."

I would nod with young interest as I tore into those mangoes.

Dad also often complained that soon the family would have no riches left because it used its land for equity. So every time something was needed in the family a plot of land was sold.

After Ogonna told me about the Surname Achikeobi. I next blurted out my dream. Once again he stared at me strangely and said with quiet consideration,

"That dream is a message. It is a message about you changing your name to Ezolaagbo. One Who Returns the Lineage Home."

He said this without any hesitation. My heart opened up like a flower. It felt right. I could feel Grannil Rosalie smiling. A week later I changed my name legally to Ezolaagbo and Adaugo (another name he gave me) Adaugo was to be my middle name. Ogonna explained it meant Daughter of the Eagle.

After my name change my dreams became even more pronounced, and it felt like an electrical current was pulling me towards something to do with the ancient past. I just never knew exactly what to do with the ancient past it was pulling me towards.

After SOAS I fell within the deep embrace of my first love, writing. An opportunity to work as a feature news writer on the prestigious National Black Newspaper called The Voice fell on my lap. At first the fast pace of the job was thrilling, but then something began to feel as though it was missing. I realized that I loved writing mostly about things that would truly help people, but then I found out Journalism wasn't all about writing what you loved. It was often about writing about things you didn't,

"and that is what a Jobbing Journalist is all about my dear," said an older reporter to me one day.

She was trying to coach me and show me what was what. But the more she spoke about the reality of what Journalism was about, was the more sunk. As every day on the paper went by I knew there was something more for me. The clarity as to what I wanted to do, came in the form of Ms. Jackie Holder, and the sun bouncing through her hair. One day she burst confidently into our small newsroom, with a story in her hand.

After speaking to her, I knew empowering women was what I wanted to do (at least for the next stage of my life). Destiny had me, and it had me for a good few years. I got well into the healing stuff. I organized empowerment workshops for women, wrote books, met HRH Prince Charles as part of the award I was given by the Prince's Trust for the work I did with women, and was generally happy. Then one day something happened, I felt all burnt out and wanted to do what normal people did – go to a nine to five job. I packed up my healing work and did just that.

Of course, I was far from happy, and had very little soul contentment, but I didn't want to be on the healing path anymore. It stayed that way until Tony, my brother, died. It was his death that got me back on track. I didn't want to see not even one other person die from not knowing their soul purpose and from the inner loneliness that can produce. In fact I didn't want to see anyone die from anything that could be aided into healing through natural remedies.

I think knowing all of this about me will help you to understand a little about how my destiny was always a strange one from the start; and why I believe it is my love of writing, and intuitive ability to analyze things (a skill you have to have as a journalist) that helped me piece together the ancient higgley piggly jigsaw puzzle that was to lay itself at my feet.

Talk about noise, chaos and festivity. That was Trinidad. It was late 2006 when mom achieved her dream of moving from London. I moved with her. That was a hard one, because I didn't want to leave Kem Ra, my son, behind. But the whole family (including his dad) agreed it would be the best thing to do. He had one more year of primary school left to do. The idea was to let him finish it and then to bring him over to school in Trinidad. We also weren't sure, anyway if we would even want to stay there. It was a kind of look and see trip, I suppose.

Once we got there we ended up living in a big beautiful round peach home which we rented from a successful Scottish business owner. The house had the waters of one of Trinidad's most sacred rivers, the Maracus River, flowing right through its back yard. The entrance to the river was guarded by two lush mango trees and arching bamboos. Cold London had nothing on this balmy paradise. We decided we would launch mom's company Island Therapy right from that house. We would offer client's holistic weight loss programs and treatments. It was a simple plan that had great success. Without any form of advertising slowly but surely we had people coming to us. All our clients were well to do. They loved our treatments because they were natural and worked. The thing with Trinidad you have to realize is that people talk, and when people over there talk good about what you are doing that is your best advertising.

Initially life was sweet on in that round house. Over a few months our client list steadily. We had fun too - dinner parties packed with exotic treats, and a constant stream of festive occasions to go to.

29

Then somewhere into our seventh month of being there Poppa, mom's father, showed up. Not literally but in my dreams. He came and ruined the whole party I was having by appearing in the middle of a dark spot wagging his finger accusingly at me. I just wanted him to go away, but he wouldn't.

"You see you. You see you. You are not listening. We are going to done leave you," he said in the finest of Jamaican vernacular.

In the dream it was clear to me that he was referring to two repetitive dreams I had a few days before. Ones where a beautiful woman sat in the middle of a room and asked me to help her. I don't remember anything about her face, or what she was wearing. I just remember she was beautiful and sitting in the middle of the room. I also remember her saying she had something urgent she wanted me to help her with. It had something to do with helping the planet.

Poppa was right. I had not listened to the dreams. Deep down I knew that those dreams were destiny and a Water Goddess who had saved my life (the Yoruba's of West Africa call her Osun) calling.

A few years ago Osun, had saved my life. Things had been going pretty bad for me as a single mother living in London when a friend of mine suggested that I see a traditional priest who was the right hand man and cousin of one of the most revered Kings of Nigeria, the Ooni. I was willing to try anything and took a long drive into the English suburbs to see him. Mom came along with me. Chief Adelakan was quite an impressive sight with his traditional blue flowing lace robes. He was obviously proud of his culture and it became clear very early on into meeting him that he was also very knowledgeable about ancient wisdom.

When Chief Adelakan sat me known on his faded blue green orange divination mat, he took out a large conch shell and held it to his ears. He explained he was one of only a few priest who could divine using this particular method. He held the shell tightly to his ears for quite some time. Every now again he would nod his head. Then eventually when his invisible conversation seemed over he rested the gigantic shell on the mat and looked up at me,

"Your guardian angel is the Mother. When you were born it is she who agreed to look after you. In my tradition she is called Osun. You are like a bottle of sparkling water with the cork on. You need an initiation into the Mother in order to release the water within. Do you understand what I am saying?"

I did, so I nodded my head. But I was not interested in no initiation. Even though I was born in London I grew up very much in a Caribbean culture. We took spiritual stuff seriously. Living with spirit was deep in our bones. We knew that once you made a commitment to following a spiritual path you had to follow it. We also knew the rules to the path were strict. So as I wanted to be normal I did not want to follow a spiritual path in that way. I did not want any spiritual responsibilities more than what was given to me through my dream state.

Well, that reading was in December 2002, by May 2003 I became bed ridden with a strange illness. No one could work out what was going on with me, because it didn't seem to be anything at all. The doctors ran a battery of test on me but they couldn't find anything. I grew skinner and skinner, weaker and weaker with each passing day. Then one day when I woke up from a deep slumber feeling more exhausted than refreshed I saw a wispy stream of white smoke leaving my body. I remember just staring at it peacefully floating away from me. Then I heard an audible voice say,

"if you don't get initiated you will die. You must go to Nigeria with your mother. "

Now mom was on her way to Nigeria in a weeks' time, so I didn't know how I could go with her even if I wanted to. But one thing I knew for sure was that I would be dead by the time she returned. I knew it, because for some inexplicable reason I knew that wispy smoke I could see visibly leaving my body was my life force.

When I told mom that I thought I was dying, she wasted no time for she felt in her bones that I was truly dying. She said,

"you are a child of the ancestors. You are the next woman in your father's lineage carrying the responsibilities. You must get initiated. I know it will save your life."

My father's sister agreed with her. She said,

"Your grandmother refused the calling. She was the next one in the lineage to carry all the powers and wisdom of it, but she was not interested. She decided to turn her back on the ancient ways. As a result all her off spring have suffered some kind of tragedy in their lives."

She paused then continued,

"I believe because of her actions there is a family curse. The ancestors are not happy. You are the one to break the curse. You cannot refuse to take up your responsibilities."

What could I say after all of that was said. Deep down I knew I had to carry the lineage. Then in that flash of the possibility of me losing my life I understood what my name Ezolaagbo was guiding me towards. The name was the message.

The day I had my initiation was five days after my birthday.
It was June 10th 2003 and the earth was baking hot. All my
fears about my duties on the spiritual path were vanquished
under the heat of the day, and by the enthusiasm of one
hundred men, women, royal priests and chiefs who turned up
for the day's event. Mom and I were staying in Nigeria with
Chief Adelakan and his family. He had organized the whole
event, and I must say he did a grand job. It took us an hour to
get to the source of our destination, which was right near the
source of the sacred Osun River. It is said that the river was
the body of Osun herself. When the van pulled up outside an
ancient row of well-formed clay buildings the road was filled
with drumming, children and lots of activity. I am told it is
bad luck to speak about this initiation in any detail, but the
one thing I can let you know was that as I stood near the small
stream (that later became a mighty river), and the priestesses
were about to give me my name the drumming suddenly
stopped The priestess began to look into the water and
whisper earnestly in their mother tongue amongst themselves.
This went on for some time, and suddenly the drums started
up again, doubly loud. The priestesses began to dance, sway
and sing with new vigor.

"Omileye! Omileye! Omileye! Omileye! Omileye!"

They gently grabbed me, and made me dance to the
rhythm of my name. Latter my translator explained that the
Priestesses had a name for me, but a lone fish appeared in the
clear Osun waters and gave the name Omileye. It all sounded
quite incredulous to me but I knew from past experience that
anything can happen on ancient lands. I asked the translator,

"What does Omileye mean?"

"Water Gives Me Joy, Honor and Dignity," she replied.

A few days after my initiation I noticed that my health was as right as rain. I loved Omileye so much, that I decided to make it my first name, and Ezolaagbo my second. I could see Grannil Rosalie smile, and knew she was pleased with that arrangement too.

Oyekun Meji

Girl: Mother tell me about Oyekun Meji
Mother: Oyekun meji talks about light coming out of darkness.
Girl: Can you tell me a story from Oyekun Meji mother.
Mother: Of course. Here's one:

One day Death decided he was hungry. It was going to come to the people of the world and consume them. The people of the world decided to gather for a meeting as they were scared. They knew that death wanted to take them one by one. So they decided to go to an old priest for divination.

"Old priest what are we to do? Death is coming to eat us and we don't know what to do" they lamented.

The old priest thought about it and consulted the oracle. After some time of consultation he came back and told the people,

"There are two things you can do. One is to put stones in your banquet food. When you eat throw these stones on the floor. The second is to tie a chicken to a place by the door."

They did as the old priest suggested. True to form Death came along to their meeting. He spied on the people trying to decide how he was going to start attacking them. But then he noticed something. He noticed that they were eating and some of the food fell on the floor. Out of curiosity he decided to taste some of the morsels that fell on the ground. He picked it up and try as he might he just could not chew it. These people are very strong, he said to himself and was filled with fear of the humans.

Just as fear filled him up suddenly the sound of a cockerel cascaded through the air, "cock a doodle doo!" Now don't laugh but we all have our Achille's heels. That includes Death. He had this strange phobia about the noise of chickens. He was scared of chickens and when he heard that cockerel sounding off he went running off out of that place so fast. He was petrified of these powerful people.

The people of the world were so happy they had defeated the evil conniving Death. Well, almost because Death decided he would send his wife Sickness and the God of Accidents to take the people of the world. This they did now and again, which worked out better than the whole human race being completely swiped out.

I didn't know what likely hood there was of a great diviner from Africa arriving on the small island of Trinidad. Especially, in the light of having three repetitive dreams that needed interpreting. But one did arrive, and his name was Chief Solagbade Popoola. His arrival was announced by an excited family friend who convinced me and my mum that "this man was the real deal".

Between sucking mangoes (as Trinis called eating a mango) or going to this purported great man's lecture on health and spirituality I definitely knew, as a mango lover, which one I preferred to be doing. Yet, try telling that to our over eager family friend. He was not hearing the words, "I want to stay at home today to suck mango". He was convinced this was an opportunity we should not miss. He kept his feet planted firmly in our house until we were all dressed in our cultural refineries (in this case, African attire) and ready to go.

We got to the meeting about an hour late. We tried our hardest to squeeze quietly and daintily through the chairs and bodies. But when you have sixty people sitting in still absorption that is hard to do. None the less we did our best not to be completely disruptive in reaching the few empty seats left. Once we settled into our chairs the first thing I noticed was the lowered head, crisp white simple robes, and humble attitude of the man who stood behind the podium.

His lecture was remarkable, delivered with clarity and great wisdom. He was truly a great man. My friend was right. Yet he was so humble. I was impressed.

Latter, after the lecture, an acquaintance present told me that Chief Popoola (who was also affectionately and respectfully known as Baba which means father in Africa) was the Head of Scriptures and Ethics for the International Ifa Council which governed the ancient tradition of the Yoruba's wherever it traveled over the world.

37

That same acquaintance had heard about my dreams (Trinidad is a small place) and said,

"why don't you get a divination done about your dreams?"

"I'm good," I replied (meaning I was not interested).

But he was not letting it go,

"when are you going to get the opportunity like this again?"

"I don't have any money on me to get a reading," I replied truthfully (I was really happy I didn't have any money on me).

The friend still was not letting up.

"I will lend you some. You can pay me back latter."

"Seriously, I'm good," I told the friend.

He still was not letting up and shoved $350 TT dollars into the palm of my hands.

"Go get your reading done."

It was clear that everyone wanted a reading from this great man, because the queue was long. The weather was very balmy so I didn't want to stand in a long line for hours on end just to hear what the great African man had to share with me from the equally great ancient oracle. But, the money from my friend was sitting there all hot and bunched up in my hands so I didn't seem to have a choice. There was another thing about the readings, and that was that they weren't exactly private. That was how it was in Africa. The readings were often done in front of quite a few onlookers. So now Africa was in the Caribbean. At least I was not one of the ones who wanted to know if I should stay in a marriage that was on the rocks.

It felt like hours before I got to speak to Chief Popoola, but eventually I came face to face with him. He politely

38

gestured for me to sit on his bright blue yellow divination mat, and then got straight to the point.

"What is your question?" he asked in a very gentle voice.

I shifted uncomfortably from side to side. I was sitting before him to have my dreams read on, but deep down I really didn't want to know the answers. There's something strange about asking destiny what does it have in store for you. Tanti, always use to say to me,

"my child, what's in the dark doesn't hurt you."

Why couldn't my dreams stay in the dark? Yet, in my culture it was disastrous to ignore our dreams, especially those where the ancestors were involved. So with this in mind my shoulders slumped as I resigned myself to fate, and shared them with him.

His divining tool was something called the opele. It was made up of big funny looking pear shaped objects which were seeds attached to a chain. There were eight of those objects in total. Each was attached to a chain which connected them all together. The idea was that the opele would be held in the hand and raised into the air and allowed to fall to the floor. The configuration it fell in would be marked by lines in a sandy looking substance called Iyarosun by the priest or priestess. Just like the Chinese I Ching the pattern of the opele's configuration would indicate the answer to the person's question. For each had a corpus of wisdom attached to it.

Well, when Chief Popoola raised that Opele up into the air, I became tense all over. The tension grew greater as the opele slowly dropped onto his divination mat, and he silently contemplated its configurations. Time ticked by slowly. Eventually he raised his head up. I dared not breathe.

"Well, the oracle has spoken." He said in very good clear English and without changing his tone   (he seemed to have the knack of keeping his tone very even).

He paused, and that too felt like hours again. My stomach churned.

"The oracle says that your dreams are accurate. Osun, the Great Mother is calling you to do healing work for humanity."

My heart fell.

"The oracle also says "why have you taken so long. You should have started this work a long time ago" "

My heart fell even harder. Destiny was hard on my case again.

"What type of healing work are you talking about and what do I need to do?"

"Osun and your spirit will let you know," Chief Popoola replied matter of factly.

By now my heart was on the floor. I thanked and paid him, as I raised my body slowly of the mat.

That night I tossed and turned in my bed. A tropical night breeze blew gently through my open bedroom window. Instead of making me feel calm, it seemed to only serve as an irritant. It was about 3 am when I decided I really couldn't sleep, kicked my sheets off, and sat in the dark room by a simple Osun alter that I had set up on a cardboard box covered with a white cloth. On top of the box was a brass Indian looking water jug, and next to that was a small jar of honey.

I sat staring at the shrine objects on the makeshift table feeling as though my life had ended. I wanted normal, but now I felt the idea of normality was no longer an option. It was as though something large had swallowed me. Was it the family lineage I was born into? The contract I had made from heaven? One or both? As I prayed I had to accept the burning truth was - I was born into a family with a strong African ancestry pulling at it, a family with deep cultural responsibilities, and a family with ancient wisdom chiseled into its bones. That family truth ran through every vein of my body, and I could not escape it, any more than I could stop breathing in air.

Yes, I had gone to a white middle class convent school in one of London's most prestigious areas – Blackheath Common. Yes, I was born in London, and lived like a middle class child. Yet, I was what I was – the next woman to carry the lineage. I was Rosalie, the namesake of my maternal Great Great Grandmother; Ezolaagbo, One Who Carries the Lineage Home; Now Omileye, the one that water gave joy, honor and dignity to. Under my honey brown skin I was all of those things. The older I got was the more I could no longer deny my feet walked in two worlds. Now the roads of both those worlds were beginning to meet in the middle.

With all these thoughts flowing through my mind I lay wearily next to Osun's water pot. My eyes eventually closed and I had a vision. I saw myself wearing what seemed like a slim piece of leather with beads hanging from it. There was some kind of small peak in the middle. In the middle of the small peak was a symbol. I couldn't see what the symbol was. Then it was revealed there would be four others who would wear this head piece.

I woke up around 5 am. My bones ached. I did my morning prayers feeling sore. It was during my meditation that I heard a voice gently direct me to go back to Chief Popoola with the night's revelations. Here, would be a good place to explain that I have what I now know to be called an auditory gift. Besides seeing visions, and having prophetic

41

dreams, I receive streams and reams of information through hearing it. I groaned at the instruction. The man would think I was a pain in the butt, but with all that ancient lineage running through my veins I dared not disobey spiritual directions.

When I went back for my divination the following day it was as humid as ever, but the queue to see the great Chief Popoola was much shorter than the day before. This time I only had to wait an hour to see him. Once again, when I got before him he politely directed me to sit down on the divination mat, and got straight to business,

"How can I help you this time?" he asked as gentle as ever.

"Well, I had a vision, and I received the spiritual instruction to come back to you to tell you about it."

"Okay," he nodded for me to tell him.

I described the strange head piece I had seen on my head shared the message there will be four others who would wear this head band.

"Can you please draw a picture of the head piece," he asked pushing a small piece of paper in front of me.

I did and pushed the paper back to him when I finished.

He stared at the picture, his face appeared calm but his eyebrows knitted ever so slightly together. After a few moments he looked up from the drawing.

"What you drew is something very ancient. It is a Crown of Osun, but a very old old one. Only the very oldest people in our community know what this crown looks like. No one in the West has ever really seen this crown. It is made from a slender piece of leather and it has beads hanging down. It has a peak in the middle and in the middle of the peak is normally an emblem of the Mother."

42

When he saw the perplexed look on my face he continued,

"Whoever is chosen to wear this crown of Osun has been chosen to carry her energy at the highest level."

"Yes, your message is also right. There are supposed to be four others who are to wear this crown. You are to choose them."

He explained he would divine on the five titles to be carried, and would divine on which title I was to have.

"The oracle says that your title is to be Yeye Olomitutu, Mother Who Heals with Cool Water."

I should have been flattered by all these revelations, but I really wasn't. My energy was getting more and more depressed. I wiggled back and forth on the mat, and eventually I blurted out.

"Baba, truthfully I am really not interested in any of this. So can I just not bother?"

Chief Popoola, who seemed to never quite reply to a question without divination, raised his opele high into the warm air. It dropped and rattled onto the table. His head bowed to contemplate the findings. Once satisfied he understood them he said,

"The oracle says this is your destiny. You were born to do this. It is not something you can choose not to do. In fact, it is was the contract you made before you left heaven."

I felt the wind leave my chest, and I tried to hold back the tears, and onto the threads of normality. I really was not interested in proceeding in this destiny stuff, but deep down I knew that was it, destiny had spoken. My lineage had spoken. The ancestors and Holy Ones had spoken.

Chief Popoola or the oracle were not finished with me.

"The oracle says that this is your destiny, but there are those who will doubt the source of your inspiration. There are those who will be jealous of you. There are those who will try to ruin your name. There are even those who will try to kill you..."

He paused as he saw the horror settle on my face. No more trying to look all calm.

"But the oracle says this is your destiny and you must go ahead with everything. The oracle says that the Mother will bless you abundantly. She will protect you and bring great honor to your name. The oracle says that you did not come looking for this blessing, you were chosen to walk this path."

"Baba, I don't want to do any of this!" I suddenly cried out almost jumping of the mat. Only respect kept me anchored to it.

"The oracle has spoken," he said kindly but firmly. Then his voice softened and he told me, and those present a story.

"When I was younger I had a great career going for me as an engineer. I could have got very high in this career. Then one day something happened where things were not working out for me so well. So someone suggested I go for divination. I went and I was told that I must leave my engineering behind and be a priest. I refused to do this and still tried to pursue my career. But things just would not work out for me. Don't matter what I tried. It got so bad that eventually I thought I had no choice but to follow my calling. Then when I did, I was poor. Really poor. I could not feed my family anymore, and I thought what kind of thing is this? I faced much humiliation. Many people ridiculed me and told me I was a lazy man. My family, all but one daughter, left me because they said I was lazy and starving my children and wife. But I just had to keep on doing what I had been called to do.

I remember one day I had to walk almost many miles home because I had no money. I cried big big tears once I got home. It was a bad experience. Then one day this old man told me that all will be well for me. Then after a few years suddenly I was in demand, and now my whole family is so proud of me.

I am telling you this story to say that when you have a calling you must follow it. Things may feel hard at first and people may try to shame you because of it. Often it is not even a calling you want at all, but eventually because you did the right thing you will be greatly rewarded for your faith and service to humanity." He paused and said,

"I will come back about June to do the Crowning Initiation for you and the others that you pick."

"But what do I do Baba? How do I do this work?" I begged to know.

Chief Popoola looked at me and said calmly,

"the answer will come to you."

Somewhere on this journey I discovered Joseph Campbell and his book "The Hero with a Thousand Faces". I remember once telling a friend I wish I had encountered him and this book earlier. It surely would have helped me in many junctions of journeying through the labyrinths of life. After further contemplation I told her,

"actually it wouldn't have. It would have pre-empted too much of what I was supposed to experience."

Now I believe there is much of one's journey that one has to navigate alone. The Joseph Campbell's, and others come along the way to give some guidance and clarity. We must all work through the gate of Mysteries by ourselves. As Bon Jon Jovi stated, "map out your future but do it in pencil."

45

In his book *"The Hero with a Thousand Faces"* Campbell states a person could be going on with his life only to be called in some way or another. Normally, it is in a way that he least expects it. He gives the story of a young Princess who was playing with a golden ball. But on one of her throws the ball did not end up in her little hands but bounced on the ground and rolled right on up into the water.

The Princess followed the ball, but the ball ended up sinking deep into the bottom of the spring. The Princess began to cry and cry. Then a voice emerged from the waters. It turned out to be that of a frog's,

"Princess what is wrong?"

She told the frog she had lost her ball in the water. The frog said,

"that's no problem. I will get your ball on one condition that you let me eat at your table, be your companion and play mate."

The Princess promised him all his wishes, but she had no intention of keeping her promise to that old frog. As soon as he came up out of the water with the ball in its mouth and gave it to her she scampered off back to her palace.

Campbell explains,

"This is an example of one of the ways in which the adventure can begin. A blunder – apparently the merest chance – reveals an unsuspecting world, and the individual is drawn into a relationship with forces that are not rightly understood."

Campbell continues by further explaining, " as a preliminary manifestation of the powers that are breaking into play, the frog, coming up as it were by miracle, can be termed the "herald"; the crisis of his appearance is the "call to adventure." The herald's summons may be to live, as in the present instance, or at a latter moment of the biography, to die.

It may sound the call to some high historical undertaking. Or it may mark the dawn of religious illumination. As apprehended by the mystic, it marks what has been termed "the awakening of the self."

As I contemplated the phenomenon of the golden ball I came to believe we live in an era where there are plenty of them being thrown to many.

Early March 2007 and my bones seared with pain. My muscles felt exposed as though no skin covered them. Baba Folami our friend and chief ancestral priest on the Island had my limp body in his arms and carried it into a cool room where he had his prayer things.

"It's Mama," he said to the ten people present, gently laying me next to an ornate brass pot he had for Osun.

"She is here," he announced.

Eventually I sat up from the floor, and began to speak. Apparently my voice was a little deeper, slower and tinted with an African accent. I say apparently, because I only know what I was told. My mom who was one of those present said that I was completely out of it.

"I am here to help the world," Osun said. "I did not want to come, but I had to, Oludamare wanted me to come, and the Council of Elders."

I paused and breathed heavily,

"you all, humanity, have five years to help the world."

I paused, again. Then after what seemed like a moment of contemplation Osun said,

"perhaps ten."

After that mom said that Osun gave her blessings to all present and I collapsed on the floor. When I came through, mom said I had been asleep for a good half an hour or more. I awoke in a deep panic. I didn't understand what was going on. I didn't understand the messages that had been given. I didn't understand why my world had been turned upside down. I didn't understand how to handle any of it, and what any of it truly meant. Judging from even Baba Folami's response he didn't understand it either, but he was deeply moved.

"This is serious you'll. This is serious. Our Mother is here amongst us and she is telling us our humanity is in a mess. We must look after this girl," he said referring to a bewildered me.

Soon after that incident Osun indicated that she was birthing her energy in me and I needed to go into isolation. I had two priests, one included Baba Folami, and one person who had been assigned as an escort virtually guarding me at all times. I was not allowed to go anywhere unless it was urgent. This went on for a frustrating four months until the day of the Osun Crowning initiation which Chief Popoola came back to Trinidad to do.

Baba Folami and mom tried to get hold of Chief Popoola a good couple of times to see if there was anything that we had to do, in what was looking like an ancient process occurring. Getting through to Nigeria is not the easiest task. In our moment of need for enlightenment it became a virtually impossible one. With the ability of getting hold of Popoola thwarted we were basically left on our own to cope with the situation until he came back in June.

My life became a daily routine of waking up, meditating, having herbal baths in the sacred river and drinking herbal concoctions. I was not happy. I just wanted normality, but all I kept on hearing were Chief Popoola's gentle but firm words, "the oracle says you have to do this. This is what you were born to do. You made a contract in heaven to do this."

On the days when I cried everyone told me to stop crying. It was not good for my spiritual energy to cry. I tried to be positive but I just felt so miserable about the whole thing all the time. In spite of my miserableness and disbelief, I could feel the strength of Osun's presence grow daily within me and at my side. It began to feel like we had a direct line to each other.

"Girl you have to stay positive in these times," Baba Folami would say in his thick Trini.

"That's easy for you to say. This whole thing is weird," I would mumble.

One day over dinner mom's then partner provided a little nugget of information.

"You know I was thinking of that five year time scale that Momma Osun gave us the other day. I hadn't thought about it, but it dawned on me that date falls on 2012 when the Mayans say the world is going to end. Maybe not end, as people think, but at least go through turbulent changes where the old way of doing things ends."

"Where did you get that information from?" mom asked.

"I came across the Mayan calendar in my research some time ago. That calendar ends 2012," he said munching on a chicken leg dripping with curry.

"Really!" mom and I chorused in together.

"Wow, isn't that interesting!" mom said turning to look at me. I knew what her eyes were saying, "This stuff is for real."

"Yep," I said munching on my diet of salad, stewed beans and rice.

March 2007 and the news about the divination ebbed and flowed around the Island. Don't try and keep anything secret amongst Island people. We have our own talking drums. As there was a huge spiritual cultural community and many followers of Osun present living on the Island, it was not too hard to call a meeting, and pick four more individuals to catch the golden ball too.

What was hard was the big party we had to throw. We really didn't have a lot of money, but we knew we could not do any skimping (Island people did things in a big way, and so did Osun.) She was after all the Mother of charm, joy, grace, laughter, music and all things fine. Getting the logistics of the divination sorted out also was a little challenging. We needed two good priests. Eventually we found two whom we could trust and whom we knew were good.

On the day of the picking party fifty people who were initiated into Osun turned up. An auspicious number as Osun's number is five (any number that was a multiple of five is seen as Osun's number.) The plates, food, drums, and river all flowed. Everyone partied hard, in and out of the river that ran at the back of our yard, as they honored the Great Mother Energy and the Holy Ones. The atmosphere was charged, the excitement was tangible.

"This is historic," an older lady came up and told me. Several other people came up and said the same thing.

"This is the first time all the Osun's have gathered in one place," some people shared.

Some even revealed they too had received messages from the Mother conveying her desire to help the world.

"We have been having a lot of dreams about Osun recently," others informed.

After the good food, the singing and dancing it was time to divine on the other four who would carry the Mother's

Crown. A good few people put their names forward for divination. After an hour the divinations were done. Breaths were held as the names were announced.

The drums raised their voices in jubilation, and the dancing started all over again. Everything finished well after midnight.

But all good things come to an end, for within the next few days lots of rumors came my way. There were many people who were disgruntled that their names had not been chosen. There were even some elders saying that I was too young to be carrying such a responsible ancient title as Crown of the Mother. Even though these elders believed in the oracle, they didn't want to accept the oracle had picked someone so young to give this title and responsibility to. If Only they knew I would have given it all away in a heartbeat.

As myself and the four others got to know each other (or more to the point as the four others got to know me, because they already knew each other) the mere rumblings began to turn into a viscous hate campaign. You name it, it was said and even done. I was upset, but not totally taken of guard, as the oracle had predicted much of what was to happen (forewarned, forearmed). What did surprise me however, was the level of viciousness that occurred from some quarters. What happened to spirituality? I wondered.

Amongst the flow of honey and acid Chief Popoola arrived in the June, and as promised he did the Osun Crowning initiations. It was an extensive ceremony which lasted three days, involved a lot of organizing, and people. The ceremony was to help us carry the energy of the Mother well, and help us to be good ambassadors for her.

The final day culminated into a dynamic public celebration sponsored by the Trinidadian Ministry of Culture and Gender. The first day of the initiation had been overseen by the ancient flow of the sacred Maracus River which ran through the back of our yard.

If you want to party then go to Trinidad. The last day of the celebrations was quite an affair held in the famous Queen Park Savannah that hosted things like the King and Queens of Carnival, large concerts and the sorts. I was happy because, it also marked the last day of my imposed isolation.

Amongst the ancestral dancers on tall tall sticks, colors, drums galore, traditional dancers and awesome singers - were the speeches of important dignitaries such as the Minister of Culture and Gender Affairs, Her Honorable Joan Yuille – Williams. Even Chief Popoola gave a speech. Over Five hundred people from various cultures, dressed in their cultural fineries, turned up for the day. They charged the air up with their ancient songs, chants, and prayers.

Us five crowns were escorted into the event under the cover of one of the priest's heavily ordained African robe. Fresh out of initiation our faces weren't allowed to be seen until we were seated on the stage. All five of us wore traditional dresses made from yellow cloth to represent Osun. When we were seated on stage or faces were uncovered. I squinted against the glare of the sun, and looked out into the crowd present. I was astonished at the colorful sight that unfolded before me.

I was moved found it hard to fully fathom the total reverence and excitement of those present. Being an Island girl born in London (a place devoid of indigenous wisdom and spirituality) it was hard for me to totally comprehend how much this meant to the people present.

Even the Minster of Cultural and Gender Affairs, Her Honorable Joan Yuille-Williams, Minister of Cultural and Gender Affairs was filled up with so much emotion,

"This is truly a historic event and affair on this island that we all embrace."

She was referring to the fact that this was the first time in history that someone outside of Africa had been spiritually chosen to carry the sacred ancient title and position of Crown of Osun. For a Westerner to understand the weight and responsibilities of this position would be hard. For we don't have these ancient cultural practices present in our lives. But in Africa Osun is seen as the great Mother of all. She is not just a figure who exist only in the heavenly sphere of mythology, but she is revered as a living fully present figure in the lives of all.

Osun is not just kept to the spiritual arena, but she is very much a player in the political one. She is in fact a Queen of the spiritual and physical realm (literally). The King of Osogbo (a busy trading area in Nigeria, which is part of a bigger state called after the Goddess herself. Osun is in fact seen as the real ruler of Osogbo) has to re-pledge his allegiance to her in her annual festival. Osogbo, a busy trading area, is only prosperous by the grace of Osun. He to only exist because of that grace too.

To have Osun's presence amongst us is seen as an enormous blessing to be respected, loved and honored. For she is seen as the quintessential feminine principle and one of the few Holy Ones who goes back and forth between the realm of heaven and earth, because she cares about our affairs that much.

Once on stage I was also surprised at how many people came up to receive blessings. Even the ministers and public figures did. Despite all the jubilance, I could not help but still wonder how did this "ordinary" Island girl from London's life take on this strange twist. I felt as though I was Alice in Wonder who had landed in another world.

The day after what became known as the Crowning Coronation I read a few papers. There were some very interesting articles. I enjoyed reading the popular Trini View article, which seemed to sum up the event very well.

Me Blessing the Minster of Cultural and Gender Affairs,
Her Honorable Joan Yuille-Williams at the Crowning Coronation

Me with mom (lady with big head wrap)
and other individuals who had received
ancient title Crown of the Mother

*Chief Popoola doing divination
during private part of the Crown of the Mother Ceremony
to give us our dos and don'ts*

TriniView Article

TriniView.com Reporters
Event Date: June 22, 2007
Posted: June 30, 2007

On Friday 22nd June, 2007, the Orisha community celebrated the spiritual rebirth of the feminine deity, Osun (also Oshun), at a special Osun Coronation Ceremony which was held at Queens Park East, Port of Spain. Osun, in the Orisha tradition, is the deity of sweet water, representing the feminine aspect of nature, harmony, motherhood, fertility and purity. One of the elders present at this historic event remarked that her spirit is so powerful that five people were needed to facilitate her manifestation. Four Orisha women and one man were honored as the crowned heads of Osun. The five crowned heads were clad in vibrant yellow wear, clearly reflecting the celebration of Osun whose colour is yellow.

The ceremony, led by Orisha elder, Chief Alagbaa Awo Ifatayese Adelekan Aworeni, included moko jumbies, fancy sailors, singing, African drumming and dancing. The moko jumbies and fancy sailors, part of our African Carnival ritual, were present in the beginning of the ceremony to signify a part of Trinidad and Tobago that still bears the tradition of our African ancestry. They danced at the front of the tent, greeting in stylish fashion, the five manifestations of Osun.

Before this, drummers had assembled in a small space under the tent to play in merriment, the coming to earth of the Orisha entity. They were joined by the singing and chanting of other Orisha worshippers.

The formal part of the ceremony began with the entry of the five manifestations of Osun into the tent where the audience was gathered. They entered hidden by large fans covering their faces, or in the case of one of the manifestations, hidden behind the robes of two Orisha devotees.

After entering the tent, the programme immediately began with prayers being offered to the Orishas and in particular, to Osun, whose visit to earth was celebrated. It was indeed a festive yet holy occasion as members of the gathering rejoiced her coming and kneeled in reverence to receive her blessings through her five manifestations.

The very old to the very young approached the chosen five intermittently during the proceedings and some even gave brief speeches professing their devotion to Osun and asking that she continues to bequeath to them blessings.

Other devotional rituals were performed by 'Brave Boy' who sang a worship song in tribute to Osun; dance performances by Ah We People Theatrical Horizon and N'belese dance groups; inspirational songs by Calypsonians Abbi Blackman and Fred 'Composer' Mitchell; and songs played on the Steelpan by legendary Pannist, Len 'Boogsie' Sharpe.

Speakers on the auspicious occasion included Chief Folagbde Popola from Ile Ife, Nigeria; SWMCOL Chairman Ray Brathwaite; IRO president, Noble Khan; and the Minister of Community Development, Culture and Gender Affairs, Senator the Honorable, Joan Yuille-Williams. In her address, Mrs. Yuille-Williams indicated that the journey from Africa was not a pleasant one referring to the slavery experience. Because of this difficult experience as she put it, it was even more of a struggle to keep their cultural traditions alive. Thus, she commended the efforts and the commitment of Africans

58

here in Trinidad and Tobago to keep the African traditions alive. The Senator also stressed that it was a policy of the government of Trinidad and Tobago that all should practice their religion freely and that they encourage Orisha worshippers to follow in the same vain.

The moment that all awaited, the deliverance of Osun's message came next. Speaking through one of the manifestations, she said Osun brought blessings to all world-wide and that she had come to bring balance to the world.

Chief Popoola was right. After all the festivities had died down, it was time for us Crowns to get to work. Like Chief Popoola said, we would hear from Osun as to the way forward. Well, we did. The only thing was that the message was vague.

"Start at water," was all I was all I heard during one of my nightly of meditations which had become more frequent.

Don't tell a hardnosed journalist something that vague. It just doesn't wash. Journalist need hard facts.

"What do you mean?" I whispered into the dark trying to get an answer.

"Start at water," was the only reply I heard back. Along with the words, "document everything."

I didn't understand the message but the following day I shared it with the others. We all decided to take the message literally – we literally went to the waters. We chose several sacred rivers that ran across the land of the Island and began to do healing prayers for the world at their water's edge. I also religiously began to document everything in my journal.

BOOK TWO: IN WATER'S FLOW

IWORI MEJI

Girl: Mother what of Iwori Meji
Mother: Yes, here it shows us that even when we think life seems insurmountable it is not.
Girl: Give me an example of a story Mother:
Mother:

One day there was one of the most senior priest of the God of Wisdom, Orunmila. He was a very powerful and great diviner who trained many priest who lived in heaven. However, he was very arrogant and conceited so many of his great heavenly works are not known because he did not want his heavenly priest to come down from heaven to tell all. However, a few of his heavenly works have been told by some of those who benefited from it. In heaven this very senior and powerful priest was known as Iwori Meji. One of the stories that is loved by many is how the sun became powerful. It goes something like this:

One Iwori Meji made divination for the sun, the moon and the darkness when they were coming down to earth. They were all three brothers and he advised them all to make offerings so that they will be honored, respected and admired by the people of the world.

More importantly so that they would not be looked on with contempt. He explained the sacrifice would make them to be viewed as indispensable to the world.

Well the moon said, " I am too handsome and popular to worry about doing any offering." So he didn't do one.

Darkness said, "do you see how handsome I am. Everyone will respect me." So he too did not do the offering.

The Sun said, "I will do my offering".

Now something interesting followed after all of this. The Moon who had done an offering earlier for love, as a result he was not seen as all powerful but was loved by all in the world. Because of his offering is why everyone when they see the face of the new moon they feel great love in their hearts for it. Then there was darkness everyone in the world hated darkness. The sun was given back the bundle of brooms he had made sacrifice with and was told that he should hold the broom in his hand and point it at anyone who dared to stare at him. The broom became the suns rays that dazzle the eyes of all living beings. However, the Sun is greatly admired, respected and honored by all because of all the things it does for the world such as generating heat and life force for the whole planet.

.

The Belly of The Whale is a strange place to be. Once you're in it that is it. You are in it hook, line and sinker. There is no escaping from that humongous strange looking place. No one to call out to, unless they are in there with you. It is the part of your calling where to enter the mysterious land of the ancients. It is the place where you, according to Joseph Campbell, go through a "metamorphosis". You have "died to a time and returned to the World Womb, the World Navel, the Earthly Paradise".

Being there you have moved beyond the First Threshold and you are now the hero who has moved into a "dream landscape of curiously fluid, ambiguous forms where he must survive a succession of trials." It is here that you as the hero "is covertly aided by the advice of amulets, and secret agents of the supernatural helper whom he met before his entrance into this region." Or it may be that you discover "for the first time that there is a benign power everywhere supporting him in his superhuman passage.

Campbell explains the mystics call this "the second stage of the Way". A time of self-purification. A time when you enter "intentionally or unintentionally into crooked lanes of his own spiritual labyrinth." Where all sorts of symbolic figures are met. In this world, "In our dreams the ageless perils, gargoyles, trials, secret helpers, and instructive figures are nightly still encountered; and in their forms we may see reflected not only the whole picture of our present case, but also the clue to what we must do to be saved."

Even in the most ancient stories the Goddess herself enters through the gates of metamorphosis. In the Sumerian myth of the Goddess Inanna descends to the nether world.

From the "great above" she set her mind toward the "great below",
The Goddess, from the "great above" she set her mind toward the
"great below",
Inanna, from the "great above" she set her mind toward the "great
below."

My lady abandoned heaven, abandoned earth,
To the nether world she descended,
Inanna abandoned heaven, abandoned earth,
To the nether world she descended,
Abandoned lordship,
Abandoned ladyship,
To the nether world she descended.

As Innana descended she approaches the temple made of lazuli and at the gate she is met by a chief gatekeeper. He demands to know who she is and what brings her to this world. She tells the guard that she is the Queen of Heaven where the sun rises. Then the guard looks with all puzzlement and ask her why on earth has she come here "to the land of no return." She replied she was there to attend a funeral. The guard nods for her to be let in. She must pass through seven gates. At each gate she has to remove an element of her clothing.

At the first gate her "Crown of the Plains" is removed; the second her rod of lapis lazuli; the third – her lapis lazuli necklace; the fourth – the precious stones of her breast; the fifth – the gold ring on her finger; the sixth – the breast plate that protected her; the seventh – all her garments that covered her body. Standing naked in the underworld she is put to death.

Campbell says that this represents the journey of the hero which strips him of all the things that divide him from his opposite. He states, "the hero must put aside his pride, his virtue, beauty and life and bow or submit to the absolutely intolerable. Then he finds that he and his opposite are not of differing species, but one flesh."

Carl Jung explained it like this - life there is something called "the other side". It is not another world but just something we cannot see with the invisible eye. He said that we have a No. 1 and a No. 2. The latter belongs to the realm we cannot see. He stated it was "the second poet, director of the dream." It is "spirit, the active dynamic aspect of the psyche. Spirit is the real culture creating factor in the human being".

He made it known that he believed it would be "erroneous" to imagine consciousness to be as "a kind of here and unconsciousness as of sort of there". Because the psyche is really a "conscious unconscious whole". An all-embracing whole.

For Jung the No. 2 was the "new King" who had to be liberated from the depths of the collective unconsciousness. The "Old King" represented the ways that no longer worked in the inner and outer world. It was the ways of the ego.

He believed that the revitalizing force of No.2 was to be brought in by a balancing world Archetype. Archetypes live in the collective unconsciousness. They are the ordering function in the physic field. They are also the unconscious dynamic energies behind the conscious collective representations of the world such as mythological stories, dreams, symbolisms and messages.

For Jung myths, dreams, symbolisms and messages had no meaning if we did not realize there was a living shaping archetype behind those things. Which gives it its true feeling and relevance. Now interestingly enough he believed that the feminine shaping force of the world – the feminine Archetype would begin to emerge in order to balance the over domineering and destructive forces of the male Archetype. It is the flowing feminine grace which he believed gave us an intelligence and world that was more receptive, graceful and balanced. Stating,

"The larger mind bears the stamp of the feminine. It is endowed with a receptive and fruitful womb which can re-shape what is strange and give it a familiar form."

He called this ability of the feminine "the rare gift of the maternal intellect".

He postulated that,

"a greater power is needed to match the one-sidedness of purely aggressive behavior. That other power is the constellation of an opposing archetype, which today is the archetype of the feminine and which so far never has been adequately integrated into our religions and our scientific images of the world."

If the Crowning represented the initiation into the Hero's Journey, and its very beginning with all the praise and criticisms represented the guarded threshold of that journey. Then what was to follow was to mark the crossing into the Belly of the Whale where the mysteries of the fluid No. 2 world and its information matrix was to unfold the greatness of its knowledge and depths.

IDI MEJI

Girl: Mother what of Idi Meji?

Mother: Yes, Idi Meji talks about how things come to prosper from bad circumstances.

Girl: Tell me a story from Idi Meji.

Mother: Now there is an interesting story in Idi Meji I want to tell you.

There was once a man called Ode (Outside) whose three wives had deserted him. When he became too poor to satisfy them materially. The name of the three wives were:

(1) Ire or play
(2) Oyin or Pleasure
(3) Ujo or Dance

It is said it was these three beautiful and active wives whose support and cooperation gave ODE his identity. When Play, Pleasure and Dance left Ode legend has it that he became very dull. It goes without saying that Outside only becomes attractive and interesting when there are outdoor plays, pleasantries, music and dancing. People go outside to play and dance. When people are enjoying themselves they feel great pleasure and from this feeling many good things are manifested. Anyway, Ode got tired of his dull life and was determined to get his wives and wonderful life back. He wondered what to do and was finally advised to go visit a priest for divination.

So what advise was Ode given? He was told to sacrifice one goat and to slaughter a second goat for a feast in his house. He was to cook yam on the fire and was assured that while the yam was cooking on the fire, his wives would return to him one after the other.

Now Ode followed the advice to the letter. When he cooked the yam and goat he invited many people to come and feast with him. Well The God of Opening the Way, Esu, went to each of Ode's wives. When he got to Play's house he told her she had made a big mistake to have left the husband merely because his fortunes suffered a temporary eclipse. He remarked that since eclipses were transient and ephemeral, ODE was already back in prosperity in a big way. The proof being that right as he spoke to her there were so many people feasting in his house. This was going on a daily basis.

Then Esu went and told the other two wives the same story. Each wife decided to go to Ode's house herself to see if the story was true. Indeed when they got to the house they found the yam cooking on fire and people feasting on the food already cooked. They all decided to chip in to help Ode, and they all agreed to stay with Ode for good.

Well Ode found that once again his prosperity blossomed. And all was well again.

It seemed to emerge from the misty blues of time. That was the Caura River, all lush, and sparkly like a beautiful woman. It was now March 2008, and we (the five Crowns) had eventually got it together enough to organize a small Water Blessing at the Caura River. The idea was to pray for world peace, and environmental healing. The river was just one of five waterways we had picked to do this at. Caura seemed to like our prayer for when we finished her waters winked back a thousand sparkles at us. We all stood there in marvel.

After the prayers we proceeded to dip our chocolate bodies into her clear waters it was hard to imagine the beautiful Caura as the scene of so many heinous crimes, but she was. Just last week a young woman had been raped there. It was just one amongst many incidents. Imagine flowing hundreds of miles from the Northern Mountain range of Trinidad only to be greeted with total ingratitude. But that was Caura's lot at the moment. Her beauty was one of an abused woman.

As I submerged my head under her coolness I prayed for the crimes to stop. Still new to the idea of Water Blessings I could not help but wonder if a prayer to water could really change anything. It was the thousands of sparkles that greeted us back that had made me think maybe, just maybe water hears our prayers.

It was 2 am in the morning, when I was woken up by an invisible nudge. That familiar electrical current that has been pulling my life for so long, lifted me up from my bed, and made my stubborn legs walk to the downstairs study. I grumbled as I stood there in the darkness wondering why I was there. I found myself rummaging through the old books on the shelf. I pulled one out. I held it carefully for fear it

69

would fall apart. The musty smell of the book rose into my nostrils making them flare out and twitch a little. I knew that I was to flick through the book. So I did. I strained by eyes against the dim street light that shone through the study window. It was a book on Yoruba mythology. Nothing in the book really caught my attention, then it.

Osun was pleased that I had. She rose gracefully from the pages and pulled me into her watery abode. My eyes slowly scanned the world of Gods, Goddesses, and an endangered world.

One day God decided to send seventeen enlightened beings to earth. The only woman amongst them was Osun, the Goddess of Water, beauty and wisdom. God instructed the enlightened beings to make the earth (which was young) pleasant to live.

The enlightened beings began to carry out God's instructions to the letter. They arrived on earth and did just that. However, while they habituated and beautified the world they left Osun out of everything.

In fact, poor Osun was relegated to just taking care of everyone, giving them food and all the nice things they needed. However, Osun knew her own power and just observed all the things they were doing. She did not protest to them out aloud but just looked on quietly.

In the meantime the sixteen men began to notice that everything that they did failed. They prayed for rain but rain did not fall. Eventually illness, bitterness, and restlessness spread all over the world. The world had got into a sorrowful state.

The sixteen men did not know what to do. They asked everyone and everything (except for Osun, of course) for help. No one could help them. Frustrated and worried about their impending extinction they returned back to God to ask for his help. They didn't even think of taking Osun with them.

After a very long journey they reached God. God noticed that Osun was missing. He listened to all the men's complaints quietly. Once they had finished he asked them,

"how many of you went to earth?"

"Seventeen," they answered.

"Where is the seventeenth?" he asked. The men looked uneasy and replied,

"we left her on earth".

God then told them something quite startling,

"in Osun I gave all the wisdom of the world."

He instructed them to include Osun in all their affairs and to beg her for her assistance and all the issues on earth will be resolved. The men went back to earth. The God of wisdom Orunmila went to beg Osun for her assistance. She told him if the baby she was about to birth was a boy she would help them if it was a girl she would not.

Orunmila reported back to his colleagues what Osun told him. When the God Oosaala looked at Osun's womb with his awo (power of knowing secrets) he found a baby girl there. He then pointed his ado Asure to Osun's womb and commanded that the fetus change into a male. It so happened after this that when Osun went into labor. She gave birth to a baby boy called Etura Meji.

I re-read the story several times. Each time I did an excitement surged through my body. To find a traditional story that confirmed it was our archetypal Mother who saves the day felt extremely precious. I knew there was an unseen force that made me find that story. I thanked it, her. For I believed that invisible force was the Mother herself. Little did I know there were many more that would land at my feet to unravel the ball of our history.

"So Osun saved the day," I whispered into the darkness hugging the book tightly.

71

"Not only did she save the day but God said he gave her all the Wisdom of the world," I shared with Derrick the following day.

Just to tell you Derrick was my husband. I know what you're wondering "husband, where did he come from?". We met at the Osun Coronation event, stayed in touch by the phone, and destiny did the rest. It was so good to have his listening ear, albeit all the way in America. We had not decided where we would live together. So in the meantime he was over there, and I was still in the land of mangoes, and sacred waters.

"That's interesting sweetie, very interesting," he enthused.

The following evening I was gripped by that electrical current again. It drew me to reading a little book I had simply called "Hinduism" by Karen Singh. I settled down on my bed, and opened it as I enjoyed the balmy Caribbean breeze tickling warmly stroking my arms. Recently I had been drawn to reading on Hinduism. There was something about that ancient world that beckoned me forward and deeper into its faded brown edged story.

As I dug into the book, the page fell onto a paragraph with two lines about a Goddess known as Durga. I had never heard of her before, but I read on. The world was facing a crisis, and the Gods didn't know what to do. Eventually they produced the Goddess Durga from their deep concentration on the problem they were facing. She emerges from a sea of light to help save the world.

The same story, as Osun saving the world. Now my mind was going. How comes? I didn't know. How comes there was one story from India of the Goddess saving the world, and one from Africa, and they were similar? I had no answers to the barrage of questions that flooded me. The electrical current that had pulled my body started tingling and sizzling. I was on to something, but what I didn't know.

Both Osun and Durga seemed to smile at me from their primordial waters. Little did I know the process of being put in the role of spiritual detective had begun, and those two sisters were there to help lead the way.

Later that evening the electrical current had me walking the hot dusty road that led from our house to the small bookstore that I loved to go to. Our house was now in the humid arid region of Chauguanas, which use to be the land of the Chauguana Native Indians. Now it was the land of industrious Indians with more new money to spend than they knew what to do with it. The spanking new mall that housed the bookshop was a testimony to that fact.

I missed the coolness of Maracas Valley, but loved the crazy famous bustle of Chaguanas, especially that little bookstore. As I trudged to the bookstore with car dust blowing up in my face and onto my clothes, I was acutely aware I was being spiritually led. When yet another book on Hinduism fell of the shelf (quite literally), and into my hands, I was definitely certain I had powerful ancient forces at my side who seemed determined to reveal ancient things. The Osun Crowning initiation seemed to have allowed me to be a privileged child in an old world. The book had a nice cover to it, and enticed me to open it up. I did, and my eyes were caught by the enticing skirt tales of an awaiting story,

One day a sage notices a scorpion has fallen into the water. He reaches down and rescues it. He is stung by the scorpion. Latter in the day he notices the scorpion has fallen into the water again. He

once again rescues the scorpion only to be stung again. An observer to the events exclaims, "holy sage, why do you keep doing that? Don't you see that the wretched creature will only sting you in return? "of course," the sage replied. "It is the dharma of a scorpion to sting. But it is the dharma of a human being to save.

I had heard about Dharma before, but on the way home I decided to stop at the internet café which had computers with plenty of viruses. I wanted to do a search on dharma. There were lots of different definitions which all amounted to revealing dharma as the natural universal laws whose observation enabled us humans to live in contentment, happiness and balance. Observation of those natural laws was what saved our tails from degradation and suffering. Hindus considered dharma to be the very foundation of life. It took me next to no time to realize that was what the two Mothers were doing. They were obviously trying to save the dharma.

I could almost feel the invisible force leading my life clapping its (or was it their hands) with glee. From there on in the ball of wool never stopped unrolling.

IROSUN MEJI

Girl: Mother what of Irosun Meji?
Mother: Yes, Irosun Meji. Here you have many stories on how men and animals alike experienced better lives.
Girl: Mother tell me a story from Irosun Meji?
Mother: Okay then.

One day when all the divinities were leaving heaven they went to Irosun Meji for divination. In heaven Irosun Meji was called Akpejo Uku, that is, the man who can alter the course of death. He advised the 200 divinities before leaving heaven that on getting to the earth, they should refrain from laying down inflexible rules and regulations because – rigid laws breed avoidance and evasion.

He told them to seek the support of Esu by offering a he-goat to him. None of the divinities did it because they did not like the trickster God Esu. However, the God of Wisdom Orunmila is the only one who followed Irosun Meji's wise advice and gave Esu a he-goat. After seeing Irsosun Meji all the divinities left for the earth.

As soon as they settled down on earth, the first law they put into effect was that as soon as a divinity's hair became grey he should return to heaven. So they would die at the turn of their hair being grey.

Eventually, the God of Wisdom – Orunmila's hair turned grey. The other divinities took glee in reminding him it was now his time to die and go back to heaven. He told them he knew.

One day he decided to do a divination to see what he could do about his dilemma for in all reality he was not ready to go to heaven. Through divination he was told to offer a he-goat to Esu. He was also to grind dried water yam mixed with ashes. He was to place the ashes in the bag, and tie the bag to the main entrance to his house. After he had done all of that he was to offer a pig to Ifa and make a feast to all the remaining divinities on earth. He did as advised.

All the divinities came to the feast for they thought it was his sending of party. By tradition it was forbidden to enter the house of any divinity with a hat. So each person was asked to take of their hat before entering Orunmila's house. They each obliged and as they entered through the entrance of the doorway Esu rubbed each person's hair with the yam powder inside of the bag at the entrance of the door. Once past the entrance each divinity put their caps back on so they did not know that their hair had turned grey. After everyone had a jolly good time feasting they all bade Orunmila farewell.

Orunmila said, "well it looks like we are all going back together."

The divinities looked at him as though he had gone mad

"What do you mean?" they asked.

"We all have grey hair," he said.

"No we don't," they replied..

"remove your caps and see," he said.

Confused as to why they were all grey they quickly passed a unanimous resolution that when there was the appearance of grey hair the person did not have to die and go back to heaven. Thus, the God of Wisdom helped rid the world of a very unreasonable law.

The Maracas River must have been pleased that we came back to visit it. For after a small Water Blessing where ten of us sang and prayed our hearts out – the primeval world of energy swirled all around me. Prakruti most have been pleased to, for she leapt from the pages of my former BS. Ayurvedic notes, and began to stomp the place to life. Each step that touched the Earth began to unfold the story of our primordial universe.

One day Purusha, the one who witnesses creation, and Prakruti, the feminine active creative will of consciousness decided to engage in a dance called Leela. The first part of the dance of creation Prakruti manifest herself as supreme intelligence which becomes the seat of the individual budhi (intellect). From Mahat becomes manifest ego which is known as Ahamkara. The three dynamic forces of creation then influence Ahamkara. These three forces are known as satva, rajas, and tamas. Satva becomes responsible for clarity, perception and spiritual awareness. Rajas in turn causes movement, sensation, feelings, emotions and mental awareness. While Tamas is the dynamic principle of inertia, darkness, heaviness, physical awareness. It is responsible for periods of confusion and deep sleep.

Now from the essence of Satva the five senses are created. They are the ears to hear, skin to perceive touch, eyes to see, the tongue to taste, and the nose to smell. The essence of rajas is manifested as the five motor organs, namely mouth, hands, feet, reproductive organs, and organs of excretion. The mind arises from satva. In the mind the life force is a manifestation of Rajas.

From the essence of Tamas originates the five subtle elements known as Tanmatras. They are sound, touch, sight, taste and smell as the primary stimulus. From the subtle elements are manifested the five primordial elements known as panchamahabhutas. They become the building blocks which create all manifested things in life. These elements are known as space (akash), air (vayu), fire (tejas), water (aap), earth (prithvi). Space is birthed from the sound AUM which creates vibrations throughout the whole universe. This vibration creates movement and thus the principle and element of air. The motion of movement causes friction which creates heat and radiation and thus the principle and element of fire. Which in turn gives rise to the moisture of the principle and element of water. Water gives rise to cohesiveness which gives rise to the principle of earth. Finally prana, the universal life force enters all form and structure setting in motion the evolution of life.

To get the main points of the story straight in my head again, I made a few notes:

- *All things come energy*
- *The central stage of this energy unfolding is the Inactive energy of the male Purusha and the active quality of female Prakriti*
- *This energy gives birth to five subtle energy levels: ether, air, fire, water, and earth*
- *This subtle energy state gives rise to a grosser form of the energy levels of: ether, fire, water and earth*
- *Each grosser energy state has four parts of the subtle energy state of similar nature which forms its center and one part of each of the others which form around it. So an Earth particle would have four parts subtle earth energy as its center and air, space, fire and water which form around it.*

As I made those notes Prakruti's stomping increased, shaking my latent memory to life. Hadn't my lecturer equated the ancient concept of levels of energy to the structure of the atom? I checked my notes. He had.

Ayurveda which means the Science of life is over 3000 years old (some say it's older). Its reveals that layers of energy are the building blocks of life: Space, Air, Fire, Water and

Earth. These layers of energy are the equivalent of the Western concept of atoms and quarks. In fact the Hindu sages said those layers of energy constituted Paramu, which my lecturer had taught was the same word for atom.

The Western atom has at its center a nucleus which is made up of the positive charge of protons, and the neutral neutrons. It is the proton which tells the observer what type of atom they are looking at. So all carbon atoms have six carbon protons. Now, the Earth element of Ayurveda has at its center four earth energy particles. Just as the Air element would have at its center four air energy particles.

Back in my days I was taught that there were electrons which travelled in neat circles around the nucleus. Now science talks about electron clouds within which the electron exist.

In science class I was also taught that the central proton is equal though opposite to charges on all the peripheral electrons put together. My Ayurvedic lecturer highlighted the fact that the Hindu Sages declared the contents of the central radical of a paramanu is equal to the contents of all the peripheral units put together.

Today scientist say they have discovered something called Quarks. Six to be precise (with perhaps a seventh). Today they believe these are the smallest building blocks of life and not atoms. The lecturer also pointed out that Quarks are synonymous with Ayurveda's Tanmatras (the subtle energy states from which arise the grosser energy states which give rise to matter)

Prakruti kept leaping and dancing. There was no stopping her. She had unlocked the fact that the ancient language of energy, which was very much wrapped up in the mythological stories, was none other than a very scientific language of pure existence and the rules that govern it.

As if to prove her point the rhythm of her frenzied footsteps led my mind back to the Yoruba creation story, I had recently encountered. Feeling her rhythmic pulse in my body, I trembled as I recalled it.

One day Oludamare (God) called Obatala (the God of White Cloth and Consciousness) to the realm of the ancestors (Ikole Orun). He wanted him to create dry land on the waters of the earth (Ikole Aye). However Obatala stated he did not know the mystery for doing so. In response to this Oludamare (God) informed Obatala he would give him the power to make land on earth. He gave him a snail shell filled with earth, palm nuts and a chameleon. On receiving these items Obatala wanted to know how was he going to make his way from the ancestral realm to earth. Ogun, the deity of iron, stated he would create a chain to help him achieve his journey down.

On making the chain Ogun flung it down to earth and the chain attached the realm of heaven and earth. Thankful, Obatala began his journey down to earth. When he reached the last rung of the chain he noticed that he was far from the primal waters.

At that point he removed the snail shell from his pouch and sprinkled some soil upon the Primal Waters. He then removed the Guinea Hen and dropped it on the land. The hen began to scratch the land and spread the dirt across the primal waters.

Once Obatala noticed the ground had become firm he removed a palm nut and dropped it on the land. It grew to its full height and reached the last

rung of the chain. Once it did this Obatala stepped from the Chain to the palm tree. Upon climbing down from the tree Obatala started to mold humans from the clay in the earth. As he worked he became tired and decided to rest. He took fruit from the palm tree and made wine and drank until he was ready to return. The human he molded while drunk did not resemble the others. He did not notice. He kept on drinking till he fell asleep.

On awakening Oludamare banned Obatala from drinking again. When he saw what happened to the humans he had created while drunk he agreed to protect all children for future generations. He said he would never again let his white cloth become soiled.

Then I started to decode the story. As I did so a thrill rushed through my body.

Orunmila (God): is the silent witness of creation which in the Ayurvedic story is Purusha.

Obatala: is"the Prakriti aspect of creative will which sets about creating everything. The role of Obatala is reflected in his other name Oloona Orun "Owner of that which emerges from the invisible realm. He is also known as the "Molder of the World".

The Ladder and ascent down the ladder: perfectly represents the coming forth of creation. The rungs of Obatalas ladder represents the different stages of universal evolution which in every culture is shown differently. The rungs of the chain Obatala climbs down are a perfect depiction of DNA. For our DNA very much resembles a spiral chain. DNA is made of double strands like a ladder. Therefore Obatala's ladder represents the pre-atomic stuff life is formed from.

The ascent down the ladder: As Obatala climbs down the ladder we have a commentary on the complicated formation of life itself. The climb down the chain actually corresponds to the Ayurvedic stage of creation where the motor organs of life form are created. They originate from the Rajas state (motion state) of pure consciousness.

The formation of life: When Obatala forms all inanimate and animate life from the earth and water. This corresponds to the Ayurvedic story of creation where all the elements arise from the principle of Tamas from which all the five building blocks of creation arise. The five building blocks of life are said to join together into a combination of different quantities to form the physical and spiritual constitution of all animate and inanimate things in the universe and on earth. The state of Tamas inertia is also represented when Obatala falls into a deep sleep and slumber, and wakes up in a state of confusion. While he is in a half sleep he is still forming creation.

The elements of life: All the five primordial elements in the Ayurvedic story of creation are very present in this ancient Yoruba story. In the same order. Ether is represented by Obatala's presence in heaven; air by his descent down from the chain where he obviously starts to come into contact with air; fire by the formation of the chain by Ogun (we know metal can only be forged in fire and Ogun represents the element of fire); earth by the earth he carries in the snail's shell; water by the primal waters he sees and drops the earth on.

Prakruti paused for a while. I was panting from the rush I was getting. She was amazing. There it was, right there in the Yoruba creation story, the story of DNA itself. The story of life itself unfolding.

Prakruti was not finished with me. This time she began to dance in a slower rhythm. Her feet stomped slowly, her waist rotated the primal pattern of energy. There seemed to be no stopping her or me. A thought engulfed me. It wouldn't let me go. *The Gods are the elements, the elements are the Gods. The body of the Gods contain the code of all life.*

My fingers trembled. I trawled through more old Ayurvedic notes. I wanted to read on the elements, as I did so my mind began to decode the Gods and realize it was true. It was true. The elements were the Gods, and the Gods were the elements. They held the code of life itself. I made profuse notes. It was tedious going, but it felt worthwhile. Excitement crashed and collided through the nether regions of space, as I made those notes.

Notes on the Elements

The concept of Space

Ether/Space is seen as the first elemental building block of life. It is none other than the manifestation of pure consciousness. The expansion of consciousness is space. Space is all inclusive of all things and it serves as the abode for the other four primordial elements of life and all objects in the universe. It is because of space why one thing can be differentiated from another.

Everything in the world contains space: vacuum in the intestinal tract, blood vessels, lymphatic, intercellular spaces and vacuum anywhere in the body, and other animate or inanimate objects is the manifestation of the element of space.

Our sense of hearing and our sense organ the ears are connected to the element of space. Space governs the Satva Guna (quality) of the mind. This is the principle which is said to contain the cosmic memory of the entire creation. This principle of the mind also endows the individual with compassion, empathy, universal love, deep feelings of spirituality, deep desire to follow truth, righteousness, good manners, moral ellamma and conduct. An individual with Satvic qualities are not easy to get upset or angry. They are not attached to material needs and desires. They are creative, humble and respectful of their teachers and elders, committed to doing good for humanity, caring of people, animals, trees and all life form. They also have a balanced intuition and intelligence.

The element of space is related to late winter and is related to the quality of lightness. Space resides within the clinical energy point of the Crown Chakra (which means energy vortex) within the human or other living species. Within the planet its clinical energy point is the universe and the realm of the sky. Space as mentioned earlier is also contained within all intercellular spaces and vacuums within the body, inanimate and animate objects. In fact it is the vast space within the atom where our energy particles are in flux. It is the space within our cellular and visceral spaces which give freedom to the tissues to perform their normal physiological functions. The solidity of a structure is only an illusion. When the element of space is out of balance within the human body or planet pathological conditions are created.

Gods and the Element of Space: Such Gods such as the Yoruba Wisdom God Orunmila, and the Hindu concept of Purusha correspond to this element.

84

The element of air

The movement of universal consciousness determines the direction along which changes of position in space take place. This course of action, causes subtle activities and movement within space. This movement is the principle of air. Air as a primordial element is the cosmic magnetic field which is responsible for the movement of earth, wind, and water. Movement is a very important function of air. Within the body the principle of air is the biological energy responsible for the movement of afferent (sensory) and efferent (motor) nerve impulses. When something touches the skin that tactile sensation is carried to the brain by the principle of movement, which is the sensory impulse.

Then there is a reaction to the impulse, which is the motor response, which is carried from the brain to the periphery. Our breathing is due to the movement of the diaphragm and intercostals muscles, our circulation is facilitated by the movement of the heart and blood vessels, and our digestion by the movement of the gastro intestinal tract. The subtle cellular movements are also governed by the principle of air. The movement of thought, desire and will are also governed by this principle.

In fact our entire universe is held together by the principle of air. Planets are held together and rotate as a result of electromagnetic energy.

The season of late winter, spring and summer are related to air. The time of the day dominated by the element of air is 2-6 in the morning and evening. This is when the system mind is capable of the greatest, clearest and most creative thought processes. The stage of life that the element of air relates to is the latter stages such as old age, the end of a process.

As this element governs movement, it also governs change and creativity. The special sense of touch and the sensory organ of the skin is related to this elemental force. Clarity, lightness, minuteness, coolness, soothing, drying, and soothing are all qualities related to the element of Air.

Gods and the Element of Air: The Yoruba embodiment of this particular energy is God of White Cloth, Obatala; the Yoruba Goddess of Wind and Transformation, Oya.

The ancients on the element of Fire

Wherever there is movement there is friction, which creates heat, so the third manifestation of consciousness is fire, the principle of heat. The element of fire is the elemental force of nature which governs all things to do with transformation including digestion, absorption, metabolism and assimilation. It is present in the eyes allowing us to perceive light. The luster in the eyes and skin is a result of the principle of fire. Our understanding, comprehension and appreciation is governed by the principle of fire in the brain as grey matter. The constant transformation which takes place in our cells process heat.

The primordial element of fire through the sun is the main source of energy in nature. This element endows the quality of lightness, roughness, sharpness, clarity, hotness, and speed to things. Its special sense is vision and special sense organ the eyes. It is an element which is related to the satvic and rajas mind due to its energy.

As we saw before the satvic quality of the mind governs clarity of perception, calm, and goodness. While the Rajas quality gives us the power to transform what is perceived externally into thoughts, concepts, visions and dreams. The principle of rajas maintains the memory of all species and the balance within nature. Individuals with pre-dominant rajastic qualities are energetic, ambitious, aggressive, proud, competitive, perfectionist, hard working, honest to their inner consciousness.

Blood is predominated by the primordial element of fire and is the main biological home of this energy. This energy is the clinical energy seat is the solar plexus which governs our ability to have clear perception, good judgement, and strong self identity, and balanced idea of power. The Clinical energy point in nature for the primordial element of fire is the Sun.

Gods and the Element of Fire: *The Yoruba Gods Ogun and Sango embody this element. Ogun is also related very strongly to the primordial energy of earth as Ogun is related to stability, minerals, vital energy to get things done, passion to do and survival. However, this God is also related to the primordial element of fire because he governs the ability to have clear and good judgment, the ability to transform raw materials into an end product, and is related to the concept of power.*

In fact there is a wonderful story in the Ifa Wisdom tradition where the positive side of Ogun's fire is illustrated. In this story Ogun seeks advise from a priest to discover how to gain popularity. He is told to make various sacrifices. One includes carrying a sword around with him. He complies with the advise. During his journey he meets two people fighting over a fish. He listens patiently to their stories after which he solves their problem by cutting the fish into two so that they both can share it. The sword he carries, how he uses the it and the profound solution to the individual's problems indicates good fair judgment and the use of the power of fire in a balanced way.

The ancients on the element of Water

Because of the heat of the fire, consciousness melts into water. According to chemistry water is a compound of molecules of hydrogen and oxygen, but water is also more than this. It is a primordial building block of life which embodies the principle of cohesiveness and pervasiveness. It is a remarkable primordial element which can be a gas, liquid or solid. All life forms are about 60-70% water. It exists in our bodies as plasma, tissue fluid, cytoplasm, serum, saliva, secretions, cerebro-spinal fluid etc. It is crucial for our sensation of taste, digestion and electrolyte balance. In fact all bio chemical reactions that take place within a living organisms body need water. Without water cells cannot live.

It is interesting to note that the entire earth's surface is covered by water. The parts of the surface we see above sea-level carve out the familiar shapes of continents we recognize today.

The qualities of the element of water are massiveness, fluidity, softness, inactiveness, sliminess, coldness, largeness of molecules , viscidity, wetness, healing, nourishing, cooling. Its special sense is taste and its special sense organ is the tongue. The quality of taste related to water sweet, slightly, salty and sour.

The element of water is related to and predominates the nerve tissues, plasma, reproductive tissues, breast milk, fatty tissue. Including the waste product of stools, sweat and stools. The sacred energy home of water is the Sacral channel which governs the healing of emotions, and trauma. It also governs creativity, sexuality, and the ability to explore the world in a creative way. The sacred energy home of the primordial element of water in nature are the rivers which act as a good monitoring point for whether this element is in or out of balance.

The Satvic quality of the mind is related to water along with the Tamas quality of the mind where there is darkness and the birthing of things good and bad.

Gods and the Element of Water: The Yoruba deities which represent and comment on this primordial element are Osun, Olukon, and Yemonja Osun is symbolized by fresh clear water, Olokun by the depth of the Ocean and Yemonja by the primordial waters, sea and in some areas of Africa the rivers. All these deities all symbolize different aspects of the element of water. The Egyptian God and Goddess Nu and Nut also represents the primordial waters from which life is birthed. While in India Ganga is the Goddess of fresh water.

The ancients on the element of earth

The manifestation of consciousness is the earth element. Because of the heat of the fire and water, there is crystallization. Properties of the earth element are massiveness, roughness, hardness, slowness, inactiveness, steadiness, firmness, clarity, denseness, largeness or bulkiness, coolness. Its special sense is smell and special organ the nose. It is related to the taste of sweet, sour and astringent. And is nourishing and healing. Earth is also the energy which predominates Spring, Monsoon, and early winter. It is also related to the tamas quality of the mind. It forms the muscular tissue, fatty tissue, bone tissue. The waste product it forms is the stools. The sacred home of earth within the body is the base Chakra which is responsible for the solidity and stability of the body and mind. The sacred home of earth within the environment itself is the earth all things are based on in the planet.

Gods and the Element of Earth: Ogun is the Yoruba deity of earth. This deity is said to govern minerals, iron ore, solidity, structure and getting things done. Like the Base Chakra where this energy is homed Ogun is the deity responsible for getting things done, and being the pioneer of trail blazer. This is the very role of the base chakra within

89

the body. It is interesting that the center of the earth is actually made up of a solid iron inner core more than 5000 km below the surface and is enveloped by a molten iron nickel outer core. Surrounding the outer core is a mantle of semi-molten rock of viscous consistency ranging from 30km to almost 3000 kilometers in depth. Above all of this is the Earth's crust which ranges averages 30km in thickness.

After writing these notes two things jumped out at me from the pages of two different written sources. The first was on a concept called Transformational Physics. Gerald H. Vind, Quantum Physics Scientist revealed quantum physics now believes in a world that we do not just observe but where we are part of the reality we perceive and "We too change along with what is observed." He claimed this new physics is known as Transformational Physics.

This new shift in physics recognizes that "there is a self-organizing principle of nature" which we in modern and ancient times have been referred to as consciousness. The belief that self-organization was the exclusive property of living systems has changed, because self-organizing forces are observable in nonliving things such as ocean currents and weather patterns.

The concept of self-organizing systems was popularized some fifteen years ago by Erich Jantshc, in his book, *The Self-Organizing Universe* where he reveals,

"Self-organization is the dynamic principle underlying the emergence of a rich world of forms manifest in biological, ecological, social, and cultural structures. But self-organization does not start with what we call life. It characterizes one of the basic two classes of structures which may be distinguished in physical reality, namely the dissipative structure that are fundamentally different from equilibrium structures. Thus, self-organization dynamics link between the animate and the inanimate. Life no longer appears as a thin super structure over a lifeless physical reality, but as an inherent principal of the dynamics of the universe."

The second thing that jumped out at me were some old notes I had written about water. In the light of Prakruti's dancing they caught my attention in a fresh way. For suddenly I could see Osun in physical water. Not only could I see her, but I realized she was indeed the mythological and physical waters of life itself.

The physical properties of water were all reminiscent of Osun: adhesion (Osun sews and holds things together), attraction (she is said to be highly irresistible and attractive to all. None can resist her), three states – gas, liquid, and solid (Osun was seen as an ethereal spirit of light, physical water itself and as an earthly woman).

As I re-read my notes on water I had made earlier, I found a renewed respect for it and the great Mother whom embodied it.

MY WATER NOTES

- Water molecules were highly attractive to themselves and other molecules. This was a result of something called their polar nature. Caused by the composition of water molecules which form an angle, with hydrogen atoms at the tips and oxygen at the vertex. Since oxygen has a higher electro negativity than hydrogen, the side of the molecule with the oxygen atom has a partial negative charge. An object with such a charge difference is called a dipole meaning two poles. The oxygen end is partially negative and the hydrogen end is partially positive, because of this the direction of the dipole moment points towards the oxygen. The charge differences cause water molecules to be attracted to each other (the relatively positive areas being attracted to the relatively negative areas) and to other polar molecules. This attraction contributes to hydrogen bonding, and explains many of the properties of water, such as solvent action.

- Water also has high adhesion properties because of its polar nature. On extremely clean/smooth glass the water may form a thin film because the molecular forces between glass and water molecules (adhesive forces) are stronger than the cohesive forces. In biological cells and organelles, water is in contact with membrane and protein surfaces that are hydrophilic; that is, surfaces that have a strong attraction to water.
- Water was one of the only elements that naturally occurs in three states: liquid, solid and a gas.
- Water has a high level of attractiveness caused by the strong cohesion between water molecules, the highest of the non-metallic liquids. This can be seen when small quantities of water are placed onto a sorption-free (non-adsorbent and non-absorbent) surface, such as polyethylene or Teflon, and the water stays together as drops.
- As a result of the forces of adhesion and surface tension, water exhibits capillary action whereby water rises into a narrow tube against the force of gravity. Water adheres to the inside wall of the tube and surface tension tends to straighten the surface causing a surface rise and more water is pulled up through cohesion. The process continues as the water flows up the tube until there is

enough water such that gravity balances the adhesive force.

Spent, eventually Prakruti releases me after days of having me in the rapture of her ecstatic dance. Exhausted I fall into the pages of my diary to make sense of some of the thoughts swirling around in my head, and around me. I sit up in my bed, prop myself against my plump pillows and write,

When I close my eyes and think of the word Earth Based Religion I realize that chaotic images of people jumping around wildly come up in my mind. Images I had been taught to believe were true from young. Images I know the whole world carry around in their head. But now I am becoming aware that science is not an invention of modern times but of those who came long before us. Their understanding of the universe was impeccable. Can we really move forward without looking backward? Without continuing to tap into this vast wise pool of knowledge? I am beginning to think not. I suppose we have pushed away what was not initially understood, and seen it as only the wild gesticulation hands. Recently I read a book about how to fix the planet but where was the mention of incorporating indigenous knowledge in this fix? Nowhere. Nowhere.

I am wondering what is so bad about the wisdom of our ancestors that we don't want to hear it. What is so threatening about it that we deafen our ears to it. More technology is not seeming to me like more wisdom in our case today. Tanti, my great aunt and Mum a Nen her sister use to give me so much wisdom. Tanti particularly use to like giving this wisdom from her old wooden rocking chair. Weaving tale after tale to illustrate some point or another. I use to love it, I use to find it so edifying. That is how I see the cultural systems of the indigenous people of the world, like my great aunt and grandmother.

Somewhere against these footsteps I have been walking I read a speech by the Dalai Lama called *Thinking Globally: A Universal Task* where he stated,

"*Ancient cultures that have adapted to their natural surroundings can offer special insights on structuring human societies to exist in balance with the environment. For example, Tibetans are uniquely familiar with life on the Himalayan Plateau. This has evolved into a long history of a civilization that took care not to overwhelm and destroy its fragile eco-system. Tibetans have long appreciated the presence of wild animals as symbolic of freedom. A deep reverence for nature is apparent in much of Tibetan art and ceremony. Spiritual development thrived despite limited material progress. Just as species may not adapt to relatively sudden environmental changes, human cultures also need to be treated with special care to ensure survival. Therefore, learning about the useful ways of people and preserving their cultural heritage is also a part of learning to care for the environment.*"

The echoes of this walk are beginning to lead me to believe that the songs of all the earth's people are needed to make things right, healed and creatively dynamic again. Buddhism and Hinduism have played significant parts in raising our level of understanding on a global level of what it is to be at one with consciousness. The voices of more indigenous people's from around the world will join in this song too. The ancient practices of Africa, the Indigenous Native Americans, amongst others will help us to heal. I think nothing is wrong with Science. Modern science. I just think it needs to join hands with ancient knowledge. This will us to heal from a place of remembering and true Earth harmony.

We all have our own song but my spirit and the spirit of the Mother has led me to know that this is not a time for the spiritual ownership of wisdom. Many cultures have particular wisdom and

94

spiritual systems attached to them. Many wear their wisdom systems like a badge of honor, while others hide theirs. Whichever way, I sincerely believe that the wisdom systems around the world were given to each for safe keeping, maybe for a moment like this.

On a final note I encountered this statement by John Gray, a modern day empowerment teacher. The book was entitled *Practical Miracles for Mars and Venus*. In this book he talks about how the man and woman of today can experience their inner potential and reach the heights of their spiritual potential. As a prerequisite to the book's many empowering exercises Gray talks about the new role of religion. He states, "to found a new religion is to deny the value of other religions. At this point in history it is not necessary. Anyone who feels the need to start a new faith is clearly not qualified. If a person were capable of knowing the truth, then he or she would already see the value of our present religions and not feel compelled to form another. Rather than a new better religion we are ready to experience the underlying truth that is present in every religion, and through the experience provide a unifying basis to support peace and harmony in the world".

I thank the Mother and ancestors for all they are showing me. It feels as though a very dark veil is lifting from my eyes.

Carving of Osun holding the wisdom of the world up, through
supporting the board of divine wisdom on her head.

*Indonesian depiction of Prithvi in ancient regal
attire as Mother Earth at Indonesian
National Monument*

OWANRIN MEJI

Girl:

Mother: what of Owonrin Meji?

Mother: Yes, In Owanrin Meji, Owonrin Meji has to overcome many obstacles which are in the form of troublesome enemies. However, he eventually prospers. Before he left heaven it is said that one of his most important works was when he did the divination for two brothers: Fefe (the wind) and Ale (the earth).

It so happened that the brothers wanted to come to the world. So they went to Owanrin Meji to discover what they needed to do to ensure they were successful when they arrived.

"Well you will have to make an offering of one palm frond and one parrot feather. Oh, and you must give a Sheep to your guardian angel and a he goat to the Opener of The Way, Esu," he said.

"Brother, what do you think?" asked Ale.

"I don't think the old fool knows what he is talking about," said Fefe

"I think he is a very wise priest. I think we should do as advised," said Ale.

Fefe did not agree. So Ale did the offering on his own. Both headed to earth to make a life. When they got to the boundary that divides heaven and earth they both went separate ways.

Ale did his sacrifices. Fefe was on the other hand, very swift, rascally and full of alacrity.

Ale became very successful on earth. He became important to all of living creatures on the planet. It so happened that any plant and animal which came to the world was advised from heaven to first pay respect to earth (Ale) by touching their heads to the ground.

While Ale enjoyed respect and stability, Fefe could not settle anywhere on earth. He took to going between earth and heaven. Also he was invisible to the naked eye and was noticed by no one.

It was the end of March 2008 and after our third Water Blessing that I discovered that water really did respond to love and gratitude. One day in the little book shop I loved I decided to browse in a different section. I normally loved going to the history section, that day I decided to go look at the section that had book's on healing. There I encountered a book by Dr. Masaru Emoto's "The True Power of Water". It was one of the most exciting finds to me. I jumped up and down, and made a complete fool of myself in front of the heavily painted Indian shop assistants. They looked at me like I had no sense (and in Trinidad it was not a good thing to act like you had no sense. It was quite scorned on). If only they knew how many years I had been waiting to come across a copy of that book. I had heard about it on and off over the years. The first person who ever mentioned it was my Ayurvedic lecturer. The book documents Dr. Masaru Emoto's amazing discoveries and findings with water. I couldn't wait to read Dr. Emoto's findings for myself, and could not get home quick enough.

Dr. Emoto's work and discoveries came from the simple thought "are there any identical snow crystals?" A question that was inspired by a book he read that stated no two snowflakes were identical. He pondered the question and before long found himself on a hunt to see if it was possible to look at water crystals. After much concerted effort he found a way to do this, and eventually, he stumbled on a profound discovery – water reads the essence of messages.

Dr. Emoto's research began with an examination of tap water, distilled and mineral water. He wanted to know if they all formed the same type of water crystals. He discovered that tap water did not manage to form crystals, some mineral water did and distilled water did. What he really found out was that their ability to form or not form crystals reflected water's state. When in a "good state" it formed stunning and breathtaking beautiful crystals. When not in this state it often formed broken crystals.

During this process Dr. Emoto came up with a hypothesis, "water shows different shapes of ice crystals depending on the information it has received." It drove him into further experimentation. He taped messages onto bottles of water, froze and unfroze the bottles and then took pictures of the water crystals (see the full method and experiment in his book).

He discovered that water did indeed read and respond to messages. It formed beautiful, strong and elegant crystals when exposed to positive messages and broken crystals (or non at all) when shown negative words. The words "thank you" and "love" seemed to make water form the most beautiful crystals which "opened up as if a blossoming flower". While water formed fragmented crystals when exposed to negative words such as "war", and "you fool".

Dr. Emoto took his experiment further and further. He exposed water to music, pictures and some messages in foreign languages and discovered that water could read the essence of messages and always responded with beautiful crystals to positive words..

He also discovered that if he labeled water with a negative message, took a crystal picture, then labeled the same water with a positive message and took another crystal picture. There was a change in the crystal formation. Concluding water changes its form according to the message it is exposed to.

Then there was his observation of water when exposed to prayer. One day he went to Lake Biwa, Japan's Mother's of

101

lakes. He took 350 people with him. A prayer session was held there led by Dr Nobuo Shioya, a former assistant professor at Keijyo Imperial University, Department of Medicine, in Seoul, Korea. The prayer performed was known as the *Great Declaration*. It was repeated 10 times.

Now Lake Biwa is known in Japan to be a very dirty lake with a smelly odor. One month after the prayer, the Kyoto newspaper ran a large article, July 25th 1999, declaring that for the first time in a very long time. Lake Biwa had "no abnormal growth of algae this summer, zero smell".

Dr. Emoto also conducted experiments on the quality of food when exposed to positive vibration and negative vibration. For these experiments he partnered with Dr. Sugahara, a graduate of University of Tokyo department of medicine and founder of the Sugahara institute.

Through measuring the energy of food with a device known as a hado machine they discovered that food responded to positive and negative vibrations.

All of Dr. Emoto's discoveries led him down the path of working with the healing power of water and he now works with hado medicine to help heal people's ailments.

After reading Dr. Emoto's book excitement filled me up. For after every Water Blessing I had conducted I noticed how much the waters had bounced alive with sparkles. After the first time it happened I gave the experience the name, "sparkling water effect".

I was eager to repeat the rice experiment Dr. Emoto had documented in his book where a Japanese family, inspired by his work, decided to try saying negative and positive words to cooked rice and then observe its impact.

They cooked a pot of rice, and divided it into two containers. One was labeled "I love you" and the other "I hate you". Every day they spoke positive words to the "I love you" rice and negative ones to the "I hate you rice". They found that the "I love you rice" did not go off, but the "I hate you rice" did.

I repeated the same experiment for three weeks with the same results. The rice I had labeled "I love you" and said those words out aloud to formed a top layer of fungi but was quite fresh underneath. The one labeled "I hate you" and had those words spoken to it became maggot ridden and quite stinky.

However, initially the experiment did not go to plan. In the first week I noticed something strange. The rice I said "I love you" to was going off faster than the one I said "I hate you" to. At first I thought the rice experiment was obviously not repeatable. But, the journalist in me tried to figure out if I was doing something wrong. Eventually, it dawned on me I hate saying hurtful words to people. So when I said, "I hate you" to the rice labeled with the same words I was saying it with a lot of love!

After that realization I changed my approach. That is when the rice labeled "I hate you" became over run with maggots. That was when I realized Dr. Emoto was correct – water reads the essence of the words.

Soon after successfully completing the experiment I came across a traditional Yoruba story. Another story, another code.

One day Osun had fought with her sister Yemaya and decided to set up a separate Kingdom. She walked and walked until

103

she reached a place where each one of her steps turned into a river. There she established herself with her husband Inle. The latter, eventually grew indifferent to her charms and she became so poor that her dress turned yellow from repeated washings.

One day Sango, the spirit of lightening, went to Osun's home and advised her to seek Orunmila's counsel. She did this and the Lord of Divination instructed her to offer an ebo. He further instructed her to deposit offerings at a very specific spot and not to be afraid of anything she might witness. Osun followed Orunmila's warnings to the letter and upon arriving at a curve on the road, she discovered a large palace owned by three brothers: twins and Iduo, the youngest sibling.

The twins engaged in a quarrel and killed each other. Osun was ready to flee but Iduo called her back and told her not to run. He told her all that she saw would belong to her as he was going to die soon. He said upon his death he will give everything to her. This is how Osun acquired her wealth.

An owner of a leading sanitation company revealed to me one day that one of the rivers they had helped to clean up was initially black. As they began the river clean up the water began to change from a very murky dark color to a clear one. He further stated that he believed the color of water indicated its health.

I realized that right there in that story of Osun, was a confirmation of what Dr. Masaru had discovered – that water changes its state according to how it is treated.

The ability of water to respond to positive words was according to Derrick one day demonstrated by Georgia's governor Sonny Perdue. It was late 2007, and Atlanta was experiencing a drought. Well after twenty months of no rain Perdue thought you know what we need to pray for rain. He stood right there on the front lawn of the State House and prayed for rain. His prayer went something like this,

"God we need you. We need rain".

His prayer was met by horror by some, fascination by others, and total disbelief by many. However, as Mark Strassmann CBS News's reporter pointed out his actions were natural for

"in desperate droughts, praying for rain goes back thousands of years, from African tribal groups to Indian rain dancers".

"Did the rain stop, sweetie?" I asked.

"Yes, it did," he said.

To illustrate that everything responds to a certain type and level of vibration. Dr. Emoto gives the example of three Tuning Forks. Forks and 1 and 2 have a frequency of 440 HZ and Fork 3 of 442 HZ. Which means that Fork 1 and 2 are designed to vibrate at 440 times per second, while Fork 3 vibrates 442 times per second? If Tuning Fork 1 is hit with a rubber hammer, Fork 2 (which has the same frequency) will give off a sound but Fork 3 will not.

According to Dr. Emoto a vibration can have a positive or negative effect. When it is negative a disturbance at a subatomic level is caused resulting in an intrinsic imbalance. This disturbance can be corrected by sending positive vibration to the intended subject matter.

He elaborates on this phenomenon by showing that wave fluctuations have a pattern of valleys and peaks. In order to cancel out a wave fluctuation you have to override it with one with opposite valley and peak formations. He gives the example of Dr. Yoshio Yamsaki of the Science and Engineering Laboratory of Waseda University. Who was reported by the Yamiuri newspaper in April 1991 to have successfully created a quiet soundless space in a room filled with music. The method used – to examine the wave shape of peaks and valleys of a sound to be silenced and produce a sound that had the opposite wave shape of peaks and valleys. Dr Yamsaki's results were presented at the International Symposium on Active Control of Sound and Vibration in Tokyo in the year of 1991.

Gerald H.Vind, MA, quantum physics scientist elegantly puts it this way in his essay, "The Light of Transformation, Future History"

Different molecular structures each have a characteristic oscillatory (vibrational) rate and, much like a bunch of crickets, molecules are constantly chirping their identity and location. The fundamental nature of life energy is information, and this information is modulated in electrical fields, magnetic fields, and quantum fields that interact in resonant patterns and harmonics that flow throughout (and beyond) the body. Information is a vital part of the process of self-organization.

OBARA MEJI

Girl: Mother tell me about Obara Meji.

Mother: It is said that Obara Meji was well known for his concern about the poverty of God's creatures. He taught people that the outcome of their lives was a result of their own choices.

So for instance one day when the Coconut was leaving heaven for the earth with her other sister, the Royal Palm, they both went for divination to a priest called Jeemfidihee. The name of Obara Meji in heaven was Jeemfidihee. He made divination for them and advised them to make an offering. On getting to the world both sisters became married to Ode (that is outside). The coconut produced a lot of fruits which made her the favorite of all people. On the other hand, the Royal Palm, although more beautiful than her sister, the Coconut, remained an object of barren decoration to her husband, lacking in any significance to anyone else.

Obara Meji also did a divination for the Frog when she was coming to the world. He advised her to make the same offering prescribed for the Palm sisters. She did it, and she began to multiply as soon as she got to earth. After helping several others in heaven, he saw a lot of poverty on Earth and felt moved to help people and animals rise above poverty to find prosperity.

It was early April, 2 am, and another night of sleeplessness which led me to sit in meditation. As I took deep long breaths I reviewed some of the things and revelations that had come my way. I was getting used to the feeling of being constantly surrounded by a battery of helpful helpers, including the archetypal Mother herself.

My deep breathing finally took me into a blissful state where all my fears and trepidations downed the veil that kept me locked in the physical world. In the moments when that happened it was easier for me to hear the sweet voice of the great universe in the form of our World Mother talking. At some point my breath became still. I was breathing without breathing. A dialogue began between my soul and the soul of the Great Mother who I was beginning to realize had many faces, and ways about her.

Mother: human beings have moved away from the Inner Most Sacred.
Me: What is the Inner Most Sacred?
Mother: It is that which teaches us how to live and be right in the world. It is the part of our nature which teaches us the fundamental laws of existence. Whatever we decide are the rules of existence are often far removed from the fundamental truths of the universe. The fundamental truths of the universe do not change. The sun sets at the same time every day and the stomach stops digesting after 6.30 pm all over the world.

Move away from the Inner Most Sacred you move away from the ability to create health and balance within the personal inner and outer world. Human's now believe they can create a world without the input of The Inner Most Sacred. But by ignoring the Inner Most Sacred they are connecting with the part of the mind that only can cope with Outer Most Objectification.
Me: What is the Outer Most Objectification?

Mother: *It is that which is connected to the left side of the mind. It sees a stone on the ground and says that is a hard object sitting down there. Without the connection to the Inner Most Sacred we lose the rest of the picture. For the Inner Most Sacred will say, "that object sitting down there is hard, it is round and it is made up of the very universal essence of God. It is wise because it holds the memory of the wisdom of the earth within its particles and it holds the essence of God within every fiber of its being".*

Me: *How do we connect with this Inner Most Sacred?*

Mother: *We all hear the voice of The Inner Most Sacred when we are at peace, sitting quietly by ourselves or with nature. In those moments we come the closest to who we really are. The ancients were in touch with the Inner Most Sacred. Through it they learnt much about the truths of who we are, why we are here and how we are meant to function with ecological human and universal harmony. Through allowing themselves to be taught by this aspect of Self they were able to stay harmonized.*

The Outer Most Objectification now had its purpose in the rightful place because anything it created, made, decided on was from a wisdom point of view. It would say – "this building needs to go up because these people need shelter. But it would say but this land is sacred and everything on it is too. So let me ask the spirit of this tree if I have permission to cut it down, let me appease the land I am going to build on, let me make sure I build something that the human spirit can reside in happily".

The Inner Most Sacred in ancient cultures was known as that which was a passive observer (thus wise and all knowing). It was symbolized by the moon, water, and inner activities. So the turning of an apple into blood is the function of the Inner Most Sacred. The Outer Most Observer was known as that which was engaged in outer activity and doing. It was characterized by action, the sun, fire, and getting things concretized in the outer world. Both principles were known respectively as the Feminine Principle and the Masculine Principle.

The Inner Most Sacred was nothing more than me The Great Mother. When we think of a mother we think of pregnancy, inner nurturing, caring, teaching principles to the child, looking after, loving, Beingness, correction, trying to bring balance and harmony. In traditional cultures The Great Mother is epitomized as: Wise, sensuous, hard-working, all knowing, an abundance bringer, a giver, a good care-taker, endowed with the ability to manifest all that is beautiful and harmonious, the keeper of the secrets.

Me: *Do you think we have moved away from you?*

Mother: *Of course. You all have moved away from the ancient knowledge that kept everything in balance.*

I think that dialogue had been triggered of by one single simple episode of a large Indian potbellied man (who must have been about fifty something) standing in the middle of a hospital ward chatting a cute nurse up. That was the day I went to the hospital with my mom to see about a clot that had appeared suddenly in her leg.

He had been telling the nurse how successful he had been until he fell sick from too many late nights and overeating rich foods – namely roti, doubles and curry chicken. He was sad that he could no longer do what he loved doing. Now he was beholden to his illness (he never mentioned what it was). From the dark marks heavily lining the under surface of his eyes, and from my Ayurvedic training, I ascertained he had serious liver problems.

For some reason what the man said, his deep regret for his lost passion – his music career, and the stamp of illness all over him disturbed me for the whole day. I could not figure out why. Then it came to me. I was disturbed and even angry that no one had taught that man the simple ancient wisdom of self-care and balance.

The thought had made me think of the billions of people all around the world who suffered unnecessarily because of the same reason. The wisdom of the ancients does heal, save and balance us. Those were the thoughts I had taken into meditation with me.

Sacred Maracus River that ran
at back our house in Trinidad

OKONRAN MEJI

Girl: Mother tell me of Okonran Meji.

Mother: Yes, Okonran Meji. Now Okonran Meji is quite interesting. In many of the Okonran Meji stories we see that one is never too small to have a good life, and never too big to have a great fall. When we live in accordance to sacred advice given to us nothing is ever to small or to big to overcome.

Girl: Mother tell me a story from Okonran Mejji.

Mother: Well, you know before Okonran Meji left heaven he did many good deeds and gave much good advice. Let's start with the mighty Iroko tree.

When Iroko was ready to come to heaven, so was the Araba, that is the name for a great spiritual leader. They both went to Okonran Meji to ask him what they needed to do before they left heaven for the world. Well, Okonran Meji told them both to give the God of the Crossroads, whose name is Esu, a goat. Now the Araba did as he was advised. But not Iroko, oh no. Iroko thought he was too big and strong. He did not believe anyone would trouble him, and generally that was the case. Everyone on Earth feared Iroko.

Anyway, after Esu had finished enjoying his delicious goat from the Araba. He got to work. He told everyone on Earth that the Iroko tree wood was good and strong for making doors. Well, no one was interested in cutting Iroko down. For one he was very mighty and powerful and two the mystical Witches of the night always met at the Iroko tree.

Esu did not give up on his mission. He gave the people an axe to chop the Iroko down with. People were at first reluctant to do anything to attack the Iroko tree. With Esu's continual urging the people began to chop at the mighty Iroko tree. Eventually, the great Iroko fell and it made such an almighty crashing sound that reverberated throughout the whole forest. The Araba heard the sound and went rushing to the place. When he saw the Iroko dead on the floor he gave up praise that he had headed Esu's advice.

Now interestingly enough, the ant was also ready to come to earth. However, he had a different problem. The ant was so small that he wondered how he was going to be able to survive and make a living on earth. Well the ant was advised by Okonran Meji to make an offering so that he will be able to have a happy and great life on earth. He was told that if he made the offering he would have rulership over all the food in the home.

The ant followed the advice. The prediction of Okonran Meji came to pass. The ant treads and feeds freely on all household food even to this day.

A few days after my meditation insight I went for a hot sultry walk to the internet café. I was missing Derrick terribly and decided to send him an e-mail. Telephoning all the time was getting pretty expensive. As usual once I got on the computer I began to idly surf the net. I was interested in finding out more about the state of the waterways. An interest that had been triggered of by a visit myself, mom and Kem Ra (he was now with me in Trinidad) had made to the famous Caroni Swamp of Trinidad.

Despite the off putting word, swamp - the Caroni turned out to be a stunning place. At first it tricks you, as you amble into the old wooden boats manned by guides, and travel up its narrow stretch of murky brown waters.

However, that murky brown strip of water opens into the most magnificent sparkling blue expanse I have ever seen. On the edges of its body are the trees that the endangered red Scarlet Ibis of Trinidad fly into for resting and nesting. This bird is Trinidad's national symbol, and when you see it you can totally understand why.

When the guide anchored our boat we had to wait for almost an hour until the sun started painting the sky orange, in order to witness being filled with the full red of the Scarlet Ibis feathers. It was hard for the heart not to stop beating for a moment in wonderment, at the startling sight.

We had a good guide that day who informed us that the word Caroni was from a Spanish word that meant "Daughter of the Moon". He admitted he was not totally sure if that was the true meaning or source of the word. However, he was quite sure about everything he knew about the endangered species that the Caroni Swamp held.

"You know this river is really dying he said. You know this because many of the species that use to be in it are disappearing."

We were all riveted to our guide and nodded our heads.

"Global warming," he said in his thick Trini Indian.

What I found from my internet search shocked me. Not only was the guide right about the Caroni Swamp dying, but I discovered a water graveyard on the net. All the rivers seemed to be dying. I came across article upon article that spoke about this river dying, or that river dying. With each river I found dying a piece of me felt as though it died to. How comes I didn't know this stuff? How comes I didn't know how bad things were? I asked myself.

Instead of e-mailing Derrick I spent the rest of my afternoon reading article after article about the state of our waterways. I saved quotes and information on my thumb drive, hoping I wouldn't end up with a virus on my computer again. That night I went back home, compiled the quotes that had moved me, and wrote "River Eulogy".

I shared it with mom, Derrick and Kem Ra. I was hoping they would find it, as fascinating and compelling as I did. They did in the same way I did. For part of them died at with each revelation too.

"Sweetie, the world has to know about this. I now feel committed to the waterways and planet healing even more. We have to know what we are doing to our waters, and planet. If our waters die, if our planet dies - we die too. Water is sacred. Everything is sacred. We cannot treat things like this sweetie. Everything is dying and why don't we truly know that?"

116

"Yes, it is true," Derrick said agreeing with me saddened by the information.

From that moment on I felt a burning fire grow inside me. A conviction to help the waterways, planet and humanity was fuelled. I wanted our children to have a future. "Going to Water" was beginning to make sense to me. Not only was water dying, but its dying voice seemed to be unfolding an ancient song that mapped the road back to wholeness. Caught in its vast current I let myself go allowing it to take me to where I next needed to be.

Once I finished the River Eulogy document I e-mailed it over to Derrick.

RIVER EULOGY

"Water responds to even delicate energy"
Dr Joan Davis

Glaciers are melting, sea levels are rising, cloud forests are
drying, and wildlife is scrambling to keep pace. It's becoming
clear that humans have caused most of the past century's
warming by releasing heat-trapping gases as we power our
modern lives. Called greenhouse gases, their levels are higher
now than in the last 650,000 years.
National Geographic

Africa does not produce any significant amount of greenhouse
gases, but it's our lakes and rivers that are drying up. America
has refused to ratify Kyoto and it is our lakes that are drying
up.
Guardian Web, 2007 on Lake Chad

Experts are warning that the lake, which was once Africa's
third largest inland water body, could shrink to a mere pond
in two decades.
40 years ago, lake Chad was 25,000 sq km and the daily fish
catch was some 230,000 tonnes; It was fondly referred by locals
as the "ocean" now it is 500 sq km with a catch of barely
50,000 tonnes. Now reduced rainfull and damming of the
rivers of Logone and Chari which empties into the lake means
only half of the water now gets into the lake. What use to be
an abundant lake creating joy and sustenance for all now has

fisher men arguing about borders. With the 30m- strong shoreline communities now competing for access to water and pastures.
BBC News Website January 2007

Some 27 years ago when I started fishing on the lake, we used to catch fish as large as a man. But now this is all the fishermen bring in after a whole night of fishing," he says pointing at tiny catfish piled on the ground in Doron Baga's once-famous fish market. BBC News Website January 2007 on Lake Chad "I tell you even animals and birds have been dying around here. There are fewer of them now," says Musa Niger, a fisherman in Duguri, an island village in the middle of the lake
BBC New Website January 2007 on Lake Chad

A recent study by Nasa and the German Aerospace Centre blames global warming and human activity for Africa's disappearing water.

Two hundred million people [are] facing a waterless future. The groundwater boom is turning to bust and, for some, the green revolution is over."
Fred Pearce author of When the Rivers Run Dry

We must change our mindset now or pay the price in the not so distant future
Tickner.wwf

Those who dispute that climate change is taking place, such as Melanie Phillips of the Daily Mail, like to point out that that the predicted effects of global warming rely on computer models, rather than "observable facts". That's the problem with the future – you can't observe it.

But to have any hope of working out what might happen, you need a framework of understanding. It's either this or the uninformed guesswork that Phillips seems to prefer.

The models can be tested by means of what climate scientists call back casting – seeing whether or not they would have predicted changes that have already taken place. The global climate model used by the Met Office still needs to be refined. While it tracks past temperature changes pretty closely, it does not accurately back cast the drought patterns in every region. But it correctly reproduces the total global water trends over the past 50 years.

When the same model is used to forecast the pattern over the 21st century, it uncovers "a net overall global drying trend" if greenhouse gas emissions are moderate or high. "On a global basis, drought events are slightly more frequent and of much longer duration by the second half of the 21st century relative to the present day." In these dry, stodgy phrases, we find an account of almost unimaginable future misery.

The Guardian 2006. The Fresh Water Boom is Over

In the report, World's Top 10 Rivers at Risk, released ahead of World Water Day (March 22) WWF The World Wild Life Fund lists the top 10 rivers around the world that are drying-out or dying as a result of climate change, pollution and dams. The report concludes that poor planning and inadequate protection of natural areas mean we can no longer assume that water will flow forever. The list includes Europe's Danube, the Americas' La Plata and Rio Grande/Rio Bravo, Africa's Nile-Lake Victoria system and Australia's Murray-Darling, but also highlights the profound problems facing Asia, where five of the 10 rivers listed in the report are found – the Yangtze, Mekong, Salween, Ganges and Indus.

Problems highlighted in the report include dams and dykes along the Danube River – one of the longest flowing rivers in Europe – which have already destroyed 80% of the river basin's wetlands and floodplains; and over-extraction of water from India's Indus River for agriculture leading to water scarcity and severe threats to freshwater fish populations – the most important source of protein and overall life support systems for tens of millions of people worldwide.

The report calls on governments to better protect river flows and ensure more sustainable water allocations in order to safeguard habitats and people's livelihoods and ensure a secure environment for businesses. Businesses themselves, especially those that rely on thirsty food and fiber products, should look at their own water use and should encourage supply chains to be more water efficient.

My summary of the WWF Report

A veterinary pathologist at the University of Montreal says one in four beluga whales in the St. Lawrence River is dying of cancer. The new study says the cancer is linked to toxic emissions from aluminum smelters which dot Quebec's Saguenay region. Martineau says the belugas are being poisoned by polycyclic aromatic hydrocarbons. PAH are a carcinogen he says are produced and released by aluminum smelters. Martineau says whales feed on sediment at the

121

bottom of feeder rivers, which have been polluted by
companies, including Alcan.
CBC 2002, Belugas dying of Cancer

Eight of the 10 largest cities on earth have been built beside the
sea. They rely on underground reservoirs of fresh water
floating, within the porous rocks, on salt water which has
soaked into the land from the sea. As the fresh water is sucked
out, the salt water rises and can start to contaminate the
aquifer. This is already happening all over the world.
As the sea level rises as a result of climate change, salt
pollution in coastal regions is likely to accelerate .
George Monit. A Burning World

Dozens of paddle steamers with their rich cargoes of wool
once plied the waters of the Darling River. But the industry
declined and over the years so did the river, to the point that
where the steamers sometimes once travelled there is now
barely a trickle.
Despite recent rains there are still persistent warnings that the
Darling River is dying – the victim of drought and poor
planning.
With too many irrigators and not enough water, the
Federal Government will next month order the taps be turned
off in the Murray-Darling Basin. Darling River dying as
irrigators ponder zero water allocations.
AM – Friday, 15 June , 2007 08:21:00. Reporter: Mark Willacy

Yangtez River, dying from pollution

They say a river system dies from its mouth, and if you ever need proof of the desperate state of our once great Murray Darling, it's where it flows into the ocean at a place called the Coorong.

The Coorong is a hauntingly-beautiful wetland, an area renowned for its plentiful birdlife and rich farmlands, a place so enchanting it inspired the classic movie Storm Boy.
But now the Coorong is dying – the wildlife's vanishing – entire communities disappearing – and we're to blame.
You see, for almost 200 years we've plundered the Coorong's lifeblood, the Murray-Darling. We've all but sucked it dry.
This week the Rudd Government announced a multi-billion-dollar rescue bid for the Murray-Darling but, as Charles Wooley reports, for the Coorong, it may be too little, too late.
River's End, Charles Wooley, Sunday 4 2008

Their occupants no longer try to fish. It is more profitable to forage for rubbish they can salvage and trade – plastic bottles, broken chair legs, rubber gloves – risking disease for one or two pounds a week if they are lucky.
On what was United Nations World Environment Day, the Citarum, near the Indonesian capital of Jakarta, displayed the shocking abuse that mankind has subjected it to.
Is This The World's Most Polluted River, Richard Shears, 25th June 2008

It used to be that in the Andes of Ecuador, toads were so abundant you had to be careful not to step on then," recalls Duellman, who is also curator emeritus of herpetology (reptile and amphibian science) at the University of Kansas Natural

History Museum. "Now, they're gone." And not just in South American rainforests. Frogs have existed on Earth for nearly 200 million years. "That's a pretty impressive amount of time to be around," says Coven "We can only hope they hang on through whatever this is.

From: Science World | Date: 3/11/2002 | Author: Masibay, Kim.

There's a joke in China today that you can tell what colors are in fashion by looking at the rivers.

CHINA: Ravaged Rivers by Jane Spencer, Wall Street Journal.
August 22nd, 2007

Last summer, Chinese government investigators crawled through a hole in the concrete wall that surrounds the Fuan Textiles mill in southern China and launched a surprise inspection of the plant. What they found caused alarm at dozens of American retailers, including Wal-Mart Stores Inc., Lands' End Inc. and Nike Inc., that use the company's fabric in their clothes.
Villagers had complained that the factory, majority owned by Hong Kong-based Fountain Set Holdings Ltd., had turned their river water dark red. Authorities discovered a pipe buried underneath the factory floor that was dumping roughly 22,000 tons of water contaminated from its dyeing operations each day into a nearby river, according to local environmental-protection officials.

CHINA: Ravaged River by Jane Spencer, Wall Street Journal.
August 22nd, 2007

Prices in the U.S. are artificially low," says Andy Xie, former chief economist for Morgan Stanley Asia, who now works independently. "You're not paying the costs of pollution, and that is why China is an environmental catastrophe. He states About 20% to 30% of China's water pollution comes from manufacturing goods that are exported. We want them to know we're watching from China," says Ma Jun, a prominent Chinese water-pollution activist who has launched a Web site that aggregates data about polluting factories.

Ganges, India. Dying from pollution

Last month Punjab has been declared as the over all best state in the country by India Today news magazine for the third conjunctive year. It is good to have a prize for Punjab and state government has immediately taken this as an opportunity to have publicity campaign for its achievement. But there is another side of the picture also which shows doom, distress and destruction is fast engulfing this land of five waters. It is a Water-Chaos in the Punjab.

We can see farmers committing suicides due to failure of pumps, neighbors in farms killing each other over the quarrel for irrigation water, Women are bound to fetch water on their head from as far as 3 kms, and a vast majority of people have no option other then to drink sub-human water. We can see long queues around certain hand pumps adjacent to canals for potable water; we can find farmers fetching water on trolleys, bullock carts, jeeps, and village made jeep-the jogards, motor bikes and bicycles in several villages.

Land of Five Rivers in Water Crisis and Chaos, By Umendra Dutt,
05 October, 2006, Countercurrents.org

The water crisis is so vast that it had engulfed every nook and corner of the state. You can find farmers demonstrating in Talwandi Sabo, Pathankot, Fazilka, Malout, Muktsar, Hoshiarpur and Garhshankar. Then there are demonstrations by urban people at Amritsar, Jalandhar, Ludhiana, and list is end less.

Land of Five Rivers in Water Crisis and Chaos, By Umendra Dutt,
05 October, 2006, Countercurrents.org

In Malsingh Wala village one could see peoples toeing water not only to drink, but also for bath and for their animals. It is 100% water importing village. Malsingh Wala has already declared itself as 'village for sale'. Even earlier village Harkishanpura which was first village to put itself on sale has also severe water problem. There is no water for irrigation neither for drinking. The water crisis made village insolvent and compelled villagers to put village on sale. The situation is almost same in whole of Malwa region. The severe water crisis is also becoming a social stigma upon some villages. It is tough to find a bride for village youths as no body wants to marry his/her daughter to these villages.

Land of Five Rivers in Water Crisis and Chaos.
By Umendra Dutt, 05 October, 2006, Countercurrents.org

The Ganga, which is virtually synonymous with Indian civilization, is dying. Pollution, over-extraction of water, emaciated tributaries and climatic changes are killing the mighty river, on whose fecund plains live one in 12 people of this planet.
This grim prognosis was made by conservation group WWF on Tuesday. Apart from Ganga, Indus, Nile and Yangtze are among the 10 most endangered rivers of the world. Ganga Among 10 Dying Rivers.
Times of India, Neelam Raaj, 20 March 2007,

India is named for the Indus River, along whose fecund banks a great urban civilization flourished more than 4,000 years ago," writes American historian Stanley Wolpert in his well-known book A New History of India. But the 3,000-kilometre-long river that is the lifeline of Pakistan's economy is dying a slow death due to thinning of Tibetan glaciers and building of dams and barrages upstream.

The glaciers of the Tibetan plateau are vanishing so fast that they will be reduced by 50 per cent every decade, according to The Independent. Citing the leading Chinese scientists, it says the glaciers have been receding over the past four decades, as the world has gradually warmed up, but the process has now accelerated alarmingly. "The melting threatens to disrupt water supplies over much of Asia. Many of the continent's greatest rivers-including the Yangtze, the Indus, the Ganges, the Brahmaputra, the Mekong and the Yellow River rise on the plateau

The International, The News 4.13.2008

Biodiversity underpins the health of the planet and has a direct impact on all our lives so it is alarming that despite of an increased awareness of environmental issues we continue to see a downtrend trend," said WWF campaign head Colin Butfield.

World Species Dying Out Like flies Say WWF, Friday May 16th 2008, Jeremy Lovell

WORLD MARKS ENVIRONMENT DAY "DYING FOR WATER

Reuters, June 5, 2003

It is a new trend that now farmers in Punjab are committing suicide as their tube wells are going dry. As water level is going down drastically day by day the farmers are forced to spend money to get water from new depth. In some of areas this is very common phenomenon. This also adds more debt burden on Punjabi farmers

Land of Five Rivers in Water Crisis and Chaos, By Umendra Dutt,
05 October, 2006, Countercurrents.org

Israel's Dead Sea is, ironically, as old as life itself. Hidden in
the world's deepest valley and protected by majestic desert
mountains, the Dead Sea is one important feature in a land of
mysteries, miracles and biblical legends that we must see
before it's too late. In another three decades, the evaporating
Dead Sea could possibly become the dry sea.
Dead Sea is Evaporating and Shrinking.
ABC News, Nov 24th 2005

The Dead Sea is dying," Bromberg said. "The Dead Sea is
shrinking. It's falling by a meter in depth every year."
The Dead Sea relies on the fresh water of the Jordan River.
And, that once-wide river is now just a contaminated trickle.
As the sea's water disappears, it creates large sinkholes that
make it dangerous to even approach the sea in certain spots.
"If the Dead Sea goes away, we lose the ability to connect
what's really central about Earth and humanity and,
ultimately, the divine," Feiler said.
BBC News, Nov 24th 2005

The river has lost so much volume because farmers use it for
irrigation. Israel's success in growing crops in the desert
climate is a great source of pride, but the use of water has
become unsustainable.
Bromberg said. ABC News Nov 24th 2005

This is the Sea of Galilee, one of the world's largest fresh water lakes and the source of nearly all of Israel's drinking water. The Sea of Galilee feeds the River Jordan and the Dead Sea further south. For thousands of years the waters flowing out of the Sea of Galilee have nourished the River Jordan and have been the only source of fresh water for the Dead Sea. These clean waters enter the River Jordan at Yardenit where the baptisms take place but just a few kilometers south is where the river begins to die.

November 2 2006. Voice of America

Just out of eyesight, sewage from communities along the Sea of Galilee is dumped into one of the world's most sacred rivers. The environmental group, Friends of the Earth in the Middle East, says action must be taken to save the River Jordan before it is too late.

November 2 2006. Voice of America

Untreated toxic fluids released from several dying factories in Bhaluka upazila is polluting rivers and canals, posing environmental and health hazards. The pollution which is going on for several years is threatening fish resources, crops and the greenmery. There are at least six big textile dyeing factories are operating in the upazila without any provision for waste treatment. They release toxic water which flows into the waterbodies, sources said. The water of Khiru river and canals flowing through the upazila is getting polluted by the coloured toxic water, local people alleged during a recent visit to the area by this correspondent. The water also affects crops and land fertility, they said. Alal Uddin of Ashka village near

131

Khiru river said that in dry season, the river water becomes colured and emits bad smell. Fishes die in the river and they can not use the water for irrigation because crops turn yellowish, he said. Aminul *Islam, Daily Star, July 17, 2005*

The sound of water running throughout African mountains is the latest sign that the glaciers are turning into trickles.
Glaciers are Dying.
December 26th 2006, Charles Hanley, Associated Press

From 1.6-kilometre-high Naro Moru, villagers have watched year by year as the great glaciers of Mount Kenya, glinting in the equatorial sun high above them, have retreated into shrunken white stains on the rocky shoulders of the 5,150-metre peak.
Climbing up, "you can hear the water running down beneath Diamond and Darwin," mountain guide Paul Nditiru said, speaking of two of 10 surviving glaciers.
Glaciers are dying, December 26th 2006, Charles Hanley, Associated Press

The total loss of ice masses ringing Africa's three highest peaks, projected by scientists to happen sometime in the next two to five decades, fits a global pattern playing out in South America's Andes Mountains, in Europe's Alps, in the Himalayas and beyond.

Almost every one of more than 300 large glaciers studied worldwide is in retreat, international glaciologists reported in October in the journal Geophysical Research Letters. This is "essentially a response to post-1970 global warming," they said.

Glaciers are dying, December 26th 2006, Charles Hanley, Associated Press

The waters of the rivers of the Amazon Basin routinely fall by some 30-40 feet- greater than most of the tides of the world's seas – between the wet and dry seasons. But last year they just went on falling in the worst drought in recorded history.

In the Mamiraua Reserve they dropped 51 feet, 15 feet below the usual low level and other areas were more badly affected. At one point in the western Brazilian state of Acre, the world's biggest river shrank so far that it was possible to walk across it. Millions of fish died; thousands of communities, whose only transport was by water, were stranded. And the drying forest caught fire; at one point in September, satellite images spotted 73,000 separate blazes in the basin.

This year, says Otavio Luz Castello, the water is draining away even faster than the last one – and there are still more than three months of the dry season to go. He adds: "I am very concerned."

Dying Forest, One Year To Save The Amazon. Geoffrey Leon, July 2006, The Independent

A lawsuit filed by the Oklahoma Attorney General against Arkansas poultry farms over pollution of the Illinois River is one of many new interstate environmental disputes growing out of relaxed federal enforcement. State and local governments increasingly reach beyond their borders to control pollution that they say the federal government should have prevented.

This controversy is detailed in an August 28 Washington Post story by Juliet Eilperin. The Natural Resources News Service developed the idea for the story and provided examples of interstate environmental disputes to the Post.

Oklahoma's complaint, filed last year, seeks injunctive and monetary relief from 14 large food processing companies in Arkansas. Oklahoma says the companies dispose of poultry waste by piling it on fields in large amounts that belie their claim that it is meant to be fertilizer. "They're not fertilizing; they're dumping," Oklahoma Attorney General Drew Edmondson told Eilperin.

The Illinois River draws large crowds of canoeists, fishermen, and other nature lovers to its wooded banks and feeds the once clear Lake Tenkiller. Oklahoma calls Tenkiller its "crown jewel of lakes." People used to come from hundreds of miles to scuba dive there. Recreation from the Illinois River is worth more than $50 million per year to Oklahoma, according to Ed Fite of the Oklahoma Scenic River Commission.

But Fite regrets that the river is now cloudy all year, fish die from anoxia, and the whole thing becomes a putrid foul-smelling mess in the spring and fall when the algae turns over. Most people wouldn't know they were swimming in chicken excrement if it weren't for the algae which thrive in the nutrient-rich water of the Illinois River. "It's not very appetizing," Fite grieves. "People don't want to get in it."

Oklahoma Arkansas Dispute Exposes Natural Problem. Christopher Law, Tuesday 29th August 2006.

An unprecedented drought stretching across the southeastern United States has forced some of the region's largest cities to declare water emergencies.
The situation has become so serious that officials in Atlanta, where rainfall totals are more than 16 inches below normal, said they could run out of drinking water in a matter of weeks.
"Without any intervention, we are likely to run out of water in less than three months," said Carol Couch, the director of the Environmental Protection Division in Georgia. The drought has been sucking the city and its water sources dry.
Atlanta Dyng of Thirst (80 days of water left), October 24th 2007, Now Public

PORTLAND, Ore. (AP) – Scientists say the deaths of thousands of adult salmon in California's lower Klamath River can be linked to the Bush administration's decision to divert water from fish to farmers this year. The fish are casualties of the warm, polluted waters of the river that biologists trace back partly to the Oregon-California border, and the
farming operations that dot the region.
Oregon Wild Salmon Dying In Lower Klamath River, September 24th 2003

One of the world's greatest rivers has been reduced to a trickle in places by a series of giant Chinese dams and engineering works which are threatening the livelihoods of up to 100 million people in south-east Asia.

A body representing four downstream governments reported yesterday that the Mekong was at its lowest recorded level, flowing "close to rock bottom" near the end of a 3,000 mile journey that takes it from the Tibetan plateau, through China's Yunnan province, Burma, Thailand, Laos, Cambodia and Vietnam.

The Mekong's downstream countries, which are almost completely dependent on the river and its tributaries for food, water and transport, fear that China's plans for a further Six dams could be disastrous.

Damned and Dying: The Mekong and its Communities face a bleak future. John Vidal.
The Guardian. March 25th 2004

WWF river dolphin initiative coordinator Anna Forslund said China's Yangtze river, the Mekong river in Cambodia, the Ganges river in India and the Indus river system in Pakistan were among the world's most endangered rivers as evidenced by their dwindling river dolphin populations.

Ms Forslund said many people had never heard of river dolphins, which were smaller than marine dolphins, had a longer snout and were often blind, but they were one of the most threatened species in the world with some populations now comprising between 1,000 to just a handful of wild creatures.

She said dolphin populations had been suffering from damming, overfishing, bad farming and mining practices, pollution and sewage since the 1970s.

"You can see the link, river dolphins are dependent on the water and the people are dependent on the water so the levels of toxicity is probably the same in people living there – low levels of dolphins means unhealthy water," she said.
River Dolphin Population Dying.
The Australian Press Associate. Monday 3rd September 2007

Beijing admits fish in Yangtze River are dying
an official report reveals that the amount of solid and liquid waste, including industrial pollutants, pesticides and ellamma pumped into the Yangtze runs in the billions of ella. All life in the river is at the risk of extinction, even the common carp. The river provides 35 per cent of China's freshwater resources.
Asia News. IT. 4.16.2007

Now I knew that the rivers were dying, us and the planet with them, it seemed that someone up there had decided it was a good time for me to discover the ancient notion of Cycles of Existence.

That night after e-mailing Derrick the "River Eulogy" document I decided to chill with a little book simply called "Hinduism" by a Dr. Karan Sing

As I read through sections of the book, something caught my attention. It was the whole concept that the Hindus believe time is cyclical not linear. The universe is anadi-ananta, without beginning and without end. It is "recurrent phases of manifestation and dissolution".

According to Singh each manifested cycle is divided into four yugas or stages: Satya, Treta, Dvapara and Kali. In Satya yuga – virtue is in ascendant but it diminishes as we get to the last stage Kali-yuga where it virtually disappears. It is at the end of the final stage where there is "tremendous destruction, pralaya" after which appears the golden age.

There are those who believe that the universe repeats these cycles. Then there are some who say it is the first time we have reached this Kali-Yuga cycle. So the universe does not repeat itself. Whatever the small disagreement on this point – the majority of scholars and interested parties seem to believe we are now in the Kali-Yuga cycle.

Through a little more research I discovered that Hindu prophets believed that in this stage our levels of spirituality declines; while violence and immorality go up. We basically loose the last remains of our humaneness.

Over the months that followed this revelation I also learned that other cultures had the same cycles as Hinduism. They varied in length and numbers, but the concept was exactly the same. Also all cultures agreed we were in the final cycle which would be marked by chaos, a decline in how we treat each other, the earth and all things in life.

As I read more details on each of these cultural prophetic revelations it was hard to ignore the cosmic voice warning its children.

I want to share here with you what I discovered (or more correctly what was revealed to me) other cultures believe about the cycles of time:

JANAISM

In Joseph Campbell's "Hero with a Thousand Faces" he shares some facts about the Jain religion and its concept of cyclic existence. Janaism is known as having a doctrine of nonviolence towards all life form. It states there are two cycles of life. The first set is called the "descending" series (avasarpini), and begins with the age of the superlative giant-couples. This superlative cycle runs its full course, terminates and enters the "ascending" series (Utsarpini).

In the "descending" cycle life becomes less and less blissful. For the age of the "superlative giant-couples" last for ten millions of ten millions of one hundred millions of one hundred million periods of countless years (yes, that is quite a number!). It then fades slowly into a time where men are only half as happy and four miles tall. In the third period happiness becomes mixed with sorrow and virtue with plenty of vice.

At the end of this period men and women are no longer born as couples. The descent of mankind continues into the fourth stage and then the fifth stage which is the present era we now live in.

This stage began in 522 BC. It is a period that is said to be one of intensified evil. The tallest human being is only

139

seven cubits tall and the longest life span they have is only one hundred and twenty-five years. People have only sixteen ribs and are said to be very violent, lustful, proud and full of greed.

If things are terrible now it is said that by the sixth stage of the descending age, life and the state of man will be even more terrible. The longest life will only be twenty years. We will have only eight ribs and one cubit meter tall. It has been predicted that the days will be very hot and the nights cold. Disease will be rampant and chastity non-existent. Strong winds will sweep over the earth and become worst as the cycle increases. It is said that in the end all human and animal life will be forced to seek shelter in the Ganges caves, and in the sea.

When this period goes into the "ascending" cycle the planet and human life will be refreshed once again.

THE HOPI

Now the Hopi are a group of indigenous Native American people who primarily live on Hopi Reservation in northeastern Arizona. The Hopi Reservation is entirely surrounded by the much larger Navajo Reservation.

Renowned for their prophecies the Hopi also believe in the cycle of deterioration and renewal of man. They believe that the era we live in is marked by our choices. The choices we make now will determine if we go into an era of deterioration or renewal.

Near Oraibi, Arizona, there is a petroglyph known as Prophecy Rock which symbolizes many Hopi prophecies. The picture below is found on this petroglyph and it speaks of this era we live in "The Age of Choice".

The Hopi Prophecy Rock

- The large human figure on the left is the Great Spirit. The bow in his left hand represents his instructions to the Hopi to lay down their weapons. The vertical line to the right of the Great Spirit is a time scale in thousands of years. The point at which the great Spirit touches the line is the time of his return.
- The "life path" established by the Great Spirit divides into the lower, narrow path of continuous Life in harmony with nature and the wide upper road of white man's scientific achievements. The bar between the paths, above the cross, is the coming of white men; the Cross is that of Christianity. The circle below the cross represents the continuous Path of Life.
- The four small human figures on the upper road represent, on one level, the past three worlds and the present; on another level, the figures indicate that some of the Hopi will travel the white man's path, having been seduced by its glamour.
- The short line that returns to the straight Path of Life is the last chance for people to turn back to nature before the upper road disintegrates and dissipates. The small circle above the Path of Life, after the last chance, is the

141

Great Purification, after which corn will grow in abundance again when the Great Spirit returns. And the Path of Life continues forever...

- The Hopi shield in the lower right corner symbolizes the Earth and the Four-Corners area where the Hopi have been reserved. The arms of the cross also represent the four directions in which they migrated according to the instructions of the Great Spirit.
- The dots represent the four colors of Hopi corn, and the four racial colors of humanity.

IFA

Now in the Ifa theological system of the Yoruba of West Africa it is also believed that our earth has gone through and continues to go through cycles of human consciousness. I have included the Ifa story of creation which was provided by Chief Popoola, Head of Ethics and Scriptures for the International Institute of Ifa, It is very rare to see this whole creation story, so I feel extremely blessed he shared it. I have shared this story and its wisdom without changing his words. It is interesting to note that like Hinduism the Ifa Corpus of Wisdom also places us in the fourth stage of existence:

The Ifa Creation Story

From Odu: Osa-Agunleja (Ogunda)

Stage 1:

Akamara created the universe. Akamara is known as the universal spirit of the universe. Akamara created the universe

142

with a huge explosion. During this time period, there only existed very hot gases and dews throughout the whole universe. No physical matter existed.

Akamara then decided to create the first Irunmole named Origun. Akamara ordered Origun to cool down the gases and dews and turn them into solid matter. This is how the stars were created. After this, the stars began to crash into each other. This Irunmole continues to cool down the gases throughout the universe to this day.

Stage 2:

Akamara created another Irunmole named Baba-Asemu-Egun-Sunwa and ordered him to give all the stars a set rotation and pattern so that they would stop crashing into each other. This Irunmole accomplished this task and gave a set pattern to all the stars and a fixed rotation. This Irunmole continues to give all stars a fixed rotation and pattern throughout the universe.

Stage 3:

After ordering Baba-Asemu-Egun-Sunwa to give order to the stars, Akamara created another Irunmole called Olu-Iwaye. Akamara gave this Irunmole the task of creating planets. Olu-Iwaye achieved this task and created all the planets from the stars. Olu-Iwaye continues to do this work in the universe.

In our solar system, Olu-Iwaye created 7 planets in the beginning. The other two planets were created later. When our planet was created, Olodumare gave our planet to a female Irunmole named Aye. It is important to note that Aye is not part of the 401 Irunmole. And since Aye was given the earth, our planet was given the name of Ile-Aye (The home of Aye).

During this stage of the creation, only Irunmole were able to travel to the planet because the planet was not able to support other types of life. The Irunmole would just come every once and awhile to visit but they never stayed to live. There were no permanent residents on the planet. After some time had passed, Aye started becoming sad because she was feeling lonely living on the planet. She wanted to have permanent residents living with her. She then spoke to Olodumare and asked if she could have permanent residents on the planet. Olodumare heard what she asked for and decided to give Aye permanent residents.

Olodumare then ordered Ogun to go the planet to make the planet habitable for other beings. Ogun accepted the job and went to the planet with his group of Irunmole. Some of them were Ija and Osoosi. When Ogun arrived on the planet, he started working but since Ogun had only brought wood with him to live, Ogun and his group had to return to heaven and tell Olodumare that they could not complete the job. This is when Ogun was given the name of Baba Jegi Jegi (Father of the wood eaters).

Olodumare then ordered Obatala to do the job of making the planet habitable for other beings. Obatala went to the planet and followed the same path Ogun had already charted to get to the planet. Obatala then came with his own group of Irunmole like Alaanu, Oloore, Magbemiti, etc. After some time had passed, Obatala also had to return to heaven with his group because he had only brought water with him to live on the planet. Obatala and his group then returned to heaven without completing the job. This is when Obatala was given the name of Baba Mumi Mumi (Father of the water drinkers)

Olodumare then ordered Orunmila to go to the planet to make it habitable for other beings. Before Orunmila left for the planet, Orunmila consulted Ifa with a group of Awo in heaven known as "Agba dudu Oriimo". They told Orunmila everything he would need to bring with him to have success on his mission. Some of the important items he was told to bring was seeds and food. They also told him to use the wood and the water that Ogun and Obatala had already brought. Orunmila did his ebo and brought all the materials indicated by the group of Awo in heaven. Orunmila was successful in making the planet habitable for other beings. And that's how Orunmila was given the name of Baba Jeun Jeun (Father of the food eaters).

During this time period, only 6 holes existed on the planet in where water was located. Orunmila started cultivating the land and planted seeds. The first plant to germinate was a plant called Tete-Agbalaye, which in Ifa this is the most sacred plant in the world.

When the planet was ready and had water, plants, animals, etc. Olodumare sent to the planet some beings called Eniyan so that they could live with Aye permanently. These beings for a long time lived in harmony with Aye on the planet but as time passed, they began destroying the planet and other planets. They were corrupted because of the power they had. Olodumare then became angry and after giving them many chances to change their character, Olodumare finally decided to try to kill them all. This is when Olodumare ordered the waters that were underground in the world to rise and drown the Eniyan. Many of the Eniyan tried to run away and save themselves. Some climbed to the highest mountains in the world, other hid in caves, and others climbed into the holes of trees, etc. Some of these Eniyan survived. In other words, not all of them died. And some of these Eniyan still live on the planet with us to this date.

Stage 4:

The world was full of water and Olodumare decides to rebuild the planet. Olodumare decides to send Obatala again to make the planet habitable. Obatala accepts the job but fails again. Olodumare then orders an Irunmole called Olofin-Otete, also known as Oduduwa to make the planet habitable. Before starting the job, Olofin-Otete decided to consult Ifa with Orunmila before going to the planet. He completes his ebo and follows all the instructions Orunmila gave him. Oduduwa rebuilt the planet: he spreads earth over the water, lowers the waters, grows plants, creates animals, etc...

Olodumare then decides to create a different type of life called "Human Beings" which are also called Eniyan. (It is important to note that the first beings and us human beings are both known as Eniyan but the accents on the word Eniyan are different).

When it was time to create the first human beings, Olodumare decided to create the first human being himself. Olodumare decided to create a human being named Nini Binini who was a woman. In other words, the first human being created was a woman and not a man like the Bible indicates. Olodumare created this woman. Olodumare then decided to give this woman to Odudwa as his wife and told them to procreate. The procreated and gave birth to 8 sets of twins. 16 children. It is not known for sure how many of these children were males or females but it is important to state that these first 16 children have nothing to do with the first 16 Odu Ifa. They are different.

As time passed, these children began growing and maturing and they began to look at each other in a sexual way because they were starting to go through puberty. One of the

Irunmole noticed this and informed Olodumare what was happening and in order to avoid incest (Because Incest is a taboo in Ifa) Olodumare ordered Esu Odara, Ogun, Obatala, and Orunmila to create more human beings so that they could procreate with the first 16 children. Esu Odara was in charge of supplying the clay, Ogun was in charge of creating and oxidizing the bones of men and women. This is why men are known as Okunrin (Hard Iron) and women are known as Obinrin (Soft Iron). Obatala was in charge of molding the bodies of men and women and Orunmila was in charge of consulting Ifa during the whole process and supervising.

The first human beings created from the clay by these Irunmole were black in color. These Irunmole created 2000 human beings using this clay. As time passed, Olodumare began to think and decided that 16 and 2000 human beings weren't enough to cover the planet so he ordered Esu, Ogun, Obatala, and Orunmila to create more human beings. They accomplished this task but this time they decided to not use clay but parts of animals, plants, trees, birds, etc. to create 2000 more human beings. This second group of 2000 human beings was red and yellow in color.

After the process was finished, one of the members of Obatala's group named Oluorogbo with the help of some of the other members of Obatala's group decided to create even more human beings. They are the ones who created the white group.

It is also important to know that during the whole process of creating the black, red, yellow, and white groups one of the members of Obatala's group named Edun Beleje (the monkey) who was very mischievous, is the one responsible for causing deformities of all types in human beings. Many blame Obatala for this but it wasn't Obatala's doing but the fault of Edun Beleje who was a member of

147

Obatala's group. The blame was put on Obatala because as we all know, when the member of a group does something wrong, the leader is always held responsible for what his members do.

During this stage the ground on the earth was united. In other words it was one, Pangaea, and all human beings lived together during this time period. But as the ground began to spread apart, the groups also began to separate. We are still in the 4th stage but we are now moving into the 5th stage. Ifa says that during the 4th stage human beings will be doing almost the same things the first Eniyan (beings) did. In other words, we'll be destroying the planet, we're going to have many powers (technology), were going to have many wars, many are going to die, and were going to reach a stage where we'll be forced to return to a more balanced and traditional way of living to save ourselves. Ifa says that not everyone is going to want to live traditionally but many others will do it.

What does it mean to live traditionally?

Answer: Living in the way our ancestors did. In other words, living in balance with nature and with everything on the planet. We need to stop wasting and using up all our natural resources in an ignorant manner, we need to stop the abuse of our fellow man in all parts of the world, we need to stop using technology that destroys the environment and contaminates it, we need to stop wars, we need to stop destroying the natural environment, etc. We have to relearn to live in harmony with all that exists on the planet. We must live in a communal fashion in where everything we do: our jobs, our relationships, how we make money, how we use technology, etc brings benefit not only to the individual but the community.

What is considered to be the community?

Answer: The community is everything that exists on the planet. In other words, it's not only your neighborhood, your city, your region, Nigeria, The United States, Colombia, Europe, Asia, etc. The community is the planet and everything that lives on it. Its taboo to do something that only brings benefit to the individual. Also, we need to start doing things that not only bring benefit to human beings but to the animals, plants, trees, birds, fish, the earth, etc...

Stage 5:

Ifa says that after all the chaos that will happen, those that survive will be more intelligent, wise, and they will know how to use technology and our natural resources to maintain balance in the world. These people are going to have a philosophy of life that is more communal than individualistic. They are going to know how to work not only with communities where human beings live, but with the communities of the fish, birds, plants, etc...

SCIENTIFIC CYCLES

It is interesting to note that modern science confirms what our ancestors have said about earth's cycles. For it is said the earth has experienced several major evolutionary changes including up to three changes of its atmosphere. For the atmosphere of earth to change indicates these were periods of great evolutionary changes as humans today are oxygen breathing.

The first atmosphere of the earth consisted of hydrogen gas together with helium and would have evaporated into space relatively early in Earth's existence, when the planet was still molten. When the surface cooled sufficiently to crust over, volcanoes formed and Earth's gravity would have held the volcanic gases close by, forming a second atmosphere comprised primarily of Carbon dioxide and water vapor.

The water vapor in the atmosphere would have rained down to form oceans, in which carbon compounds would provide the breeding ground for bacterial life and later planets, which would give the atmosphere oxygen. The situation then would have become ripe for the nitrogen cycle to begin eventually resulting in atmospheric nitrogen.

According to science we have been through five extinction periods and presently face our sixth extinction which for the first time is caused by one species, and one species only - man.

BOOK THREE

MEETING THE MOTHERS

OGUNDA MEJI

Girl: Mother tell me of Ogunda Meji.

Mother: It is said that Ogunda Meji was one of the most powerful diviners in heaven and earth. He combined the strength of the God of Iron, Ogun, and the wisdom of the God of Wisdom, Orunmila. Many stories of Ogunda Meji are interesting. They tell of how no suffering is too great that it cannot be overcome when sacred advise is followed. So it is in Ogunda Meji that the Boa Constrictor was saved from starvation and learned to hunt.

Now in Ogunda Meji is also a story of when the Divinities came to Earth for the second time. The story goes something like this:

God asked the God of Iron to come to earth to blaze the way for its second habitation. He accepted the challenge, however he did not go for sacred advise through divination. He was given 400 men and women by God. They were to accompany him to earth and became known as his followers.

No sooner had he gone to earth he realized it would have been better for him if he had gone for divination. His followers became very hungry and asked for food. However, without the wisdom of sacred advise Ogun had not even thought about the issue of food and had only brought sticks for his followers to eat. Needless to say, that did not satiate their hunger and many of them starved to death. It was all quite disastrous and Ogun went back to heaven and reported his mission a failure.

After hearing about Ogun's woes and experiences, God decided to send Olokun, God of Water to Earth. Maybe, he would do a better job than Ogun had to make the earth a livable place. He gave him 200 men and 200 women to take with him. They were to be his followers, just like the last lot had been the followers of Ogun.

Just like Ogun, Olokun had not bothered to get the wisdom of sacred advise through divination. When his followers got to earth they of course became hungry. He told them to drink water. Of course, that did not work and many of them starved to death. Olokun dashed back to heaven to tell God that his mission had failed.

God listened to all his woes and problems. After which he made the decision to send Orunmila, the God of Wisdom to earth. Maybe he would be able to make the earth habitable for humans. Now there is something you should know about Orunmila, he never did anything without consulting the divine oracle first. So he went for divination and sacred advise. He was told to give Esu, the God of the Crossroads who opened up the way for things, a goat. Also he was told to take one of every plant and animal from heaven down to earth with him. He followed the advise without fail. Then God gave him 200 men and 200 women to accompany him on his mission. They were to be his followers.

Now as soon as Orunmila leaves heaven Esu got busy. He rushed to Ogun and told him that Orunmila was travelling to earth through the route which he, Ogun, had established. On hearing this Ogun went to block the route with a thick forest. When Orunmila's party came to the forest, they did not know what to do next. He sent the rat to find a path through the forest.

Before the rat returned, Ogun appeared to Orunmila and queried him for daring to proceed to earth without informing him, and to add insult to injury to use the route he had grafted to establish.

153

Orunmila was surprised at this accusation and said he had asked Esu to inform the God he was going. Ogun remembered that it was Esu who had indeed come to alert him. As a result he quickly cleared the forest for Orunmila to proceed on his journey. Before leaving him, Ogun told Orunmila that the only other obligation he owed him was to feed his followers with the sticks as he had done with his. Orunmila promised to do so.

While all of this was going on Esu was busy talking to Olokun whom he told about Orunmila going to earth via the route he had established. Olukun was very angry and caused a wide river to block Orunmila's way. When Orunmila came to the bank of the river, he dispatched a fish to find a passage through the river. While waiting for the fish to return, Olokun appeared to him and queried why he dared to embark on a trip to earth without obtaining clearance from him. Then to add insult to injury he was thinking of using the route he had established.

Orunmila explained that he had sent the God Esu to inform Olokun that he was going to earth on the mission. Olokun remembered it was Esu who had informed him of Olokun's mission so the God must be speaking the truth. He immediately cleared the waters for Orunmila to proceed on his journey. He however warned Orunmila that he had a divine obligation to feed his followers water just like he had done. Orunmila promised he would do so.

With no more obstacles in his way, Orunmila proceeded on his journey to the earth. When he got to earth he advised all his male followers to clear the bush and to construct temporary huts roofed with mats. When they completed the assignment they got out the seeds that Orunmila had brought with him so they could plant them the following day. As they slept Esu got busy. He planted the seeds, germinated them and made them fruit. Now when Orunmila and his followers woke up in the morning they were shocked to see these miracles had taken place.

154

After their chores Orunmila's followers said they were hungry. He told them he made a promise to Ogun and Olokun that they would eat the sticks and drink water just like those who had come to earth before them. The people proceeded to follow this obligation. Then Orunmila said they could feast on the fruits of the land. Now what is interesting is that up to this day in traditional African societies people still start their day by chewing sticks. This stick is known as the Chew Stick and it is very good for cleaning the teeth. They then rinse their mouth out with water. So their day starts with sticks and waters before feasting on food.

Once everyone had finished eating Orunmila's friend Okpele (which is the divination tool which Yoruba priest use today) came to earth. Esu promised he would come to earth and help Orunmila to succeed while he was on earth. Before arriving, Orunmila asked his followers to build a hut for Esu. He also gave Esu a goat to eat. Esu was very happy. Orunmila promised he would always keep Esu well fed.

Well, meanwhile in heaven Olokun and Ogun wondered whether Orunmila had succeeded in his task of making the earth a good place to live. When he didn't return back to heaven Ogun and Olokun both left heaven to find out what was going on. When they saw that Orunmila had indeed accomplished his mission successfully they both begged for his forgiveness. They went back to heaven and asked God's permission to go earth to live with their followers. With permission given they left to help Orunmila make the earth a good place to live. Ogun, was the God of technology so he was real useful to have around. Oh, with Olokun and Ogun came the God Ule as well.

Once everyone was on earth Orunmila made a declaration:

"Whatever respect is given to me, should always be extended to Ule. Olokun will always reside in the waters to be the dispenser of

wealth and prosperity for mankind. Ogun will always be used for man's great achievements."

Soon after he said those things, a strange thing happened. Ule suddenly dropped dead. From his dead body sprung many houses. One was very grand and that is where Orunmila set up home. Because of the God Ule all inhabitants on earth now had nice homes to live in. Ogun, who is very proud and loves to do things for himself refused to live in any home provided by Ule. He proceeded to make his own hut.

Meanwhile Olokun did not want to be outdone by what he considered to be the feats of Ule. As a result he turned himself into water to make up the body of the oceans, seas, and rivers of this world.

As life went on, on earth, the followers of the respective deities: Orunmila, Olokun and Ogun soon began to intermix and marry. They multiplied profusely. The offspring became the priest and followers of the divinities who had originally populated the earth.

Just after my birthday which is June 5th, I collapsed on the floor clutching my heart. I was having terrible palpitations. Their intensity lay me up in bed for days. I felt weak as though I was dying. Each day when I tried to get out of bed, I would collapse on the floor, clutching my heart.

In between sleep and waking state I could hear a faint inner whisper,

"go home. I need to go home."

That was all I would hear and say before whispering the words out aloud, and falling into a deep slumber. Derrick immediately contacted Chief Popoola in Nigeria. He immediately consulted the oracle. The oracle said I was to immediately go to Nigeria. There was something important that I had to get. Something needed to help with the journey.

How were we going to get to Nigeria? We really didn't have the money to do that. On the fourth day of everyone pondering on this dilemma my brother Jeff called. He didn't have a clue as to what was going on. No one had bothered him with the incident.

"Hi mom, Just want to let you know that I want to send you and Omi some money to help you guys out over there."

The amount? The exact money that was needed for my flight to get to Africa. It was a miracle. Latter Jeff explained that he had been looking at a bottle of water in his kitchen and had the strong urgent feeling that he needed to send us some money. He didn't question the feeling; instead he immediately acted upon it.

It was by many twist of fate like that how myself and Derrick ended up in Africa for two weeks. It was our first time seeing each other since our January wedding and one night of honeymooning. We were to spend our first night with Chief Popoola. Then his two sons plus brother were to take us to the Osun Palace, Osun's chief seat of residence, where I was told I would have a seven day initiation period in order to receive an implement called the Sacred Calabash. The seat of Osun's ase (power). After which we were to spend another week with Chief Popoola and his family.

Our host at Osun's Palace was a short slim dark young man with about ten braids in his hair. I noticed his hair because I had never seen a man in Nigeria with braids in his hair before. Not to say there weren't men with braids in their hair, I just had not seen one. Which made me think it wasn't that common. His braids seemed to be a sign that he was a special devotee of Osun. Indeed, his mother was the head honcho of the Osun Palace, and had the title Yeye, like me, which meant Mother.

The first thing OsunKolode did was to show myself and Derrick to our room. The walls were painted in a kind off faded blue. Its only furniture was a traditional worn mat. The ceiling was a brown sack cloth looking type of material held together by cross wooden beams. As myself and Derrick had only one honeymoon night together, we joked and said this would be our honeymoon suite. Despite the bareness and simplicity of the small square called our room, I loved it. It felt familiar to me. I lay my things down, and said

"I think I am going to really love being here."

Derrick felt the same way.

Once we settled into the room our host gave us a tour of the rest of the Osun Palace. It didn't take very long because there were just a few ancient low rise buildings and one large room that acted as the main meet and prayer area. Next to our room was an outdoor shower from whose shower head no

158

water came. Next to it was the well. Much of the water for the Osun Palace came from that well.

One day OsunKolode showed us the water in the well as he drew it out for me to have a spiritual bath. I was excited because I had never seen the inside of a well before. As I looked down its long ancient shaft I could see that the water was well below the water mark. Derrick noticed it too. There was something very eerie about seeing a sacred well, on an ancient Water Goddess's sacred grounds running empty. Something about that felt like a poetic statement from the universe.

Looking down the well made me think of "River Eulogy", and the information I had just read about such as the drying of the Ogallala aquifer which once held more than 3 billion acre-feet of water, roughly the equivalent of 3 billion acres of land covered in a foot of water. The aquifer's depth varies by state. In parts of Nebraska, there are still 1,000 feet of water saturating its sand and gravel. But in parts of Texas, Oklahoma and Kansas — states that had less water to begin with — the water table has dropped steeply. Today the Ogallala Aquifer, groundwater has almost run dry. If this aquifer goes dry, it is said that more than $20 billion worth of food and fiber will vanish from the world's markets. Even more astonishingly scientists say it will take natural processes 6,000 years to refill the reservoir.

There are several Aquifers in the world. The Ogallala is the largest one in the world. What's the importance of Aquifer's? Well, let's just say about 97 percent of all water is in the oceans. Three percent of the worlds water is available to us as fresh water. 69 percent of which is locked up in glaciers and icecaps, mainly in Greenland and Antarctica. You might be surprised a lot of the remaining freshwater is below our feet, as ground water or in our rivers and lakes.

Aquifers are critically important in human habitation and agriculture. Deep aquifers in arid areas have long been water sources for irrigation. Many villages and even large cities draw their water supply from wells in aquifers.

Municipal, irrigation, and industrial water supplies are provided through large wells. Multiple wells for one water supply source are termed "wellfields", which may withdraw water from confined or unconfined aquifers. Using ground water from deep, confined aquifers provides more protection from surface water contamination. Some wells, termed "collector wells," are specifically designed to induce infiltration of surface (usually river) water.

Aquifers that provide sustainable fresh groundwater to urban areas and for agricultural irrigation are typically close to the ground surface (within a couple of hundred meters) and have some recharge by fresh water. This recharge is typically from rivers or meteoric water (precipitation) that percolates into the aquifer through overlying unsaturated materials.

I looked down the well again. Osun, the Mother of Sweet Waters, had brought all the intellectual stuff about our dying waters and planet alive right on the grounds of her home.

Next we were shown where prayers were done every morning and all Osun activities were held. It was a fairly large space which on the far right side of the entrance existed an old brown antiquated looking wooden door. We were told that this door led to a room which only a few priest were allowed to go into. That room was where the Ase (primordial power) of Osun was homed in its sacred Calabash.

The Etiquette at the Osun Palace was to greet Osun every morning. This was done by bowing ones head onto the ground before the heavy wooden door which led into her private room. The first time I did this routine I felt a cool refreshing breeze float around me and stroke my cheeks. It happened to Derrick too.

It was that same morning that I also took note that nearly every inch of the walls of the meet/prayer room were painted with large fish. There were a few huge paintings of Osun, as a beautiful mermaid, lovingly holding a fish in either hand. No wonder it was strictly forbidden to eat fish in the shrine space or anywhere else on the grounds of the Osun Palace. Fish were seen as her children and also signified her blessings of wealth, abundance and fertility. So to eat them was seen as an affront to her. Anyway, why would you eat your blessings?

As I raised my head from the ground from which I prayed I also noticed a couple of large wooden statutes which seemed to have some age on them. Their stillness had an unruffled air of authority. Latter I was to find out they were images of the divinity known as Babaluaye, who helped to cure all sorts of dreaded illness, and who cared for the poor. He was closely associated with Osun.

Besides the etiquette of praying every morning to Osun, it was also seen as good manners (in fact, essential) to spend some chill and mediation time in the Shrine space. So we followed the etiquette and encountered an interesting phenomenon as we did so. Every morning there would be a multitude and array of individuals looking for divine guidance from the Yeye Osun of the place and healing direct from Osun herself. Some of these individuals looked very wealthy and some looked really poor. Whichever category they fell in Osun obviously did not discriminate for she promised each what they had come for: wealth, children, home, relationships, successful studies, fertility, and love. The phenomenal levels of faith we saw placed in these healings was something indeed to behold.

From my previous trips to Nigeria I remembered people had told me that Osun bestowed many fertility miracles on people. I half believed it, but I didn't see how that was possible. How could a Goddess help you to get pregnant? I was told when you pray to her and drank her sacred waters you would become pregnant, for sure. At the time it all sounded like well-intentioned mumbo jumbo to me. That was until one day Chief Popoola returned to Trinidad just before the trip I had to make to Nigeria.

I went for a divination, and one of the main things that came up (to my surprise) was the topic of children.

"the oracle says you have children waiting to arrive. You must hurry up and have them," Chief Popoola said in his very gentle firm African way.

"I have been infertile since having my son and that was almost thirteen years ago," I told him thinking it was okay for some elusive oracle to tell me to "hurry up" and have children.

He lifted his Opele high in the air and let it fall to the ground. I had never quite gotten over the habit of holding my breath while waiting for the opele to fall to the ground and its configuration to be interpreted. I mean it was like watching your destiny fall to the ground and not being sure which way it would go until someone told you.

"The oracle says that all you have to do is pray to Osun and drink her waters."

Now Chief Popola had kindly gifted me some stones on that trip. They were apparently highly sought after sacred river stones of Osun, known as Otan stones. He told me the stones bring fertility, prosperity and many more good things to their keeper. The only one prerequisite is that you look after

162

them properly. He even said the stones multiply. I am sorry to say that little Westerner inside of me screamed,

"mumbo jumbo,"

But latter on when I moved to the States to live with Derrick he kept on finding replicas of the stone every few months, in very strange places. He had this way where we would be somewhere, and suddenly stop. He would then stoop down and put his hand on the ground and come back up with a fat juicy looking Otan stone. It was after this happening on more than one occasion that I shared a thought with Derrick,

"Chief Popoola was right. The stones do multiply. Just not how I was thinking they did."

Now in terms of drinking Osun Water and getting pregnant - this bit of the divination happened almost two years later when myself and Derrick decided to do a forty day fast period and try for a baby. I ate very healthily, exercised, drank the sacred Osun water I had, and the waters from the North Carolina Healing Springs (also known as God's acre). On day forty one and after almost fifteen years of a dry spell in terms of my fertility, I was pregnant with baby Omololu. It was a miracle.

I loved everything in the Osun Palace, except for the toilet set up. Soon after we had arrived on the shrine's hallowed grounds I was actually dying to do a number two. Our kind host directed me to a place and space that was supposed to be the toilet.

"Where is the toilet?" I asked holding my nose from the high stench that was hitting it.

163

"Right there," he pointed right at an open pit filled with shit, and flies.

I was horrified.

"What am I supposed to do?" I felt stupid and Western for asking the question.

"Just do your stuff in this piece of newspaper and toss it in the pit," he said casually.

When he saw the horrified look on my face he began to apologize.

"we are making plans on building a toilet there, but we are still sorting out all the finances."

A well that was running dry, a toilet filled with flies – all on the sacred grounds of a Water Goddess. As these thoughts ran helter-skelter through my mind I remembered that Osun was the Queen that held the mirror. Was Osun mirroring our chaotic destructive attitude to the Earth herself? I realized it would quite befitting and appropriate for her to do so.

If something could feel long. It was being at the Osun Palace. Linear time just seemed to vanish. It felt more like what the ancients called cyclic time.

When my initiation stuff was not going on my free time was spent strolling, sitting quietly in the Shrine room watching the visits come and go, going for walk abouts through the bustling local town lit up by hundreds of lamps at night or visiting historical places with Derrick and OsunKolode.

Now OsunKolode was a cool person to hang with. He knew the history of Osogbo very well. He was also well acquainted with every local shrine don't matter how old their histories. One day he took us to a shrine that he said was a couple of hundred years old. The roof was a rusty galvanized thing, and the whole place had this eerie feeling of abandonment. That was why I was surprised to know that people still went there to drink the water from its sacred iron water pot.

"Come and drink the water," OsunKolode obviously felt we would feel honored and eager to drink the holy elixir he beckoned us towards.

I won't lie I was scared to drink the water, even though I knew it was coming from a sacred pot. Myself and Derrick had existed so far on sipping water from a filter bottle he had brought on the trip with him. Every day we counted the drops we drank so that we did not run out of clean water. There was no real choice of drinkable water in the town. There was the expensive bottled water or the dubious water that had been bagged in plastic. The latter is what the locals mostly drank. It never seemed to affect them but it was known to hurt the sensitive bellies of foreigners like me.

I tried not to seem rude as I declined OsunKolode's Holy Waters.

The reality of a waterless world was everywhere. Even when we had spent the night and day at Chief Popola's home in Lagos we witnessed that reality. People from his locality often collected water from his water tank. A cousin of his said he never turned anyone away, even if it meant he and his family had to go without water. It made me think of people in the West who have so much more, yet fight tooth and nail to retain "theirs".

Water in Nigeria was not just the issue, it seemed like everything to do with basic human needs was. The electricity supply was limited – it would cut of many times during the day and often stayed off (Unlike the West it had nothing to do

165

with if you had paid your bill or not. It was all about how erratic the national supply was).

Driving through Lagos we witnessed the horrifying conditions of human existence: people who lived in homes with no windows, unfinished roofs, half built walls; piles of rubbish (mainly plastic) piled up high; children running barefooted after cars trying to make a penny. I witnessed first hand children who had not eaten for days. I remember being somewhere where the children who had not eaten for many days found some leftover chicken bones from an old meal and cooked them with onions and all the grace of experienced chefs. They were so hungry they ate the tiny bits of flesh left on those bones like it was the best gourmet meal they had ever eaten.

You could feel the accumulated stress and tension in the air of people trying to survive. On one walk, that Derrick took by himself, he said he had witnessed a river that had run completely dry.

All the realities of what a waterless world was like, and the effects of us humans moving away from honoring Mother Earth seemed to exist right there in the dust of human existence in Lagos, Nigeria.

OsunKolode happily slurped the holy water from the old iron ladle, correctly guessing it was useless to continue beckoning us come drink. I am sure in his mind he thought,

"foolish Westerners have missed out on a big blessing."

In ours, however, we thought we had probably missed out on a good dose of malaria. I hoped the Gods would understand.

At the back of the shrine was a mighty choppy river.

166

"This is where men pray for fertility," Osunkolode declared as he led us to the river's Tempestuous banks.

"It's amazing," I replied trying not to slip on one of the large river rocks.

"This river is the body of the God Erinle. He is a Water divinity," Osunkolode revealed shouting over the roaring water.

He then proceeded to give us quite a long story of the river. There had once lived a human being who did many great and wonderful things for people when he was alive. When he died he turned into the Erinle River. According to Osunkolode, this was a common occurrence, and all the great rivers were once real living people (this included the mighty Osun river).

"By turning into rivers these great people can continue to bless people in their afterlives." Osunkolode said without blinking an eye lash.

His attitude of total belief in these stories reminded me of growing up in Trinidad for those few years when I was younger. There were some wild stories that use to go around. I remember one about the Lajabless. It was a woman who dressed in red, came out during the night time, had a cow foot for her left foot, and seduced unsuspecting men. The Lajabless was so sexy that apparently no man could resist her. However when she asked her victim to light her cigarette (and she always did, according to the story), its illumination would reveal her cow foot. Well, that would be it. The victim would run away as fast as he could. I had heard many men, including my Uncle Bobby, swear they had seen and escaped from a Lajabless.

167

When I was not strolling through the streets and historic sights of Osogbo, I was spending my time in initiation activities. Much of it was in the Osun Palace, as well as her sacred Osun Grove

Designated as a world heritage site it was lush and all embodying. You could not help but move through its green overarching lusciousness through which the long brown seductive body of the Osun River ran through. The river is said to be the Goddess Osun herself.

Even though you have to take a short drive from the Osun Palace to the Osun Grove, the two are seen as intrinsically connected. It is said that the first palace ever established in Osogbo was by a hunter called Larooye. Many centuries ago there were two hunters, Larooye and Olutimehin, who travelled from a nearby village in search of water. It was in Osogbo they found the water they needed. Happy with their find, they announced it to their people. Everyone migrated and settled in Osogbo. The place they settled is now the Sacred Osun Grove.

It is said that life started of quietly at first, and all was well until one day the grounds were being prepared for the planting season. A huge tree fell with a crash into the Osun River. From the waters emerged a beautiful and upset voice which called out,

"Larooye! Olutimehin! You have destroyed all my dying pots!"

They discovered that the voice in the water belonged to the Goddess Osun, who in fact was the rightful ruler of Osogbo long before they had arrived. The Goddess gave permission for the new settlers to stay in Osogbo, but on the condition that they moved away from her river.

The King and people obeyed the Goddess, not wanting to get on her wrong side. The King's palace was abandoned.

That palace became the Osun shrine which one sees inside the Grove now. The second location the King moved to is today part of the Osun Palace Shrine complex where we were staying. The building is situated in the bustling heart of Osogbo. The King's Palace is virtually attached to the Osun Palace residence, and is just a few footsteps away.

In fact we were invited to visit the King. We had to just walk five footsteps to the iron wrought gates of his palace. Once through its threshold we encountered an impressive iron cast statute of the first King of Osogbo, Larooye, holding a fish in his hands. It was revealed, by one of our host, that this fish represented the pact the King and the people of Osogbo had with Osun - to keep on honoring her. This relationship of honoring between Osun, the King and the local people is taken pretty seriously, and is renewed on an annual basis at the popular Osun Festival.

Osogbo is a thriving artesian, creative and trading center. The people believe it is through Osun's blessings that they are able to enjoy such success. Believing that if the original pact with Osun is ever broken their success would be taken away by her.

Another interesting fact about the Osun Grove is that it was a white Austrian artist, Susan Wenger, who rebuilt the Grove. Gathering local artist she restored many of the buildings and sacred art works that were part of its lands. Her husband was a professor at the local University of Ife. She latter left him, married a local, became a head priest, and the rest is history.

If it wasn't for Ms. Wenger catching the Golden Ball the world most probably would not have been able to enjoy the sacred grounds of the Osun Grove, as they do today. Ms. Wenger dedicated her entire life to restoring the grove. It was that thought I often had on my mind as myself and Derrick

169

strolled through its hallowedness and passed under the shade of its thick canopy which spread it's cool touch over the land.

Part of my initiation was to take a few river baths right there in the Grove. Well, the rain falls had been heavy before we arrived, the water was brown, and once again my fear of getting Malaria rose to the surface. For my first river bath Osunkolode smiled a lot and urged me into the water saying it was very blessed and clean. The rains had just made it come up brown. I was hearing him, but not quite feeling him.

However, what would happen if I didn't take the bath? Wasn't being blessed in the waters of Osun partly what we had travelled thousands of miles across the ocean for. Wasn't this a blessing direct from the mother that shouldn't be missed? How could I continue on my water journey if I could not become one with the sacred waters of the Mother herself? If I could not come into union with her?

"I think you will be okay," Derrick whispered in my ears.

I looked at him doubtfully. As if to prove his point he stripped down to his bathing shorts and began to pour the first waters of blessings over himself. Ten minutes later, he stood there on the banks of the river with a big smile on his face. He appeared to be glowing, with light bouncing of him. Maybe, it was a trick of my eyes, but the light wouldn't stop pouring from his aura.

"Go on," he teased until eventually I caved in.

I stripped down to my swimsuit and began to pour Osun's holy waters over me. Osunkolode had disappeared and left me to have my privacy. Soft silk sheets being pulled slowly over my body. Yes, that is what the waters felt like. Like a lover's caress. As I allowed the water to wash over me again and again I did a silent prayer for myself, family, earth, waterways, and humanity's wellbeing. It was fifteen minutes later that I stood there dripping in ecstasy. I and Osun were one. I had met the Mother in person, been part of her divine essence. Not just through washing in her waters, but walking on her blessed body, the land that belonged to her.

Almost every day we took a stroll in the mighty Osun Sacred Grove (which I had failed to mention was 185 acres). With each visit I was able to sense Mother nature on a deeper and more refined level. I could feel her seeping through my pores and dancing in the center of my being. With each day we went the peace within grew more and more certain. Here in Osogbo, at the Osun Palace Shrine, and in the Grove, I was discovering water. Not as a physical object, not as a sacred object I read about in history books, or as a concept intellectualized about. Instead I was discovering water as a true living essence. Who was as real as touching you or the next person next to you.

The deep belief that the priestess of the Osun Palace Shrine had in this concept of water as a living essence, and the Mother as being fully present was reflected in their daily reverent actions. One day we had the privilege to accompany them to Osun's Sacred Grove on one of the days they fed all the divinities, including Osun. For the land was alive, and it was those divinities who protected it.

The feeding was done every five days. So much love went into preparing the black eye beans and rice. The walk through the Grove was accompanied by joyful heartfelt singing, as the food was laid tenderly down at various spots. The feeding of the divinities was an ancient action which had been done the same way for hundreds of years. Deep down I envied the priestess for living in a world where it was still okay to feel such deep conviction and love for Mother Earth, and her sacredness.

It was on one of those moving blessed walks through the Grove that I wrote in my diary,

"my Mother is indeed beautiful. The way she nestles in the lushness of green, the blueness of the sky, the brownness of the earth. I realize that the world inside the grove represents the world how it could be if we harmonize with her within and without. The world outside the Grove with its lack of water, collective desperateness, anxieties, greed, hatefulness, human deprivation, smog, dust, and excessive noise represents a world that is out of step with the wisdom and heart of nature. Which world would I prefer to live in? the one we can create like the grove or the one we have already created outside of it?"

Carving of Osun on wall of Sacred Osun Grove

It was three days before leaving that I eventually received what Osun had really wanted – a sacred Calabash. I received it with much jubilation. What's in there I cannot truly tell you, but I can tell you her Ase (power is there), and that I had been made whole. At the end of the day's festivities I was given the Calabash and told to wrap it up well in a white cloth. I was shown all the things in the calabash, how to use them, along with how to treat the Calabash herself. That's right; the Calabash was not to be treated as an object but as the living essence of the Mother herself. So it was not an "it" but very much a She.

I knew it was a great honor to receive the Calabash, and promised to look after her.

Eventually we got to meet the woman who had made our walks through the Grove possible, her honorable Susan Wenger. For days Derrick had been asking Osunkolode if we could meet her, and for days he replied,

"She is very old now. She does not see visitors anymore. She is in her nineties, you know."

But Derrick is a funny one. He has a very strong sense of intuition. Two nights before we were due to leave the Osun Palace, and our bare little honeymoon suite he said,

"my spirit is telling me we are going to see her."

"Really?" I said not believing a word of it.

"OsunKolode said that is not going to be possible. The woman is in her nineties," I reminded him.

"We will see her tomorrow," he said before rolling on his side to fall asleep.

I did not feel totally sleepy. So I stayed up meditating for a little bit. As sleep began to drift over me so too did a soothing beautiful voice with this message.

173

If something is happening to the water how could I not do something about it. Each river is like one of the veins in my body. When one goes wrong my capacity to help humanity diminishes. When water goes then I go. When I go there is no more humanity. Without water there is no more life.

We say the earth does not need humans but just as flowers are to the earth, is how humans are to God. Humans were given the ability to make the planet beautiful. Human beings are pleasing to the eye of God when you are all fulfilling your purpose for living. The planet can live physically without humans, that is true, but spiritually it is not true. God needs humans.

If that was not the case, then human beings would not be on the earth. God does not do anything without a purpose. The purpose of human beings is to make the whole world beautiful, as well. God's purpose for the world is simple, and it is happiness. It is not as complicated as we think of it. When everything is moving around energetically and harmonious, everything looks beautiful in the eyes of God.

It was the following day. The day before we had to go back to Lagos. The morning came and went quite uneventfully. I teased Derrick and told him his intuition was way of track. But the last laugh was on me. At lunch time over Jollof rice, red sauce, and plantain OsunKolode dropped into our little honeymoon suite and said,

"Why don't we go and see Susan Wenger today. She might be up to seeing us."

He didn't explain why he had a sudden change of heart and we didn't question it. As we ambled up from our little mat, I tried not to look Derrick in the eyes because I knew they would be saying, "I told you so."

174

If you have never been to a living museum then you have not been to Susan Wenger's house. It was a fifteen minute drive away from where we were staying. The road was pretty dusty and kicked up through the window onto my white African lace outfit. Who cared? We were on our way to see Susan Wenger.

The four wheeler hummed and bumped along the dirt roads until it pulled up smoothly outside a house that had an air of aged antiquity. We jumped out like excited puppies. And passed through the state of the art carved primordial door. Which opened into a bigger art piece – the interior of her house.

Her house was an impressive piece of living art beautified and embedded with African sculptures, totem poles and masks – all made by her. Her living space was awe inspiring. It seemed just as amazing as the carvings and energy in the Sacred Grove itself. Which made sense as many of the art pieces there she had directed or personally done with her own hands.

Standing in the midst of all that impressive art brought on a realization that whispered ever so softly to me

true conviction to contribute something to humanity is something we must live, not just through words but with every breath we take and every action we do.

We waited anxiously on the ground level floor of the house. Were we going to get to meet the artist or weren't we? Osunkolode had gone upstairs to find out if she was feeling well enough to receive visitors. The anticipation made me restless. Waiting for the answer was far from boring. There were dozens of art pieces to oooh and ahhhh over. Which included numerous finely carved totem poles which propped up the very foundation of her house.

Then it happened. After waiting for a few minutes on the ground level floor of what we discovered was a three storey house. Our host came down, nodded in our directions, and ushered us hurriedly up wooden living art stairs. We were taken through a door and suddenly there she was. Sitting dignified, nicely matured and full of spirit, and art.

It took no time for the small room to be filled with us the visitors, and her assistances (some of the priesthood from the Osun Palace). Meeting Miss Wenger was a moment I would never forget. Swamped in the reverence, art and aura that filled the room I felt as though I was meeting history itself and the type of servant my watery guardian Osun was now asking me to be. As I knelt before Ms. Susan Wenger for a traditional blessing, I thanked Osun. For suddenly I felt I understood all that she wanted me to be. The kind of dedication, commitment for humanity and the planet I had to embrace. I thanked her for being able to be graced by the presence of this legend before us. Who despite her age had honored us by granting an audience with her.

Susan Wenger's feeble hand touched my head lightly and I sunk into the sacred sea of her prayers. Something inexplicably began to transform and transfix itself in me forever. I could not explain it but tears rolled from my soul. The world needs us. All of us. My heart whispered.

Meeting Susan Wenger was a moment I would never forget. She reminded me of the self less love of water itself and seemed to embody all of what the Mother was: loving, caring, healing, wise, selfless, creative, motherly and tireless.

Despite the awe, despite the historicness, despite the immersion I knew I could not miss the opportunity to ask some questions of Ms. Wenger.

Question: What do you think of water as an agent of healing?

176

Ans: Water knows when you need it. It doesn't lose its power. You must seek its energy.

Question: What inspired you to reconstruct the grove?

Ans: I just went there one day to enjoy and walk in it. I wasn't there to change it. I was just like a child. Every time I went to the grove I had a new experience like a husband or wife has with their partner. Every time you experience that person you experience something different.

Question: How has the water of the Grove changed?

Ans: when you have a beautiful child it is always beautiful.

With Derrick's nudging insistence I read her a piece that I had written the night before on the grove.

I cannot sleep and it is because Osun has me thinking of many things. The grove is one of them. The Grove shows the power of Osun to inspire people into action and devotion. Not only is it visionary but it would have taken a serious commitment to action. To rebuild its ancient space you would have to have an outstanding level of commitment, stamina and vision. The grove is a symbol of individual commitment but also joint action and devotion from which something beautiful came out of it.

When I read this piece out to Miss Wenger the whole room listened including her carved masked She called her family. That's how connected she felt to the spirit of art and wood. On finishing the piece she looked at me strangely with her virtually cataract covered sea blue eyes. Then she hugged her arms to her body.

"You are young. You are new, but you have a very very ancient Osun in you. She is in you. I can see her. You are very privileged."

177

That night I woke up from a dream. I am not sure what it was, but in between sleep and wake I heard a soft gentle whisper speak to me.

"I want you to begin a water project. I want it to be something that helps the waterways, the planet and the humanity. I want it to help humanity to connect with water and the natural world. I want humanity to see that they are a reflection of the planet and the planet a reflection of them. Ask Derrick for the name of the project. He will know."

Derrick was in a deep sleep when I nudged him awake about 2 am in the morning. After he got over his initial grumpiness on being woken up so abruptly he listed to my insights. He immediately said, "Humanity4Water. That is what the project will be called.

The small boy chased the four wheeler. It was lunch time and the day after our moving visit with Susan Wenger. My initiation was all finished. I had the Sacred Calabash carefully wrapped up in white cloth and placed even more carefully in a bag. We hurtled back to the smog and noise of Lagos. The boy was trying to sell us boiled eggs to snack on for our long journey. We bought some.

"Esheo! Esheo!" he shouted his thanks.

The four wheeler driven by Chief Popola's brother sped on its way. The Osun Palace grew further and further away. As it did so, the world humanity had created for itself began to swamp us once again. Somehow I knew I had to hold my experiences close to my heart. I never wanted them to go.

178

But there was no worry about that. Osun had sown them securely there.

Back at Chief Popola's house. Children played, people came in and out for divination, and prayers constantly floated up to the heavens. Despite his business he greeted us with his customary kindness. After enquiring about our trip he divined to see if all went well with the initiation. He confirmed,

"Ifa said all is well."

Then he made the surprise announcement.

"Ifa say you are to receive a second Crown title, Yeye Tayese, Mother Who Mends the World."

"I already have a Yeye title!" I exclaimed trying not to appear rude, but truly astonished at the suggestion of having a second Yeye (Mother) title.

"Is God trying to make doubly sure I don't escape from my destiny!" I jested.

The whole room, including Chief Popola laughed.

That same day the oracle honored Derrick with a chieftaincy. I laughed when I heard it, "General of Generals". It so summed him up.

Carving at King of Osogbo's palace of the fish that Osun
gave to the first King of Osogbo as a blessing and permission to settle in Osogbo

On the way to Nigeria reading Yoruba language book

Myself and Derrick at the Sacred Osun Grove,
World Heritage Site

Me, OsunKolode and his Mother
Yeye Osun at Osun Palace

The beautiful Sacred Osun River I had the privilege to bath in

Trying to get a picture with one of the peacocks at the Osun Palace

Myself and Derrick with King of Osogbo

A Blessing from Susan Wenger

Sitting with Chief Solaagbade (right) and
one of his gifted diviners, after the oracle had given me
title Yeye Tayese (Mother Who Mends the World)

184

OSA MEJI

Girl: Mother Tell me about Osa Meji.

Mother: The Odu Osa Meji talks about beings who are powerful forces of nature, which in this case are known as divinities of the night. Here it shows how careful and respectful you have to be of all the forces of nature.

Girl: Tell me one of the stories from Osa Meji.

Mother: Oh, the stories are very interesting. I will tell you one.

One day Osa Meji is leaving the realm of heaven. However, he does not pay any respect to any of the sacred forces and does no offerings or divination before he leaves. You know through divination it was believed you could find out the best way to do something. The best way that was in harmony with the forces of nature and life. Anyway, Osa Meji did not bother with any of that.

He just decides to leave heaven. As a result he gets totally lost on the way. Eventually he reaches the edge of heaven and to the last of the rivers before he gets to the world. There he meets the Mother of the the Divinities of the Night, Osoronga. She had been there for a long time because no one wanted to take her across. She was on her way to the world but she was too weak and feeble to cross the bridge of the river which was not the strongest of bridges. She asked Osa Meji if he could help her.

Osa Meji told her that the bridge would not take both their weights. Well, Osoronga came up with a plan. She told Osa Meji that he could swallow her and carry her in his stomach. He agreed to do this. When he got to the other side safely he told her they had reached their destination. But Osoronga said that his stomach was comfortable and she would stay there.

Osa Meji was quite horrified at that idea. He tried to trick her out, by telling her she would die of hunger in there. Osoronga was not buying that. She told Osa Meji don't worry about her dying of hunger, as long as he had a liver and organs she would be just fine. Just to prove her point she took a bite out of his liver.

Now Osa Meji was in pain and worried. He went for a divination and was told to offer a goat, palm oil and white cloth. He did as advised. He cooked the goats heart, liver and intestines. He put the food out and told Osoronga there was food for her. Well, the smell was so delicious that she could not resist coming out. Then she said, she could only eat out of the sight of anyone. So he used the white cloth from the offering to create a tent for her.

As she is eating he quickly escapes and runs into the nearest womb he could find. When Osoronga was finished she could not find Osa Meji and started screaming his name, "Osasa! Osasa! Osasa!". This is apparently the cry of the Divinities of the Night, even to this day.

The Catawba River was big, brown, mesmerizing, undulating, and pondering. It reminded me of the mighty body of the Osun river. But there was a difference. Whereas the body of latter seemed rather elegant, abundant, graceful and alive. The former was a sacred river that was more silent, contemplative and full of sorrow. What was its sorrow about? Why was the Catawba so sad? I wondered.

Now the answer was not to come in a dream. There were those to. But more in the form of beautifully white haired, creamy peachy skinned Becky. Becky was a Catawba Indian. But not just any old Catawba Indian. Her Grandfather who was now passed had been the Catawba Chief, Chief Blue. Now I knew nothing about Chief Blue before I met Becky. I also knew nothing about Catawba Indians, until I met her. I also didn't know about white skinned Native American Indians until I met Becky and others.

In fact, the most I knew about Native American Indians was the fact that my great grandfather was a Carib Indian from Trinidad; I use to watch cowboy and Indians on television when I was younger and always favored the Indians (they had this amazing deeply in touch with earth culture). You may have guessed that being born in London made me pretty ignorant about Native American Indians in general. We don't have Native Americans in London. I had the honor of meeting the Carib Leader of Trinidad once. But besides that I had not met any Native Americans.

There are plenty of Londoners who wished they could meet Native Americans. I think we all have visions of sweat lodges, trancing out to drums, and vision questing which we believe will lead us by some miracle into our ultimate transcendental nature. I was no different I had that dream in my head too. So when I got to meet Becky, a real life Native American (not just Native American but a medicine woman to

187

boot), I was, just a little bit over happy. It was Becky who made me realize why the Catawba River looked so mighty and sad. She lent me quite an impressive hard back book that looked like it was definitely part of the corridors of time and history.

Her great grandfather was there in its pages wearing a glorious feathered head dress ablaze with blues, reds and yellows. Then there were the facts shared about the Catawba River. Explorers discovered the Catawba River and the people called the Catawba. They were confused. They asked "who is the Catawba? The river or the people?" The chief simply replied, "we are one of the same."

It must have been nice fishing in the Catawba River. Becky explained that she had grown up with the Catawba river virtually rushing through her back yard. For part of the Catawba River nestles along the edges of the Catawba Reservation. Beckee once told me and Derrick as we all stood contemplating the river quietly.

"We use to be able to fish in this river. But now I would not even think of eating the fish from it."

I later discovered that the Catawba River was considered by the American Rivers to be the most endangered in the United States.

Latter Derrick said to me sadly,

"Imagine being called River People yet you cannot use the river that runs through your own backyard. You cannot use the river that you are physically and spiritually part of. You have the river right there and you cannot eat its fish. You cannot bath in it."

It was really more than sad. Just as the river seemed to be so endangered so did the Catawba. For the more we listened to Beckee's stories was the more we heard the echoes of the Native American people's suffering. We learned that the Catawba people had numerous problems with Sovereignty, had faced terrible past atrocities, were constantly struggling with the question of self-sufficiency. The more I heard was the more my London fantasy about the golden lives of Native Americans disappeared like melting snow.

In London when we talk about Native Americans we do so with a kind of reverence. Now it seemed like there was not much of that going on in their own land. A fact that as an Islander disturbed my spirit. For venerating the ancient ways and the ancestors was an integral part of our culture. Not to remember those who had walked the land before was well.....nothing short of disastrous.

Now what is interesting is how we came to meet Beckee. One day, as I did my usual meditation and prayers in Trinidad, I had an insight. It was about going to America. Now, Derrick still lived in America. But this insight wasn't about the mere fact of me joining him. It seemed that my Watery Guardian Osun wanted me to continue my calling of "going to water". However, not in Trinidad but in America. I didn't like the sound of the idea. I was not too sure about the States, but the usual divinations were done by Chief Popola who confirmed,

"Ifa said you must go. There is work for you to do there."

Myself, mum and kem Ra arrived in South Carolina in July 2008 – one month after going to Nigeria. By the time we met Becky it was latter in the year. We met her at the lively

Catawba Yip Yew festival which was an annual celebration of the Catawba people. It was a nice day. One that broke my belief that all Native Americans were dark skinned with long plaits drapsing down their backs. For at the Yip Yew festival I remembered entering through the doors of the local university building where it was being held and thinking, "where are the Native Americans? I even asked Derrick where they were. He wondered too.

Even though he was born in South Carolina. He had in fact spent his college days upward living outside of South Carolina. So he too didn't know about the Catawba Indians. Well, hardly anything. It was after half an hour of being at the festival, with my disappointment getting heavier and heavier that Derrick whispered in my ears,

"I think the women and men in Native American clothing are the Catawba."

I looked at him incredulously, like you gotta be kidding me.

"How?"

He shrugged his shoulders. He didn't quite know, but he turned out to be right. The creamy skinned looking people in leathers were indeed the Catawba and some other Native Americans from other nations. Amongst them I didn't see not one dark skinned Indian. How could that be? I wondered. Being from London and the islands I was confused. For in the Islands the Carib Indians were still very brown skinned. I didn't know it was possible to be white and Native American. But once I met Becky I discovered it was.

Becky was all Catawba Indian and very proud of her heritage. She helped me, us, to understand much about the Native American history and issues. In terms of the Catawba's current skin color she explained that they had, along with other nations, experienced much intermixing with the white foreigners who had come to make the home of Native Americans their land. Color was not important for brown or white skinned most Native Americans still are proud of their culture.

Becky is quite beautiful. When I first laid eyes on her she was on stage. We had missed the beginning of her fascinating talk which now turned its attention to turtles. I really don't remember what she said in detail, but it was fascinating enough for me to remember it was about the fact that the markings on the back of the turtle divides exactly into twelve months. There was so much more she said and it would have been good to share it with you, but I really don't remember what it was.

What I really want to share though, is as Becky stood up there I was fascinated by her clothing. She wore an all white leather outfit that matched her perfectly white and beautifully groomed hair and skin. Then there was something else I noticed and it was the white aura that surrounded her. Now I knew about auras. A kind of halo around people that is said to represent their energy body. It is said each person's aura is different as it reflects the different states of their emotions and health.

However, I have never seen an aura, not until that day when I saw Becky. I had no doubt that the big white light I saw so visibly around her was her aura. At the time I didn't know she was the Catawba Medicine Woman. But her white aura seemed to be talking to me and this little voice in my head kept on saying, "that's the Catawba Medicine Woman."

Being in what Joseph Campbell called the Belly of the Whale leaves much room for synchronicity. Meeting Beckee and

191

being at the Yip Yew festival was one of those moments. The story goes something like this. It was almost two months since I had arrived in South Carolina. I was so busy enjoying marital bliss, the Pine trees and the fascinating drawling accents that I forgot all about my mission. Well, not really. I was kind off sort off wishing it would just slide away like a snow drift. It seemed as though I was getting away with it until one morning Derrick looked me in the eyes and said,

"you know you need to start going to water again."

Now I really didn't want to hear that. So what did I do? I just shrugged my shoulders and agreed. After that I thought the issue would definitely go away. But every week Derrick proceeded to sound like somewhat of a stuck record.

"Baby, you have to go to water."

Now, as most people know South Carolina is quite a Christian place. I had never really encountered the South Carolinian brand of Christianity before. I mean in the Islands we have plenty of Christians, but they are still Caribbean and even though they reject certain aspects of Island culture they still believe in dreams, signs from the heavens, ancestors, and donkey's with gold teeth. Now London has, well not so many Christians. But the ones who are Christians are kind of flexible.

So back to the South Carolinian brand of Christianity. It seemed rather…well..kind off excluding of other cultures and things. The mention of words like Indian flutes, honoring nature, yoga, and healing just got people running in the opposite direction. Now that was not everyone but it was a lot of people. I didn't quite understand it because I had gotten so use to finding value in so many other cultures and ways. It just seemed strange to me. Especially since 99% of my client's for my natural health clinic in Trinidad had been Christians.

So when Derrick kept on trying to do the right thing and remind me of my calling I just didn't want to know. In my quest to get on Mr. Normal's right side I was once again willing to abandon my own unique path, and the responsibility of the ancestral lineage that flows through my blood. I wish I had something like those ten second reads I now receive every day in my Facebook. They are by Paulo Coelho and they are really to the point and centering. He had one about the path which read:

"I am willing to give up everything", said the prince to the master. "Please accept me as your disciple."

"How does a man choose his path?" asked the master.

"Through sacrifice," answered the prince. "A path which demands sacrifice, is a true path."

The master bumped into some shelves. A precious vase fell, and the prince threw himself down in order to grab hold of it. He fell badly and broke his arm, but managed to save the vase.

"What is the greater sacrifice: to watch the vase smash, or break one's arm in order to save it?" asked the master.

"I do not know," said the prince.

"Then how can you guide your choice for sacrifice? The true path is chosen by our ability to love it, not to suffer for it."

You really can't just abandon your path like that. You have to love your path. Loving your path is one of the greatest things of life. I remember once someone telling me a story in Trinidad. It was about a man who use to go picking up rubbish from the local streets and he would sell whatever he could. The man enjoyed what he was doing so much that he eventually got a bigger cart, a bigger, then even bigger one. Until one day the man had fleets of lorries where he collected

193

rubbish. The man who told me the story happened to be the grandson of the man who became a tycoon.

I digress slightly. Back to Derrick. I didn't feel like embracing any calling but he wouldn't stop nagging me. Then one night I had a dream where a fish was standing on the edge of the Catawba River. It had feet and could speak like a human. The fish looked poignantly at the water and said to me,

"the water is too dirty I cannot get in."

The fish looked so sad. I felt sad looking at the fish because I knew it was going to die. I felt bad for what humans had done to the water. Then I woke up. I woke up feeling all sad, depressed, deeply disturbed and with a renewed sense of conviction to continue on destiny's path. How could I just enjoy marital bliss and not continue to help the planet? Destiny won the day.

The first river we chose was the Catawba River. How we came upon this choice was that we both agreed that the Catawba was at least a local river. Surely it would be good to start with the river in one's own backyard.

"How on earth are we going to do a water blessing?" I asked Derrick anxiously.

"It will work itself out," he said with his usual quiet confidence.

The longer I knew Derrick was the more I was beginning to realize he was a true disciple of pure faith. That boy had some faith. I tell you.

"What do you mean it will work itself out?" I was not convinced.

"It will, you will see."

Three days later I was browsing through the local paper which had advertised a festival called Yip Yew. It was to be held by the Catawba people. For some reason it felt like a good luck omen. I rushed down stairs and showed it to Derrick.

He smiled quietly. The rest is history. We went. Had a good time. Met Beckee, who said we could access the Catawba river from the Catawba reservation, and helped us to organize our first water blessing.

A very nice Charlotte Observer reporter, Dan Huntley, came down to see us all. He was not only extremely bright and pleasant, but also seemed like a darn good journalist. He had a serious love of water and knowledge about the Catawba River.

"There was a time when you could hear the roar of the Great Falls from 3 miles away. Now you can barely hear it at all," he said.

We also discovered not only was the Catawba river 220 miles long, but we had chosen a river that was considered one of the "Most endangered rivers" in the United States by the American Rivers.

"They say the spirit of the Catawba is dead," Dan further informed us. Referring to the eleven dams that break the flow of the Catawba river.

Beckee agreed with him about the death of the Catawba. They both said the Great Falls was a spectacular feature of the Catawba. It was approximately 4 miles long, with a total elevation of 121 feet. The creation of dams at the Great Falls resulted in the top 2 miles of it being completely dry (de-watered) except during times of very high flow. The bottom portion of the Falls is drowned by a dam known as Cedar Creek.

A few days after the interview Dan had an article in the Charlotte Observer about our up and coming Catawba River water blessing called: *A Prayer for The River*. It was a pretty cool one.

Never rely on numbers before you take up your calling. It was January 2009, 8pm and beyond freezing cold. Only ten people braved the weather that day of the Catawba water blessing and I really couldn't blame the ones who didn't. It was really really cold. Even though, I couldn't blame the ones that didn't show up I was still a little disappointed with the low attendance. But amongst the ten people who showed up there was a good mix of cultures and warmth too. Before the ceremony we all chatted over bowls of homemade Island lentil soup I had prepared. It felt strange but it was as though we had all met before. After eating we warmed ourselves up with drums, rattles, and Native American flutes. For ten people we didn't do too badly on filling the whole air up with a sacred joyful noise.

As we all created music - myself, Beckee and Derrick wondered where would be the best place to hold the ceremony. The original plan had been by the river, but it was wet, muddy, and real dark outside. Beckee decided it would be better to have a bucket of Catawba River water and pray around and over it.

My heart sunk a little. A bucket of water didn't quite seem the same as standing by the river to me. But, Derrick assured me it would be all okay. In fact, he came well prepared with five candles to float in a bucket of water. That day he had observed the weather forecast which had predicted heavy rains. Becky had also listened to the weather forecast and came prepared with a pre-collected bucket of Catawba River water.

So it was all decided, we would do the water blessing ceremony outside around the bucket of Catawba River water. Interestingly, enough Beckee told Derrick that five was actually a very sacred number for the Catawba people. I also latter discovered that five was also a sacred number for the Chinese. It represented numerous things including: the basic elements of life: earth, wood, metal, fire and water; totality; the geographic directions of the earth: North, East, South, and West plus the center; the Five Blessings: Long Life, Wealth, Peace, Virtue and Fame; the Five Virtues: Piety, Uprightness, Manners, Knowledge and Trust. Five was also Osun's sacred number.

In terms of the Water Blessing and the bucket of water it was years later, one of the attendees who had become a friend of ours, said her and her partner had a good little laugh amongst themselves about praying around that bucket of water. She was newly dating the guy she had invited along, and revealed she was thinking, "oh, my lord I know he is thinking what am I doing here praying around a bucket of water, in the freezing cold, in the middle of the dark?!"

Ironically it was soon after this revelation that I met with a wonderful kindred spirit, Ann Rosencranz (an amazing healer and Program Director for the Center of Sacred Studies, and The Council of 13 Grandmothers). During one of our chats she spoke about a water ceremony herself and her husband do for their sweat ceremonies. Guess what? Their prayers are directed to a bucket of water! She sent me a picture of the bucket and it had been turned from an ordinary silver bucket into something quite ceremonial looking with two pictures of beautifully painted water and fire birds. Myself and Derrick had a good giggle about the whole bucket thing,

"you see, spirit always knows what it is doing, even when we don't!" I laughed.

197

The Catawba Water Blessing, despite some obvious obstacles, ended up being a beautiful ceremony. As we prayed and sung for world healing and the health of the waterways our voices raised into the cold damp air, and warmed us to the bones. The whole ceremony took about an hour to do, and we all left feeling warmer and better than when we had arrived. It had all been worth it.

When myself and Derrick got home he down loaded the pictures from the prayers. We both looked at each other puzzled when we saw what looked like white finger prints all over some of the photos. The mystery deepened when we noticed only some of the photos had those white finger print things on them.

"Sweetie, our pictures are ruined with those finger prints. We should have cleaned the lens," I complained.

"They are not finger prints. I don't think so, because they are not on every picture," Derrick replied still staring at the photos with his eyebrows raised to the sky.

"What do you mean they are not finger prints?" I quizzed.

He shook his head, as puzzled as I was. About a year later at our first Humanity4Water awards ceremony we met the impressive couple Gary and Debbie Fourstar for the first time. We were honoring them with a Humanity4Water award for Outstanding Commitment2Action. They had travelled down from Atlanta with several suitcases full of stuff to display. In one was a photo album which had photos with large finger print looking things on them. I froze when I noticed the same markings as in our Catawba Water Blessing pics.

"What's that?" I asked Debbie.

"Orbs," she replied matter of factly.

"What are orbs?" I asked curiously.

"They are benevolent ancestors and spirit guides" she replied. "They often show up during sacred moments like these.

"We have pictures just like these," I told her.

"Yes, it is quite common," she said.

Her explanation made me and Derrick feel as though the Catawba Water Blessing really was a blessed affair.

I have to say working with the Native Americans became an experience I always came to look forward to. Interesting, mystical things always seemed to happen. They came in the form of spirit animals, dreams, whispers of wisdom, fortuitous events and cosmic bumps.

In fact after the Catawba water blessing my dreams became even more vivid than usual. I felt a growing sense of oneness with nature, and awe for those mind blowing moments of synchronicity. It's as though the spirit of the Native American ancestors were rising from the ground and entering through the soles of my feet flying right up into my soul. It was a good feeling, a happy feeling. We must have been doing something right, for I suddenly felt a great joy in the simplicity of honoring the waters and land.

A few weeks after the Catawba Water Blessing I was to experience the unexpected – the strong gentle whispers of the Catawba River itself. I had no idea that this was the intensification of a gift that had opened up in Trinidad. A gift that I had not even been aware had been there. It was Beckee's brother Dan who eventually made me realize I was experiencing the gift of "hearing water".

"You know how many times I have sat by water and tried to hear what it is saying. This is the gift that our people have, especially the older generation. It is a wonderful gift to be able to hear the spirit of water," he explained putting a large hand on my shoulder before continuing, "you are so lucky that you can hear water, many have lost this gift."

Ironically the whispers of the Catawba came five times. Just like the five candles we had lit in the bucket. It as if each revelation had been sparked by their sacred fire.

The first Whisper of the Catawba came in the form of a dream that I remembered very little of. It was a dream that made me truly begin to realize the connection between water and the rest of ecology. Small things really can make a big impact. For the part of the dream that I remembered was small but it has had a lasting and profound impact on me. Someone was showing me things in nature. Then suddenly they showed me the inside of a tree that was next to a dirty waterways. The inside of the tree's trunk was riddled with the most shocking disease. I was horrified at what I saw. Somehow in the dream I felt a compassionate connection with the tree and screamed out "the trees!". The scream entered my world of reality and immediately woke Derrick up. Half awake, half asleep, I trembled. Derrick was shocked into action, and shook me fully awake,

"what's the matter! What's the matter!"

All that shaking woke me right up. I explained to him I had a nightmare.

I could see his concern etched against the night air, and felt really stupid when I told him I had a nightmare about a diseased tree. I waited for him to burst out laughing, but he didn't. Instead he proceeded to tell me what he thought the meaning of the dream was.

"In your dream state you became completely one with the tree and you felt its pain. I believe the dream was showing you the connection between the waterways and the rest of ecology including trees. There is something about the trees and their significance to water that the dream is indicating needs deeper consideration."

Derrick was a serious tree lover and he impressed me with his dream interpretation.

One morning he decided to come walking with me.

"I want to take you somewhere," he revealed mysteriously.

We took a scenic route lined with beautiful Southern Pine and Cedar trees. It led us to a medium sized stream that looked intriguing but seemed to be dragged down by pollution. We had to amble down a small hill and go into the woodlands to access the stream properly. We noticed that the dream had been true for all the trees that were near the waterways were dying. Many had fallen, some were leaning over precariously, and others were rotting. It made us realize that the health of trees was one of the ways to assess the health of the waterways. We had never thought about trees properly until that point. It brought back something a good family friend, and leading Caribbean geologist had said to me once,

"if you're going to look at the question of water you have to look at the forest and trees. The two go hand in hand".

I was so green around the ecological edges that I did not quite understand what he meant. I also did not dwell on it further. Well, not until the dream happened.

The Second Whisper of the Catawba River followed shortly after that dream and came in the midst of my morning meditation as a gentle quiet voice,

201

How you heal your clients is how you heal me. The road to healing is the same for everything in life. When you heal someone you have an idea of how a healthy human being is meant to be. This you have learnt from the knowledge provided from your training. You then spend time with the person. You talk to the person and you become aware of their story. The story of how they have reached to where they are today. Through awareness you are able to begin the process of pin pointing the problem. You want to help the person to heal the problem. You find solutions of what you can do to help them and they can do to help themselves.

A river is no different. You need to know what does a river and water do. You need to know the river's story. The one of how did it get to this state, what are the issues that are causing the problem and what are the solutions to turn the issue around.

To skip any of these healing stages out means that you cannot truly bring healing to a situation. Most people look at rivers and they are trying to put in place a solution. But how many people care to know everything about the river's story, its sacred history, its past, what state it needs to be returned to, what the real causes of its problems are?

I shared this insight with Derrick. We tossed it around for a few days. One thing I knew about healing was the importance of locating what I call "the pain". If there is a client with weight problems just adjusting the diet may not solve his/her problem. Often listening to her story carefully and pinpointing the true source of the pain is crucial. This made me think of the river and nature as a client. The waterways are polluted and dying along with the rest of nature. But what is the real source of the pain? Why was this truly happening? So now these were the questions on my mind, the ones that I carried around with me from that point on.

The Third Whisper from the Catawaba answered the question. It came in my meditative state, like the whisper before.

If you look at water and start with the perception of compassion you begin to see it differently. You say, "Ah". You begin to see it and notice things about it. You begin to open your heart up and now you want to know something more about it. The compassion of traditional societies made them look at nature closer and notice its nuances and personality. So with water they said,

"oh it gives us so much, it helps us, it's very attractive, I feel clear headed when I am near it".

That is where the personification of nature came from. Through getting closely acquainted with it. So as a person if you experience an increase in compassion for nature and the things around you - it will make you open minded. It will make you start thinking "that's interesting. I want to know more about this thing".

Compassion will give you a spirit of adventure. It will make you want to explore your relationship with nature, people and life on a deeper level. Making you suddenly feel okay about going out of the box and asking questions about nature you had not even considered.

As your compassion takes you into a deeper relationship with nature - nature becomes your friend. Someone you want to look out for. You begin to think what can I do for my friend? Your compassion starts making you see things differently. Your friend is in pain.

"Why?" you ask.

You explore deeper. You see the pain, and what is causing it. Then you try to help. Compassion also takes away the anger you may act with. There are people polluting the waterways, but compassion tells you "don't be angry with them. Let's develop an understanding and find a better solution for both of us, together."

As with the first whisper I discussed this insight with Derrick. We both agreed that somehow our relationship with nature seemed to be broken.

"It's all about relating," Derrick said quietly. "You feel compassion for your friends so you care about what happens to them." He paused and continued, "so why don't we feel a relationship with nature? I know that we somehow have become more distant from it, but what is really the root of our distant feelings from nature?"

The Fourth Whisper seemed to be the answer and came riding on the back of my breathless son.

"Mum guess what I asked the science teacher today?" the whole of his just turned thirteen year old self plopped onto the bed.

"What?" I was really interested in knowing what had him so breathless and excited.

"Well, we were in class today and we were just talking about things that are living and things that are not. I asked my teacher if water is alive?"

"What did she say?" I interjected. "

"Miss said that water is not alive. It does not have a cell and it cannot reproduce".

"What do you think?" I asked.

"I think water is alive".

"I agree with you. I believe it is too," I acquiesced.

With a bright smile my son disappeared out of the room.

Derrick had been present and actively listening to the whole conversation. The belief that water was not alive bothered us both. For days and days we discussed the concept of whether water was alive or not. Then by the third day we came to a conclusion.

"That's the problem – if we don't think water is alive then no wonder why we treat it that way. No wonder why we treat Mother Earth the way we do".

The question, "Is Water Alive?" Would not go away. It seemed to highlight a fundamental perception of humanity's attitude towards life itself. Somehow it seemed that the Mother Waters now had us looking at the very essence of life itself and the perceptions we hold about it. When I was at the Sacred Osun Grove, water was very much alive. It was a living healing essence. Somehow it began to feel important to prove that water was alive.

I knew that Dr Masaru Emoto, author of "The True Power of Water", had shown that Water had crystals that changed according to the words or images exposed to it. I also knew I had done the rice experiment and seen the effects of loving and hateful words on the cooked rice for myself. I had not documented the results though. I wished everyone could do that rice experiment. It was such a simple validation of a fundamental truth – nature is alive, and responds to our love.

The Fifth Whisper. If the first three whispers were quiet; and the fourth one came in the form of a breathless teenager; the fifth one came in the form of a Middle School Science Fair.

Kem Ra came home with a sheet of paper. It stated he had a Science Fair and there was going to be a competition for the best project.

For two weeks different ideas passed between Kem Ra and Derrick. Till eventually one day they agreed on the idea of

205

doing the question "Is Water Alive?". They decided on repeating the rice experiment.

I was excited to know Kem Ra was going to do the rice experiment. However, eventually a lingering doubt crept over me. Was the experiment repeatable? I even tried to talk Kem Ra out of the experiment, but he really wanted to go ahead with it. Eventually, I went with the flow. Myself and Derrick decided to shadow the experiment.

*Me with Beckee Garrison, the Catawba Medicine
Woman, just before the Catawba Water Blessing standing by
Catawba River. The Catawba River is one of the most endangered
Rivers in the United States*

The famous bucket of Catawba Water we prayed
over and those auspicious orbs

Me, Derrick, Beckee, and Dan Huntley from the Charlotte Observer.

EKA MEJI

Girl: Mother tell me about Eka Meji.

Mother: The stories in Eka Meji talk about Eka Meji being a good diviner but absolutely ignored since he was the oldest amongst the apostles of God who came to earth. As a result Eka Meji initially had no prosperity. He was very poor. However, before he left heaven he had did a divination where he was advised to do an offering to ensure he did not meet amongst insurmountable obstacles. He did as was advised.

Well, one day while Eka Meji was on earth suffering, God decided to come down. Esu, the God of the Crossroads was making mischief and disrupting Gods work on earth. God wanted to know who was causing problems in his creation and what to do about it. Before he came down he disguised himself so that he would not be recognizable.

The first person he came across on earth was Eka Meji. God asked him for a divination. Eka Meji agreed to do it. He informed the mystery visitor that Esu was the cause of all his problems and he had to offer a goat in order for the problems to stop. God said he did not have the money to do that. Out of compassion Eka Meji decided to do the offering for him. After thanking him God asked how he could find the other priests who were senior to him. Eka Meji directed him to the house of Eji Ogbe.

When God, in his disguise, arrived at Eji Ogbe, he was turned away. Eji Ogbe said he had no time for the stranger. On his way back God found out that Esu had stopped all his mischief. On hearing this he returned back to earth in his full glory. He told Eka Meji who trembled before his presence that he would have all the prosperity in the world, and told all the senior priest and priest that anything Eka Meji said must never be challenged. After that Eka Meji lived an abundant life.

Mother: Now there is one more story I want to tell from Eka Meji. It is short but I like it very much.

Before leaving heaven Eka meji was approached by the small oil and the small thread for divination. The lamp was told to make an offering. He did this. Thereafter he was given a human to serve him for the whole of eternity. This is why to this day it is the human being that rekindles a lamp when it is about to extinguish.

They came to this water just like the Native Americans had. It was the latter's secret initially. Eventually, it was a secret they shared with some soldiers of war. It was a secret that healed those soldiers from their bloody wounds and near death experiences. Like all secrets, once discovered it could not be kept anymore. The cat was out of the bag. "God's Acre Healing Springs"(fondly known as The Healing Springs) was now everyone's secret

Now how we came to be standing on the hallowed grounds of the Healing Springs on a warm February day in 2009 was yet another testimony to the magic of the journey, synchronicity, and those spiritual guides that carry one along the wings of the universe.

It was soon after the Catawba Water Blessing that Beckee decided to invite myself and Derrick to a meeting of Native American Chiefs to speak about our Water Blessings. Nervous at the idea, I initially didn't want to go, but with a bit of cajoling from Derrick I changed my mind. I couldn't decide what to wear. The image of Native American Chiefs dressed in regalia of all sorts propelled me to wear a cream and gold African lace outfit. I had worn it on more than one occasion to one of several weddings and political occasions at the King of Ife's Palace in Nigeria. So if it was good enough for the palace then I reckoned it would be good enough for a Native American Chief's meeting. Anyway, I had left most of my African outfits behind in Trinidad due to weight restrictions (those outfits can be heavy). Derrick decided on wearing a stylish cool grayish gold batik number.

The meeting had already got started by the time we arrived. I felt a little more than ridiculous shimmying on in with my big African head wrap of silver and gold. Especially, when I saw that the Chiefs present did not live up to that fancy image that had danced around in my head. Instead they were dressed in simple down to earth clothes, like jeans and t shirts. I consoled myself with the thought - at least I am representing.

Sovereignty, education, land rights, were all the issues of the day. I felt honored to be allowed to sit in on such a meeting. At the end of the meeting myself and Derrick were called up to talk. I got nervous and felt kind of foolish as we squeezed up to the front podium.

"We have two people here who would like to talk about us honoring Mother Earth, the waterways and rivers. They want to talk to us about the water blessings they are doing," said the speaker introducing us.

Stupidity was now definitely the order of the day. It kept on roaring with laughter in my face. I just wanted to sink into a deep hole. I looked over at Derrick who looked as cool as a cucumber. The speaker and Derrick looked at me with their urging eyes. I forced myself to greet everyone. Then I forced myself to go beyond my fear, and talk. However, once I got started there was no stopping me. I talked about the calling; I talked about how important Mother Earth was and how absolutely essential it was that we begin to treat her waters as sacred again; I talked about how the journey of honoring Mother Earth had begun to change my life and open me up to a deeper more spiritual me; I talked about the Catawba Water Blessing and how honored we had felt to work with Beckee and the Catawba nation on this venture; I talked about the fact we were planning a second Water Blessing and would like to once again partner with the Native American people to do it.

As I talked the words just flowed out surprisingly fluidly, against an even more surprising backdrop of total silence. Eventually, I stopped talking, and my heart seemed to

212

also stop beating. Oh Lord I was a total failure. I wanted to hide in a corner with that big old head wrap of mine, and run before they all started to stone me. Then in the midst of planning my escape I heard a thunderous round of applause like the rising of a storm. It took my heart and lifted it on the glories of the Red Road. I smiled shyly, breathed a sigh of relief, and thanked the audience. Trying to get back to my seat was a challenge for all sorts of people wanted to speak to myself and Derrick. Their eagerness and oozing love for Mother Earth and her waters surprised me. It amazed me that there were still people that felt this level of intense love for our Great Mother. The overwhelming sincerity of emotions swept me away on a wish that everyone could care this deeply and this much for the web of life we are all a part of.

An average height woman with a glorious beautiful Mother Moon face grabbed me by the arm and steered me outside into the quiet of the hallway. I did not have a chance to get my bearings properly before she grabbed me and pulled me into the warmest biggest bear hug ever. I could feel something wet seeping through my lace top wetting the flesh of my shoulder. The wetting was followed by a muffled voice choked up with emotion,

"thank you, thank you, thank you."

Those thank yous travelled through my ears and landed right in the garden of my heart. At last River Flows (that was the name the woman introduced herself by) set me free. She scrambled through her bag and pulled out something I recognized instantly to be a CD. She pulled out the cover and gently pushed it into my hands.

"Read!" she commanded softly.

I dared not disobey her instructions and began to read what had been placed in my hands. The front cover of the CD read, *Tribal Waters Music by Native Americans*. While the back of it read,

Water

One of the elements sacred to all existence offering us the gift of life. Native people have always honored and respected the natural world. If we take from nature we give back with prayers and songs. There are ceremonies for the Water Spirits. When it rains we pray and give thanks to the creator for the wonderful rainy day and for everything that will grow.
The salmon have a song they sing as they travel together moving water has a song all of its own that inspires song in ourselves.
By Agnes Parker

"All the things you spoke about are here, right in this CD. I am part of a group and that's what we do, we sing healing songs to water. We Native Americans, this is one of our duties to look after Mother Earth, to look after water. It's one we have not been fulfilling. We have broken our promise."

The last sentence seemed to cause the tears to well up again.

"I think you should do your next Water Blessing at the Healing Springs. It is a beautiful place. I go there to meditate all the time," said the beautiful Moon faced woman to me.

I was feeling her. I was all ears.

"When I meditate there I always see a huge eagle in the water. For my people Eagles are very important. They are a very sacred symbol."

I could see the eagle too, rising in my mind's eye. I smiled at the image.

"Go to the Healing Springs."

214

Later, on through follow up conversations with River Flows we discovered she was the founder of a Native American group called The Little Horse Creek Fellowship Circle. They gathered together in an eclectic mix of Christianity and Native Americaness to worship the Great Spirit. After our conversations with her we knew that the Healing Springs would be the sight of the next Water Blessing.

A week after the Native American Chief meeting we went to visit it to see if it would be suitable. We arrived to witness a lively stream bouncing through happy looking trees, artesian wells flowing freely with water (there were no taps to turn the water flow off), and droves of an array of earth's beautiful people reverently collecting water from the endlessly flowing taps. We gave gratitude to the water and joined the others who collected it. Refreshing sparkling water filled our cups, and plastic containers. All in the cloak of silence that engulfed the place. For despite the amount of people present, the only sound one could hear was that of the water flowing from the taps.

We took our time filling our containers, so that we could soak up the soothing atmosphere. Riverflows had invited us over to the Native American meeting place she attended, Little Horse Creek. We had been told it was only a short drive away from where we were. So on finishing at the Healing Springs we headed on right over there. Apparently their head, Chief Randall, wanted to meet with us, and let his group know about the planned Water Blessing. It was a good day to let them know about it, as they were having a Sunday social.

I just want to back track for a minute. Before we left the Healing Springs to visit Chief Randall and the Little Horse Creek, the journalist in me wanted to find out what was it about these waters that so attracted people to collect it in absolute devout silence. So I decided to ask one woman who had almost forty empty bottles, and was going about patiently filling all of them. Her answer to my question was not a long winded complicated one, but was simple and heartfelt,

"I totally believe in the power of this water. I have faith in this water."

After her answer I wanted to taste the water. It had been calling me to do so, anyway. I bent over and let it touch the edge of my waiting lips. Then I drank it in with that same devout silence that each individual collected it with. The water tasted beautiful. My mother followed suit and found a stomach pain that had been plaguing her all day instantly disappeared. Derrick just kept on saying,

"this is good water."

While Kem Ra, just stood mesmerized with two other children at the edge of the river's bank. He played in the clear water and then did something unusual. He washed my face, Derrick's face, and my mum's face with all the heart felt sincerity in the world. Although taken by surprise, we allowed him to perform the simple ritual that some ancient force in his spirit had seemingly directed him to do.

After he did this we all stood together and with the cool water dripping from our faces we each prayed to the waters and Great Spirit in silence. I prayed that there would always be clean cool waters. It's a prayer I have taken to always saying, even when showering. I thanked the Healing Springs for giving so much, so freely to everyone. I prayed reverently and at the same time drank the water, as if this action would magically seal my prayers.

On finishing my prayers I heard a gentle inner whisper,

*"you know you guys are not healing water. Water is healing
you. There is nothing wrong with water. The only thing wrong with
water is what you guys are doing to it. Water is doing you a favor it
is healing you."*

This revelation took me by surprise. "Water is healing
us?" Then I thought back on how the Osun River nestled in
her lush grove had lent her waters to healing a bump on my
head I had gained from going through one of those low rise
traditional buildings, and how she had healed my soul. I
thought of how she lends her water every day to the healing of
people who visit her in droves, just like the Healing Springs
does. Then I thought back on the Catawba again. It seemed to
represent something old, something aged, something dying.
Dying with all its wisdom because of the ignorance of the
world.

Yet, like the generous power of the Mother Waters the
Catawba still gives us its self generously, even urgently.
Maybe, it knew that we could not do without its voice of
consciousness. For it is the Catawba that had revealed to me
how to heal the environment, and offered up a message of
compassion.

As I drank, prayed and thanked the Springs for all its
healing I thought of Katie Price's Healing Horses. The rivers
were just like the horses they reflected back our condition to
us, absorbed and healed it. Katie Price, was an English woman
living in South Carolina, who healed horses through her
organization the *Healing Horses*. She once told myself and
Derrick,

"it was a horse that was dying that showed me how to
heal other horses."

We never doubted her. She was renown in South
Carolina for her ability to literally heal almost any horse. On

many occasions myself, Derrick and kem Ra had witnessed her awesome ability with the horses. There was no doubt she had a real gift with them.

The first time we met Katie she showed us a beautiful white horse called Sharman. I can't remember what breed Sharman was, but he was splendid looking and nervous. The poor horse had been treated very badly by its owners.

Katie recognized Sharman as a powerful healer. She treated him with all the tenderness and love he deserved. A few weeks latter when we went back to see Katie and her Healing Horses, Sharman was surprisingly more confident, calmer and plumper looking. He was obviously happy and well on his way to being rehabilitated. According to Katie, he and other horses like him that she had at her ranch would help others to heal by mirroring their behavior, absorbing it into their bodies, and then dispelling it out through their hooves.

The social gathering at Little Horse Creek was in full swing. It was all pasta, tomato mince, sodas, garlic bread, and up to fifty people with good will to spare, jubilant singing interspersed with lots of community announcements. As soon as we stepped into that vibrant flow of activity we felt at complete ease. We all agreed, it felt as though we were home.

The activities went on in full swing for about two hours. As they tailed off into an atmosphere of calm contentment Chief Randal introduced me and Derrick to the crowd. He asked us to explain the Water Blessings. We shared all that we could. Just like when we had visited the meeting of the Chiefs the whole room was quiet. Once again, I thought this must not be going down very well. Only to be informed differently by the thunderous round of applause that burst forth like claps of lightening.

It was after the meeting and many handshakes of enthusiastic thanks that we had a chance to talk to Chief Randall. He was once again a white skinned Indian. But you could see the Native American all over his features (whatever, that means). He had snow white hair that was pulled into a neat one at the back of his head. He was slim and had a simple humble demeanor about him.

Derrick liked him immediately. We all did. He kept us talking for quite a while after the meeting informing us he was interested in his group, made up of various nations, collaborating with us on the Water Blessing.

"Water is very special to us. We honor water, we honor the earth," he said.

He revealed to us how he use to keep horses but had to give them away.

"No one to look after them," he declared.

That was part of his answer to telling us how the Little Horse Creek came to be called by that name. He loved horses and felt especially connected to them. When he heard that since doing the Catawba Water Blessing I kept on dreaming horses he said,

"and you too. The horses come to you."

Days latter, after meeting the crew at the Little Horse Creek Riverflows called and shouted excitedly down the phone,

"We have lots of interest! There are quite a few people saying they want to come along to the Water Blessing.

It was during that conversation that we set the Healing Springs Water Blessing for 4:30 p.m, Saturday, March 14. Riverflows had left the best for last,

"there's a reporter who wants to carry an article before and after the Water Blessing in the Orangeburg Times and Democrat newspaper."

219

We were thrilled.

Now the history of The Healing Springs was quite fascinating. Riverflows had told us enough about it to get our palettes whet. It was sacred waters to Native Americans. When a white general found that the Native Americans seemed to take their sick somewhere in the bush, and then come out of it with healed people he wanted to know where they went. A Native American Chief eventually led him to the springs. Some say he did so willingly, others say that he had been forced to show and tell. Whichever, was the truth the oath to guard the sacred secret of the Healing Springs was broken. Once broken, it is said the Native Americans never returned to that spot again.

After our visit to the Springs we discovered a little Amish shop, just a stones throw away from where everyone collected water. It was filled with enough sweet treats to get ones hand stuck in the cookie jar. But the greatest delight was finding a little book written by Everette Stanley McDonald, called "The Natural History Buried In Blackville". That little book was a real find, as it gave the whole history of the Springs.

We discovered that the Healing Springs was situated in Blackville which had the largest number of black water streams in any one place in the world. Mc Donald revealed,

"The Edisto (river) may be the longest black water streams in anyone place in the world. If not the longest".

He also shared the Healing Springs was attached to the Edisto river.

According to McDonald the Healing Springs was not a real spring in the true sense of the word but an artesian well.

An Artesian well is a well-made by boring into the earth till water is reached which forms internal pressure, and flows up like a stream.

McDonald elaborated on the story of how the Healing Springs secret got let out of the bag. Sharing that the Irish moved into the Northern part of a place called Barnwell District. Daniel Walker (referred to as General Walker) started to travel into the area north of Blackville along the Indian trails. He traded with the Indians for skins and furs. One day General Walker noticed the Indians went into an area that was thick with vegetation and saw an old Indian Chief washing his face with water from a small hole in the ground. He enquired about the use of the Springs (some say he intimated the Chief to tell him all). The Chief had ordered his people never to tell the white man about the springs. However, when Mr. Walker insisted on knowing it was the Chief himself who informed him the Springs were used to heal the wounds of the sick and lame.

The day after the Chief told Walker about the Springs it is said the Native Americans left the area never to return again. General Walker developed a community near the Springs now known as Walker's Station.

Further historic accounts reveal that in 1776 the American Revolution began. The fighting that took place in the Blackville area was mainly partisan but there was one battle of great importance that took place. It was called the Battle of Slaughter Field. The exact location of the battle was never recorded. However it is known that it occurred North of the Healing Springs.

It is said that many died and four British troops were severely wounded and left at the Healing Springs to die. Two able bodied men were left to care for them, with instructions to return to their base in Charleston after the men died and were

221

buried. It is said that the water of The Healing Springs was used to help nurse the wounds of the men and six months later all of the men returned to the Garrison in Charleston.

After passing through six different owners and failed attempts to commercialize it, the Springs ended up in the hands of a Mr. L.P Boylston who decided to deed the Springs and an acre of land to God. Part of the record of the deed read,

"To have and to hold all and singular the said before mentioned unto said Almighty God forever; In Trust, nevertheless, for the public use, especially for the diseased or afflicted to use the precious healing water that flows from this God given source, reserving, however to myself as long as I may live full and complete control and supervision of the said described property herein conveyed".

As a Result of Mr. Boylston's deeding of the land to God, the Healing Springs became known as God's Acre Healing Springs.

I had not mentioned it earlier, so I will mention it here - the dream I had before we went down to view the Healing Springs for our possible Water Blessing. I share it as I wrote it in my diary,

In the dream I was walking in this place and on this land with my husband. It was South Carolina. My husband had to go somewhere. When he went I saw a Orangutan and her young baby. Then I saw an eagle. I called to my husband. He answered, "what is it?" I shouted "come! Come!". As he approached the eagle flew away. Then

222

it came back. With it were other eagles. I was astounded at their beauty. One eagle was fluffy and white etched with lilac purple. Its face was very wise and very old. It turned and looked at me. I pointed the eagle out to my husband and said, "something is going on. Why are we here?" Then I thought this is a sacred sight I will always go to.

The day after having that dream I just had to find out more about the Healing Springs. I was especially curious to see if eagles were associated with the Healing Springs site. I discovered that it was known in the past to have many birds flocking to it and many unusual animals too.

Two weeks before kicking of the Healing Springs Water Blessing, Kem Ra's Rice experiment was getting into full swing. Getting it of the ground had been hard going. Not so much because he didn't want to do it, but because he had never participated in a Science Fair before. In London we don't have them. I loved the idea. Thought it was a great way to get young people engaged in science.

The good news was once Kem Ra got started on that experiment there was no stopping him (myself and Derrick matched his eagerness, as we got our rice experiments going too). After cooking a pot of rice we each took some rice and divided it between two jars. One got labeled "love" and the other "hate". If there were going to be any results I was expecting them by the second week. But something strange happened. By the third day of the experiment Kem Ra's "Hate" jar began to smell very foul while his "Love" jar began to smell sweet.

By day four the rice in his "Hate" jar of rice had a thick layer of green fungi on it. While his "Love" jar of rice had nothing. By the end of the week his "Hate" jar of rice was covered in fungi. The "Love" jar started to sweat and ooze a sweet smell. The rice in it had also begun to melt and produce a lot of water but very little fungi. We shared a joke between us and said Kem Ra's love energy was literally getting that rice to sweat.

By the fifth day of the experiment I noticed that my "Hate" and "Love" jar of rice were looking the same. I was not sure what was going wrong with my experiment. Derrick's "Hate" and "Love" jar of rice were displaying similar results to Kem Ra's. His "Hate" jar of rice was getting covered in dark fungi and his "Love" jar of rice was quite fresh looking.

I decided to spend the night of the fifth day of doing the experiment to meditate on the problem. Then something struck me. It was something I could have easily missed. I hate saying nasty things to people. So I had not noticed that instead of saying "I hate you!" with all my might to the "Hate" jar of rice. I was saying the words, "I hate you!" with all my love. Once I realized the problem. I made sure I put all the venom I could muster and pour into my "Hate" jar. It worked. By the sixth day a little black fungi appeared at the bottom of the jar of rice. My "Love" jar of rice had no fungi at all. By the second week the black fungi had almost consumed my "Hate" jar. My "Love" jar remained sweet smelling with only a little bit of white fungi on it.

Every day or other day I took pictures of the changes. The results took us all by surprise. Both I and Derrick noticed that Kem Ra started saying "thank you" much more often. He also started doing nice things for people, such as making us breakfast more often (something he had only done once in a blue moon). He was also displaying much more care about everything.

"I had heard you talk about this experiment and even though I am seeing it with my own eyes but I still can't believe what I am seeing," Derrick enthused.

Interestingly, just as a small side experiment we decided to sow some seeds and water on one tray of seeds with water infused with "I love you" words. The other with water infused with "I hate you words". Seeds normally take 7 days to start germinating. By day two the "Love You" tray had sprung up several seeds. By day three one of the seeds had reached one and half inches and by day four it was two and half inches. We took pictures. The hate tray had not germinated any seeds until days later.

But now I was realizing that this experiment held no flukes. The water in the rice was really responding to positive and negative words. Or it would be more accurate to say "the intention behind the words".

I gave Kem Ra a hand with doing some of his research. That threw light on an interesting subject – the question of what is living. Derrick encountered something called biophotons when he came across a website where a Mr. and Mrs. Excel founded a company called Hexahedron 999. Mr. Excel shared research the couple had done with biophotons. We discovered that up to forty scientific groups from around the world were doing research into biophotons.

Through the Somatoscope microscope which magnifies things by 30,000 times, Mr. Excel and his wife discovered the presence of biophotons in water. He discovered that there were three types of biophotons present in water: Regenero Active Biophotons which has the ability to regenerate life, Genero Active Biophotons which have the ability to sustain

225

life and DegeneroActive biophoton which have the ability only to recycle life.

They (Mr. Excel and his wife) discovered that well water had more Regenero Active Biophotons than City Chlorinated or distilled water which often had very few biophotons and often Degenero Active Biophotons. They further discovered that Renegero Active and Genero Active Biophotons had hexagonal shapes. While the last of the category – DegeneroActive biophotons had a more broken shape (this was reminiscent of the work of Dr Masaru Emoto where water in its healthy state formed beautiful hexagonal shapes; while water that was not had broken, distorted or no hexagonal shape at all)

It is said by all researchers in the field of biophotons that a biophoton is a fine emission of light energy that all living things emit. F.A Popp is a respected leading scientist in the field of Biophotons. He revealed that all things continuously emit biophotons. It is said that biophotons are emitted through the cones at the end of the chromosomes which are called telomaze, they transmit electromagnetic impulses (the silent language of DNA), they control all metabolism, cells regulation, growth and reproduction in the body.

Apparently biophotons can be measured in units per centimeter squared. A new born baby can emit at least 200 units of biophoton per second per centimeter squared; the average adult radiates between 80-120 units of biophotons per second per centimeter squared; while an elderly person's biophotons drops to 60-50-30-10. The conclusion is that the quality of life is determined by the quality and quantity of biophotons.

Scientist are currently researching the following: if there is a difference between the quality and quantity of biophotons in normal or abnormal tissues; if knowing the quality of biophotons can help us to access the quality of food; how biophotons can indicate bacterial contamination; if biophotons can be used to assess blood and the health of the body. Interestingly enough I came to call biophotons little dancing lights of life's love.

On the third morning of the Rice Experiment I was lying in bed when I saw a clear image of Osun dancing in front of me smiling. Her smile was dazzling, and even more dazzling was the mirror she held up in front of her. It was her famous mirror.

THE MIRROR. THE MIRROR.
THE MIRROR. THE MIRROR.

Her voice seemed to sing the words like the ripples that gently move across the surface of a clear lake. The song literally lifted me out of my bed and onto my feet, and led me to my biophoton notes and Mr. Excel's biophoton research. I flicked quickly through the pages of those notes. My heart was racing. I stopped at the section that the voice led me to. In summary it read that the Regenero Biophoton had a full hexagonal shape. Mr. Excel revealed the middle of that shape "looked as though it was like a mirror".

I stopped. My heart stopped. I re-read the passage. It was clear what Mr. Excel was saying - the biophoton was a fine emission of light energy that all living things emitted and it had a center that looked something like a mirror.

Right there and then I exhaled. My journey was over. It was at the end. I had reached the end. I felt an elation swirl through me. I was bursting to tell Derrick, the end was here. But he was sleeping and I didn't want to wake him up. Of course, the end wasn't really near. I was soon to realize the journey was a long protracted one. As Derrick was sleeping I decided to write a note in my head instead, which turned into its own joyous song of redemption. It was one I would transfer onto paper the following morning.

Picture of Regenero Biophoton

My Watery Guardian, Osun has revealed that the Mother energy of the world is the source of all life. The biophon was proof to scientist that all things were living beings. Her mirror, that mirror that was suppose to represent her vanity to the unknowing eye, actually represents her being the source of all life. All life is ONE and she is the invisible pin that brings it all together. She was the oneness, the light that existed in all things. Her waters were merely like her oracle. They behave like a mirror that helps man monitor his existence with the whole. The whole within and the whole without. To help him know if he was on or of track. Because we have grown so far away from nature we no longer know how to read water's symbols, much less now to have an understanding as to what those symbols mean.

When I lived in the Islands between the ages of ten and thirteen, my great aunt had taught me how to read the sky. I always knew if it was going to rain that day. I also knew that when it rained if it was going to stay a rainy day. I was taught how to identify a "passing cloud". A passing cloud has a particular look about it. It makes you think it is going to rain all day, but the look of the cloud tells you it is not.

Ongoing back to the West (London to be precise) I noticed my friends had no idea when it was going to rain and how long those rains would last for. My great aunt, taught me many more things. She was from the old school. What I call The Old People's Ways School. As I got older I realized that the things taught by the old school were good things. They helped you to live with the land and even each other very well. My father trained as an engineer, but he was not interested in engineering. He found living in London difficult and moved back to Trinidad. There he spent his life painting people's homes. His true greatest happiness was spending time with the earth and planting.

One day when I went back to Trinidad on holiday, when I was in my twenties and had Kem Ra as a one year old on my hip, he told me something.

"When I plant there are certain moons I plant by. I have observed that when you plant at certain moons the crops turn out a particular way. So with one moon the roots go right into the ground and the crops grow very strong. While another moon the roots of the crops are very short and then there's another moon where the crops come out very stout and sturdy. I have come to know that all those modern day farmers they don't know about these things."

So water was and has always been Mother Earth's oracle. Her litmus test. You know where you are when you observe it closely. It will tell you. If the waters are polluted, it is letting you know you must be too. The Native American's say "Something is

229

wrong with the frog that drinks its own water" (The frog is either deluded, mean, crazy, out of step or has serious amnesia. Most probably all those things together.)

When the waters are polluted then you better get doing something. Because polluted waters mean that other things are dying with it. Other things are affected by our behavior and those other things are affected by a forgetting that we all belong to one sacred thread. Water has the ability to talk to the whole planet. One message we all understand from water is that if it goes then Bye bye baby.

That's it. Caput. Polluted water's mean we are abusing our Mother Earth to the max and we need to stop. Mother Earth lives within everything. We cannot survive without her and that is why the ancients venerated the Mother Earth and her Mother principle which embodies Love.

Yes, it's love we are missing. It's love. That's what the water experiment is showing. It is showing that things go rotten with hate. Water is showing that it is LOVE we need. Water shows us LOVE is ONENESS, which leads to LIFE. LOVE is the answer

The ranting of my thoughts stopped dancing in the light of self-awareness. They had been illuminated by the waters of my Mother's mirror. I felt elated. I felt that at last I understood the beginning of this journey's message - "go to water". For water was going to show me the way and through its celestial mirror I was going to see the reflection of the whole Earth, along with all its problems. Once again, I also discovered that the mythological body of the Mother Goddess when decoded held the secret language of water and life itself.

As Synchronicity would have it, a few days after my biophoton illumination the family got invited to the University of South Carolina, Lancaster (USCL). The event was entitled, *An Evening with Naturalist Rudy Mancke.*

We had no idea who Rudy Mancke was but we were eager to go find out. The meeting was held in the University's library, which seated about fifty people. We arrived late, but a considerate hostess helped us to find some empty seats without disturbing what turned out to be a very cheery faced down to earth man talking with all the animation of the Gods on the subject of plant life on this planet. We had entered the meeting in the midst of laughter. For we were soon to find out Rudy Mancke could really make a crowd laugh with his natural sense of humor. His fascinating insights into nature made learning taste like nectar.

As we settled into our seats Rudy Mancke's voice boomed,

"Human beings are more connected to nature than they think. I believe that is why many people like to be by nature".

That got me sitting very upright; I don't remember slumping back in my chair for the rest of the meeting. I was riveted from the laughter, to the voice, to the words and to the knowledge. I saw Mother's Nature's mirror dance before me, as his whole talk constantly went back to the message - "everything is related in a oneness."

The talk flowed on what I realized must be his trademark – laughter and knowledge. I was happy that my mum, who was due to go back to the UK any day, was able to hear the talk. Kem Ra and Derrick were obviously enjoying it to, judging from their smiles, laughter and vigorous head nods.

It was actually, impossible not to enjoy Rudy Mancke's considerable knowledge wrapped up like a tasty sweet. It was easy to see how he had gained the title - leading Naturalist of South Carolina.

After the meeting I just had to make a nuisance of myself, and try to catch him for a chat. Mum and Kem Ra hung around with me. They watched him with all the fascination of a child, as he showed a small group of people gathered around him a long dried out snake skin. I had a bit of a long wait to see him as there were a ton of people wishing to speak to his majesty of the natural world. But my patience eventually paid of.

Now, I may be amongst the most curious people in the world, but I am also one of the shyest. So before talking to Mr. Rudy Mancke I took a few deep breaths and began,

"I was really fascinated by what you said about oneness. I noticed you brought it up more than once."

"After having a long career as a Naturalist I am of the firm opinion that life recycles itself. We are all made of the same stuff. It is particles that come from collapsing stars that make us up. It has been shown that the atom in the rock is the same atom in us. We're all Stellar really," he said letting out a hearty warm Southern laugh, before pausing to continue,

"Every Naturalist has come to know that what is in one place affects another place over there".

What he said reminded of a conversation I had, just a few days ago with my brother, Jeff, who works as a scientist at the Royal Kew Gardens.

"You know if people realize that everything is energy moving. The chair we sit on is energy moving, the floor we stand on is energy moving. They are all energy moving at different rates. The more solid an object is, the slower the energy is moving. They would realize that everything is one. I think the real message of Osun is that we are all one energy body. If we realize that then we will stop hurting the earth, the trees, and each other. Come on, if your hand starts punching your face, it's going to hurt and why would the hand punch the face? If the hand starts punching the face then it represents that something is seriously wrong and needs to be corrected."

Stellar. It was a word that played on my mind a few days after Rudy Mancke's talk. It made me want to find out more about stars, their substance and how they related to us and the planet. Being the thirsty researcher that I am I began to read everything I could put my hands on and got totally caught up in stardust.

I discovered that there were stars called Massive Stars (they were greater than five times the mass of the sun). When the hydrogen of Massive Stars becomes depleted, they convert helium atoms into carbon and oxygen. Then there follows a fusion of carbon and oxygen into neon, sodium, magnesium, sulfur and silicon. With later reactions transforming these elements into calcium, iron, nickel chromium, copper and others. Then these old, large stars with depleted cores supernova creating heavy elements (all the natural elements heavier than iron) which spew them into space and forms the basis for life.

I was fascinated. The stuff from stars indeed contained all the elements of life. I kept on researching and discovered that our planet revolves around just one star and that is the sun. Planet Earth is part of the Solar system. But this one star is part of the Milky Way galaxy which contains thousands and thousands of stars. This milky way galaxy is part of a group of galaxies known as the Local Group and that is part of a bigger cluster of galaxies known as the Virgo Galaxies; and millions of Galaxy clusters are strung together like a spider's web. These spider webs are made up of billions of galaxies, and trillions and trillions of stars thousands of other galaxies. The area between the strands of galaxies are just empty space. It is said that you would have to travel hundreds of miles just to find one atom.

Galaxies come in many shapes. It is said the most beautiful type of galaxies are Spiral Galaxies. Their long twisting arms are areas where stars are being formed. Imagine a ripple in a pond, the spiral arms seen in this kind of galaxy are circling waves. These waves cause new stars to form. They are like star farmers planting star seeds where ever they go. Some of the new stars created in the wave are very large.

Because of their size these large stars glow brighter than their smaller cousins, causing the nearby dust clouds to glow brightly. Thus, any area near one of these waves glows like a fluorescent light. You can't actually see the waves, the spirals that we see are the glowing clouds illuminated by large, hot stars. As the waves move on the clouds behind them dim down, no longer glowing until another wave passes through. The Milky Way is one of those beautiful Spiral Galaxies.

I latter discovered some interesting facts about the Milky Way. The Egyptian connected it to the Egyptian Goddess Hathor, who was also connected and interchanged with the Sky Goddess Nut. The four legs of the celestial cow which represented Nut or Hathor were sometimes seen as the pillars on which the sky rested. While the stars on their bellies constituted the milky way on which the solar boat of Ra, representing the sun, sailed.

The Egyptians considered the *Milky Way, The Nile In the Sky*. In the sacred Indian language Sanskrit the Milky Way is called *Akash Ganga* which means Ganges in the Sky. It is said the Ganges River and the Milky Way are considered to be terrestrial-celestial analogs of each other. In ancient China the

Milky Way is known as Heavenly Han *River*, and in Japan it is known as the *Silver River System*.

All the stars that the eye can distinguish in the night sky are part of the Milky Way Galaxy, but aside from these relatively nearby stars, this galaxy appears as a hazy band of white light arching around the entire celestial sphere.

The facts were dazzling. The ancients had once again proved themselves to be wise. Not only wise but high scientist of the first order. They seemed to understand, long before modern scientist, that our universe was part of an arching celestial world. One which they depicted as none other than the Goddess herself. As if to confirm this finding I discovered two beautiful pictures – one of the Goddess Nut arching protectively over the earth; the other of the Milky Way gently bent over the earth. The two pictures looked identical to each other. Together they made it clear – the Mother was the nurturing universe.

The Milky Way arching over part of the earth in Chile

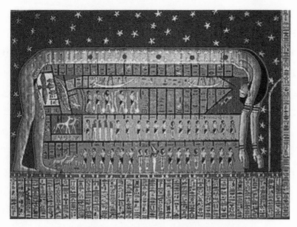

The Goddess Nut arching protectively over

the planet and all its inhabitants.

The things I encountered made me think of something else my brother Jeff had said,

"If only people realized that the nucleus in an atom is absolutely tiny. Most of the atom is just energy space."

Reading about the spider web formation of galaxies and the huge empty space within them brought my mind back to his statement. As I thought about the galaxies I could see Prakruti smiling, as she stomped out her swirling Dance of Leela. Purusha, sat watching her in still peacefulness, as together they co-create the world.

All that empty space in science is called dark matter. 90% of the mass of the universe is said to be made up of dark matter. Once again, ancient and modern science seemed to be on the same page – for from Tamas came the whole of life.

The invisible forces of the universe were working it. There was no stopping the ancient song of oneness it was unfolding from its cosmic waves. On the back of the Milky Way and dark matter came an interesting Buddhist phenomenon known as Indra's net. This concept is also known as Indra's Jewels or Indra's Pearls. Indra's net is said to symbolize an interconnected universe where everything in it forms one community. This interconnectedness was embodied in the Hindu God Indra, whose net hangs over his palace on the sacred Mount Meru (which is seen as the center of the cosmic and real world). Indra's net is seen as having a multifaceted jewel at each vertex, and each jewel is said to be reflected in all of the other jewels. This concept is expressed well by Francis Harold Cook, in his book the "Hua-Yen Buddhism: The Jewel Net of Indra":

> *Far away in the heavenly abode of the great god Indra, there is a wonderful net which has been hung by some cunning artificer in such a manner that it stretches out infinitely in all directions. In accordance with the extravagant tastes of deities, the artificer has hung a single glittering jewel in each "eye" of the net, and since the net itself is infinite in dimension, the jewels are infinite in number. There hang the jewels, glittering like stars in the first magnitude, a wonderful sight to behold. If we now arbitrarily select one of these jewels for inspection and look closely at it, we will discover that in its polished surface there are reflected all the other jewels in the net, infinite in number. Not only that, but each of the jewels reflected in this one jewel is also reflecting all the other jewels, so that there is an infinite reflecting process occurring.*

The Dance and song of oneness just wouldn't let up. After Rudy Mancke, after the Milky Way, after Indra's Net, came David Bohm. I don't know how I came across David Bohm, but I did. He came, I suppose, as part of the grand plan of Mother Universe telling her/our story. There seemed to be no coincidences on this journey.

Now David Bohm, I was to discover, was quite an interesting chap. He had a deep interest in science from a young age and became fascinated by the world of quantum physics. He fast came to the conclusion that everything in our universe is part of "an undivided wholeness in flowing movement". He believed that all that separated objects, entities, structures and events in the visible world around us are relatively autonomous, stable and temporary sub totalities derived from a deeper implicate order of unbroken wholeness. In his book "Wholeness and Implicate Order" he uses the analogy of water in the form of a flowing stream.

On David Bohm's flowing stream, one may see an ever-changing pattern of vortices, ripples, waves, splashes etc, which evidently have no independent existence as such. Rather, they are abstracted from the flowing movement, arising and vanishing in the total process of the flow. Such transitory subsistence as may be possessed by these abstracted forms implies only a relative independence or autonomy of behavior, rather than absolutely independent existence as ultimate substances.

Bohm believed that the whole universe can be thought of as a kind of giant, flowing hologram or holomovement, in which a total whole order is contained in each region of space and time. He believed that the outward order of things we see is a projection from higher dimensional levels of reality.

The apparent stability and solidity of the objects and things composing it are generated by a ceaseless process of enfoldment and unfoldment. For he suggested that subatomic particles are constantly dissolving into the inner order and then re-crystallizing.

While Bohm worked at the Lawrence Radiation Laboratory he did landmark work on plasmas (a plasma is a gas containing high density of electrons and positive ions). He was surprised to find that once electrons were in a plasma, they stopped behaving as individuals and started behaving as if they were part of a larger interconnected whole. He later extended his research and discovered that electrons in metals behaved in the same manner.

It was while writing his book on "Quantum Theory" where he began to doubt the conventional physics view that subatomic particles had no objective existence and everything happened by chance. Six months of conversations with Einstein led him to go deeper into this thought process. Along with a young researcher Yakir Aharonov he further discovered the interconnectedness of all things. They found that in certain circumstances electrons are able to "feel" the presence of a nearby magnetic field even though they are traveling in regions of space where the field strength is zero. This phenomenon is now known as the Aharonov-Bohm (AB) effect.

In 1982 a remarkable event took place. At the University of Paris a research team led by Physicist Alain Aspect performed what some say may turn out to be one of the most important experiments of the 20th century. Aspect and his team discovered that under certain circumstances subatomic particles are able to instantaneously communicate with each other regardless of the distance separating them.

It doesn't matter whether they are 10 feet or 10 billion miles apart. They discovered that somehow each particle always seemed to know what the other is doing. Bohm and a colleague John Bell laid down much of the latter theoretical framework regarding this experiment.

Bohm believed that the reason subatomic particles are able to remain in contact with one another regardless of distance separating them was not because they are sending some sort of mysterious signal back and forth, but because their separateness is an illusion for they were part of that "flowing whole". That is not static but in a constant state of flow, and change.

This flowing energy state Bohm revealed "could equally be called idealism, Spirit and Consciousness." Bohm further believed, much like the ancients, that Consciousness, the flowing whole, was not disorganized. He believed from his experiments and deep contemplation on the matter that subatomic particles such as electrons are not simple structureless particles but highly complex dynamic entities. He rejected the view that their motion was fundamentally uncertain or ambiguous. He believed that they followed a precise path. Not one determined just by conventional physical force but also by a more subtle force which he called quantum potential.

He believed that the quantum potential guided the motion of particles by providing "active information" about the whole environment. He gave the analogy of a ship being guided by radar signals: the radar carries information from all around and guides the ship by giving form to the movement produced by the much greater but uninformed power of its engines.

I made another mental note,

The flowing universe, Nut/Hathor's body arched over us protectively and bejeweled. The River in the sky. The Goddess who holds up the mirror of our existence.

As oneness sung to its zenith. My mind went back to the cheery Rudy Mancke. Then I remembered the ethereal sound of a Native American flute that had floated through the air as everyone mingled eating cheese, fruit and crackers. It subtly floated through the air in the most haunting, unobtrusive, and beautiful manner. But there was no doubt in my mind that it was that flute and its song that kept the whole atmosphere, sea of thoughts and chatter alive.

It came from an equally unobtrusive Monty Hawk and an elegant cedar wood flute. Both seemed to draw me and my family over like Peter the Piper. We followed its vibration and call to the corner of the library from whence it emanated from. Monty Hawk sat behind the large sweep of the library stairs.

He was slim built, affable and a Catawba Indian. He showed us several types of flutes. One was a small very thin one made from River Cane. It looked quite inconsequential but when he put his practiced lips to its mouth it released the most haunting and surreal sound. Even more beautiful than the larger Cedar wood flute.

It was in between blows that Monty Hawk said,

"the reason why we are in the terrible state we are in today because we no longer listen to the tunes of nature. There was a time when we would be quiet and we could hear what nature and life was saying to us. We did not see ourselves as separate from the song of nature but as part of it."

Bohm put it this way in his book "Wholeness and The Implicate Order",

"It is proposed that the widespread and pervasive distinctions between people (race, nation, family, profession etc) which are now preventing mankind from working together for the common good, and indeed, even for survival, have one of the key factors of their origin in a kind of thought that treats things as inherently divided, disconnected, and broken up into yet smaller constituent parts. Each part is considered to be essentially independent and self-existent."

This brought to mind a traditional Yoruba tale where:

One day all the women moved away from the men and King. The village suffered as a result of the women living away. The King wanted the women to come back, He beseeched everyone far and wide but no one could succeed at the task.
Then one day Osun came along and said I will try. She simply took out a little drum and went to the village where the women were now living. She played the drum and did not speak a word. Then something happened all the women begin to sway and dance. Osun danced out of the village playing on that small drum. Peacefully and in the stream of Osun's music the women returned back to the village of the men. To make a long ending short – all lived in peace and harmony again.

Maybe I just was not getting it. Or maybe my watery guardian wanted to make sure I got it. Or maybe its song was so joyous that it just could not stop singing, for the lessons of oneness and what it brought to the world just kept on flooding into my space just like that Milky Way filled the sky up.

It was a few days before the Healing Springs Water Blessing when it felt like the revelations of Oneness moved from the mind in my head to the mind in my heart. For my thoughts of Oneness suddenly opened like a light filled flower into the realm of compassion. I woke up from a dream. I am not sure what the dream was now, but the words,

"water is showing us how to be at one. Water is showing us how to be compassionate."

Kept on ringing in my head. Compassion. It seemed like a far reach in the society we live in today.

COMPASSION

The word kept on bejeweling and anchoring my inner net of awareness. Then as if that was not enough I heard a voice move gently within me. It moved slowly but surely,

"if you can say thank you to water. Care enough to want to heal it. Then you can have compassion for anything. It is compassion that fosters healing".

The ferocious wave of oneness and compassion had broken its banks and would not stop. It was one day as I shopped at our local supermarket that a book by the Dalai Lama poked slightly out from one of the book shelves. It was called "Expanding the Circle of Love". I felt drawn to open it. There it was, the dance of compassion and oneness stomping gently across every page.

Compassion and oneness were far from done with me. As Derrick and mom were taking their time with the shopping I decided to quickly pop into Hall Mark which was just a few shops away from the Super Market. I headed to my favorite place, the book section. I randomly reached for one of their wisdom books and the page fell open onto a section called, of all things, COMPASSION!

By now Compassion had me dazzled and befuddled. What's up with this Compassion stuff? Was my main thought. Later that evening I sat with my diary and wrote,

Mother Osun is obviously wanting me to know that the feelings of oneness leads to compassion. The mirror of water leads us to the song of compassion, the song of oneness. The ancient Egyptians say that Hathor and Nut are the ancient Heavenly Cows whose milk feeds the universe and all its inhabitants. Now I know the milk of the Heavenly Cow is non-other than the Milky Way that flows through the celestial realm. It is the heavenly waters in the sky which mirrors the heavenly waters on the earth. Both nourish our existence. As it is said in the bible, "Thy will be done in earth, as it is in heaven."

Now I don't think it was a coincidence that at this time I received an e-mail from a very irate individual. She did not seem to think the Water Blessing Ceremonies were valuable. She believed they did nothing for the environment. Then she gave me some good advice, "why don't you clean up rubbish instead!"

This woman had not bothered to find out what we were trying to do. She obviously did not believe that awareness brought change, and repaired our damaged relationship to the environment. The woman's e-mail raised my heckles but what could I do but admit that many people were like her – they just didn't get it. I use to be one of them.

LOVE CURES EVERYTHING. All that compassion stuff made the voice of my inner awareness dance before me. I decided to look up the definition for compassion. I liked the one I found on Wikipedia:

Compassion is a profound human emotion prompted by the pain of others. More vigorous than empathy, the feeling commonly gives rise to an active desire to alleviate another's suffering. It is often, though not inevitably, the key component in what manifests in the social context as altruism. In ethical terms, the various expressions down the ages of the so-called Golden Rule embody by implication the principle of compassion. "Do to others what you would have them do to you – Jesus Christ (Matthew 7:12). Ranked a great virtue in numerous philosophies, compassion is considered in all the major religious traditions as among the greatest of virtues.

The Dalai Lama stated in his teachings on Compassion,

"Ultimately, the reason why love and compassion brings the greatest happiness is simply that our nature cherishes them above all else. The need for love lies at the very foundation of human existence. It results from the profound interdependence we all share with one another. However capable and skillful an individual may be, left alone he or she will not survive".

He further links compassion with the question of oneness,

"Interdependence, of course is a fundamental law of nature. Not only higher forms of life but also many of the smallest insects are social beings who, without religion, law or education, survive by mutual cooperation based on an innate recognition of their interconnectedness. The most subtle level

245

of material phenomena is also governed by interdependence. All phenomena from the planet we inhabit to the oceans, clouds, forests and flowers that surround us, arise in dependence upon subtle patterns of energy. Without their proper interaction they dissolve and decay."

Months later compassion came singing again, this time in the form of Amma, "the Hugging Saint". Known as such because to date it is said she has hugged, blessed and consoled more than 25 million people throughout the world. I discovered that many times she has often been asked the question,

"why do you receive every person who comes to you with a loving embrace?"

Her reply is always,

"if you ask the river, why do you flow? what can it say?"

Amma believes that by helping and connecting with nature we learn how to be compassionate beings.

The song of compassion did not end. It must have been that important, for all the spiritual masters to line up and say their piece from here and beyond the grave. For soon after Amma, a book by Gandhi appeared, jutting out from a bookshelf just as the Dalai Lama's had. I discovered that Gandhi believed compassion is a way of selfless existence. A way of true love, a way of giving, a way of courage, a way to walk well in the world. Through Compassion balance can be brought back into our inner and outer worlds.

Compassion led Gandhi to care deeply about his nation, and have the heart to sacrifice his own life for the better good. He desired to see a free India, but above all it appeared that his deepest desire was to see peace and love on earth.

If Dalai Lama, Gandhi and Amma was not enough. My spirit and mind turned onto Susan Wenger and what I had shared with her in Osogbo, from my diary in June 2008,

My Mother has realized that her compassion is what called Susan Wenger to rebuild the Grove. She wanted her waters and presence to be preserved so that they could reflect the wisdom of what a loving world can create. They wanted us to see the difference between this world and the world we are now creating. Have now created. It was Susan Wenger's compassion that made her stay in Nigeria to take on this calling. Now there is a Grove for us all to walk in and to feel this divine sacred presence called water, oneness, the Mother, love and compassion.

Had compassion finished with me? You would think it had, but oh no, it followed me all the way to a little jaunt we did at the conservation spot, and sacred Native American land, 40 Acre Rock. I walked with Derrick, mom, and Kem Ra on that big beautiful mysticalness which was a vast stretch of hardy land.

When you climb down the surface of 40 Acre Rock you encounter a flowing path of pristine water filled with fish. You follow the path and fish then come across a refreshing water fall. You feel tempted to lay in that water – I rested my feet up to my legs in it. Then you feel only silence. Beautiful silence. Your brain falls away. You forget everything. Then something happens. You remember only who you are below the surface of your flesh. You remember the other you. The you that knocks everyday at the door of your heart saying, "hey remember me!"

You remember Sparkling clear abundance. Right there and right then with the sun softly touching your skin and the water lapping over your feet – your heart opens up and compassion sings its song.

It was in this moment of awareness, with my eyes closed that I heard a gentle voice within whisper like the quiet rustle of the leaves,

"if people are silent they will get it. They will feel the connection for themselves. All the answers they have been looking for they will receive. People do not need to read a book to know they are one with nature. People do not need to read three hundred pages of a book for them to know they need to protect nature. People do not need to be told the importance of these things. For in silence they will know. If they stand by a beautiful waterway or in the heart of nature, how can they not know these things. And if they do not feel any of these things then something is wrong. Something is very wrong".

I was truly humbled in my silence. Yes, silence was important to compassion. For to be compassionate we have to know silence. Then I thought of another spiritual person I encountered the day before at Barnes and Nobles browsing through the books on sale. It was a small one by Mother Teresa. Her face looked up and out of the cover. I flipped it open and the page fell open on these words,

"the only way we can come to know God is through silence."

Just as Compassion and its dance of oneness was about to release its grip on me. It had that final destination for me to attend, The March Healing Spring's Water Blessing. It had come up fast on us. Kem Ra's "Is Water Alive?" experiment was finished. The Conclusion – yes it was. Despite his teacher's umming and aaahing the results were right there for them to see – the "Love Rice" was white after a few weeks, and the "Hate Rice" was covered in dark mold. The words "Love" and "Thank You" had produced the profoundest positive effect on the rice.

In the light of all these findings we gathered, the song of compassion and oneness burst forth in its final crescendo. About 40 adults and children, several flutes and drums, sung up a storm. The warm day began with Chief Randal, I and Derrick walking a circle around the space, praying and thanking all the great spirits of the land and Mother Earth. We sprinkled sage as we did so. Then the rest of the sage cleansed the surroundings and each person with its fragrant smoke.

We were people of all different faiths, nations, traditions, and cultures gathered together. There were Christians, Native Americans, Protestants, and others. The sound of our voices, flutes, drums, prayers and thanks to water and the Great Creator melded together into one song. In the midst of all that singing Cathy Nelson, a Native American science teacher who also taught Native American sacred songs and the flute to others, spontaneously began to bless people with the Healing Springs water, from the edge of its river bank. We all drifted into line for those blessings. I remember the feel of the cool water flowing through my hair and down onto my face as she sang a beautiful almost melancholic water song for healing. Its melody seemed to stretch its hands from some ancient almost forgotten past into the present. Afterwards, I felt free as though something had gotten left behind in those waters.

In the midst of our singing it was as though hundreds of people were present. Together we closed the end of the day with prayer and more healing water songs. Even though it had been a warm day the rain came down in warm splatters for about two seconds straight after the prayers. I remembered how the elders in Nigeria had taught me that rain is a blessing from the Mother. It meant that all had been accepted. So when that rain lightly touched my face and shoulders I could not help but smile. Mama had blessed us.

As we all mingled and prepared to go home. The song of oneness and compassion kept on going. The flute players kept on playing and Derrick received a beautiful hand carved drum from a grey haired woman dressed in traditional Native American clothing. She hugged him tightly and said,

"In our culture we always give back what we have received. What you have given to us was a true blessing. Thank you."

I received a big hug from Riverflows who informed me,

"this was very special, very historic. This is the very first Water Blessing that has been done since the Native American Chief and his people abandoned this spot. We should have blessed these waters a long time ago. We had promised the ancestors we would take care of this land. Thank you and your family for making this happen."

"No thank you and everyone else," I whispered back.

A few days after the blessing Cathy Nelson, the Native American Science teacher (the one who had been blessing everyone with the waters) e-mailed a reply to my query – how did she find the day?

"The event was respectful, uplifting and very traditional of Native American spirituality. Water Blessings are important because

250

when all is said and done, we will only be stewards of what we care about. If we do not care about our water resources, we will only poison ourselves and our environment. In the late 1800's Chief Seattle taught that we did not weave the web of life, but we are a strand of that web. What we do to the web we do to ourselves,"

After reading her reply I urged Derrick to download the pics from the camera, and there they were - the orbs. Many of them floating around the singing smiling gathering. Once again, not all of the pictures had them, so we knew for sure these were no fingerprints. That along with the article about the Water Blessing in the Times and Democrat made our day.

I feel ashamed to say but I had no idea that soon after the Healing Springs Water Blessing, it was Earthday. I had no idea until we received a phone call from a woman called Lisa Moore, who announced she was a magazine editor from Natural Awakenings. She had seen the article "A Prayer for The River" by the Charlotte Observer which had heralded in our first water blessing event, and she was interested in doing an article on us too. Were we doing anything for Earth day? She wanted to know.

"We hadn't planned to, but now we know Earth Day is around the corner we most definitely will," we replied.

"Where do you think it will be?" she asked.

We told her we would get back to her soon.

After making a few phone calls, most of them to Beckee, the matter was resolved. We would go to another part of the Catawba river, where the second Catawba reservation sat. This second reservation was called Green Earth. Whereas, the first reservation was home to the Cultural Center; the second was the Catawba Nations living quarters.

We informed Lisa of the arrangement and she proceeded to interview us for an article she planned to carry.

"I think we are going to get a good response from this article," she informed.

Just before the Water Blessing, Beckee took us over to see the Green Earth reservation, and introduced us to her cousin who lived there. He informed us of a nice spot we could access the river from. To get there you had to go through a small wooded area. I was okay with everything until his wife said,

"there might be a wild dog or two. If you see one just keep on walking, they shouldn't hurt you."

Him and his wife were really excited by the idea of the water blessing. There excitement was contagious. As we all began the trek towards the woods that led to the river, I was once again surprised by the deep connection Native Americans still felt towards the land, and waters. When we arrived at the ragged outer edges of the woods, Beckee (like a true Native American) asked permission from the spirits of the land to enter. When she felt satisfied we had received it she allowed us to proceed. It was a simple yet touching gesture. I mean who still did things like that?

The woods were alive with energy, but as we ambled along the path I somehow doubted this location was the right one for a Water Blessing event. There was something awkward feeling about the whole trail. I doubted anyone would want to go through so much hassle just to get to a little bit of river. When I say a little bit of river, I really believed that was all we were going to see.

I whispered my concerns to Derrick, and he whispered back with his usual infinite wisdom.

"I think this will be a good spot."

I didn't say anything more, but deep down I still wasn't convinced.

Now there is something about being around nature with Native Americans. Interesting conversations start up. As we navigated our way through the trees a conversation started up with Beckee's cousin's wife. It went something like this,

"I love trees,"

"me too," Beckee replied.

"My father use to be able to speak to the trees. Said that each tree had a different personality and they could speak."

"Really?!" we all said in Unisom.

"Yep. He said that you could tell what the trees were saying by observing their movements. He use to try and convince me that I should speak to the trees. I would tell him

"Pa, get out of here trees can't talk. " But one day I tried it and found out that they really did!"

I was riveted. Derrick too.

"Now I can tell what the trees are saying. I can tell what each of these trees are saying right now just by looking at the way they move."

To prove her point the cousin's wife began to point and tell us,

"that tree is very sad"..."that tree is very ancient"...."that tree is the wise old man".

We all looked on quite fascinated. Suddenly I wish I could hear the trees talk too. However, something shifted in me and I began to look at the trees quite differently. The trees no longer looked like just trees. They looked vibrant and alive.

They truly did resemble what Zulu Wisdom Keeper Credo Mutwa called "Growing People".

That was what I loved about being amongst the Native Americans (native people in general) they made you believe in the natural world again. It wasn't separate from them, it was a part of their breathing reality.

We continued walking through the woodlands. It was a longer walk than I had anticipated. The cousin's wife had stopped talking. Silence. Nothing spoke except for the trees. A serene peace enveloped. Each person became lost in their own thoughts. Each footstep we took on the land echoed into an awakening consciousness, and no there was not one wild dog in sight.

"Almost there," the cousin's wife broke the silence to let us know the river was nearby.

I could hear the sound of the water gently singing. Despite, the beauty of the singing water I was still not convinced we were at the right spot for the water blessing we planned.

"Why can't we do it at the other reservation? The one we did it at before?" I whispered in Derrick's ear.

"It's okay," Derrick said as though he were politely swatting a nuisance mosquito from his ears.

We followed a little curve, went down a little hill and there we were. I stood still. My breath stood still. We had reached the source of the singing. It was not a little bit of river but a large beautiful clear body of flowing water. It was spectacular, elegant and feminine as it bounced right pass us. So different from the masculine sad silent river I had encountered earlier. As I looked into the vast stretches of its watery flow I was filled with awe. The Catawba river was full of surprises. Its vast flow definitely seemed to have more than one personality. As it sparkled and bounced pass us. It seemed to stop for a while to wink at me and say,

"told you so."

The told you so was to say there is always something more awaiting your expectations than what you thought. It was a simple wink which spoke a million words. It was a wink that allowed for the light to bounce of the water.

"Wow, this is beautiful," I exhaled. Derrick did too.

"Yes, I love this spot," the cousin's wife said with her husband agreeing.

Derrick was so inspired that he took out a flute that Beckee had gifted earlier that day to Kem Ra. Oh, didn't tell you about Kem Ra, Beckee and the Cedar wood flute. Well, before arriving at her cousin's house Beckee had gifted Kem Ra her very precious much prized cedar wood flute. He was obviously in with the luck that day, because he also received a Native American name from her brother - "Eagle Boy". He was well pleased. He had adored eagles from the time he was so high and they had played a prominent part in his life from young.

When I was pregnant with him an eagle appeared on the roof top of our urban apartment in London. In a place called Vauxhall, a place filled with smog and grime. If you know London and knew this place you would understand there was almost zero percent chance of seeing an eagle mosey on by. But this eagle did mosey on by and it stayed right there, up on that roof, for the whole duration of my pregnancy and until the day after I got out of the hospital with Kem Ra. One day latter, the eagle flew away, and no one ever saw that eagle again.

What's even more interesting is that the very first book Kem Ra ever wanted when he could talk and ask for one was called "Birds of Prey". He also insisted at the age of four that

255

the barber shave a baby eagle in his head. The barber showed his seasoned skills of, as he shaped a perfect baby eagle in the back of Kem Ra's head. It was a work of art that grabbed a lot of attention.

Now how Kem Ra got the flute is a nice story, because I had originally had my eye on that flute. Earlier that day when Beckee said she wanted to gift the flute to one of us I expressed how much I really wanted to play the Native American flute. However, it was Kem Ra whom she gifted the flute to. I tried to use all my wiles to gain that flute from Kem Ra, but nope they didn't work. He was holding onto his gift with all his in born characteristic tenacity.

That day I learned something. What is for you is always for you. That had been the translation of the name of an old boyfriend I had from Nigeria. Well how Derrick ended up with the flute that day was a true testimony to sharing. Kem Ra opened his heart right up and decided we could all share the flute with him indefinitely.

Notes soared through the sky. Derrick had never played the flute before that moment. When he had initially pulled it out for playing, I admit, I kind of shuddered. I mean there were all those expert Native American flute players around us. Gosh he was going to really embarrass us now. But he didn't. He pulled that flute out and started playing it. Everything went silent. The notes of the flute soared through the sky. I could almost see the eagle from Kem Ra's birth floating on its gentle yet haunting rhythms.

All of that is to say – Derrick's flute playing was exceptional. Maybe he had played it in a past life. For he surely handled that flute like a pro. Even our Native American companions were completely blown away by his soul wrenching eerie tune. The whole universe seemed to lament.

When the notes came down from their great heights there was a deep silence and then a thunderous round of applauds.

"Awesome!" Beckee's cousin's wife congratulated.

We all joined her. She was totally impressed, we all were.

"Who taught you to play like that?" she asked.

"No one," Derrick answered truthfully.

"This was my first time playing the flute."

"Wow!" was all she could say.

Everyone wowed with her.

Since that day in the woods by the bouncing elegant Catawba river I have noticed that Derrick seemed to have developed this awesome gift for music. If water had given me the gift of hearing it, it had given Derrick the one of playing for it and others. Since that day he plays the drums as though he has been taking lessons for thousands of years. Yet, he has never had a drumming lesson in his life. When he produces sound it always seems so ethereal. It comes from a place of dark matter beauty. Music like that can only come from such a place. It's the ultimate soul music. Right then I wondered if I could understand the trees what would they say about his gift. Would they confer that the spirits of the land gifted it to him? Or would they say the spirits of the land merely opened up a portal that had always been there within?

The actual Earthday Water Blessing went well. Beckee saged us all twenty people who turned up, including David Merryman, the Catawba River Keeper

The trees sheltered us from the fierce baking hot sun as we held hands and prayed for a more loving world, and beautiful waterways. Together we sang, shared thoughts, and heart. David Merryman was genuinely impressed by spot we had picked for the blessing revealing,

"this part of the Catawba river represents one of the longest stretches of water from the river that is clean and free flowing."

I was touched at how genuinely moved everyone present was by the beauty and grace of the water we stood by. Everything about the spot moved them and us. The water, the land, the trees and the latter's thick sheltering canopy which now lovingly protected us from the sun.

The Natural Awakenings people did turn up, but a few minutes after we had left for the river. They could not find us. Although clear directions had been given, it was still difficult to find the spot we were going to do the blessing if you had never been there. The good news was that once the water prayers had been completed we all had the good fortune to bump into each other in the car park we had used as our meet up spot. We were pleased when Lisa Moore, the editor, informed us they had a good drum and sing session at the spot they had chosen. Two blessings in one. That was cool, I thought.

One thing I can say. When you do spiritual work that has been approved by the spirits of the land there is always something called a significator. Now a significator is a little bit like getting a tick from your math teacher. It's a good sign that tells you are on the right track. The significator for our day came in the form of an Eagle feather discovered by Beckee. Straight after the Water Blessing her eyes spied this beautiful baby eagle feather which somehow had floated down from one of the trees and landed right by her feet. She smiled and said it was

"a darn good omen."

"This means everything has been accepted," she said smiling broadly.

Then with true Native American generosity she gave one of the participants present the feather. She really appreciated it. That participant seemed to have been in need of a lot of healing. That was not a guess, it was a fact she had openly shared with all present. She was going through troubled times and had come to bless the water but had also come to receive blessings. When she received the feather it was like giving someone a pot of gold. Her face lit up with a beaming smile. She gently tucked that feather into her bag like it meant the world to her, and said her healing had begun. The feather had made her feel acknowledged. Like there was some inexplicable force out there that was saying,

"I see you. I hear you. I heal you."

After the water blessing life went on as normal. Then I had a dream that seemed to herald something in. The dream was quite short,

I dreamt I had a beautiful African gown on and a female friend of mine who is very spiritual was pleased. This beautiful gown was made from crushing the juices of pink flowers.

When I went to write the dream in my diary, something happened - I couldn't stop writing. Something poured out of me like water, literally. I began to write poem upon poem. They were all about water and the environment.

259

Then when I went to surf the net for a Native American quote on the environment, I found myself caught up in a sort of dream world drama of ancient wisdom.

My hands did not stop writing, did not stop typing, did not stop searching for quotes until some four days latter. When it did stop, I was spent. I came out of what felt like some trance like state. I couldn't believe it, I had written over four hundred pages that documented ancient thoughts, celebrations and attitudes about the earth, water, trees, birds, bees, eco system and humanity. I even had people like David Bohmn in there too.

I looked around myself bewildered. The space where all of this happened looked like the land had folded in on itself. I had books and papers everywhere in that little corner. The collection of things I had pulled together even gave itself a name. It called itself "Dreamtime Awakening". I immediately knew I had just channeled a book. I had to publish it. I plucked up the courage to e-mail it to Lisa Moore, the Editor of Natural Awakening, to see if she could write something for a jacket. A few weeks later Lisa sent this review of the book back,

Dreamtime Awakening is a heartfelt homage to the Earth, Sun, Moon and a precious resource we often take for granted – water. Achikeobi – Lewis's collection of ancient wisdom, personal reflections, and meditations invoke an impassioned plea to unify in order to begin healing our planet. Her mission to deepen ecological awareness and elevate universal consciousness brilliantly shines through.

I was very touched, no chuffed, that she had taken the time to even read it. Now how the title came about is somewhat of a mystery. During those four manic days of discovering, writing, discovering and more writing I stumbled across the concept of the Aboriginal Dreamtime. A time when the ancient laws of the land were laid down. Then one day during my morning meditation I heard a gentle whisper nudge me, "call the book "Dreamtime Awakening"". I didn't question it for the title seemed so apt. For it seemed as though the Dreamtime had indeed awoken. Not only had it awoken but it seemed to be in a darn big hurry to get out. A bit like the birth of my second child Omololu, who appeared after a forty five minute birth. Her first name means "My Child is My Hero". Her middle name is Iyanu which means "Surprise!". That's exactly what Dreamtime Awakening was like, a big surprise that gripped me in the throes of its labor pains. One that wouldn't let me go until it had arrived. The things that came out of me during my Dreamtime Awakening sounded somewhat like this,

The Whites too shall pass —perhaps sooner than other tribes. Continue to contaminate your bed, and you will see night suffocate in your own waste. When the buffalo are all slaughtered, the wild horses all tamed and the secret corners of the forest heavy with the scent of many men, and the view of the ripe hills blotted by talking wires. Where is the thicket? Gone. Where is the eagle? Gone And what is it to say goodbye to the swift and the hunt? It is the end of living and the beginning of survival.

Those were the words of Chief Joseph. Then there were the words of those such as the Native American Mourning Dove who lived from 1888 to 1936,

everything on earth has a purpose,
every disease an herb to cure it,
and every person a mission.
This is the Indian theory of existence.

And the reminder of the Native American proverb,

treat the earth well.
It is not given to you by your parents,
it was loaned to you by your children.
We do not inherit the Earth from our Ancestors
We borrow it from our children.

The knowledge that revealed itself to me held me in the throes of awe. I was awed by how the Dogons of Mali, West Africa, have a four hundred year old artifact that depicts the configuration of the Sirius star in the Siguia ceremony they have held since the 13th century. It celebrates the cycle of Sirius A. The ceremony takes place every 65 years and can take several years to complete. If all of that was not fascinating enough. There was something even more fascinating. The knowledge of this star was only known to the West with the development of modern day astronomy.

Then there was the ancient knowledge about the sun, moon and all other life forms. The ancient Aztec sun stone calendar was originally carved in the 15th century and was a 25 ton 12 feet long stone slab known as the Eagle Bowl. This Sun stone was used to calculate auspicious days for religious, agricultural, and daily activities. It rounded the year into 365 days. And what about the Cherokees celebration of the thirteen moon cycles?

I seemed to pay homage to the trees, the earth, the grass, the sun, the moon, water, and the great mother. *The Tear For Every Fish* seemed to sum up the energy that moved like a vast swooshing current inside of me,

262

Dear Water,

They loved to play in you.
You know your children?
You know the ones that are dying,
the ones that can no longer breath your beautiful aura, or have
a home that is safe.

.

Now I dream of them on the land looking out at
you wistfully. Wanting to jump right on in
but afraid of the only home they know,
the only home that they can call home.
They line the bottom of the rivers.
They line the graveyards of the ocean.
They die silently hoping that
one day their mother will be a safe home once again.

As I wrote I could feel the heart wrenching cry of the ancestors
and their wet tears fell on my soul. It felt as though whoever
they could talk to and through they would. They didn't care if
that person was caught in the glass house of our "modern"
day life. They seemed willing to smash through that glass of
"modern" existence in their compassionate attempt to save us,
and pull us back to our mother's bosom. That soft warm place
that keeps the balance of our health and nurtures the very core
of life's being. Those tears and ancestral appeals to our
sensibilities seemed to be reflected perfectly in a poem, "The
Ocean", written by my son Kem Ra, who was then thirteen.
He wrote it while on Summer Camp at a place called Adopt –
a – Leader.

The Ocean

In the deep ocean floor the balance is gone.
The animals want to go to that cloudy home,
Because of human's irresponsibility to help
Nature is gone, gone for so long you got to
wonder what have we done.
That poor Clown fish has lost its common sense
to defend its home of the poisonous touch.
All due to the horrible chemicals on the ocean floor.
You got to wonder what have we done.
Sea birds look at the ocean with no enthusiasm or
adventure in their eyes.
Looking at the black oil covered ocean they can't see
the reflection of Mother Nature's beauty.
So they want to die,
die for so long.
You got to wonder
What have we done.

In my Dreamtime haze I discovered that there was a sacred era in which spirit beings formed creation. This era is what became known as "The Dreaming". It was in this Dreamtime that all the patterns and laws of life were laid down.

Everything that we see in life existed in the Dreaming first. The meaning and significance of particular places and creatures is attached to their origin in The Dreaming, and certain places have a particular potency, which the Aborigines call its dreaming. In this dreaming resides the sacredness of the earth. For example, in Perth, the Noongar believe that the Darling Scarp is said to represent the body of a Wagyl – a serpent being that meandered over the land creating rivers, waterways and lakes. It is taught that the Wagyl created the

Swan River. All features of our landscape and world are seen as either the physical embodiments of the first spirit beings or are the results of their activities. The dreaming and travelling trails of the Spirit Beings are the songlines.

It is said that before things came to the world there was no separation, just one big world soul. Then when it was time to come into material existence. The animal and plants were created first, and humans last. A pact was made between all three, "each one will look after the other." This pact was never to be broken.

The conditions and requirements of the Dreaming are said to be kept when people live according to law, and live the lore which is maintained through initiations, songs, dancing, paintings and how we live our lives.

Right there in the Dreamtime something else seemed to be happening. Other things began to rise up from its milky cosmic waters. They were the signs. The signs of the Dreamtime. The ones we have forgotten how to read. The signs that tell us when a cloud is just a passing so there will not be a heavy rainfall; or one that means there is a run out of your way storm about to happen.

The ancients obviously knew how to read these signs. There are peoples around the world who can still read these signs. I remember my great aunt, Tanti, could read these signs very well. Now the younger generations of traditional peoples and those in the West have on a whole forgotten how to read those all important signs. If we hadn't forgotten how to read the signs we would be noticing those of the Dreamtime and that they, like the clouds I had learned to read during my childhood, were trying to warn us of our up and coming disasters.

During the four days my pen sped through the Dreamtime I noticed one of those warning signs – the honeybee. I discovered the honey bee was not dancing too well these days. According to scientist they were disappearing so fast that no one knew why. Pollution, chemicals, genetically engineered crop have all been cited as reasons. But, no one seems to know for sure what is going on. One thing that everyone seemed to know - was that bee keepers, along with farmers, were complaining about the honey bee's historic disappearing act.

The honeybee is said to be one of the last wild pollinators in the world. So another thing everyone seems to know for sure – if the honeybee completely disappeared (70% already have) the world would starve. Literally. One year latter after learning about the honey bees plight my brother Jeff told me that he was eating his lunch at Kew Gardens (where he works) when he noticed a strange phenomenon – bees falling into the lake in droves. He said he didn't even think about taking a picture of the event. He wish he had. He shared,

"you know Einstein said that if the Honey Bee disappeared the world would have only four more years before it starved to death."

After the honey bee sign, came White Buffalo Calf Woman. She appeared gloriously in the pages of Indian Country Today, a Native American newspaper. In a story about two sacred buffaloes (one white, one black) who were living at an animal zoo. The zoo was closing and the animals were now in danger of falling into the wrong hands.

Many Native Americans had been doing pilgrimages to see the two buffaloes that they claim were birthed by immaculate conception. The paper pointed out that the white buffalo was connected to the Lakota prophecy of White Buffalo Calf Woman. She had appeared to the Lakota two thousand years ago in a time of great strife and famine. She taught them their sacred ceremonies and rituals, gave them a sacred bundle and sacred pipe. She told them that one day she would return for the sacred implements. Which are still in the hands of the Lakota.

She prophesized when she returned it would be a time when the earth was undergoing great changes and humans would have to change their damaging ways and bring back the boundaries of respecting the spirit and earth again. Now it seemed as though White Calf Woman was back with a warning message for the whole of humanity.

After the White Calf Woman came Kem Ra and his White Lions of Africa. After overhearing me talk to Derrick about some of the ominous ancient signs I noticed while writing "Dreamtime Awakening", he insisted that I read about the White Lions of Africa.

"Mommy they say that when these White Lions appear the world is breaking laws."

So of course I read the story. In 1975 two white Lion cubs were birthed in the area of Timbavati, South Africa. A place where the first white lions had been spotted in 1928. Recently in 2008 an unusual occurrence happened where five white cubs were birthed in the same area. South African natives and Shamans say that this area is sacred and the white lions are sacred to this area. They also state that these White Lions bring a message to humanity that it is time to stop the inappropriate ways that are destroying the earth and return to the proper laws of Mother Earth.

Bees, Cows, White Buffalo Calf Woman, Lions. I contemplated these signs further after I had come out of my writing haze. They were all different, but they all had the same message. Then I noticed something else – all the symbols belonged to the signs of the mother. The Bee was sacred to Osun. I was latter to find out it was sacred to other versions of the World Mother Goddess. Cows/buffalos were also sacred to her too. Lions, I was soon to discover were sacred the World Mother Goddess in her Egyptian form of Sekhmet "the Lioness Goddess" and the Hindu Goddess Durga.

This realization made goose pimples crawl all over my skin, and brought with it an inexplicable fear. The more I examined the symbols and signs was the clearer it became to me that they rang a warning bell from our Universal Mother – "Desist before it is too late".

Yes, our Universal Mother was talking to us in a myriad of forms, and faces. Weren't we privileged that someone still cared about our wellbeing?` However, there was one problem – we no longer understood Mother Talk. Dreamtime Awakening deepened my growing conviction that ancients had coded much of the language of life in the body and symbolisms of the great Mother Goddess. Our only job was to show up and read those signs. Each one seemed to be like the corners of her famous yellow dress. I was filled with the inner knowing that I had to keep on decoding the symbols, signs and stories with the help of the universe. As dramatic a feeling as it was, it seemed as though our lives depended on it.

That knowledge and all the revelations of "Dreamtime Awakening" weighed on my heart like wet laundry in a basket. Exhausted, the last words I wrote for the Dreamtime flowed, spattered and splashed right onto the paper,

Yes, it is a lot like dancing for just a moment.
I thought of the joy I felt.
Of how cool it was.
How beautiful it was to be
connected and then I felt nothing but despair.
I thought about the world
I lived in and how much like dancing it wasn't,
and suddenly I just didn't want to dance anymore.

Picture of my mom at the Healing Springs on
Day we went to see if it was a good location
For a Water Blessing

Group from Healing Springs Water Blessing.
Chief Randall is standing right in middle

Healing Springs Water itself

ETUROPON MEJI

Girl: Mother tell me about the Eturopon Meji.
Mother: Well, Eturopon Meji is the odu that governs the birth of intelligence into the world.
Girl: That sounds interesting.
Mother: Yes, girl it is.
Girl: Can you tell me a story from Eturopon Meji.
Mother: Yes, there is this one.

One day Eturopon Meji did a divination for Egherun, who was the most beautiful birds in the heavens and for Ugun the Vulture. Now Egherun had all sorts of suitors wanting to marry her. All the eligible birds from the Kingdom of birds wanted to marry her. But she turned each and every one down. The vulture decided he would be the one to be successful. He worked out a plan on how to blackmail her into marriage.

Now he knew how much Egherun loved fresh palm fruits. So he went into the forest and picked some from the tree. He lay them on the road knowing Egherun would pass by at some point. Well, on her way back from the market she saw the most attractive palm fruits on the road side and could not resist the urge to take a few. As she was about to set off home. Ugun came out of his hiding place and accused her of stealing.

Egherun was so embarrassed at being caught and scared to. For the offence of stealing back in those days carried the penalty of death. Well, she begged Ugun not to tell. When he just stared at her blankly, she then told him she would offer him any amount of money to compensate for her crime. You know Ugun was not interested in that either. Eventually he told Egherun for her hand in marriage. Well, the vulture was so ugly she really did not want to. She had many sleepless nights about this blackmail offer by Ugun.

Eventually she decided to seek spiritual advise and went for a divination. She was told to make an offering of two cocks. One of the cocks was split open and offered at the cross roads. She then went into hiding as directed. It was that day that Ugun had left home to look for food to feed his bride. Now it is common knowledge that the vulture cannot resist the sight of dead meat.

On the return home he saw the cock at the crossroads. He settled down and began to eat it. He parceled up the remains of what he had not eaten. As he started on his way to go home, Egherun came out and accused him of stealing. Well, Ugun said a husband could not be accused of stealing from his wife. She insisted she did not make the offering on the road side for him. Ugun soon realized he was not going to win the argument. He asked what could he do to be reprieved of his crime. She told him the only thing he could do was to rescind his marriage to her publicly.

Ugun had no choice but to agree, for the other choice was the death penalty. After that Egherun was a free woman again.

Joseph Campbell appeared to be right when he stated the Hero has the "inevitable meeting" where the soul concludes its exile in the world of organized inadequacies to reunite with the bliss that was before that.

What is this bliss that Campbell talks about? It is: "the comforting, the nourishing, the good mother - young and beautiful – who was known to us, and even tasted in the remotest past".

Poetically he continues, "time sealed her away yet she is dwelling still, like one who sleeps in timelessness, at the bottom of the timeless sea."

We meet her not only as her beautiful, young form but as the good, bad and ugly too. For each appearance represents an encounter with her that eradicates the illusion that keeps us away from Truth – the truth of true harmony and bliss.

But who is the Mother really? Campbell reveals,

"The mythological figure of the Universal Mother imputes to the cosmos the feminine attributes of the first, nourishing and protecting presence. The fantasy is primarily spontaneous; for there exists a close and obvious correspondence between the attitude of the young child towards its mother and that of the adult toward the surrounding material world."

He informs us in the Indian Tantric books her abode is called Mani-dvipa, "The Island of Jewels." The words conjured up an image of luscious beauty, wealth and abundance. In Mani-dvipa,

"Her couch and throne is there, in a grove of wish fulfilling trees. The beaches of the isle are of golden sands. They are laved by the still waters of the ocean of the nectar of immortality. The Goddess is red with the fire of life; the earth, the solar system, the galaxies of far extending space, all swell within her womb. For she is the encompassing, nourishes the nourishing, and is the life of everything that lives."

Campbell lets us know it is the Mother, who teaches us to see beyond all things material so that we can see into the clear light of life itself. When we can learn to do so we become like the Irish Prince who inherited the Supreme Power we really crave for. The story goes something like this:

One day there were five sons of the Irish King Eochaid who went hunting. They became thirsty on their hunt and decided to go and look for water. One by one they went in search of water. The son called Fergus went first. He found a well where an old woman stood. She was wild and disheveled looking. He asked her if she was guarding the well and she lets him know that she was. He then ask her "dost thou license me to take away some water?" The old woman replied she did. Requesting that before she allowed him to do so he had to give her a kiss on her cheek. He tells her, "my word I give that sooner than give thee a kiss I would perish of thirst!" With those words he left.

Then Olioll, Brian and Fiachre, went to the well to get water. Each came back empty handed because each refused to give the old woman a kiss on the cheek. Finally it was the brother called Niall who went in search of water. When he came across the well the woman told him the same thing as all the others. He answered her, "forby giving thee a kiss, I will even hug thee!" Then Niall bent over and kissed the woman.

The old woman who is referred to as an old hag throughout the story turns into a woman who it is said no woman in the world could have matched her beauty. Niall ask the woman who she is?

"King of Tara! I am Royal Rule…"

She then states, "Go now to thy brethren, and take with thee water; moreover, thine and thy children's for ever the kingdom and supreme power shall be."

275

It was soon after the completion of Dreamtime Awakening and in the heat of June 2009, the pieces of the Universal Mother began to cement themselves together. In fact, the Mother appeared to begin her full ascent from the primordial waters in which she had been resting. Her significant rise into our waking world seemed to be marked by two really significant things that happened to me. The first was meeting the picture of Tutankhamun, again (I will explain why I say, "again"). The second was the visiting of the endangered Catawba Spider Lilies. Both occurrences actually happened on the same day, and began with mine and Derrick's desire to visit the Lilies before their last blooms disappeared.

The Catawba Spider Lilies are known as Rocky Shoal Spider Lily or the Cahaba Lily. They are beautiful, white, elegant and quite mesmerizing to the beholder's eye. This plant exist in large streams and rivers in South Carolina, Georgia and Alabama - areas which usually consist of the rocky shoals and bedrock outcrops that provide anchor points for this beautiful Water Queen. It is a plant that grows best in clean flowing waters. Thus, why it is now endangered.

It was David Merryman, the Catawba Riverkeeper, who informed us that the Catawba Spider Lilies make their home in the middle of the Catawba River. Which boast the largest colony of Spider Lilies in the world. He encouraged us to go and see these rare flowers blooming in their glory mid May to mid-June. We took his advise (well, on the visiting part anyway). By the time we decided to rush and see the lilies it was late June. Derrick was convinced they would still be in full flower. The day we decided to go he proceeded to pack the car. As he did this I killed time by browsing the internet. After half an hour I started shifting in my chair. What was taking him so long? When he came bursting through the door like a gale storm wind, I was pleased to see him. I rose from my chair to grab my things, so that we could leave. Instead of Derrick saying, "come on let's go," he said,

"I don't want you to look or peak. Just close your eyes."

I closed them unwillingly.

"Keep them closed," he said mysteriously.

I kept them closed for a few seconds. Then he said,

"Now open your eyes."

I opened them.

There in his hand was an almost life size original oil painting of Tutankhamen and his wife.

There are some things that make you freak out and there are some things that don't. This was one of those things that made me freak out.

"Oh, my God! Oh my God!" I exclaimed feeling like the female character in the movie Hitch, when Hitch's romantic surprise turned into her living nightmare.

"Where did you get that picture?" I asked shaking.

"I found it here in the garage. I think it was one of my brother's artifacts."

I tried to sound calmer and control my shaking, but I didn't do a good job of it.

"Oh God! Oh God!" My head started to spin again.

Derrick's eyebrows began to look like a piece of knitting gone wrong.

"What's wrong?" he asked worried.

"That picture your holding I have seen it before. My father who use to paint a lot drew that very picture on a large wooden canvas when my mother was pregnant with me. He

277

colored the whole thing in with ink pens. It was a stunning picture. You would have sworn he painted it. He did a slightly more stylized version of the original. For some reason he drew Tutankhamun with breast. Now what's interesting with that picture was that it was the only picture that my mom said survived a move she made when we were small. It eventually got lost when we recently moved to the Islands…."

I paused only for a second. Then continued.

"Now Kem Ra's dad had this beautiful picture commissioned by this white guy when I was pregnant with Kem Ra. He kept on talking about it, but wanted it to be a surprise. When he eventually brought the picture home he unveiled it and I froze. It was the very picture in my mom's house. The one my dad had painted.

The strange thing is he had never really noticed that picture. It was easy for him not to notice the picture properly because it had this way of blending into my mom's patterned wallpaper. It was also in much duller colors. I think it was those ink colors. They were much less vibrant than if the picture had been done in paint. It was mom who told me my father had drawn the picture of Tutankhamen when she was pregnant with me. At the time, I felt as though there was some significance to these two strange coincidences but I never quite figured it out. Now here you are showing me this picture again!"

I could tell that Derrick found the story highly intriguing by the way his eyebrows relaxed out of their messy knitted poise and rose into a smoother arch. As I finished the story Derrick shook his head and said,

"that's deep stuff sweetie."

Then he dashed back to the car to finish packing our things before the Catawba Lilies really did wilt away for good. In the meantime I went back to browsing the net. Still shaking

278

I now wanted to find out more about Tutankhamun and the picture. I was determined to begin to get to the bottom of this life mystery that had been following me around in the form of his painting.

After following loads of leads and links I discovered that Tutankhamun's original name was Tutankhaten which means "Living Image of Aten". While Tutankhamun means "Living Image of Amun".

He was a boy king who was born in 1341 BC, and was said to be the son of Akhenaten (formerly Amenhotep IV) and one of his sisters. In 1922 he was rediscovered by Howard Carter and George Herbert, 5th Earl of Carnarvon. His intact tomb was found and apparently sparked a renewed public interest in ancient Egypt.

It seems as though he latter ascended to the throne in 1333 BC, at the age of nine, taking the reign name of Tutankhamun. His wet-nurse was a said to be a certain woman called Maia, known from her tomb at Saqqara.

When he became king, the majority of historians speculated that he married his half sister, Ankhesenepatan, who later changed her name to Ankhesenamun. They had two daughters, both stillborn

In his third regnal year, Tutankhamun apparently reversed several changes made during his father's reign. He ended the worship of the god Aten and restored the god Amun to supremacy. The ban on the cult of Amun was lifted and traditional privileges were restored to its priesthood. The capital was moved back to Thebes and the city of Akhnetaten abandoned. This was the period when he changed his name to Tutankhamun.

As part of his restoration, the king initiated building projects, in particular at Thebes and Karnak, where he dedicated a temple to Amun. Many monuments were erected, and an inscription on his tomb door declares the king had "spent his life in fashioning the images of the gods". It is said that the traditional festivals were now celebrated again. He has a restoration stela which reads:

Temples of the gods and goddesses ... were in ruins. Their shrines were deserted and overgrown. Their sanctuaries were as non-existent and their courts were used as roads ... the gods turned their backs upon this land ... If anyone made a prayer to a god for advice he would never respond – and the same applied to a goddess.

The restoration of Egypt's religion back to the old one in order to restore the glory of the Gods and Goddesses seemed to be a very significant fact.

That electrical current that normally pulls me forward and deeper into history began to tingle in my bones. There was something more I had to know, I knew it. Amun smiled at me, and urged me to keep on moving forward. I decided to find out what all the fuss about Amun was about - to discover there were various reasons why he was held in such high esteem by the ancients. One important factor about Amun seemed to be that he was seen as a champion of the less fortunate. Why? Because during the invasion of the Indo Aryans, the Egyptians had many victories against them and put it down to Amun. He later joined identities with Ra, the Sun God and became regarded as Amun-Re.

Sometimes it is just a few words that gives everything away. The electrical current kept on pulling me forward. There was more. I still did not feel I had stumbled across the other significant thing it wanted me to find. Then suddenly I saw a sentence. It was short and read "his consort was Mut". That was it. No more was said about her as she got outshone by the writer's excited and glorified exultations of the glorious radiance of Amun. But the sentence was enough to make the electrical current tingle deeply in my bones. I had to find out more about Mut, I just knew I had to.

Unbeknownst to me the rabbit had me and before I knew it I was running right after it to enter the hole of ancient Earth history helmed and adorned by a wondrous Mother Goddess. In the hole, I was rightfully greeted by the first eight ancient deities of the Egyptian Old Kingdom which dated back from the third through to the sixth dynasties (2686 to 2134 BC). The eight formed a company of Gods known as the Ogoad and were worshipped in a place known as Hermopolis.

The eight deities of the Old Kingdom period were put into male and female pairs. This pairing represented the opposing and complementary dynamic shaping principles of creation. These male and female pairs were seen as the living elements that birthed all life.

The four pairs of deities were: Naunet and Nu; Amunet and Amun; Kauket and Kuk; Huh and Hauhet. Each pair was associated with a primordial element concept. So Primordial waters were Naunet and Nu; Air or invisibility was Amunet and Amun; Darkness was Kauket and Ku; then there was Hu and Huahet for eternity or infinite space.

Amunet was the female aspect of an abstract concept for air and invisibility. As we saw her male counterpart was Amun. She was seen as the Mother of all Creation. Latter on Amunet was replaced by Mut. In the Egyptian language Mut meant mother. She was an ancient Egyptian mother Goddess whose faces changed over thousands of years.

She was mostly depicted as a white vulture and was considered a primal deity associated with the waters through which all of life was born She wore the crowns of Egypt upon her head. Her appellations included: *World Mother, Eye of Ra, Queen of the Goddesses, Lady of Heaven, Mother of the Gods,* and *She Who Gives Birth but was Herself Not Born of Any.*

It is said that Mut was originally the title of the primordial waters of the cosmos, Naunet, in the Ogdoad cosmogony. As the identity between motherhood and cosmic waters became more diversified and a separation between these two identities began. Mut gained aspects of the Creator Goddess as she was seen as the creator of the entire cosmos.

The hieroglyph for Mut and for the word mother was the same – the white vulture. The Egyptians believed that vultures were very maternal creatures and that they had no differing markings between female and male of the species. In fact the they believed that all vultures were female.

Latter it seemed that the Mother Goddess absorbed the identity of other Egyptian Goddess. Lower and Upper Egypt had Wadjet and Nekhbet as their patron deities along with Bast and Sekmet. When Thebes rose to prominence Mut absorbed these warrior Goddesses. Thebes was the Greek name for an Ancient Egyptian city located on the east bank of the river Nile. The Valley of the Kings is located in Thebes. So Mut's identity became first Mut-Wadjet-Bast, then Mut-Sekmet-Bast (wadjet having merged into Bast). Then she also became assimilated with Mehit who was also a lioness goddess.

It was later in the Middle Kingdom when the Egyptian pantheon deities were identified as equal pairs who had the same function; and when Thebes grew in importance that its patron deity Amun became quite prominent. It was during this period that Amaunet became replaced by Mut. It was said that Amun needed a more substantial partner. Who better than the creator Goddess Mut, herself.

It is said that as the authority of Thebes waned Mut was assimilated into Ra and then into the figure of the cow Goddess Hathor who was the mother of Horus and who had become identified as Ra's wife. Latter Mut-Hathor became identified as Isis where she became known as Isis – Hathor or Mut-Isis-Nekhbet. Latter the Mut –Hathor – Isis identity became just Isis. The Isis cult spread and became prolific throughout Greece, Rome, and Britain.

It is also said that Mut did not give birth to any children because she is said to have been created from nothing so could not give birth so she adopted. As the female counterpart to Amun she at first adopted Menthu, God of War. However latter he became replaced by Khonsu, the moon God because the sacred lake outside of her ancient temple in Karnak at Thebes was in the crescent shape of the moon.

I raced along in my reading. I discovered that when Akhenaten had suppressed the old religion it also included the suppression of the Mother Goddess Mut. It was Tutankhamun who latter re-established her worship and thereafter his successors continued to associate themselves with her.

As I read about Mut my head was reeling. *Mut was the creator Goddess. Mut was the Creator Goddess. Mut was the Creator Goddess. She was the Creator Goddess who had merged all the other Egyptian Goddesses together. She is, She of Many Faces.* These words kept on swirling around in my head like chocolate on vanilla ice cream. I rested my head on my desk as the weight of a sudden intuitive realization dawned on me. All these years the picture of Tutankhamun had been patiently waiting for me to one day discover the glory of the ancient Mother and all she meant to us throughout history. Was this all the picture meant? I did not know, but in terms of the Mother I knew I could not deny her historical presence. As I looked up I could see the Great Mother standing poised on the precipice of history.

Mut opened the doors, and allowed the primeval rush of water through. She ensured some of her symbols caught my eyes. Namely, that of the vulture, water, lions, cat, amongst others. I noticed there were a few that belonged to Osun. Those being the vulture, water, and the title Great Mother. I found it interesting how the word for motherhood, and Mut were represented by the vulture, and how water had been connected to the concept of Motherhood. Like Mut, Osun was seen as the Great Mother of the World. She was also the Mother of the Waters. My brain did not fail to compute the symbols that lay scattered at my feet: Mother, Vulture and Water.

I went back over Mut's fusion with Isis, Sekhmet and Hathor. For some reason this fusion fascinated me and became a highly symbolic reference point. At that moment I knew just a few rudimentary things about each of these Goddesses. I knew Hathor was the Goddess of Joy, music, wisdom, fertility and creation. Sekhmet was the fierce protective Lioness Goddess of very protective Goddess of Upper Egypt. Bast was her Cat Goddess counterpart in Lower Egypt. Isis was the wife of Osiris and was the great mother goddess associated with healing and mending things back together again.

The more I thought about these Goddesses and the unifying of their energies, a question arose in my mind and kept on growing like the Egyptian Lotus flower. Was Osun none other than the Mut who had fused with all the other Goddess? That electrical current had me again. It would not let this thought escape from my mind. Little did I know that Osun was about to act like a Goddess Rosetta Stone.

I found myself once again reading back over all the information I had come across. It seemed to me that she was. I had come to know Osun well. I knew her not just from a text book (in fact most of my knowing was not from any book), but from the depths of my being, from being told the oral stories, visiting her Sacred Grove, meeting her priesthood, receiving her age old symbols, artifacts, and energy through ancient initiations. I knew her like a child knows its mother. I could almost see that Osun seemed to represent the Motherhood that all the Egyptian Goddesses had come to symbolize when combined with Mut. She also appeared to be the joyful Hathor, and the fierce Sekhmet, as well as the watery Isis.

It was then that I also remembered that Osun had other deities in the pantheon she belonged to: Yemanje, Oya, and Olokun. It seemed that even though Osun represented the whole of the Mut combination, she also seemed to be the head of a combination where each Goddess reflected an Egyptian Mother Goddess. So Yemanje, the Mother of the Waters (like Osun), seemed to represent Isis; Oya, the Mother of Transformation and winds, seemed to embody Sekhmet; Olukun, the Mother/Father of the deep ocean, seemed to represent Nut.

In that moment I felt a bold confidence to ascertain that Osun was indeed an embodiment of what I latter came to call the Mut Composite made up of the Egyptian Mother Goddesses: Mut, Sekhmet, Bast, Hathor, and Isis. Mut seemed to be the common thread that pulled them all these Goddesses into their Universal Motherhood identity. Just as light passing

285

through a prism of glass and coming out in various colors at the other end - these Goddesses were like the light shining through the prism of glass, but they were one light. Mut appeared to be the prism of glass, and the one light. Well, that is how I saw it in my mind's eye for that moment.

Sometimes there is one thing that catches your eye and triggers something powerful of. In the queue of symbols that stood before me – it was the vulture. The image of this dark powerful bird slightly scorned by modern society (how many people can claim to love a vulture?) kept on flapping its wings before me. As it did so my mind raced back in time to a Yoruba wisdom story about Osun I had been told by a priest.

One day when the world was still very young the Gods got very tired of serving Oludamare, the Lord of heaven. They began to go against all his wishes, and were even planning an insurrection. Well, unfortunately for the Gods and very fortunately for Oludamare, he learned about their rebellious plans. He was also tired of their bad behavior and how they were treating and abusing the earth.

He showed them the immense force of his power, by simply refusing to allow, even one single drop of rain, to fall upon the Earth. Without any rain, a great drought began to spread across the Earth, and the ground, which had always provided sustenance and life, quickly began to dry up. The various forms of life, which the rain had always brought forth, soon began to die, and the Gods quickly began to realize, that without the gift of rain, the people and the Gods would all die. `

Indeed, the Gods and humankind began to starve and be thirsty. They called a conference and decided that they had to beg for

Olodumare's forgiveness. As well as, to ask him to give them back the rain.

It was a good plan, but there was a little bit of a problem. None of the God's could travel as far as heaven. They attempted to reach heaven by sending the birds of Earth; but each of them, one by one, unsuccessfully returned. They simply did not have the strength to undertake such a long and arduous journey.

The God's became very down hearted. They were running out of time. They would all soon starve and thirst to death. They thought, "that's it, we are all going to die. There is no hope."

Well, like in all these stories no one had thought about asking Osun, the Great Goddess, to help. Yet, luck of luck, one day she appears as a beautiful peacock and tells them she will go to the Palace where God resided so that the world could be saved from its terrible drought. The Gods, did not believe that this little beautiful peacock could achieve such a feat. If they couldn't how could she? However, the Goddess kept on insisting she would succeed. Eventually, they let her go.

The Goddess in the form of that little peacock flew upwards towards the sun, and towards the Palace of God, which existed high up in Heaven. The journey was an extremely long and tiring one. One that was extremely difficult for Osun to do.

However, one thing about Osun she is not a giver up. She was determined to help save the world. She continued flying higher and higher. As she flew closer to the sun, her feathers began to grow weathered and dark, and her beautiful head, became almost bare. Nothing, however, could stop her from continuing on her journey. She was completely determined, to reach the Palace of God, and save the world from the terrible drought that engulfed it. Guess what? She actually made it to heaven, but not as a beautiful peacock more like a Vulture. For by the time she got to the palace of God she was completely cinched all over.

So what does God do when he sees her? He is completely moved by her deep strength, commitment and courage. Of course he invited her into his palace, fed, watered and made sure she was healed.

Once Osun was better again, God asked her why she had made such a long and perilous journey. She explained to him, the rain he was withholding from the earth was causing all of her children to die. That was how Osun looked upon humanity; she saw them as her children. She also informed God that she had risked her own life, to make this dangerous journey, so that the people of the Earth might be saved.

God looked down upon the Earth, and saw that everything, which Osun had told him, was true. It was then that he turned to Osun, the once beautiful peacock, who now looked much more like a vulture than a peacock, and he withdrew his curse. Once again, the rains wet the earth.

Once he removed this curse God looked deep within the Goddess and he was moved by the purity of her heart. He announced on the spot that she would become the messenger of The House of God. He told everyone that she must always be shown great respect.

It was from that moment that Osun became known as Ikole, the Messenger of the House of God. She also became known as Ibu Ikole, a name which associated her with the vulture.

As the vulture she traveled back to the Earth, and with her, she brought the gift of rain. The whole planet rejoiced at what she had done. The beautiful thing about it all is that despite all the accolade Osun remained extremely humble.

She never once said to the other Gods, "there I told you so!" It was also from that point on that whenever a person becomes a priest, before he is able to gain the divine power of a God, within him, he must first travel up the river, to receive the blessings of Osun.

Going back over the story of Osun's feat to save the world moved me deeply. I could almost feel the pain of commitment she had to bear in her journey to save the world. As I examined the Mut composite some more I realized that all the Mother Goddesses in it were inextricably connected to wisdom. I pondered on this wisdom aspect of the Mother Goddesses. Then another Osun story loomed back into my mind. It was all about how Osun founded the bag of wisdom.

One day Oludamare (God) sent a message from heaven that he would throw knowledge to the Gods. Whoever picked it up would be rewarded. He did not name the specific day or say what the thing would look like. However, he told them he would be sending knowledge to them.

They all began to search for the knowledge. Osun consulted the oracle who advised her that she had to make a sacrifice of the gown she was wearing. In those days it is said that the women wore the long gowns like the men. However, Osun was not interested in giving up her gown, so she didn't do the sacrifice.

Then one day when everyone was out searching for the knowledge. She came across a little parcel and it was the knowledge itself. She did not know this. She picked up the parcel and put it in her pocket.

It is said that the Esu, the God who opens the way and also tricks people, tore a hole inside of her gown because she had made no sacrifice. When everyone got tired of searching for the knowledge they gathered back together again. Orunmila, the God of Wisdom, showed what he had found. It was the knowledge.

Osun informed him that she had found it first. Orunmila told her "tough luck" (my words not his) "I found this on the ground. So it is said that is how Orunmila became more knowledgeable than everyone else.

The relationship of Osun to wisdom is further illustrated by the fact she is said to be the owner of a Yoruba divination system known as the demerilingoe which uses cowrie shells to divine. This system is still used by Osun devotees. It consists of the first sixteen odus (Wisdoms) of Ifa. The full Ifa oracular system used by Ifa priest consists of two hundred and fifty six Odus (bodies of wisdom. That's the best way I can explain it.)

As these two hundred and sixty Odus are actual combinations of the first sixteen Odus of the oracular system I remembered how Dr. Wande Abimbola asserts in his essay "The Bag of Wisdom" found in the book "Osun across the Waters" - the Ifa oracular stories themselves hint at the fact that the sixteen cowry shell system is indeed the original and older system of divination.

He states,

"I will make the claim that Osun has much to do with the founding of Ifa divination more than the Babalowa (Ifa Priest) are ready to admit. I will, indeed, put forward the hypothesis that the entire divination system of Ifa started with Osun from whom it got to Orunmila and not the other way around."

This relationship with Osun to the sixteen Odu (bodies of wisdom) is acknowledged during her famous Osun festival where sixteen lamps are lit. Each lamp represents an Odu and the wisdom that lights the world. It is also interesting to note, the festival itself acts as a time when mankind renews its pact with the Universal Mother, who represents the nourishing waters of existence. In return she gives prosperity, long life, fertility, healing, joy and harmony to humanity.

As I re-remembered all these stories of Osun, she seemed to smile at me, as she reminded me and the world that that within the ethereal body of the Mother Goddess is all the

290

wisdom of the world. The Mother holds the bag of wisdom we so desperately need.

All these thoughts and analysis raced through my mind in the interim of waiting for Derrick to tell me he was ready to go see the Catawba Spider Lilies. We had a quiet drive down to Lands Valley Canal where they awaited us. The drive was quiet because my head was drowning in the buzz of my own thoughts

Once the car pulled up on the park's land. We trumped along a well-trodden path, one whose worn trail showed that it had been walked by many like us who searched for the same thing - the beauty of the endangered Spider Lilies.

The walk was refreshing. The waters of the Catawba River bounced along the way as it followed the entire pathway like a special guide. I noticed how the water was not sad like the first time I had seen it, nor was it simply elegant like the second time, but this time she was like a Royal Queen sitting in residence.

I would like to say that when we got to the spot where we could view the Catawba Lilies we saw them in splendid full bloom. But we didn't. From the edge of a little wooden platform we saw them wilting and bashed around by the torrent of the surrounding waters. Their glory was almost faded, yet strangely enough they still looked beautiful in a haunted kind of way. I admired how hard they tried to stay above water so that we could see them, so that we wouldn't forget them. So that we knew that we must help them to continue to exist. They reminded me of Osun, and the Universal Mother in all her forms and cultural guises throughout history and time. I closed my eyes and prayed they would never die.

It was a few days after seeing the Catawba Water Lilies that I had a dream.

I was in this house with Derrick. There was a man in the room next to ours. He seemed nice enough, but when I saw him I could see that something was wrong. I lay my hands on his brow chakra and I saw this evil male spirit in him. The longer I left my hand on his third eye was the more the spirit began to diminish. But when I took my hand off the man walked off kind off arrogantly and slammed the door. I felt disappointed because I realized I had the power to see the man but not to completely get rid of the evil spirit within him.

Then I sat at the dining table. Derrick was there He looked lovely. Eventually, he went off to try and help the man. I noticed that the house had half of it with the usual mundane activities going on. The other half had a lot of spiritual activities going on.

Then I noticed this very old washing machine was washing. Derrick knew how to work it but I didn't. I kept on pressing these buttons, Until somehow the machine started to soap up real quick.

In the next scene water flooded through the house and the whole world was destroyed by a flood. I was in all this water. I could see nothing but a huge statute of an Indian Goddess standing in the middle of the world in the water. She had a Lotus on her. She stood in the middle of the flood and then crashed into the water and disappeared. I noticed where the statute of the Indian Goddess had stood was now an Egyptian coffin. I was now standing closer to the spot. I noticed that a flat sculpture of a Goddess fell from the coffin. Then one by one there were more Goddesses made the same way that fell like dominoes out of it. Each Goddess was from a different

292

culture. They all disappeared into the water. I felt an overwhelming sadness as I watched each one disappear as if for good.

I woke with an aching sadness in my bones. The same kind of sadness that had overcome me when I saw the Catawba Lilies. I felt I was being shown the connection between all the Goddesses from across the waters, and how they had been buried by the waters of time.

After the Catawba Water Lilies, after the dream, arose a real life Mother Goddess from the primordial waters. Amma came forth from a rare lotus flower. Let me explain, it was late June and Derrick and I were busying ourselves with the Humanity4Water 2009 awards. One of our main task was to get together the names of those planet heroes we wished to honor.

Finding the names was half the joy of the awards, anyway. When you discovered the hard work of those who were trying to help the planet, their level of commitment, love and compassion it was hard not to be moved. Discovering who these individuals were and what they did was also part of our journey with water. It grew us, and deepened our understanding; in turn we did the same for others

Well, Amma who is fondly known as the Hugging Saint was to be our awardee for compassion. The internet seemed to throw her up from cyberspace into our arms, at a time when I was also trying to find out more about the connection between the world Mother Goddesses. Cosmic bumps cannot be ignored.

According to the information on Amma's website she was given the beautiful name Sudhamani (Ambrosial Jewel).

Born in a poor fishing village in Kerala, Southern India, in 1953, her father sold fish to make a living. According to her mother she was born with a beaming smile on her face.

As a small child she was thought of as unique because by six months she could walk and talk, and by the age of three she was constantly singing. By the age of five she was composing beautiful, extraordinarily profound hymns to Krishna (an incarnation of Vishnu who is seen as an aspect of the Supreme God). Her devotion to God eventually began to annoy her family and instead of being praised for it she was scolded.

As fate would have it her mother became ill. She was the brightest girl in the class but had to leave school to take care of the whole family. She had the grueling task of taking care of seven brothers and sisters. Then there were the animals to attend. She became what has been described as "the family servant" who worked "from dawn till midnight."

As she went about her chores she noticed that there was much suffering in the world, hunger and pain. She felt great empathy for individuals who suffered. It was this that made her "contemplate the question of suffering. " She began to ask herself,

"why do people suffer? What is the underlying cause of suffering?"

It was during this period of her life that she wanted to reach out and comfort and uplift those who were less fortunate than she.

Much to her families annoyance she would often give food away to the poor, cloth and feed the elderly. At night she would take refuge in her Lord Krishna. In her early teens she was sent to the houses of relatives to labor for them. This she took in her stride and stayed prayerful keeping Krishna in her mind at all times. She was indeed an unusual child for the more abuse she sustained from her family was the more she "prayed to be given more of the Lord's work. "

There was more. So I read on. It was a section of her website called "Who is Amma?" following that question is her full name Sri Mata Amritanandamayi Devi. Then we are told that Amma means "Mother of All" She shows us that "Motherhood, in its ultimate sense, has nothing to do with bearing a child, but with love, compassion and selflessness. It lies in totally giving one's self to others."

We are then shown how Amma, known as a "living saint" exemplifies the many faces of the Mother concept.

"If we look at Amma's life, this is what we see—someone who has offered her every thought, word and deed for the benefit of others. Giving is the essence. It's just that when the homeless come crying for shelter and Amma gives them a house, we call her a "humanitarian." And when the sorrowful come crying for emotional solace and she gives them love, we call her a "mother." And when those thirsty for spiritual knowledge come earnestly seeking and she gives them wisdom, we call her a "guru."

We are told that Amma refers to this type of selfless service as vishwa matrutvam—universal motherhood." "And it is to this pinnacle of human existence that Amma is trying to awaken the world through her life, teachings and *ellamma* [divine embrace]."

Then there's the fact that Amma did not study with a guru or study the sacred Vedas, "yet she speaks on the truths expressed within the scriptures with wisdom, clarity and true insight. Hers is not an academic knowledge, but the knowledge of one who is ever-established in the Ultimate Reality."

Her dream is to see "a world in which women and men progress together. A world in which all men respect the fact that, like the two wings of a bird, women and men are of equal value". Her further dream is the desire to ensure that "everyone in the world should be able to sleep without fear, at least for one night. Everyone should be able to eat to his fill, at least for one day. There should be at least one day when hospitals see no one admitted due to violence."

We are further told that since the age of seventeen Amma has been miraculously known to sit down for 22 hours embracing people. Thus her nickname "The Hugging Saint".

I found it interesting that Joseph Campbell said to meet the Mother was to go beyond non dualism. For Amma seemed to fully exemplify this truth. For we are told that "For Amma, *Advaita* [non-dualism] is not a mere philosophy, but something to be lived." We are shown that when one lives with Advaita then like Amma we see that "everything within and without is divine."

Amma's motherly compassion is further expressed in her huge humanitarian efforts done through her organization the Mata Amritanandamayi Math. As such in 2005 it was given special consultative status by the United Nations. For her philosophy is driven by the concept, "it's better to get worn out than rust away". In fact, Amma has said that she wishes to be lovingly caressing someone, consoling them and wiping their tears even when she breathes her last breath.

As I read about Amma I thought of Susan Wenger and her act of compassion in building the Osun Grove. An act of compassion because it reminded all who visited of the universal Mother Energy, and her nurturing compassion. Then I thought of the Mother herself, and how much Amma exemplified all she was about. Little did I know that like the Indian Goddess in my dream, Amma was about to herald in an avalanche of Goddesses who belonged to one lineage connected to the primordial waters of time, place and space.

It was in July that we discovered that Amma was to be in the United States - Washington to be precise. We could not believe our luck. There they were again, those cosmic bumps. The only problem was that we only had $100 left to our name for that month. Derrick was not working as yet, and neither was I. However, it seemed as though we were meant to go. We prayed on it and decided we would spend our last dime to drive down to Washington. First we rang all the appropriate people to see if it was possible to give the Humanity4Water award to Amma. We were excited when we found out it was.

Driving from Lancaster South Carolina to Washington took a couple of hours. It was much smoother than I had anticipated and the hours went by quickly. We stepped into the Washington Hilton Hotel where Amma was to give Darshana (blessings), and found ourselves drowning in a sea of white. Everyone was wearing white to see the saint. That was everyone but me, Derrick and Kem Ra.

I stuck out the most, like a sore yellow thumb (albeit a graceful sore yellow thumb). I wore one of the few African outfits I had travelled from Trinidad with. It was a beautiful yellow one shoulder African lace top and skirt (which I had in fact worn on the day myself and Derrick got married). Derrick was handsomely kitted out in a more subdued grey blue African batik outfit. Through the sea of white he got into action immediately. He was on a mission to discover how we were to hand the award to Amma.

Myself and Kem Ra followed him through the crowd as best we could. I tried not to step on anyone (there were many people sitting on the floor) or knock anyone with the pink gift bag I had put the award in. We waded through the white clad bodies to the main desk manned by two helpers.

"We have come to deliver from Humanity4Water Amma's Award of Compassion. What do we need to do?"

Derrick asked the organizer who proceeded to look down a list of what turned out to be listed guest.

"Nope, there's no Humanity4Water guest on this list," the organizer said shaking his head.

"Well, there must be a mistake, we spoke to someone who told us we could bring it down and we would be down on the list," Derrick said patiently.

"I am sorry I can't help you, you are not down here," the organizer said firmly.

"We travelled all the way from South Carolina just to deliver this award to Amma," Derrick explained.

"I really can't help you," said the organizer looking to see who was next.

"Is there anyone who can help?" Derrick asked.

"Yes, there is someone but he won't be here until another couple of hours," the organizer informed.

"By the time he arrives most of this stuff will be over," Derrick said."Is there someone else who can help us?"

"There's a lady over there" said the organizer pointing to a pretty Indian lady with hair cascading down her shoulders.

"Okay, thanks," said Derrick.

I admired him for not loosing his cool. I on the other hand began to see the sea of white turn to red. I felt totally humiliated by the way we had been treated. I could not believe at how little the assistant seemed to care about our dilemma.

"I thought this is meant to be a deeply spiritual event," I said to Derrick fuming.

"Don't worry about it," he said. Still focused on discovering how we could get our award to Amma.

The beautiful Indian woman turned out to be no more helpful. In fact, she was down right rude and arrogant. Least the assistant before her was not completely outright rude to us, he just wasn't very helpful. The beautiful woman on the other hand scanned us up and down and scornfully said,

"There is no way you will be able to see Amma. I can't help it if you drove all the way from South Carolina."

"Can you arrange to put us on the list since we were told we were on it," Derrick asked politely.

"That will not be possible," she said barely looking at us as if we were one of the untouchables from the caste system.

Then she turned on her heels and began to walk towards the sea of white which was turning bright crimson in my eyes.

"But. We...." I began to protest,

Her mobile phone went off,

"sorry I've got to answer this."

She flicked her luscious mane and then disappeared into her sacred sea of white.

At that point I thought of our last $100 we had used to drive down to the event, and I wanted to cry.

"This is terrible," I said to Derrick through clenched teeth.

Derrick is not easily fazed. His faith in divine grace constantly   amazed   me.

"Let's get a Darshana ticket. Somehow God will arrange it for us to see Amma. We did not come this far for him not to," he said. "These are all part of the test that the cosmos puts in the way. These are the test that help people to grow. You have something special to give this very loving woman. She will be very pleased to accept it."

"But, they said we are not on the list and they won't put us on the list now...." I protested and tried to tug him to the exit.

"I heard what they said. I also know why we are here. I think we will get to fulfill our purpose for being here."

I gave up the ghost of trying to leave when I heard his steely commitment. With a sulky attitude I followed his suggestion. With Kem Ra in tow we went to get our tickets for darshana. I was the only one sulking as we waited in a forever line of hundreds of devotees which stretched right into the main hall where Amma would appear. Derrick and Kem Ra chatted calmly together. They seemed pretty unperturbed by how events had unfolded so far.   Once in the main hall we waited another long period to be seated.

Now as Derrick said, "the cosmos throws things in our way to overcome." The longer we stood in the queue was the more I decided to embrace this attitude. I might as well enjoy the atmosphere. We weren't leaving. Derrick had made that plainly clear.

The more I let go of my anger was the more I began to observe the comings and goings of the hall we stood in. The atmosphere was buzzing with hundreds of people in queue, some were seated already. The energy felt like the anticipatory emotions of a highly charged child knowing its mother was about to come back home with sweeties.

Behind where I stood were people busy buying gem jewelry, flowers, apples, and all sorts of other paraphernalia to be blessed by Amma. Far to the front of me was a nicely decorated chair which was obviously where Amma was going to sit. Just as my intention to be upset slipped finally into oblivion strange things began to happen. The first was that we got ushered to the second row of chairs. Now this was an excellent place to sit because the front rows were almost right next to Amma's royal looking seat. To this first miracle Derrick said,

"See I told you so."

"How did we end up sitting here?" I asked him feeling like a leper who had been redeemed.

"When you have a good intention and the cosmos wants you to do something, everything conspires to make it happen," he said quietly in my ears.

"Wow, this is amazing," I marveled at the work of the Cosmos.

The second miracle came in the form of a blond assistant with a clipboard in her hands. She stood right by the front row.

"You know what. I remember someone saying you are allowed to ask a question. Ask the assistant if we can ask Amma a question," whispered Derrick.

I was reluctant to go up to the assistant as everyone was almost seated, but Derrick kept on insisting. Now when he gets really insistent like that I know that the Infiniteness is up to something. So I risked embarrassment, rose from my seat and approached the blond assistant to ask her his question. I braced myself for a tirade of rudeness, but none flowed forth. There was no rude outpouring from the blond assistant. She politely answered,

"Yes, that is right you are allowed to ask a question. In fact, no one has asked to do so as yet. So you, your husband and son will be the first in line. Just take these pieces of paper and write down your questions. I will read them and make sure that they are written clearly."

The blond assistant kindly explained that the Swami (holy teacher) who was assisting Amma reads the questions and interprets them for her. So the questions have to be clearly written. The cosmos was working it! My heart sung. We sat on the mat not too far from Amma's chair and began to formulate our questions. Cosmos was moving us closer to her.

Now a new and interesting dilemma presented itself. If you were told that you could ask God one question and one question only, what would it be? Well, to be told you could ask a Living Mother and Saint one question and one question only left the same dilemma. Derrick knew what his question would be.

"I want to ask Amma how I can help the world."
Kem Ra knew what his question would be too.

"I want to ask Amma does she do anything to help endangered animals."

Verbose writer that I am I could not think of one question to ask. I could only think of several pages of thoughts I would have liked addressed.

"Baby, I can't think of a question," I complained to Derrick.

"Ask her about your role with the Mother," he said.

Didn't know how to do that without writing an essay. But eventually I wrote,

"I have been given a calling by the Divine Mother. What can I do to embrace it more fully?"

I wasn't happy with the question. I was sure there was something so much more profound I could ask, but that was all I could come up with. The smiling assistant took our questions. I thought we were going to be asked to sit back in our seats until the right time to be called came up. Instead we were told that we would sit, where? Right by Amma's chair!

The blond assistant explained giving us elaborate instructions on what was going to happen next, what we needed to expect and do.

"Now, the proceedings are about to start. The Swami is going to sit right by Amma, slightly behind her. You all need to sit right up by the arm of her chair and snuggle up there. This is so she can see you and know you have a question. In between hugs the Swami will take a question and ask her it. She will give her response, and he will relay it to you. Then he will take another from you all, and follow the same procedure until all your questions are answered. Just be patient, you won't be forgotten."

I couldn't believe it. From being treated so badly and almost going home, we were now being ushered right up to Amma's chair!

"The big Mother obviously wants you to meet Amma," Derrick smiled.

I grinned happily back.

When people saw us being seated by Amma's chair there was suddenly a rush of those who now wanted to ask Amma questions. We snuggled safely by the chair, while the poor blond assistant was now flooded by request to ask questions. I admired the fact that she never lost her beautiful warm smile in the midst of the rushing throngs. We felt so blessed we were first in line for questions for the mat next to Amma's chair was only so big, and could therefore only seat a certain number of people.

"God how did we end up here, again?" I asked that unseen force that had conspired so hard for us to see her.

The event began with the Swami taking us all into a meditation. Everything became very still. So still all you could hear was the breath.

"Now you are going to breathe in. When you breathe out. You are going to release all the tension....."

His deep melodic voice went on like the gentle rolling waves of the sea. I found myself drifting away on it. His voice blended into the universe, and faded into primordial awareness. The only thing I remember him saying was

"see yourself embracing the Mother. Her light fills you up."

303

I could feel the light and a universal lightness came over me. I was filled with a bright whiteness. There was no one in the room. Just me and the light.

Then the voice faded and brought us all back to a room flooded with the hormones of peaceful indwellingness (if there is such a word). Soon after that Amma came in, or was she there before. Temporarily lost in a state of non-dualism I was a little confused on that fact.   Anyway, all I knew was that by the time I looked up and to the side of me at her chair, there she was seated on it. She was a good sized Indian woman with long dark hair. She was dark skinned and humble looking. Her smile was down to earth and yet so radiant. Do the two go together? They did with Amma.

Anytime I recount the whole incident I explain to my captive audience that I sat right at Amma's armpit, literally. For my face was right up on her arm. Sitting there something strange began to happen to me. As I sat in her presence a creeping sadness began to crawl and spread all over me until it sat on my shoulder with the weight of Mother Earth. My sadness turned into sorrow. I suddenly felt over burdened. I began to think of the responsibilities I had been given in regards to my duties with the Mother. I thought of the two titles I had been given. Why, I really don't know, but I did. Yeye Olomitutu, and Yeye Tayese. Mother who Heals with Cool Waters, and Mother Who Mends the World. In that moment they both felt too ancient and grandiose for the modern world I co – existed in and the modern girl I was. I thought about how much they bound me (often against all the logic of my mind) to a duty deeply rooted to a sacred contract, and past.

I became acutely aware of a dilemma that was always at the back of my mind. I had a sacred contract to help uplift humanity, but I was not wrapped in traditional African mud

304

cloth, I was not wrapped in a Sari, I was not wrapped in the orange and browns of a Buddhist's robes. I was just me. So what did this sacred contract really mean, how could just a normal girl like me carry it out?

My anguish deepened. My shoulders sagged. Suddenly the suffering of all the people in the world sat on them. Maybe I was picking up on Amma's empathetic feelings as she hugged those before her. I did not know what was causing these emotions to well up in me. I felt too tired and full of pain to try and figure it out. The pain washed over me, then I could feel only regret. Then came the wet hot tears rolling down my cheeks. I was filled with shame. I was ashamed of those darn tears. I chastised them in my mind and told them to go back from whence they came. But they wouldn't. They made a fool of me as they soon turned into into a sob that I had to stop from turning into a full belly wrenching wail.

Amma continued to hug people. My tears did not disturb her. She kept on hugging and blessing people. Derrick saw me struggling to not cry, and urged me on.

"It's good. Just cry. Let it out."

Let what out? I didn't know. But, let it out I did. Whatever it was that wanted to come out or was it come in? I let it be. Till it was all dried up. Then I wiped my face and nose clean.

The Swami sat almost directly behind me. It was time for a question. He asked Derrick's question first. Amma kept on hugging people as he explained it. She kept on hugging the sad, sorrowful and happy as she responded. We were expecting a small short response, but she kept on talking and talking. Eventually, she stopped. Then the Swami told Derrick this.

305

"Amma was telling a story. She said that once upon a time there was a man who wanted to help the whole world to change. So he set about doing this with great passion. But then after years of trying he noticed the world was still the same. He was quite tired and disappointed. So he decided I will not try to help the whole world I will try to help my own people to change for the better. He did this for years and years. The more he tried was the more no one changed and the more tired and disappointed he grew. This man was quite tired now. He was very sad too. Then he hit on another idea. I know I will try and change my State. By now the man had little energy but he tried to do this any way, but people did not change. Now the man was very very tired, and very very disappointed. But he did not want to give up, so the man said wearily but still passionately.

"I will try to help my family to change for the better."

This is what will be successful. Even his family did not change for the better. All tired, frustrated, angry, bitter and sad the man felt as though he had been defeated. He felt as though he had not helped to change the world to a better one. Then in all his tiredness, all his frustration and all his sadness he suddenly had a realization. "I know I will try and change myself for the better"

The Swami went onto to explain,

"Amma says the only way to create change in the world is to create the change in yourself first. This is how you help the world."

Derrick and all of us were very touched by Amma's response.

After another twenty minutes of Amma hugging individuals it was time for Kem Ra's question. She continued hugging the people as the Swami asked the question. She had a big smile and looked at Kem Ra. Her response was not as long as Derrick's but was just as considered. The Swami told Kem Ra,

"Amma says she has not done anything for endangered animals. But now she will think about doing a project to help the dogs in India who are quite abused."

Kem Ra was so pleased with the answer. He loves the idea of being a Planet Revolutionary and felt that he had helped to create a change in the world.

Another twenty or so minutes went by and the Swami asked Amma my question. She kept on hugging people. Her response was quite short, but once again very considered. The Swami said,

"Amma said concentrate on the feminine principle. On the aspect of Motherhood. Expand this notion beyond pregnancy, and spread it. She says, "this is what I am blessing. This is what I back. This is what will be successful."

It was not the answer I expected. I had no real response in mind. Yet, somehow that response moved me to tears again. I felt as though I had met the Mother. I had that same feeling when I had met Susan Wenger. After our questions had been answered the smiling blond assistant was still smiling as she approached us.

"It's a very moving experience isn't it?"

We all nodded.

"You all need to go back to your chairs and queue up for your Darshana now."

God smiled on us again. We were not too far back in the queue. I felt that I had all the experiences I needed. That was until I had that hug that drew me into a realm of endless darkness, where there was no thing. I could see nothing. Nothing separated me from the nothing. I was just there. I just was. It was cozy there in that nothingness too. It was not what one would expect in a place where there is nothing. It was all warm and welcoming. It felt homely like someone had lit a hearth fire and my mother was baking that favorite thing I loved to eat as a child. It was nothingness like I never felt it before.

It felt as though I was there not in body, not even in soul, just there in the embrace. A stream of consciousness, a stream of light, a stream of something I could not find the words for. When Amma released me, I squinted my eyes against the artificial light in the bright hall. I was back from nothingness, but nothingness was, it felt, forever inside of me. For an eternity. I realized it had always been there. It was always there.

Derrick and Kem Ra had their own experiences. After the hug Derrick seemed quite transformed. His face was glowing. Kem Ra was very quiet and still for the rest of the day. We also got a chance to give Amma the award. She conveyed to her assistant that she was very pleased to accept it. We asked if we could take a picture of her accepting the award, but this was not permitted. They did not allow pictures to be taken of Amma. We respected this, and went on our way to enjoy the rest of the day.

On the way home I felt honored that universe had conspired for us to meet Amma, just how it had conspired for us to meet Susan Wenger. Soon after our Darshana hugs we went and ate some Indian Dahl from the hotel's Cafeteria. Then we headed onto site see Washington. I stood by the Potomac River for quite some time staring into its large, brown and quite dirty looking water. Despite how it looked there was something undeniably mighty and powerful about how it carried itself. I offered gratitude to it for all its hard work, and a prayer for all the waterways.

The drive back home was quietly pleasant. The first few nights after getting back home I had two profound dreams. I wrote them both in my diary, as I did with most of my dreams. The first was about a Native American woman and a feather. I wrote in my diary,

I ended up in this house visiting this woman. There were all these men working on this construction site and she looked at me and said,
    "I can't find the feather."
    I asked, "what feather?"
    She said, "it's a red feather. A small one."
    I said, "I keep on seeing feathers. What is it for?"
    She said, "the men are dying because I cannot find the feather."
    I looked on the chair where she sat and I found a baby feather. Then I found more feathers. She chose the baby bird feather. She said she was happy because the feather would save her whole culture. She sat in the garden and started sewing a new outfit. I tried to watch but she wouldn't let me. She said I must wear a dress before she showed me how to prepare for the feather.
    I told her, "I don't have a dress."
    She said, "if you look you will find one."
    But I told her I had tried.
    Then she showed me this beautiful leather waist coat that she would wear with her dress. I was upset because I had no nice clothes. Then I found myself walking behind her and she had the feather held high.
    She walked towards where the men were working and it was as though the feather was going to rescue them all from dying.

You want to know an interesting thing? I kept on finding baby eagle feathers for months after that dream. Every time myself and Olu went for a walk we found white fluffy eagle feathers. Then one day I was in the two acre yard of his parents and found a large Kestrel feather.

The second dream I entitled "The Sacred Verse of Joy". I wrote in my diary.

"Dreamed that in the middle of my dream there was a sacred verse of joy and Amma was standing on top of it. I said to Derrick "look we don't have joy. The verse of joy is right here in the middle of my dream."

After those two dreams I found myself reading a book by Sylvia Brown. I found her past life regression technique interesting, and decided to try it. Putting myself in a deep regressive meditation I fell asleep and had this dream,

"I went to a place called the Hall of Tones. It was indeed beautiful. Beyond all earthly description. There seemed to be a lot of gold it was made of, but not gold in the human sense. It glistened ethereally. I sat waiting on a bench and someone came to see me. I asked for my personal mantra. The one Slyvia speaks about in her book. The one that exist for everyone. They let me know that I had already received it at the Amma event. I asked what is it, they said "Om Amma". It made perfect sense but I was a little disappointed because I was expecting something amazing. But then again, I guess that was something amazing

I then found myself in a place called The Hall Of Records. Everything was very ethereal down to the books. That surprised me. I thought they would be more solid looking. There was a screen. I asked to see my records. I was told I did not have permission to see my records. So I started going. Then I was sat down again to be given a little snapshot .

I was told I was a great teacher on that side and my job was to be a great teacher again in this lifetime. They really wanted me to understand this.

I felt myself drifting and then I saw this beautiful hut like structure and I was sewing. They said that on that side I sewed and made beautiful things. Then I saw another hut and this one I was studying in it. They said I studied and researched a lot because of my role   as   a   teacher.

Then I was shown a Hut of Gifts. They said that this hut was filled with all my gifts. I could glimpse a little in the gift hut and I saw lots of laughing children as I was doing a demonstration for them.

Then there was another hut and it was called The Hut of Rejuvenation and I was in there. Through some high level process my womb was being scanned and there were some dark blotches. They said I needed some healing in my womb. They did the healing on my womb."

There was a lot more to that dream. Interestingly enough a few months after that experience I became pregnant with Omololu after 40 days of fasting to end fifteen years of infertility.

After the dreams the dance of oneness seemed to make its presence felt again. The works of yoga sage B.K.S Iyengar fell in my lap in the form of his book "The Light of Yoga" I liked how he likened the true self to water.   He reveals the true self can be experienced "before the waters got ruffled"…. "When you ruffle the waters, you create. You create everything in the manifest." For "the yogi is journeying in the opposite direction from the world of things that are endless, joyful, baffling and unending, back to the stillness before the waves were ruffled. Because he wants to answer the question "Who am I?". "What is the source of my being?" "Is there a God I can know?"

He then explains what Yoga is,

"yoga is a ladder we ascend, but whereas a real ladder, when you are on the seventh (dhyana) rung, all your weight is on that rung. In yoga your weight is still equally on the proceeding rungs that have aided your ascent. Should anyone of those crack you fall."

As I re-read his words I thought of how much compassion, love, selflessness, and the laws of Dharma were important rungs of the ladder we could not afford to forget. For leaning on all the rungs of the ladder, deciding to take that lofty journey inward BKS Iyengar explains, we return to

"the innermost core of being, to the bliss body or divine body that resides within us all. The place where our soul lives and where we glimpse the universal oneness that embraces us all. This vision of our divinity forces us to once again to return to the nature of our humanity."

Giving gratitude to the water that
sustains us on day we went to see Catawba Lilies

The Catawba Lilies
struggling to survive

ETURA MEJI

Girl: Mother what of Etura Meji?
Mother: Yes, in Etura Meji one is often reminded of how truth will eventually overcome falsehood, and how abundance came to the world.
Girl: Mother tell me a story from Etura Meji.
Mother: Well one day Truth and Falsehood were having a big argument up there in heaven. So Etura Meji solved the problem by quoting them a poem,

I threw a missile;
And it hit a trickster;
Who made a long dress;
To conceal his treachery.
Whoever hides to practice;
Wickedness against others;
Will have evil endangering him openly.

After listening for a while. Truth and Falsehood began to argue again between themselves. Truth argued that he was more powerful than Falsehood. Falsehood argued that he was the more powerful one. Etura Meji listened to this whole argument and when the heat had settled a bit he said,

314

"Falsehood is transient and ephemeral. Truth is slow and weak, but it will always overcome Falsehood."

Then he sang these simple lines to the two:

"No matter how powerful wickedness is,
righteousness will always be victorious in the long run".

After Amma Osun and Durga seemed to leap from their primal waters, take their bow and begin to join the thread of time on their weaving looms. The unraveling of the ball of wool would take me months and months of reading, analysis, and meditative contemplations. I suffered from months of terrible head banging frustrations, sleeplessness, and feelings of inadequacy, but Durga, Osun, and all the Mother Goddesses seemed intent to arise from the waters from which they had been buried and forgotten. Over those months my notes were profuse along with my migraines. However, even in the midst of being heavily pregnant with Omo I allowed the mystery of the Mothers to unravel and weave themselves back together again.

Durga and Osun

Durga was quite a mighty intimidating figure. When she stood up you could not deny or rebuke her presence. I discovered that Durga was often referred to respectfully as Maa Durga, which reflected her role as the world Shakti, and Mother of the Universe. Hers was a compassionate fierce kind of love. One that kept the world in balance when threatened with chaos. I remembered early on in the journey how hers and Osun's stories of saving the world had caught my attention. They appeared to be a hotbed of similarities. Now Durga and the electrical current of the waters of time pushed me forward. Now was the time to read Maa Durga's story in full multi-colored detail.

The Gods were having real problems with the evil Mahishasur, a demon who was destroying the world. They all went to the creator Brahma to find out what they could do. They discovered all three

316

aspects of the creator God: Vishnu, Shiva and Brahma at Baikuntha, the place where Vishnu lay on the giant snake Anantya Naag. When the three aspects of the creative force were approached and informed about the going ons of Mahishasur they became so angry that a fierce light emerged from each of their bodies. From that light emerged Durga.

When Durga emerged she made it very clear that she was the form of the supreme Brahman and she was the creator of all the Gods. She then announced that she had come to help save the world from the demon, and the Gods were being blessed with her compassion.

It is said that when Mahishasura saw Durga he underestimated her powers.

"How can a woman kill me-Mahishasur the one who defeated the God trinity."

Durga obviously found this hilarious as it caused her to roar with laughter. As she did so an earthquake trembled the earth. Well, yes Mahasura was afraid.

Needless to say a battle ensued and Durga, after much battling, defeats the demon. When she has finished defeating him she turns into her gentle side Parvati. It is also said that at one point in the battle that Durga wounded the demon but was to soon find that the situation was worsened. For every drop of blood that spills from Raktabija, a clone of the demon became reproduced. Until the battlefield is filled with his duplicates. Durga is now in serious trouble so she summons up her form of Kali to combat the demons.

Kali came from her forehead armed with a sword and noose. She was decorated with a garland of skulls, clad in a tiger's skin. Her roars filled the sky. She destroys Raktabija and all the duplicate demons. It is said that Kali becomes drunk on the blood of her victims which makes her dance with a frenzy. In her fury she apparently almost steps on her poor old husband Shiva who is lying amongst the corpse. Shiva attracts her attention. She sticks out her tongue in shock then she turns into the more gentle Parvati.

317

I compared each part of Durga's classical heroic story to the original wisdom story, that had marked the beginning of my journey, of Osun saving the world. The similarities were painfully obvious. The more ticks of confirmation I put on my little table was the more I could feel the warm tingle of certainty fill me up.

Osun	Durga
Osun saves the world√	Durga saves the world√
Osun is asked to do this by the male Gods when the world is on the brink of destruction√	Durga is asked to do this by the male Gods when the world is on the brink of destruction√
The men try to solve the problem first without consulting with Osun. √	The men try to save the world first without consulting Durga first.√
When their plan to save the world without Osun fails they discover the solution lies in asking her for help. √	When they go away and contemplate what to do they manifest Durga from their light.
Osun is declared to be the Mother of Wisdom by Oludamare (God) √	In enters Durga. She makes it clear that although she came out of the God's leela she is the great mother who was self begotten.

After so many ticks of confirmation I was made to think of Osun's fierce side. For it is common to hear Osun devotees say,

"Osun, you don't want to mess with her. Osun don't mess, you know."

In fact, many of Osun ritual implements, which only the initiate gets to see, includes: swords, handcuffs and the likes. In her book, "Osun Segeesi" author Valeria Badejo shares verses from the Osun sacred songs. One verse praises, "the one who, in flowing forcefully along, hits her body against the grass, the one who in flowing furiously along hits her body against the rock." Badejo says that this verse illustrates Osun's two motherly sides as first the nurturer and secondly as the defender.

Then there was Oya, the warrior Goddess of transformation and wind. I saw her as part of the Osun Composite of Goddesses.

Parvati – Durga's Gentle Side

Parvati is the gentle side of Durga. She floated into my realm of awareness straight after Durga finished her battle. There she was all gentle, soft, and waiting. She was Durga once the battle of the Demons has been fought and won. I wanted to find out more about her. (Of course I did, isn't that how the cosmos works? Gets you all curious about something it wants you to look deeper into). I wanted to see if there was anything about this side of Durga that reminded me of Osun. With her beautiful waist hung with sacred beads she was more than a willing participant in my curiosity. She began by showing me her relationship with Shiva, the God of the Universal Dance. Her devotional ability to transcend into the world of pure unadulterated love is what seemed to mark her out. Through

319

her transcendence of all that was worldly she was able to access the coveted prize of wisdom.

I imagined a traditional poet writing these words in praise of her,

Where oust thou?

Shiva seeks you in his embrace from which the salvation of

the world is born.

From a child Parvati was interested in the stories of Shiva. She was filled with memories of her past life as his wife Sati. As she grew into a young woman her love for Shiva and the memory of their union led Parvati to do what is known as tapas (austerities). There is no true love that is not tested. Shiva decided to test Parvati's devotion by disguising himself as a person who would criticize him. Parvati's love and desire for Shiva was undeterred. Impressed Shiva decides she is indeed the woman to marry. After the marriage Parvati moves to Mount Kailash, the residence of Shiva.

In the Goddess oriented Shakti text of the Hindus, Parvati is said to transcend even Shiva and is identified as the Supreme Being, itself. Together Parvati and Shiva represent the Power of Asceticism, the attainment of balance and self realization that brings spiritual power. Then there is the reflection of a marital relationship based on the laws of balance which radiates in its midst the mirror of true transcendent love.

Together Parvati and Shiva have a son Ganesh. Personified as an elephant he is widely revered as the "Remover of Obstacles". There are several story versions as to how Ganesh makes his appearance. There is the story of Ganesh being molded from turmeric paste by Parvati.

Once, while Parvati wanted to take a bath, there were no attendants around to guard her and stop anyone from accidentally entering the house. Hence she created an image of a boy out of turmeric paste which she prepared to cleanse her body with, and infused life into it, and thus Ganesha was born. Parvati ordered Ganesha not to allow anyone to enter the house and Ganesha obediently followed his mother's orders. After a while Shiva returned and tried to enter the house, Ganesha stopped him. Shiva was infuriated and severed Ganesha's head with his trishula (trident). When Parvati came out and saw her son's lifeless body, she was very angry and sad. She demanded that Shiva restore Ganesha's life at once. Unfortunately, Shiva's trishula was so powerful that it had hurled Ganesha's head so far off that it could not be found. Finally, an elephant's head was attached to Ganesha's body, bringing him back to life. Still upset, Parvati demanded her son be made head of the celestial armies and worshipped by everyone before beginning any activity. The gods accepted this condition.

Another story that caught my eye, for good reasons is the one of the world being in trouble and Parvati gallantly deciding to help save the day.

One day Parvati the daughter of the mountain King, Himalaya, retreated high up on the hills to practice severe austerities. A tyrant – titan named Taraka had usurped the world. The prophecies said only a son of the High god Siva could overthrow him. However, Shiva was the pattern god of Yoga and was aloof, alone and withdrawn into meditation. It was impossible that Shiva could beget a son while in this state.

Parvati was determined to help the world and decided that she would match Shiva in his meditation. She too became aloof, alone and withdraw into meditation and went deep within her soul. She fasted naked beneath the fiery sun. Her once beautiful body shriveled to a brittle construction of bones, her skin became leathery and hard. Her hair became matted and wild. While her soft liquid eyes burned.

One day a priest youth arrived and asked her why would anyone so beautiful destroy herself with such torture. She replied,

"my desire is Shiva, the Highest Object. Shiva is a god of solitude and unshakeable concentration. I therefore practice these austerities to move him from his state of balance and bring him to me in love."

The young boy told her Shiva was a destroyer. He said that Shiva liked to meditate and dance amongst the dead. However, Parvati was unmoved and said.

"He is beyond the mind of such as you. A pauper, but the fountainhead of wealth; terrifying but the source of grace; snake garlands or jewels of garlands he can assume or put off at will; How should he have been born, when he is the creator of the uncreated! Shiva is my love."

After that amazing speech the boy takes of his disguise and it is Shiva who appears.

I noted that the original Osun story of her saving the world was not only similar to Durga's own, but also to Parvati's. For when the world is on the verge of extinction and the male God's eventually turn to Osun's wisdom to save the day. Pregnant by the God of Wisdom through immaculate conception, she reveals she will save the world only if the child within her stomach is a boy.

One of the priests present uses his powers to turn the baby who is a girl into a boy. So Osun has a boy who is eventually called Esu Etura, *the One who Opens the Way*. It is Esu that the Yoruba's honor before any activity is undertaken. All his qualities are similar to Ganesh's.

322

I make a mental note – just like Osun, Parvati has to have a boy child with Shiva in order for the world to be saved. It is a child made through divine concentration. Once again I wondered how the stories of the three Mother Goddesses: Osun, Durga and Parvati could be so similar. One Goddess was all the way in India and the other all the way in West Africa.

I also found Parvati's divine appearance to be of interest too. As the daughter of a Mountain God, Himalayan. She has three eyes: two normal eyes and a third eye, and is referred to as, the dark one, as well as Gauri "the fair one". It seemed that most researchers were confused by her two different complexions. Her hair, like Shiva's, is matted and like him she also wears the crescent moon in her locks. The items she carries around include a: mirror, bell, citron and rosary.

I found Parvati's energy beautiful like a breath of fresh air. The information about her exhilarated me. For in her devotional love, in her stories, in her objects I could clearly see Osun. I reviewed my information on Parvati and made a few written notes of the similarities between her and Osun:

Devotional relationship with husband: Osun's husband is Orunmila, the God of Wisdom. The two have a very close relationship of profound devotional love, just like that between Parvati and Shiva. They are depicted together often. Both Osun and Orunmila practice the oracle system and helps the lives of others through their divine wisdom.

The Birth of a Son to Save the World: The first story I encountered of Osun helping to save the world involved her saying she

323

would help if she gave birth to a son. Osun gives birth to a son. Even though Orunmila is the father, the son is born through Immaculate Conception. In the story of Parvati saving the prophecies predict she could help to save the world if she gives birth to a son for Shiva. Like Osun she gives birth to a son through an act that amounts to Immaculate Conception.

The Son Who Removes All Obstacles: Osun's son is called Esu Etura. He is the God Esu, who is said to be the "clearer of the way" and the "Guardian of the crossroads". He is honored before any activity takes place. Parvati's son is called Ganesh and his name means, "the remover of obstacles". He too is honored before any activities takes place.

The Son Who Has a Rat: Orunmila, the father of Esu, has as his famous symbol the Rat. It is interesting to note that Ganesh has as his symbol the rat too.

Oh Ye My Father, "The Mountain God": As I recalled my June 2008 trip to Nigeria I remembered that in the Grove we went to one of Osun's main shrines. Opposite the ornately carved shrine door was a big grey rock. I remembered that we were informed that we must touch our head to it before we entered the shrine, which was totally of limit to visitors. Out of curiosity I asked our host Osunkolode the meaning of the rock. He said that it was "Oke" the mountain God. I didn't ask any further questions about Oke, however now I was excited to note that Parvati's father was The Mountain God, Himalayan.

"How Fair is My Complexion?": Many researchers are confused as to why Parvati is referred to as "the black one" and as the "fair one". Making a note of the complexion issue I remembered how I too was always puzzled by something to

do with Osun. I noticed when I had been to Nigeria, and seen her on temple walls she was often depicted as light brown. I never understood why this was the case. On the walls of a host we had stayed with, who happened to be the cousin of the Ooni (King) of Nigeria and his High priest Osun was painted a very very light brown.

Their Sacred Objects: Like Parvati, the bell and mirror are very important sacred items to Osun. Parvati has the rosary she holds, while Osun priesthood have a set of important beads connected to the Goddess they wear around their necks.

In the light of Parvati and with the information I had collected thus far in the journey I concluded that the fairness of these Goddesses could be connected with the Milky Way. Now Hathor was the Egyptian personification of the Milky Way. In passing I had more than noticed that Osun and Hathor also had many many similarities. Both were the Goddesses who gave and encompassed: Fertility, children wisdom, healing, transcendent love, joy, laughter, music, social, life refinement, sacred rivers and Primordial waters (Hathor was closely connected with the Nile, Osun with the Osun River). Both also had a gentle and fierce side. The fierce side of Hathor was Sekhmet, and the fierce side of Osun was hidden within herself ready to pounce out when needed. I also saw it as being embodied within the Goddess Oya who had many similar traits to Sekhmet.

The more I thought about the similarities between Osun and Hathor was the more I realized that Durga and Parvati had the same identifying traits with Hathor too. I felt a tingle fly up my veins. A tingle that told me I was on to something.

325

Lakshmi and Saraswati – The Beautiful Daughters Of Parvati and Durga

The force of the electrical current, didn't let up. It continued to pull me along. I was led to the next two Goddesses – Lakshmi and Saraswati. They patiently waited in all their fineries (and they were fine Goddesses indeed) for me to discover them. Discover them I did for they were both the daughters of Parvati. Being the daughters of Parvati I logically concluded that Durga was also their mother, for Parvati was just Durga in restful peaceful repose.

As my mind continued to pick through the tangled pieces of Goddess wool, and Osun continued to act like the Greek language which allowed the ancient language of Hieroglyphics to be at last translated on the Rosette stone - I posed to myself this question,

"If Lakshmi and Saraswati are Parvati and Durga's daughters would they too show clear connections to Osun?"

The electrical current surged in me and bucked me forward to find the answer. It was through Lakshmi that the force of the flowing waters picked up further pace. Opening me up to the forever growing and clarifying realization - all the Goddesses in all cultures are aspects of the same universal Mother Goddess, the archetypal cosmic force that leads to the ultimate path of true liberation. For the language of liberation was right there in all their symbols, stories, and descriptions.

Lakshmi

Lakshmi danced, waiting for me, as she made festivity at the Durga Puja festival. She obviously wanted me to notice and pay attention to the event she had graced. Why? The answer became clearer as I took a closer at the whole scene that unfolded before me.

The Durga Puja, is a renowned festival celebrated twice a year between April to May and then September to October. It is according to Swami Sivananda, the founder of Sivananda Yoga,

" the greatest of all Hindu festivals in which God is adored as Mother."

He explains that the festival is to "propitiate Shakti, the Goddess in her aspect as Power to bestow upon man all wealth, prosperity, knowledge (both sacred and secular), and all other potent powers." The aim of worship is to ultimately link oneself to her energy. According to Swami Sivananda,

"truly speaking all beings in the universe are Shakti – worshippers, whether they are aware of it or not. For there is no one who does not love and long for power in some form or other. Physicist and scientists have now proved that everything is pure, imperishable energy. This energy is only a form of divine Shakti which exists in every form."

For nine days women and men go through the stages of renewal and evolution to realize the God within them. They go from the state of Individualization to the state of Self realization (enlightenment). In the first three days of the festival Shakti is honored in her form as Durga, Durga the Terrible. Her role is to annihilate our impurities and the baser animal qualities we possess (thus her story of her war against the Demons).

The second three days the aspect Shakti as Lakshmi is worshipped. It is here that I learned about who and what Lakshmi is. For her name is the Sanskrit word for "goal" or "aim". She is the goal and place we all need to be aiming at. She is considered to be the Goddess of wealth, prosperity (both spiritual and material), light, wisdom, fortune, fertility, generosity, courage, beauty, grace, and charm. The worshipper can only get to that after they have spent days conquering their ugly side. Ultimately Lakshmi embodied the spiritual world known as Vaikunta which is considered heaven. She is the wealth and heaven that resides within all of us if only we can let go of "ugly".

Reading about the Durga Puja made me think back to Diwali, "The Festival of Lights" I had experienced in Trinidad. At the end of 2007, myself, mum and Kem Ra drove to a wealthy Indian community to witness Diwali. There was no electricity on in the streets, the light came from hundreds of small oil butter lamps lining the streets and the paths of homes. I remembered standing in the middle of the candle lit streets, feeling like a boat that was being guided in the right direction by a ceaseless tide of illuminated ancient existence.

Diwali marks the beginning of the Hindu New Year. It is said that the lights are put out to Lakshmi so that she will bless the individual and their household. When she does they also obtain "pure divine qualities" and are now able to obtain the light of supreme wisdom.

Now the symbols of Lakshmi are interesting. This Goddess has an array of different ones. With a complexion of coral, seated on a lotus, she has eighteen arms. Each one carries one of the following: a string of beads, battle axe, mace, arrow, thunderbolt, lotus, bow, water pot, cudgel, lance, sword, shield, conch, bell, wine cup, trident, noose and the discus. She is often depicted as residing on the great snake with her husband, Shiva. Who is the husband of Durga, Kali and Parvati too. The snake in ancient mythologies often symbolizes divine wisdom. Pitcher of nectar in one hand and constantly ringing a bell in the other.

The following story indicates that immortality can only be obtained by acquiring the qualities of Laksmi's purity.
In Hinduism Devas (gods) and asuras (demons) were both mortal at one time. Amrit, the divine nectar that would give immortality could

only be obtained by churning the Kshirsagar (Ocean of Milk). The devas and asuras both sought immortality and decided to churn the Kshirsagar. With the devas on one side and the asuras on the other, the samudra manthan commenced. Vishnu incarnated as Kurma, the tortoise, on whom was placed a mountain as a churning pole, and Vasuki, the great venom-spewing serpent, was wrapped around it and used to churn the ocean. A host of divine celestial objects came up during the churning. Among these, importantly, was Goddess Lakshmi, the daughter of the king of the milky ocean. The last to come up was the Amrit. With this, the avatar of Kurma, the tortoise, ended. Vishnu then took up the form of a beautiful maiden to distract the asuras and gave immortality to the devas.

The Similarities of Lakshmi and Osun

The electrical currents of time pulsated breathlessly through me, lighting me up like Diwali as the Goddess lineage unfolded herself. There was still the third day of the Durga Puja to investigate, but Lakshmi smiled and would not let me go from her Lotus presence (her name also means "Goddess of the Lotus) until I put my mental observations of her and Osun onto paper. I did so with trembling tingly fingers:

Qualities of the Goddess: Lakshmi like Osun is the bringer of wealth, love, wisdom, fertility, beauty, grace, charm refinement and generoistiy.

Symbols and the Goddess: Like Osun Laksmi has weapons, the conch, the water pot, the bell, the coral bead, and nectar (Osun's nectar is honey). It is interesting that Laksmi is often shown with a pitcher of nectar and ringing a bell. The bell is very important in the worship of Osun, as well as honey.

Festival of Lights: Laksmi has the festival of lights. In her river festival Osun also has a festival of lights where the 16 lamps are lit to for her.

Milky Way: As the daughter of the King of the Milky Way Laksmi has an association with the Milky Way, like I believe Osun does.

I made a special note on Hathor, Lakshmi, and Osun:

Like Parvati, and the gentle side of Osun, Laksmi has the exact same characteristics of the gentle side of Hathor (the fiercer compassionate side being Sekhmet), (It was a little bit later on in the journey that I was to discover that Hathor was also associated with the Lotus flower).

Saraswati

After Lakshmi left me, Saraswati welcomed me dripping in painted enticing yellow, and jewels. She announced herself to be another aspect of Shakti who is worshipped on the third cycle of days of the Durga Puja. Now the aspirant has acquired purity and spiritual wealth they can now access divine wisdom in the form of Saraswati. For Saraswathi is the Mother of the Sacred Vedas. She is the Goddess of knowledge and arts. Known as the Guardian deity in Buddhism who upholds the teachings of the Buddha she offers protection and assistance to Practitioners.

Saraswati name is a Sanskrit word which means: Saras – flow; wati – woman. As a result Saraswati means flowing woman. Saraswati is the name of the river and of the Goddess. Just as Osun is the name of the river and the Goddess. In fact, in the Rigveda the Saraswati is said to be the best of all the rivers. There she is called *ámbitame náditame dévitame sárasvati*, "best mother, best river, best goddess". Other verses of praise also refer to the river as the white flowing river 'with golden wheels'. Like many rivers in the sacred Rig Veda the Sarasvati is likened to a cow who it is said she pours, "milk and ghee".

As the Goddess of Divine Wisdom she is also the Goddess who represents all forms of cosmic consciousness, music, arts creativity, fertility and power. Her dress code also aligns her to absolute truth and joy for her colors are white and also yellow. Sitting on a lotus flower she is often depicted with four arms which hold the four aspects of the human personality involved in learning: mind, intellect, alertness, and ego. These four hands also represent the four Vedas, the primary sacred books for the Hindu. The Vedas in turn, represent the 3 forms of literature: poetry, prose and music. In each hand you will often see a book which represents prose, a garland of crystal, music, a pot of sacred water. Saraswati's book represents all universal knowledge and symbolizes her perfection of science and the scriptures; her rosary of crystals symbolize the power of meditation and spirituality; the pot of sacred water represents her creative and purification powers; while her musical instrument represents her perfection of all arts and sciences.

Saraswati is often depicted with a Swan at her feet which is offered a mixture of milk and water. She is sometimes seen with a peacock next to her or sitting on one. It is said to represent her teachings of the importance of not being concerned with external appearance but with the eternal truth of the matter. Also she is strongly associated with honey. Honey is often offered to her as a symbol of perfect knowledge.

SARASWATI AND OSUN

Well, when Saraswati was finished with me I too could not help but smile. For in her were so many of Osun's symbols. Once again, I was left wondering – how comes? How were these Goddesses so connected? I put my mental notes down onto physical paper:

Owner of Wisdom: Saraswati plays a very important role as a keeper of Wisdom and the protector of it. Osun is, in the original story I encountered of her saving the world, specifically said by God to be the one he gave all the wisdom of the world to. Then there was the whole thing about Osun being the founder of the bag of wisdom (which albeit was stolen by her husband Orunmila, the God of Wisdom). Like Saraswati she is very much the guardian of Wisdom. In one of her stories, Orunmila (the God of Wisdom) has to go away. He goes away for quite a long time. It is Osun who keeps the whole community going by providing wisdom through divination for them.

Implements: Saraswati and Osun's implements are closely matched. For like Osun Saraswati has: honey, a pot of water, the peacock, the colors yellow and white (both are the two primary colors of Osun. White is what she wears when she is representing spiritual purity).

The River that is Goddess and Water: Both Saraswati and Osun are said to be women whose bodies became the flowing waters. Saraswati's name means the "Flowing woman", and according to author Valeria Badejo Osuns name means "one that seeps out".

Milky Way Complexions: In terms of complexion both Saraswati and Osun are depicted of a lighter shade. Thus they seem associated with the Milky Way. The conviction of this assumption is further deepened by Saraswati's strong resemblance to the Goddess Hathor. In fact Saraswati, Parvati, and Lakshmi seem to be synonymous with the Goddess Hathor.

Special Note: Saraswati is associated with the cow whose milk is the nourishing river. Hathor is also associated with the cow. As Nut it is said her udders produce the milk which nourishes the world in the form of the Milky Way (which is the Nile in the Sky).

Ganga

Before my journey with Water and the Goddess I knew only Ganga amongst the Hindu Goddesses. So naturally this Goddess trail made me think about how did Ganga fit into this unfolding picture, if at all? Was she part of what I was now to call the Durga Composite of Goddesses?

Ganga was to show me that she was. For she was none other than Parvati's sister. Her name, like her niece Saraswati, was the name of the Goddess and that of a river's. The identity of the two being inseparable. Ironically, in this instance the niece seemed to be older than the aunty. For the Saraswati river is seen as the older of the two rivers.

Ganga let me know that she represented liberation from the cycle of life and death. This explained why Hindus throw the ashes of their family in the waters of the Ganges - so that their loved ones can go to heaven. Like her niece Lakshmi Ganga has a festival of lights dedicated to her. In the Loy

Krathong festival of Thailand, candlelit floats are released onto the waterways to honor both the Buddha and herself. This yearly gesture is said to bring good fortune and to wash away the sins of the individual.

As a river it is said the sacred Ganges is the only river that travels from all three worlds: heaven, earth and the netherworld. This places the Goddess in a special role where she joins all three worlds together in unity. Her role and position in them is illustrated by the following story:

One day there was a King named Sagara who magically acquired sixty thousand sons. One day, King Sagar performed a ritual of worship for the good of the kingdom. An important part of the ritual was a horse which had been stolen by Indra.

Sagara sent all his sons all over the earth to search for the horse. They found it in the nether-world (or Underworld) next to the meditating sage Kapila. They believed that the sage had stolen the horse and began to throw insults at him. This disturbed the sage's meditation. For the first time in years he opened his eyes and looked at the sons of Sagara. Unfortunately, for Sagara's sixty thousand sons they were all burnt to death.

Well, the souls of the sons of Sagara wandered as ghosts since their final rites had not been performed. Bhagiratha, a descendant of Sagara, son of Dilip, learned of the fate of his relatives he vowed to bring Ganga down to Earth so that her waters could cleanse their souls and release them to heaven.

He proceeded to pray to Brahma that Ganga should come down to Earth. Brahma agreed, and he ordered Ganga to go down to the Earth and then on to the nether regions so that the souls of Bhagiratha's ancestors would be able to go to heaven. Ganga felt that this was insulting and decided to sweep the whole earth away as she fell from the heavens. Alarmed, Bhagiratha prayed to Shiva that he break up Ganga's descent.

Well, Ganga ended up landing in Shiva's head. But Shiva calmly trapped her in his hair and let her out in small streams. The touch of Shiva further sanctified Ganga. As Ganga travelled to the nether-worlds, she created a different stream to remain on Earth to help purify unfortunate souls there.

Now even though Parvati is the mother of Ganesha, and birthed him by immaculate conception. Ganga is also his mother. One story that explains how Ganga is also the mother of Ganesha says that Parvati created Ganesha out of her bodily impurities and endowed the image with life by immersing it in the sacred waters of the Ganges.

Ganga's iconography includes a full pot of water which represents the universal healing power of the womb. She also has a crocodile mount known as Makara, a hybrid between a crocodile and the tail of the fish.

As I read about Ganga she of course ensures that I once again put my mental notes about her similarities with Osun onto paper. As I do so, I cannot help but feel that there was no more boundaries between the Dreamtime and the world I viewed with my open eyes. The two had become one.

The electrical current that was pulling me along, had me more and more swimming in a world of mythological figures of Goddesses, the live archetypal forces of Jung's world. The forces which shaped our very existence. How this was possible I really didn't know. I wrestled with this unsettling thought and reality as I wrote my comparison notes between Ganga and Osun down.

Comparison Between Ganga and Osun

Goddess and River: Just like her niece Saraswati, Ganga was the name for the Goddess and river. This was the same as in the case of Osun and the mighty river named after her, The Osun river.

The Joining of Three Worlds: The same way Ganga joins all three worlds. I remember Chief Popoola informing me that Osun was the only Irunmole (being of light) who travelled constantly between heaven and earth. In fact she was a being of light who often personified herself in the form of humans and water. So she too was seen as the Water Goddess, Divine Holy Mother who joined all the worlds together.

Purification Rites of Water: Both Ganga and Osun's waters are seen as highly purifying and healing. I remember how I felt when I bathed in the Osun river and vibrated with the light of its waters.

Mother of the World: Like Osun, Ganga is seen as the Mother. She mothers all her children and looks after them with her healing waters. Thus why Ganga is often referred to as Ma Ganga.

Goddess's Iconography: Osun has the symbol of the fish and crocodile as her animals because both belong to the waters. Ganga too has these symbols which are combined into the hybrid animal Makara. Like Osun, Ganga has the full pot of water that heals all worldly angst and needs.

The Beautiful Dancing Girl of Mohenjo – Daro

Who is the Dancing Girl of Mohenjo – Daro? After I was spent from the roll call of Indian goddesses that unfolded their lineage and likeness to Mother Osun. The maddening questions tumbled over themselves in my journalistic and spiritual mind: How comes Osun and the Mother Goddesses of India were so similar?" How did these Goddesses travel across the waters? Did the Goddesses travel from Africa to India or was it from India to Africa? My head grew sore with over thinking these questions. Also how comes there were so many similarities between Osun, the Hindu Goddesses and Hathor?

One day as all these questions played havoc on my mind and tugged at my spirit I idly played on my computer.

As I did so, I keyed in various key search words and up popped the image of The Dancing Girl of Mohenjo – daro. She appeared in the form of a tiny statute which showed her off as slim, dark and elegant. I traced her image with my eyes and noticed that on one arm she wore a couple of bracelets. Their appearance reminded me of Osun's brass bracelets.

Bracelets are very important to Osun followers and her priesthood. They wear five brass ones. As my eyes continued to settle on the Dancing Girl of Mohenjo-daro I could feel the weight of my five rather ancient looking brass bracelets weighing my left arm down. I had received them with the sacred Osun Calabash on my June 2008 trip to Nigeria.

My eyes and the Dancing Girl of Mohenjo-Daro seemed to lock onto each other for an eternity. Her smile was the next wave of electrical current that urged me gently but hurriedly forward. That familiar tingling in my legs, arms and fingers told me there was something she wanted me to discover.

In the quiet of that night she greeted me. Her silent presence seemed to have one aim – to ultimately help solve the mystery and questions that were blazing inside of me and consuming my every waking moment.

In a tranquil dance she led me right to the Indus valley where she was found. Archaeologist, Indian Scholars, and Western Scholars did not seem to agree on the answer to the question, "who is the Dancing Girl of Mohenjo – Daro ?"

Some say she was a temple girl, others - a dancing girl, and yet again others believe she was a Queen or a very important noble woman. One thing they all agreed on was that she was over 4500 years old (2492 BC), and she was found in the Indus Valley in the Southern regions of India.

A long time ago I vaguely remember some black intellectuals claiming that the Dravidian people, the original inhabitants of the Indus Valley, were none other than Africans from ancient Egypt. I also remember once reading a book (way back in my days as a student of African Studies at the School of Oriental and African Studies, London University (SOAS)) by respected African Egyptologist Cheik Anti Diop, who also made this assertion. I myself had never dwelled on the question much, except when I did my Ayurvedic degree. It seemed that so much was clear about Hindu history until it came to the Dravidians. They stuck out like a sore thumb in history.

Instinctively, I felt the Dancing Girl of Mohenjo-Daro held a major key to the connection between the African and Indian Goddesses; their religions and traditions. Somehow her dancing posture seemed to scream at me (elegantly, of course) "we are of a broken circle but a circle we are still part of."

338

The electrical current whipped me on. There was a hole that had to be closed. There was a gaping wound in history. One that made us all hurt. One that if mended would heal the whole.

The electrical current whipped me again, constantly taking my mind back to my dream of the Indian Goddess standing in the middle of a vast body of water, and then all the Goddesses from all over the world falling out from an Egyptian coffin into the oblivion of the waters. The image seeped sadness into my bones again. It felt fresh all over again.

The dream, the dream. My head pounded. My temples throbbed. My analytical hat went back on.

The Goddesses came out of the Egyptian coffin.... so the Goddesses came from Egypt? If the Goddesses came out of the Egyptian coffin some how my dream seems to be indicating that the world Mother Goddesses were originally from Egypt. Now the Indian Goddess that I saw first could have been Amma, who means "Mother". For it was the whole Amma incident that seemed to lead me looking into the connection between Osun and the Hindu Goddesses which led me to this point now.

My thoughts banged on and then came to a searing halt. *If there is a connection between the World Mother Goddesses and Egypt where is the mythological story/ies that show it?*

My heart fell for I had not found any connecting stories. But the dance of oneness would not let go. Osun seemed to be the driver behind the beat. Known for bringing things together for being the mender of the world, she seemed determined to show that we are all part of a sacred circle. Living well on earth was in the old bones of the Goddesses.

339

It was like a bush of fire – the thoughts that would not die.
In frustration and in hope of finding some direction I decided
to go back over my extensive research notes. As I reviewed
them I noticed that Durga and the Egyptian Goddess Lioness
Goddess Sekhmet, who was the fiercer side of Hathor, seemed
to definitely have a lot in common.

Besides my feelings about this, was there anything that
truly related the two? I wondered. The most important thing I
was looking for was a connecting mythology. I suddenly felt
as if I was looking at one of those magic pictures made up of
dots. You know there is a picture in there because you have
been told there is. But you just can't see it. All you see is a
jumble of dots. That is until you follow the sagacious advise of
those who have managed to successfully see the picture in the
dots, "just de-focalize the gaze". Once when I did that I saw a
picture of a dolphin jumping out of the waters. Another time I
saw a garden filled with flowers.

However, in this case I decided to give up the ghost. I
sincerely believed I would find any mythological connections
between Sekhmet and Durga. Thoroughly tired and beaten
down by the force of broken history, I didn't even try. That
was until one night I had a dream. I don't remember what the
dream was but a voice kept on saying, "Look at the Goddess
Sekhmet and Durga". It kept on repeating it over and over
again, waking me up from my sleep.

At exactly five in the morning (Osun's auspicious time)
a force seemed to drag me out of my bed and back to my
notes. I groaned. However my fingers flicked back through my
piles of notes on Sekhmet and Durga. My eyes reviewed the
them. Then I began to make a written check list of the two
Goddesses to see how many similarities I could match. The
connections leapt out like a dotted picture viewed with the de-
focalized gaze of the onlooker. The dolphin leapt out of the

340

waters, the flower garden blossomed. The mythological, iconographical, and personality connections were all there, right there in my jumbled notes, which the leaping dolphin encouraged me to now sort out in a more methodical way. So I did.

Sekhmet

- ✓ Goddess of Upper Egypt
- ✓ Similar to the Warrior Goddess, Bast of Lower Egypt, but seen as the more powerful of the two as Lower Egypt was conquered by upper Egypt
- ✓ Some of her titles: Avenger of the Wrongs, Scarlet Lady (reference to blood), Lady of Flames (because her body took on the glow of the midday sun), One Who is Powerful, One Before Whom Evil Trembles, the Mistress of Dread, Lady of Slaughter
- ✓ Her breath created the deserts
- ✓ Protected Egypt from enemies and in battle
- ✓ Depicted as a lioness
- ✓ She is a solar deity and is often seen as an aspect of Hathor and Bast
- ✓ She remains a separate Goddess from Mut (The Great Mother) but she latter down the line is joined in the Mut Goddess Composite which includes: Mut, the two symbols of lower and upper Egypt: Wadjet (who is depicted as a cobra), Nekhbet (depicted as a White Vulture), Sekhmet, Hathor and Isis
- ✓ Sekmet was so important that in order to placate her wrath priestess performed a ritual before a different statue of the goddess on each day of the year. A

341

practice which resulted in many images of the Goddess being preserved. There were more than seven hundred statues of Sekhmet which once stood in the funerary temple alone of Amenhotep III

✓ Her color is red

✓ Sometimes the dress she wears has a rosetta pattern over each nipple, an ancient leonine motif which can be traced to observation of the shoulder knot of hairs on lions

✓ Tame lions were kept in her honor

✓ The festival of Sekhmet would be celebrated after battles so that the destruction would come to an end.

✓ There was an annual festival held once a year for the Goddess where lots of music was played and lots of ritual beer consumed to imitate the extreme drunkenness that stopped the wrath of the Goddess when she almost destroyed humankind. This festival is said to also relate to the excessive flooding during the inundation at the beginning of each year, when the Nile ran blood-red with silt from upstream and Sekhmet had to swallow the overflow to save humankind.

✓ There is also a latter story related to the drunken festival that says Ra, who was by then the Sun God of Upper Egypt created Sekhmet from a fiery eye which was the Goddess Hathor. He wanted to destroy humanity for conspiring against him. Sekhmet almost destroyed all of humanity. In order to stop her Ra had to trick her by turning the Nile as red as blood so that Sekhmet would drink it. However, unknown to Sekhmet the red liquid was not blood, but beer mixed with pomegranate juice so that it resembled blood. This liquid made her drunk and she gave up the slaughter and became an aspect of the gentle Hathor

Durga

- ✓ Durga is seen as the embodiment of Shakti, the feminine creative force of the universe
- ✓ She is seen as the warrior aspect of the Great Mother
- ✓ Her name means "The Invincible One"
- ✓ Depicted as having ten arms, riding a lion or a tiger, carrying weapons and a lotus flower, maintaining a meditative smile, and practicing mudras, or symbolic hand gestures
- ✓ Kali is considered an aspect of Durga
- ✓ Parvati is seen as the Gentler side of Durga and kali
- ✓ Durga is called upon to defeat the evil demon who is destroying the world. She emerges from the light of the God trinity, Vishnu, Brahma and Shiva. On her arrival she announces she gave birth to all Gods and none gave birth to her. She came to help the world out of her compassion. The Demon makes the big mistake of laughing at her and thinking "how can this woman defeat me", but she does. In the final battle with the Demon she takes a deep sip of Divine Wine before slaying him.
- ✓ However, she does not stop killing and Shiva throws himself on the ground to stop her bloody rampage.
- ✓ She stops and turns into the gentle Parvati.

My excitement bubbled over like a tasty pot of Island Red Bean soup. I could see it. I could see the connections between the two Goddesses. They were clearly one of the same. I made some further mental ticks on the story of Durga fighting the baddies.

✓ She Fights against evil doers
✓ She is seen as the Great Mother, and the warrior aspect of that energy.
✓ She emerges from light of the male Gods as does Sekhmet, from the light of the Sun God Ra. In the Sekhmet story the light of God is actually from the eye of the Goddess Hathor.
✓ She Drinks wine in the story and becomes drunk.
✓ She Finds it hard to stop her bloody rampage
✓ She is stopped by the male God, Shiva. Sekhmet is stopped by the male God Ra
✓ She Turns into her gentle side Parvati. Sekhmet turns into her gentle side Hathor.

I made a note that the only difference in that story was that Durga seems to become drunk and thus cannot stop her rampage. Sekhmet is made to become drunk so that she can stop her rampage. Even with this discrepancy there is still the theme of drunkenness connected to the Mother Goddesses rampage of defeating the evil doers and the enemies of good. I wanted to jump through the roof.

I love hot chocolate. Right there and then I felt as though I had just finished a big warm mug of one. I felt all warm, contented and whole. That morning before I even had time to bask in the glory of that feeling that persistent voice from my dream commanded in a whisper DON'T FORGET TO LOOK AT THE GODDESS KALI. The morning was coming in quick. I could see the daylight beginning to peep in through the window. The only thought I personally had was that I wanted to get some sleep. But waves from the primordial waters would not let me go. They gripped me in their current and moved me onto my next lot of notes which were on the Goddess Kali. I had made them some time ago, so they were quite jumbled. I read and sorted through them patiently and with all the carefulness of a forensic scientist.   Once again I made a mental and physical check list as I did so.

- ✓ Kali is also seen as Durga
- ✓ Kali is depicted as dark skin
- ✓ Her name means "the black one". It also means time, death, lord of death, Shiva
- ✓ She is like Durga and Parvati the consort of Lord Shiva (who is depicted as white because of the ashes that are over his body).
- ✓ She is also referred to as Bhavatarini "redeemer of the universe"; "Adi Shakti" – Fundamental Power, and "Para Prakriti" – Beyond nature
- ✓ She is mentioned as a distinct Goddess and is related to war
- ✓ She is always depicted as looking rather terrifying and is related to corpses and is found in cemeteries
- ✓ In her popular form her iconography depicts her with four arms holding: a sword, a head, a bowl or skull cup catching blood of the severed head; a trident. Before you say yuck. The sword represents Divine knowledge, the severed head signifies the human ego which must

be slain by divine knowledge in order to obtain spiritual liberation. She is also doing special blessing mudras which means anyone who worships her with a true heart will be saved and guided well in the hereafter. Around her neck is a garland of skulls which also represent the slain ego and the garland of letters of the Sanskrit alphabet. As such she is seen as the mother of language and all mantra.

✓ Shiva praises Kali in a text known as the Mahanirvana-tantra and says, "thou art the beginning of all, Yellamma, Protectress and Destructress that Thou art."

✓ In one of Kali's most popular myths which is found in the Devi Mahatmyam Durga is having problems slaying the Demon and from her forehead she gives rise to her even fiercer self Kali kills the demon and drinks his blood. She feels intoxicated with victory and she dances wildly. All the worlds tremble and sway under the impact of her dance. So, at the request of all the Gods, Shiva himself asked her to desist from this behavior. However, she is too intoxicated to listen. That is when Shiva lay like a corpse among the slain demons in order to absorb the shock of the dance into himself. When Kali eventually stepped upon her husband she sticks her tongue out. It is said that Kali represents active divine consciousness, while Shiva represents inactive divine consciousness.

Then I summarized my thoughts,

" *Kali elaborates more about Durga. They are one of the same. They are both clearly the Goddess Sekhmet who herself is the fierce*

*compassionate Mother Warrior Goddess who can be found in the
burial grounds of the rulers of Egypt. Kali emerges from Durga's
forehead which would be her third eye. Just as Sekmet came from the
eye of Ra which was said to be Hathor. She too is said to have drunk
blood of the demon and she becomes intoxicated. Sekhmet drank what
she thought was the blood of the enemies and became intoxicated. But
actually what she was drinking was wine. It seems that by
implication of her intoxication and in the light of the similarities
with the Sekhmet story Kali too was drinking wine. Which ever way,
the theme of intoxication in relation to their battle is consistent with
both Sekhmet, Durga, and Kali."*

I also make a few more added notes,

*"Durga and Kali are interestingly both said to be black and are said
to be pre-Aryan Goddess. Meaning that they belong to the Indus
Valley traditions where the Dancing Girl of Mohenjo – Daro is
found. Now I am wondering if that dancing girl figure is Egyptian?"*

For some reason I vaguely remembered that Sekhmet
who was from Upper Egypt had her warrior counterpart in the
feline Goddess Bast. The two had merged together. I had some
notes on the Goddess Bast too. Despite my powerful throbbing
headache, I decided to review them and then made a couple of
mental and physical notes:

*Sekhmet and Bast merged together. Sekhmet who was seen as
the stronger of the two took over the personality of the Goddess Bast.
Now as I can see that Sekhmet and Durga are related, it does not
seem of any coincidence they both have another warrior persona by*

347

another name– Sekhmet in the form of Bast and Durga in the form Kali.

Then I remembered how I had found out earlier how Mut had merged with all the Goddesses giving them the stamp of Primordial Mothers. I contemplated this thought and visited it over from the stance of my previous thoughts about the Primordial Mother Goddess identity originating from Mut. I wrote down:

Mut was like a thread that brought all the Egyptian Goddesses together under the umbrella title of Great Primordial Mother Goddesses. Mut had merged with Sekhmet and Bast. I found it interesting that Durga and Kali together were seen as the great Shakti, Primordial Mother. Sekhmet and Bast were also seen as the Compassionate primordial mother in her fierce protective side. When she wasn't being compassionate and protective she turned back into Hathor. Just how Durga and Kali turned back into Parvati.

I had book marked a picture of the Dancing girl of Mohenjo – Daro on my computer. I pulled her image back up. I retraced her form again with my eyes, and thanked her for where her waters had led me. I still was not sure how to close the wound of the Goddess that afflicted the heart of humanity. For the question of the "where's?" now loomed larger than ever– how on earth did Sekhmet and Durga come to be related? Which Goddess had come from where? As I had these thoughts my eyes still lingered gently upon the Dancing Girl of Mohenjo- daro. It seemed as though she held the answer within her defiant pose. The longer I stared at her, a deep intuition filled me with a certainty that she was from ancient Egypt. However, my intuitive certainty was not backed by the historical facts that I had found out as yet. For her origins still remained vague.

Dancing Girl of Mohenjo-Daro

Sekhmet   **Mut**

Kali

Durga

Guan Yin Dreaming

Exhilarated. Vibrating, excited, confused, overwhelmed waters flowed hotly over my head, over my body, falling onto the ground where my feet tried to stay planted. My days rolled into a seamless cloth, a void of no thingness. I was being breathed in my something larger than myself. Gripped in the electrical current that rolled me on, and one night I dreamt.

Suddenly I was lying in bed and Derrick was next to me. So I thought I was awake. This man was standing next to the bed and smoothing this very ancient looking dress down. It seemed to be made of light silk. He said, "Guan Yin will always be with you". I didn't know what he was talking about but he kept on saying

"Guan Yin will always be with you from now on." She is the Goddess of Compassion and she will always be with you. She will always be inside of you.

Then it went to darkness and a voice of the same man said, "Durga will always be inside of you too."

Then I felt this force rising in me and the force had its hands in a praying position above its head. Then everything went very black and Kali was inside of me. Then the voice said, "the Goddess of Wisdom will also be inside of you. You research her."

The voice then said when you wake up you will see something significant so that you will know that this is all real. I woke up and everything was dark. Derrick was lying next to me and there was a van next to the bed. I could see under it and there was a fish. The light was so dim that I wasn't sure if the fish was moving until it came up from under the van and I noticed it was swimming in the air!

I woke Derrick up and said, "baby, baby can you see that swimming fish in the air!"

352

"No baby," he replied and told me it must be my imagination.

"Baby, there's the fish. That must be the significant thing."

Then I woke up. I was faced with the quiet stillness of the early morning. All the time I thought I had been awake I had been sleeping.

I could not help it, but I just had to wake Derrick up. He was in a deep sleep. I felt guilty for shaking him out of it, but I was bursting to tell him my dream. He eventually woke up with much nudging and elbowing from me. He groaned,

"I was just dreaming about a fish swimming in the air. How weird."

I froze, realizing that the fish had been the significator from the dream. For Derrick had dreamt it too. I proceeded to tell him the dream.

"Who is Guanyin? Do you even think such a person even exist? " I asked Derrick.

"I don't know. Look to see if anything comes up on the internet," he replied drowsily before rolling over, and falling back to sleep.

The following day I tried to search for the name but came up with nothing. The problem was I knew what the name sounded like, but I didn't have a clue on how to really spell it. I tried many variations of the strange sounding name. Just when I began to doubt that there was such a person called by the name in my dream, my search engine threw up, "Guanyin".

I leapt out of my seat and eagerly tried to find out more about Guanyin. I thought Guanyin would be some kind of male sage, but what I thought was going to be a he turned out to be a she. She was a female and the Bodhisattva (Buddha) of Compassion. I was truly excited. My heart raced. There really was such a person called Guanyin. I took a deep breath in and began to read about her.

Guanyin is a derivation of the Sanskrit name Avalokiteshvara, the Buddha who embodies all the Buddha's compassion. In Tibet he is known as Chenrezig and is said to be incarnated in the present Dalai Lama. In other words the Dalai Lama is an incarnation of Chenrezig.

According to legend Avalokiteshvara vowed to liberate all beings from suffering, but when he realized the magnitude of his task, his head exploded into countless pieces. His body was then reassembled by the Buddha Amitabha and the bodhisattva Vajrapani – the "wielder of the thunderbolt". Once they put his body back together again it had eleven heads and a thousand arms. Each hand displayed an all seeing eye.

Now even though Avalokiteshvara is called a He. He is not really just a He, but a She too. For Guanyin is seen as the female aspect of this great Buddha of compassion whose name means, "sound perceiver" and literally "he who looks down upon sound" (he pays attention to the cries of humanity). Guanyin's name is a Chinese name that means the same thing.

I shifted on my chair. I could feel my breath racing jaggedly through my chest. Excited I read on. The story of Guanyin was virtually identical with Avalokiteshvara

One day Guanyin vowed she would never rest until she had freed all sentient beings from samsara or reincarnation. Despite strenuous effort, she realized that there were still many unhappy beings yet to be saved. After struggling to comprehend the needs of so many, her head split into eleven pieces. Amitabha Buddha, seeing her plight, gave her eleven heads with which to hear the cries of the suffering. Upon hearing these cries and comprehending them, Guanyin attempted to reach out to all those who needed aid, but

*found that her two arms shattered into pieces. Once more, Amitabha
came to her aid and appointed her a thousand arms with which to aid
the many.*

I paused and thought back on my dream. I could see
the Chinese man smoothing down that ancient dress and
saying Guanyin's name. Saying that she was the Goddess of
Compassion. I was astounded that once again my dreamtime
had entered my waking world. My head swam. My thoughts
raced – *a Chinese man smoothing down a woman's dress.... That
was none other than Guanyin in her male and female form..... For in
China I discovered that sometimes Guanyin is depicted as a man.....
Then there's also the fact that Guan yin is the female aspect of the
male Buddha of Compassion.*

I put my thoughts down into physical notes,

*So there is a Guanyin. She is both male and female. I guess, that is
why in my dreams the old Chinese man was smoothing down a silk
woman's dress. Guanyin is Chinese. She is connected to the Indian
tradition because Avalokiteshvara is the Buddha of Compassion from
India. She is also connected to the Tibetan tradition because
Chenrezig is the name of Avalokiteshvara and is embodied in the
present reincarnated Dalai Lama. Uhm, all the traditions seem to
connect when you follow the lineage of the Mother. If Guan Yin is
connected to India then she must be connected to the Durga
Composite of Goddesses which means she must be connected to Osun
and the Egyptian Mut Composite of Goddesses. Which means the
Buddha Chenrezig is too. Which means that all the traditions really
do connect. I feel like the wound of the earth is definitely trying to
heal itself. Who better to heal it than the Mother Divine, herself. It
seems as though in all traditions that is her job – to heal the wounds
and the souls of the lost.*

I went back to reading. In China, Guanyin is usually shown in a white flowing robe and usually wears necklaces of Indian/Chinese royalty. In her left hand is a jar containing pure water, and the right holds a willow branch. The crown she wears usually depicts the image of Amitabha Buddha, Guanyin's spiritual teacher before she became a Bodhisattva.

In some Buddhist temples and monasteries, Guanyin's image is occasionally depicted as that of a young man dressed in Northern Song Dynasty Buddhist robes sitting gracefully. He is usually depicted looking or glancing down, symbolizing that Guanyin continues to watch over the world.

In The Lotus Sūtra it is explained that Avalokiteśvara as a bodhisattva can take the form of any type of male or female, adult or child, human or non-human being. Basically whichever form is needed to teach the Dharma to sentient beings.

This text reveals there are thirty-three manifestations of Guanyin, of which seven are female manifestations. It was known to have been very popular in Chinese Buddhism as early as in the Sui Dynasty and Tang Dynasty. According to the doctrines of the Mahāyāna sūtras themselves, it does not matter whether Guanyin is male, female, or asexual, as the ultimate reality is in emptiness.

I looked at the beautiful pictures of Guanyin looking down on the world with great compassion. There I saw my watery guardian Osun, acting as the Greek language on the Rosetta Stone again. She drew my attention to water pot Guanyin held delicately in her hand. There was the water pot again. Osun had the water pot. In fact, when one is initiated into her one receives her auspicious water pot filled with her elixir like waters. The electrical current snaked through my body. Guanyin seemed to be the Chinese and Tibetan version of Osun. This awareness was to latter act as a door opener to allow the Goddesses DNA to unravel some more.

I made a mental note,

Osun's primary ritual color is white. Like Guanyin Osun is constantly listening to and compassionately answering all the request of sentient beings. She heals with water. She is the Mother of Water and is often depicted holding a water jug. There's Water again and Osun' trying to compassionately to help everyone again. Trying to hear all request from humanity's dire circumstances.

I allowed my mind to dwell on those thoughts a little. Then continued to read on. Three things caught my eye. Guanyin's connection to fish, Guanyins connection to parrot feathers and Guanyins connection to wisdom.

It is said that sometimes Guanyin is depicted as carrying a fish basket. Now that was interesting because Osun is seen as the Mother of Fish. In fact, when I stayed at the Osun Palace Temple it was strictly forbidden for anyone to eat fish on the grounds. The main worship room was also covered in pictures of Osun as a mermaid holding fish in her hand. There were also fish all over the walls. If you were in doubt about this Goddess's connection to fish you wouldn't be after being there.

It is said that Guanyin's veneration was introduced into China as early as the 1st century CE, along with Buddhism, and reached Japan by way of Korea soon after Buddhism was first introduced into the country in the mid-7th century.

In her role of the wisdom keeping compassionate Mother who saves the world Guanyin echoed the wise footsteps of Durga and her family of Goddesses; Mut and her Goddess Composite. Then most definitely Osun's Goddess

Composite. Her position in relation to teaching the Buddhist Dharma, and her ability to heal any ails seemed to single handedly emphasize the wisdom keeping role of all these Divine Mothers. It is a role I found to be illustrated perfectly in this story.

One day Shan Tsai (also called Sudhana in Sanskrit) a disabled boy from India was very interested in studying the Buddha Dharma. He heard that there was a Buddhist teacher on the rocky island of Putuo. Determined to fulfill his desire to learn the Dharma he quickly journeyed there for teachings. When he arrived at the island, he found the great Guanyin. He eagerly expressed his desire to her. She listened and then decided to test the boy's resolve. She conjured the illusion of three sword-wielding pirates running up the hill to attack her. Guanyin took off and dashed to the edge of a cliff, the three illusions still chasing her. Shan Tsai, saw that his teacher was in great danger. He hobbled as best he could uphill. Guanyin then jumped over the edge of the cliff, and soon after this the three bandits followed her. Shan Tsai, was still determined to save his teacher. He managed to crawl over the cliff edge.

Of course he fell. As he fell helta skelta through the air he was caught by Guanyin who told him to walk. He tried and found he could now walk. He looked into a pool of water and also discovered that he now very handsome face. From that day on Guanyin taught Shan Tsai the entire Buddha Dharma.

I thought back on Guanyin's parrot feathers. Osun is also associated with parrot feathers however, her ones are red. According to Valeria Badejo, author of "Osun Seegesi", Osun's red parrot feathers symbolize power. In Nigeria I remember certain Osun priestess who were considered royalty wearing the red parrot feather in their hair. It looked rather pretty. That night I wrote in my diary,

I think of Avalokiteshvara and I see the beautiful relationship of the divine feminine, and divine masculine standing like the guards to the balancing scales of life. I see reflected in the universal mirror not only Avalokiteshvara, Guan Yin and Tara. I also see their mirror reflections in Osun and the God of Wisdom Orunmila; Durga/Kali/Parvati and Shiva; Hathor/Isis and Osiris. These images swirl around me. Dancing and laughing they make fun of me. "See if you can catch us" they say. They seem to certainly know who they are even though history has confused their identities, separating them by vast oceans and rivers of time. Yet curiously enough, it is those same oceans and rivers which seem to be re-uniting them back together.

QUAN YIN AND OSUN'S SHARED QUALITIES

I went on to write a quick summary of Guan Yin and Osun's Shared Qualities onto paper:
- ✓ Fish
- ✓ Parrot Feathers (Tara's is white – Osun's is red)
- ✓ Jug of Water
- ✓ Compassionate to all beings
- ✓ White dress
- ✓ Guan Yin other half is *Avalokiteshvara* /Osun's other half is the wise compassionate Orunmila
- ✓ Guan Yin is the keeper of the Dharma Wisdom, Osun is also the keeper of the wisdom. A point illustrated when her husband Oludamare went away and she kept the place ticking over by divining for the village and healing all their issues. Also Oludamare (God) said, "to the woman Osun I gave all the wisdom of the world."

Tara

Tara was the next Goddess to step forward. As I had seen her name mentioned in relation to Guan Yin's and Avalokiteshvara, I of course decided to check her out. She confirmed my strong suspicion that Guan Yin was connected to the Durga Goddess family, thus to the Mut and Osun one.

In Tibet Guanyin's name transforms into Tara. In other words Guanyin is Tara and Tara is Guanyin. Tara is known as "the Mother of Liberation". She is regarded as the Bodhisattva (Buddha) of compassion and action. Many Tibetan Buddhist often meditate on her image to develop the inner understanding about the secret teachings about compassion and emptiness (there was the song of compassion again, I thought).

Tara as an aspect of Avalokiteshvara Tibetan form, Chenrezig. The story of how she was manifested from Avalokiteshvara struck me as hugely similar to how Ra manifested Sekhmet from his Hathor eye. For Ra seeing the corruption of mankind decided to restore order. He sent forth from Hathor, his eye, Sekhmet (Hathor's) other half to eliminate those who were doing harm to the world; and to ultimately bring the world back into equilibrium. The Tara story states,

Then at last Avalokiteshvara arrived at the summit of Marpori, the 'Red Hill', in Lhasa. Gazing out, he perceived that the lake on Otang, the 'Plain of Milk', resembled the Hell of Ceaseless Torment.
Myriads of being were undergoing the agonies of boiling, burning, hunger, thirst, yet they never perished, but let forth hideous cries of anguish all the while. When Avalokiteshvara saw this, tears sprang to his eyes. A teardrop from his right eye fell to the plain and became the reverend Bhrikuti, who declared: 'Son of your race! As you are

striving for the sake of sentient beings in the Land of Snows,
intercede in their suffering, and I shall be your companion in this
endeavor!' Bhrikuti was then reabsorbed into Avalokiteshvara right
eye, and was reborn in a later life as the Nepalese princess Tritsun. A
teardrop from his left eye fell upon the plain and became Tara. She
also declared, 'Son of your race! As you are striving for the sake of
sentient beings in the Land of Snows, intercede in their suffering,
and I shall be your companion in this endeavor!' Tara was also
reabsorbed into Avalokiteshvara left eye, and was reborn in a later
life as the Chinese princess Kongjo (Princess Wencheng)."

Within the Mandala I see Tara and Durga Smiling

For some reason as I ponder on Tara, I begin to feel moved to make something out of clay. I buy the clay, shape it into a round rough circle, and bake it in the oven. I carefully paint it yellow, red and white. Then I set a carnelian gem in the middle of it. I hold the object in my hand, and wonder what have I made. What is it? I find no answer coming forth from deep within, so I decide that it would make a good jewelry piece. I go into my bedroom and set it upon the book shelf. I place it right next to a little Egyptian pyramid that belongs to Derrick.

A few days on I have forgotten about my small clay piece. That is until day three after making it I discover something in a Jung book I am reading. I am on a new section in the book and it talks about the Mandala. Jung says he dreamt of one. He painted it and called it "The Window of Eternity". He like me had no idea what he had really created.

A year later he is given a book called the "Golden Flower" and in it he recognizes his Mandala. Jung says,

" only gradually did I discover that the Mandala is Formation, Transformation, Eternal man's reaction . And that is the self; the wholeness of the personality which if all goes well is harmonious, which does not tolerate self-deceptions."

After reading the chapter I rise from my seat and go over to the book case in mine and Derrick's bedroom. I take it gingerly of the shelf and turn it around in my hand. Then I turn it the right way up and lay it flat on my palm. I examine it and realize that I too have made a mandala.

As those cosmic bumps would have it, a day or two latter myself, Derrick and Kem Ra head to Barnes and Nobles in Pineville. When we arrive I browse through the bargain books with Derrick. A burst of color jumps out from one of the front covers. The title jumps out too. It is called the "Celestial Gallery" by Romio Shrestha. I soon find my fingers trembling and flicking through its pages. The images pull me into their deep oranges, blues, golds and greens. They beckon me forward, and soon I am staring at the Great Tara . She sits in the middle of a Mandala looking perfectly serene and divinely beautiful. I read the words of the author explaining the painting,

"Upon the orb of a moon in the center of the anthers of a soft and tender lotus, its petals full blown, the body of the goddess, sensuous, ravishing, mother of all the Conquerors: there I direct my prayers." Romio Shrestha quotes the Dalai Lama.

It is this description of Tara that makes me think of Durga. It also took me back to Durga's more gentle side reflected in holy images of Parvati, Lakshmi and Sarasvati. Then it made me think of the two sides of Osun. Also it made me think of the gentle and compassionate aspects of Mother

Mut composite of ancient Egypt.   It was clear to me that Tara was yet another face of the gentle fierce compassionate Mother Goddess of the world.

I read on and Shrestha confirms my suspicions revealing Tara as the "Mother of All Buddhas" who originated from the Indian Shakti worship. She was assimilated into the Tibetan tradition "where through multiple emanations, she functions as savouress and supreme Protectress."

My eyes are then drawn to the serene looking image of the White Tara. It is said her color and form indicates she gives longevity, protection and fulfills earthly desires "through pacifying, increasing, and subjugating." The embodiment of pure love she is divine pure love which is symbolized by the lotus flower she holds. Transcendental eyes stare out from her forehead, palms, and feet. She is smiling joyfully and peacefully. Shrestha let's us know,

"her loving kindness reflects an innate altruism that arises spontaneously from recognizing our oneness with all creation."

I close my own eyes and smile. I feel her emanating presence radiating onto and through me.

"If we see through to Tara's essence, she frees us from self – serving" thoughts and encourages us to act selflessly, and wisely, for the benefit of all beings: the surest prescription for a long fulfilling life," says Shrestha.

Ahhh. I find Tara so refreshing. So energizing. Her lightness of color makes me think of Hathor being associated with the milky way and the moon of consciousness. Then of paintings I have seen of Osun painted, on many occasions, a lighter brown than most other deities.   Then I think of Saraswati dressed all in white, with milk and water at her feet with a white swan and a peacock; along with the honey that is fed to her by her devotees. Lakshmi, she of purity, dances before me too. All sisters, all emanations of the same self. The same force. They all dance.

I sigh. I feel at peace, but not before I notice that Tara's eyes are said to be seven. I remember reading that in ancient Egypt when a child was born The Seven Hathors would appear to tell their destiny. Sometimes the Seven Hathors were drawn as Seven Celestial Cows. As she was seen as the Heavenly Cow that provided milk to nourish the universe. I find it interesting that the eye was so important to Tara. For Hathor is seen as the eye. I re-reminded myself that she was the eye of Ra. As Tara and Hathor seemed to share almost the exact same qualities. It was interesting that it was their all seeing eyes and the number seven which still connected them across time, waters, and history.

I turn the page of the book, and there I see the other Tara. She is green. Apparently there are quite a few emanations of Tara. However the green aspect of Tara Shrestha explains "represents a blending of white, yellow, and blue colors which symbolize, respectively, the functions of pacifying, increasing, and destroying." Green Tara "as a Mother protects her child, so as the cosmic Mother, Green Tara, shelters all beings in her loving embrace. Green Tara is our insurance against all harm and ill will."

He reveals that "Green Tara is said to protect beings from the "eight great terrors". This sentiment is expressed by the seventh – century Buddhist scholar Chandragomin says,

Entering upon the road, I see you, hands and feet reddened with the blood of slain elephants; upon the road I think of you, a lion trampled beneath your feet, and thus I pass into the thick-grown impassable forest.
Those who do not stop for an instant on their path of killing,

364

Wandering with roaring sound of a host of bees flying at a cheek
fragrant with intoxicating liquor: O Tara, even they are conquered
and bow down before you,
a fire blazing as high as if the firmament were kindled by the wind's
great power at the dissolution of the world: even that will be calmed
should a city but call out your name.

As I read the words a thrill of excitement runs down my spine. There was Sekhmet. I see her in her cloth of red, fiercely and compassionately protecting humanity from all ails. She is there in full three D. As I see her, her fierce compassionate loving smile fuses into Durga's own, whose smile fuses into Osun's

Now I look at both the White Tara and Green Tara mandalas. I allow my consciousness to expand into them. I allow my breath to be enthused by them. I dissolve and expand outward. I embrace the presence of the Mother and realize that somehow Tara was living true to the words I remembered reading from His Holiness the Dalai Lama about her. They were spoken at a conference on Compassionate Action in Newport Beach, California in 1989.

"There is a true feminist movement in Buddhism that relates to the goddess Tara. Following her cultivation of bodhicitta, the bodhisattva's motivation, she looked upon the situation of those striving towards full awakening and she felt that there were too few people who attained Buddhahood as women. So she vowed, 'I have developed bodhicitta as a women. For all my lifetimes along the path I vow to be born as a woman, and in my final lifetime when I attain Buddhahood, then, too, I will be a woman.' This is true feminism."

My Tara Notes: Joining Tara With Her Sister Goddesses

I go back over all my mental notes and make a physical summary of them on paper. This time my aim is to draw her lines of connections with her sister Goddesses.

Tara and Durga: Tara is clearly stated to be Shakti from Hinduism. Green Tara is none other than the fierce compassionate Durga; while White Tara is none other than gentle Parvati (along with her other forms as Lakshmi, Saraswati, and Ganga

Tara and Hathor: Tara is Hathor. For I have already aligned Durga to Hathor/Sekhemet. Hathor does battle with the forces of darkness as her fierce compassionate side Sekhmet. Who after doing battle with the demons she turns back into Hathor (the gentle side of Sekhmet). Now like Hathor, Tara is associated with the iconography and spiritual symbolism of the eye and her number seven. In fact, Sekhmet is born from the eye of Hathor who lives in Ra when the demons are wrecking the world. Just as Tara's born from the eye of Chenrizig and her sister form Guan Yin is born from the eye of Avalokiteshvara.

Tara and Guanyin: Well as Tara is the female version of Chenrizig, that makes her also none other than Guanyin, who is the female version of Avalokiteshvara.

Tara and Osun: I have connected Osun to Durga and her family of Goddesses. It is interesting to note that within Osun are all the qualities of Tara and within Tara are all the qualities of Osun.

I pause from my notes and I write:

I can see the image of the primordial Mother dusting herself of and gathering all her pieces slowly back together again. The pieces are now dust molecules but by some share force of cohesion they begin to fly into the air and float into their respectful place to form the body they all rightfully belonged to. I feel challenged. For I always speak about spirituality. I always claim myself to be deeply spiritual. Yet here I am being challenged by the universe dreaming itself. I am in that dream and the force of this dreaming is challenging my every waking state. It over whelms me with.

After reading about Tara and seeing her Mandala of sheer beauty and love, I feel moved to paint a mandala on paper for myself. I draw several circles with four cardinal points. In the center I draw a very black faceless woman sitting with a top knot in her hair. On top of the top knot is the flame of wisdom. I swathe her in elegant orange. Lovingly I drape a cloth over one shoulder. I place a pot of water in her hands and slightly tilt the hands so that the water is pouring forth into the cosmic and earthly world. The waters feed the fish I place around and inside of the circles. They are Koy fish painted in white, orange and a luminous blue.

I put the famous Conch shells of the mother that calls us to attention within the outer circle. I paint not one but several of them washing them in a light peachy cream. A white still quarter moon is made to grace the outside of the mandala. It sits on the edge of the page from where it shines its light on the Mother.

When I finish I look over the picture. It looks pleasing to my eyes. I smile. My eyelids begin to close. I am overwhelmed by the tiredness not just of that day, not just of the last few days, but by the blur of months of research and realizations the universe had flung my way. Sleep claims me. Into its arms I fall softly, softly, very softly till I am in a deep restful sleep, and dream of all the mother's singing their song of compassion together, while pouring out the soothing waters from their pots. Its rivulets wet and anoint my head.

Tara by sculptor Zanzabaar, 17 century

Guan Yin, 1656 carving, Vietnam

IRETE MEJI

Girl: Mother tell me of Irete Meji.

Mother: Amongst the many things Irete Meji helps us to understand is that to have prosperity we must understand how to act wisely.

Girl: What do you mean Mother?

Mother: Girl, I will tell you a story to illustrate this point.

Girl: Go ahead Mother.

Mother: OK.

Well, one day after creating life on earth God decided to create the Tree of Prosperity called Ege which means The Tree of Wealth. Now like all such precious gifts one must ensure that it is not misused. So God appointed protectors to the tree. The boa constrictor, the ram and the cock. They were to be the trees custodians. Well, once the Tree of Prosperity grew up all the two hundred deities who lived on earth tried to pick its fruits. However, not one was successful. For none had bothered to discover the secret to harvesting such fruits.

Well, it was Orunmila, the God of wisdom, who made the effort to find out the proper way to harvest the fruits of this tree. He went to three very good priests. Their names meant: "The person who bales out water from the river demolishes the fish"; "Only the patient man can succeed in killing a small animal called Okhuokhua who builds two hundred houses but lives in none of them."; "It is a strong headed missile that destroys evil."

Now before Orunmila made any attempt to climb the tree he was told to first destroy his home in heaven. The next thing he had to do was to build himself a house with special leaves on top of the shrine of Esu, the God of the Crossroads, and let the priest destroy it. Now these sound like very strange instructions but Orunmila followed them.

He then went to another priest who told him to make an offering of corn, yam and rats. He was also to make an offering of a goat and a ladder. All of these materials were to go in a bag that was to be placed at the foot of the Tree of Prosperity.

When Orunmila got to the tree and tried to place the offering the Boa Constrictor was the first to attack. Orunmila quickly threw a rat to the snake and it swallowed it and left him alone.

Then the cock began his attack. Orunmila quickly threw plenty of corn out for him. He swallowed it and left him alone.

Then the Ram went on the attack. Orunmila quickly threw pieces of yam out to him and he left him alone.

With the three guardians of the tree busy enjoying their meals Orunmila climbed the tree with a ladder that Esu, the God of the Crossroads put there. It was the same ladder that Orunmila had given to Esu as an offering. Orunmila climbed the tree with a ladder installed by Esu and was able to pluck the beautiful life giving fruits from the Tree of Prosperity.

It was August 2009, the days had rolled into months. The Dancing Girl of Mohenjo-Daro wouldn't stop dancing in front of me. Her elegant image haunted me, as that electrical current pulled me forward and backward into time again. I was filled up with the questions: "what happened to the Dancing Girl of Mohenjo-Daro?", "what happened to the Goddess?" that she the Dancing Girl of Mohenjo-Daro, had come to represent (in my mind at least). As if in answer to this nagging that plagued me, one day two books poked out (quite literally) from my mother in law's book shelf. One was entitled "The Power of Myth" by Joseph Campbell. The other "When God Was a Woman", by Merlin Stone.

The next couple of weeks of my life were spent reading those two books and others that fell willfully at my feet. I was surprised at how many books had been written about the Mother Goddess, I was equally surprised how most of them seemed to be stuffed at the back of shelves collecting dust. They were as hidden and lost in time as the Goddess herself. The more I read was the more the corridors of Goddess and Earth history unfolded like a gripping must read epic story. One that unfolded mainly through the voices of Joseph Campbell, and Merlin Stone.

It seemed that the story went something like this. Once upon a time there was the existence of "Mother Consciousness" (as Derrick labeled it). Where the universe was perceived as the great feminine or Mother Goddess. This Mother Consciousness existed thousands of years before the arrival of Abraham. Archaeologist trace it all the way back to Neolithic communities of about 7000 BC, and some to upper Paleolithic cultures of about 25,000 BC. When Archaeologist explored the

372

burial sites of ancient cultures they often found that the earliest form of worship was ancestral and often that the ancestral figure was represented as a female. They found numerous sculptures of women made from stone, bone and clay. These figurines sometimes dated back as far as 25,000 BC. They were often found lying close to the remains of sunken walls. These figures are nicknamed the "Venus Figures".

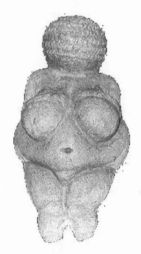

Venus of Willendorf

Why was the Goddess so prominent in ancient time? Joseph Campbell answers,

"It has to do with earth. The human woman gives birth just as the earth gives birth to the plants. She gives nourishment, as the plants do. So woman magic and earth magic are the same. They are related. And the personification of the energy that gives birth to forms and nourishes forms is properly female. It is in the agricultural world of ancient Mesopotamia, the Egyptian Nile, and the earliest planting culture systems that the Goddess is the dominant mythic form."

He goes on to explain that there are hundreds of Goddess figures found throughout Europe, but "hardly anything there of the male figure at all. The bull and certain other animals, such as the boar and the goat, may appear as symbolic of the male power, but the Goddess was the only visualized divinity at that time."

He continues,

"When you have a Goddess as the creator, it's her own body that is the universe. She is identical with the universe."

He mentions Nut and how she is the whole sphere of the life enclosing the heavens. Months after reading this I forget about his mention of Nut. However, she does not forget me and once again, shows me herself in all her glory arching over the entire universe sheltering humanity, plant and animal life.

Nut is amongst the oldest deities of ancient Egypt. Her arching image protectively covers the earth and all its inhabitants. She helps us to visually understand that the Mother energy was indeed perceived to be the nurturing supportive universe. Nut's praise names hold the song of her ancient meaning: *Coverer of the Sky, She Who Protects, Mistress of All*. She is the meant to be the birther of all the Gods, and the primordial waters from which all of life arose. She is also Hathor. Their names and iconographies are often interchanged.

Across the primeval watery of Nut it is said that sometimes during the day the heavenly bodies such as the sun and moon make their way across it. Dusk marked the time that they would be swallowed by her illustriousness, and pass through her digestive track during the night to be re-born at dawn.

Joseph Campbell goes on to explain,

"When you move to a philosophical point of view, as in the Goddess religions of India where the Goddess symbology is dominant to this day – the female represents Maya. The female represents what in Kantian terminology we call the forms of sensibility. She is time and space itself, and the mystery beyond her is beyond all pairs of opposites. So it isn't male and it isn't female. It neither is nor is not . But everything is within her, so that the gods are her children. Everything you can think of, everything you can see, is a production of the Goddess."

When I shared this with Derrick he made a good point,

"remember all of the potentiality of life is within the Mother. She contains both the potentiality of the female and the male. When scientist want to create a human part in stem cell biology they have to get the cells from the Mother not the father. So yes, I can see what people like Joseph Campbell are saying and why the ancient cultures say that the Mother helps us to go beyond the duality of existence and the belief that the material is separate from the sacred."

In terms of the concept of the Mother being seen as the first ancestress Merlin Stone revealed,

"thus as the religious concepts of the earliest homesapiens were developing the quest for the ultimate source of life (perhaps the core of theological thought) may have begun."

She further explained that the mother was regarded as the sole parent of the family and ancestor worship. This concept formed the basis of sacred rituals and the idea of matrilineal lineage. The mother was all in all revered as "Divine Ancestress"

She goes on to quote Robert Griars, a poet and mythologist, who shared, "the whole of Neolithic Europe, to judge from surviving artifacts and myths had a remarkably homogeneous system of religious ideas based on the many titled Mother Goddess, who was also known in Syria and Libya. The Great Goddess was regarded as immortal, changeless, omnipotent and the concept of fatherhood had not yet been introduced into religious thought."

I realized that although Robert Griars was commenting on mainly Europe. His comment stretched across the entire globe. I began to feel strange, as though old ancient books were knocking on my head. Merlin Stones continues,

"Upon closer scrutiny, however, it becomes clear that so many of the names used in diverse areas were simply various titles of the Great Goddess, epithets such as Queen of Heaven, Lady of High Place, Celestial Ruler, Lady of the Universe, Sovereign of the Heavens, Lioness of the Sacred or simply Her Holiness. Often the name of the town or city was added which made the name even more specific."

In terms of the later point I knew this to be true, for the State in Nigeria where Osun dominates, Osun State, is called after her.

She goes on,

"We are not confronting a confusing myriad of deities, but a variety of titles resulting from diverse language and dialects, yet each referring to a most similar female divinity once gaining this broader and more overall overview it becomes evident that the female deity in the near and middle East was revered as Goddess – much as people think of God."

Right up on the back of Merlin Stone comes the voice of Robert Graves, who translated the "Golden Ass" by Roman Writer, Apuleius, 2nd Century. In its antiquated pages the Goddess announces who she is,

*"I am Nature, the universal Mother, mistress of all elements,
primordial child of time, sovereign of all things spiritual, queen of the
dead, queen also of the immortals, the single manifestation of all
Gods and Goddesses that are. My nod governs the shining heights of
Heaven, the wholesome sea breezes, the lamentable silences of the
world below.*

*Though I am worshipped in many aspects, known by
countless names and propitiated with all many of different rites, yet
the whole round earth venerates me.*

*The primeval Phrygians call me Pessinuntica, Mother of the Gods;
the Athians sprung from their own soil call me Cecropian Artemis,
for the Islanders of Cyprus I am Paphian Aphrodite, for the archers of
Crete I am Dietynna, for the tri-lingual Sicilians, Stygian Prosperine
and for the Elusininians their ancient Mother of Corn – some know
me as Juno, some as Bellons of Battles' others as Hecaate, others
again as Rhamnubia, but both races of Aethiopians, whose lands the
morning sun first shines upon, and the Egyptians who excel in
ancient learning and worship me with ceremonies proper to my
Godhead, call me by my true name, namely Queen Isis (the Egyptian
name, Auset)."*

The story of the Mother continues her reflection in women.
In the past women were honored as the Goddess herself. For
as Joseph Campbell said, "earth magic, and woman magic are
the same." Today, like the Earth they are abused.

Merlin Stone explains that amongst our ancestors the
status of women was tied in with the status of the Goddess
herself. The status of the woman was also further increased
because family inheritance was passed through the line of
women. Social Anthropologist Sir James George Frazer
confirms that the favorable laws of the land towards women
were a result of the reverence paid to "this mighty Goddess".
Revealing,

"It is for these reasons, in fact that it was ordained that the queen should have greater power and honor than the King and among private persons the wife should enjoy authority over the husband, husbands agreeing in marriage contract that they will be obedient in all things to their wives."

Adding,

"In Egypt the archaic system of mother – kin with its preference for women over men in matter of property and inheritance, lasted down to Roman Times."

As to the status of women, Merlin Stones gives fascinating and revealing examples of real living women of ancient times. She reveals that Diodorus Siculus of Sicily, a Historian, wrote about his travels to Northern Africa and some near East places forty nine years before the birth of Christ. He noticed that there were women warriors and strong matriarchal systems. Apparently women in Ethiopia carried arms and raised their children in a peaceful communal way. While in Libya "all the authority was vested in the women, who discharged every kind of public duty."

He creates a leap in imagination (especially for today's mind) when he states,

"the children were handed over immediately after birth to the men, who reared them on milk and other foods suitable to their age."

The women he met in his travels revered the Goddess as their principal deity and set up sanctuaries for her worship. He tells us that in Egypt the Goddess reigned supreme, and the laws of the land reflected the reverence paid to the "mighty Goddess".

The status of women could be seen mirrored and played out in the relationship between the Queen and King. Diodorus tell us that it was ordained that the Queen should have greater and more honor than the king. In fact, Herodotus of Greece was awed by the fact that women went to the market places, transacted and did business "while the husbands stay home and weaved."

As to why property passed from the mother and not the father, it is professor Cyrus Gordon who explains,

"this system may well hark back to pre-historic times when only the obvious relationship between mother and child was recognized, but not the less apparent relationship between father and child."

In fact many a man in the Mediterranean could only become King or Chief by formal marriage, and his daughter not his son succeeded. This meant that the next chief would be the youth who married the daughter.

The power of and status of women was written and into the law of the lands. SW Baron comments,

"in Egyptian papyri many women appear as parties in civil litigations and independent business transactions even with their own husbands and fathers."

Women could also divorce their husbands and get paid compensation, no problem. In terms of religious practices it was apparently the women who were seen as the natural intermediary with divinities. As priestess they would preside over divinical matters. The role of the male was subordinate to hers even when he took on the role of high priest of the bull.

Gustave Glotz explains in his works "The Aegean Civilization",

"While private worship was performed in front of small idols, in public the part of Goddess was played by a woman. It is the high priestess who takes her place on the seat of the Goddess, at the foot of the sacred tree or stands on the mountain peak to receive worship and offerings from her acolytes and from the faithful."

Often this high priestess of the Goddess would also be the Queen or tribal ruler. On this Merlin stone comments that some male writers who were use to their own male orientated society being a set pattern "reverse cause and effect" suggesting that when a woman became Queen she then also gained the title of high priestess, a position supposedly resulting from her marriage to the King. However, Stone suggest there is ample evidence to suggest it was the other way around.

Apparently it was the daughters not the sons who were the inheritors of the Egyptian throne. This is why the Egyptian Princess for many centuries were married within the family and were not available for international marriage. It is interesting to note, in very ancient times the Mother Goddess ruled alone. Over a period of time she acquired a son, lover.

They came with battles and spears. I find myself peering into the ancient veiled world of the Dancing Girl of Mohenjo-daro. My mind is filled with a burning question which I direct to her,

"If you were so powerful then, how comes you are so obscure now?"

She doesn't reply. At least not directly from her lips. But her words seem to come through the further telling of the history of the Goddess through the various books I find myself buried in. From Europe came a fierce and vicious warrior people who saw the world as their dominion. They came to the Mother cultures not in one single event but in a series of migration waves which took place over a period of thousand and possibly even three thousand years.

They brought with them a storm God, a concept of light being good and darkness being evil. Their divinities were thunderbolt hurlers. The belief of "the sword and death instead of the phallus and fertility," says Bill Moyers journalist and the man who interviews Joseph Campbell in the book, "The Power of Myth".

The invasions began to happen about the fourth millennium. These northern invaders were called Indo-Europeans, Indo Iranians, Indo Aryans or simply Aryans. Merlin Stone reveals they left "no temple or tablets untouched". Apparently they had a superiority complex which was based on their ability to conquer the peaceful people's of the Goddess.

Joseph Campbell states, "they came in from the north and from the south and wiped out cities overnight. Just read the story in the Book of Genesis of the part played by Jacob's tribe in the fall of the city of Shechem. Overnight, the city is wiped out by these herding people who have suddenly appeared."

Why were these Indo Aryans so violent?

He answers my enquiring mind like fleets moving across a desert floor with night falling swiftly.

"The Semite invaders were herders of goats and sheep, the Indo-Europeans of cattle. Both were formerly hunters, and so the cultures are essentially animal-oriented. When you have hunters, you have killers. And in movement, nomadic people coming into conflict with other people and conquering the areas into which they move."

So what happened when these Semitic and Indo Aryans invaded the Mother Cultures? Once again as quick as I ask the question Campbell answers.

"The Semitic people were invading the world of the Mother Goddess systems, and so the male-orientated mythologies became dominant, and the Mother Goddess becomes, well – sort of Grandmother Goddess, way, way back."

Another question arises from my mind like the sand being blown by a hardy desert storm. How was this dominance in the mythologies achieved? I could almost see Campbell rubbing his chin as he replies,

"the way of bringing this about is by annihilating the god or goddess who was there before. That's what imperialistic people have always done."

An example or two is always fitting, and so he gives them.

"Well, the one that was there before the Babylonian god Marduk was the All-Mother Goddess. So the story begins with a great council of the male gods up in the sky. Each god was a star, and they have heard that Granma is coming, old Tiamut, the Abyss, the inexhaustible Source. She arrives in the form of a great fish or dragon – and what god will have the courage to go against Grandma and do her in? And the one who has the courage is, of course, the god of our present great city. He's the big one.

So when Tiamat opens her mouth, the young god Marduk of Babylon sends winds into her throat and belly that blow her to pieces, and he then dismembers her and fashions the earth and heavens out of the parts of her body."

He explains this motif of dismembering a primordial being and turning its body into the universe is echoed across continents. He pushes on,

"now, the mother goddess in old mother-goddess mythologies was herself already the universe, so the great creative deed of Marduk was a supererogatory act. There was no need for him to cut her up and make the universe out of her, because she was already the universe. But the male –

382

orientated myth takes over and he becomes – apparently – the creator."

Merlin Stone adds, "many of the myths written by priests by the invading tribes was to justify the supremacy of the new male deities and to justify the installation of a king as a result of the relationship of that King to the Male Deity."

Now remember we are a microcosm of the macrocosm, and the ancients more than anyone believed this. Myths were their T.V. It was where they explained their philosophical, cosmological, laws, scientific and sociological outlook to life.

If the male God of the invaders were not outright chopping the Goddess up into little pieces, he was partnering himself with her as in the case of Amun and Mut, Zeus and Hera. In many myths the Goddess is represented as a serpent or dragon who would be slain.

Merlin Stones explains that the female religion especially in the early invasion seems to have assimilated the male deities and survived as a popular religion of the people for thousands of years after the initial invasions. By the time Marduk did away with the great Mother Goddess Joseph Campbell reveals,

"by that time – 1750 B.c or so – it was finished."

It was with the Hebrews and eventually the Christians of the first century after Christ that the religion of the Mother was finally suppressed and nearly forgotten.

`The pattern of the Indo Aryans invaders was interesting. According to Merlin Stones,

"a group of aggressive warriors accompanied by a priestly caste of high standing, who initially invaded, conquered and then ruled the indigenous population of each land they entered."

Once they affirmed the right of their male God over the female Mother Goddess. They then also used this to justify their terrible treatment of women. For no longer were women to be viewed as Goddesses but as harlots, property and booty to be raped and owned. In Deuteronomy of the Old Testament it is stated, "Thou shalt not kill, thou shalt not covert thy neighbors wife – except abroad. Then you should put all the males to the sword, and the women you shall take as booty to yourself."

Merlin Stone further elucidates that through their sacred text the Aryan and Hebrew invaders recorded their views just as the Mother cultures had. Only theirs was one that would mark the demise of a world that was harmonious in terms of human and ecological relations.   When Indo-Aryan culture went to India they created sacred versus which affirmed their position. In the Rig Veda, Merlin Stone points out, they stated that in the beginning there was only Asura (living power) They then broke into two cosmic groups. One was the enemies of the Aryans – the Daravas or Dilyas, whose mother was the Goddess Danu/Diti; the other was the group in which resided the heroes of the Aryans, known as A Dityas (not Dityas. Not people of Diti).

The Rig Veda is very clear about how women are perceived in these times of the Aryan culture, "the mind of women brooks not discipline. Her intellect has little weight."

The daily worship of the Aryans was not to an ancestral mother who first gave birth to everything, but to a Father God known as Prajapati who becomes the Supreme father of all.

They brought with them the concept of light and dark because the people they conquered were dark skinned peoples known as Dravidians. With this they brought in the caste system. Where the Dravidians were at the bottom as untouchables and they were at the top as the rulers and priest.

384

Their light and dark concept also seemed to echo their belief in a God of the volcanoes.

The Dravidians believed in a Mother God and were from the Indus valley the same place as the Dancing Girl of Mohenjo-daro. They believed in a Mother Goddess who appears in the Puranas and Tantras under many names such as Durga and Kali or simply the name Devi (which combines all Goddesses under one roof). Merlin Stone tells us "her name Danu or Diti had been forgotten" I wondered if that was the name of The Dancing Girl of Mohenjo-daro. I silently ask her, but she keeps on smiling gently, quietly urging me on.

I discover that today in South India, in non Aryan circles, every village has its collection of Ammas or Mothers and their worship is the chief religious exercise of the village priest or priestess of those deities

As I learn about the Mother, I feel myself basking in the luminosity of enlightenment. As I do so two questions idly, cross my mind: Did the word devil derive from the word Devi, which means Mother? Also is that why the pictures of Kali, the great Pre-Aryan Mother Goddess, is made to look unappealing compared to her fairer aspects?

In ancient Egypt the attacks of the Indo-Aryans came about 300 BC. The two Goddesses the Egyptians held in great esteem were Nekhebet (the Vulture Goddess) of the South, and Wadjet (the Cobra Goddess) were lessened in their position. Represented on the crown of upper and Lower Egypt respectively, they none the less seemed able to hold onto their power as symbols of royalty. It became clear to me that the saving grace of Egypt's religious beliefs and system, lay in their ability to fluidly assimilate the Gods of the Aryans.

385

I love snakes, but I am afraid of them. One day while trying to take in all I had been reading I fell asleep and had a dream. It was late at night and there was only silence in the balm of South Carolina. I dreamt a snake crawling up the mosquito net of mine and Derrick's bedroom. It was long slim and black. I remember feeling petrified.

Even though most of my dreams come true, I couldn't believe that would or could. How wrong I was. About four weeks latter I was sitting on my bed reading something about the fall of the Goddess. My back was backing the bedroom window. It was a hot balmy day so I had the window opened. In the middle of reading I suddenly paused, dog-eared my page, and turned around slowly. I froze. Goose pimples rose on my arms. Right there on the mosquito net was the snake from my dream.

I didn't know what to do. In slow motion I called Derrick. He answered the phone, but all I could say was,

"the snake! The snake!"

Luckily for me, he had left work for lunch and was literally outside the house door when I called. As I heard the key turn in the door, a surge of life ran through my numbed out legs. I ran to greet him, and pushed him back outside the door, gesticulating wildly at the snake which was now on a pipe near our bedroom window. I still could not talk and once again could only manage,

"the snake! The snake! The Snake!"

He followed my wild pointing and gesticulations and saw the culprit, but before he could do anything it bolted like lightening away from the crime scene. That's exactly what it had done in my dreams when it had been chasing me.

Afterwards Derrick laughed and shook his head,

"you and your dreams."

"Have you ever seen a snake like that?"

"Never," he replied. "Not in all the time I have been growing up here which is almost forty years!"

"How long do you think that snake was?" I enquired visibly shaking.

"That joker was about 4 foot long, easily," Derrick estimated.

For a few months after that I could not sleep properly. I would suddenly awaken during the night fully expecting to see that long black snake on our bed.

I am glad to report that it did not quite happen that way. Instead not too long after that incident I found a shell in my mother-in-laws collection of sea shells. They had been sitting on the porch for the longest of while in an old battered shoe box. Obviously quite abandoned and forgotten. I had never looked in that box really. But one day I felt moved to do so. There in the box something caught my eye, it was a shell that seemed to contain a fossil image of a cobra's head. My hands picked it up trembling. I ran my fingers across it feeling all the indentations.

Then a question floated like a silver cloud across my mind - what was with the snake theme? Me and snakes really were not friends. I mean I have stroked a few in my time. I wish more people could, actually. They really are not slimy but warm and beautiful to the touch. Yet, this knowledge was not enough to alleviate my fear of snakes. I wondered where this fear had come from?

The day after the snake incident I went back to the history of the Mother Goddess, and found myself in the currents of discovery once again. Something interesting caught my attention, especially in the light of my snake incident. To subjugate the Goddess the invaders of the indigenous peoples of the earth turned all her symbols upside down. This awesome attack of Indo Aryan ideology came primarily through the Semitic people, the Hebrews. Merlin Stone quotes many good authorities such as Professor Cyrus and George Menden Hall who state that there was a close relationship between the Indo Aryans and the Hebrews.

They discuss some interesting facts about Abraham in order to show this connection. Apparently, Abraham was the father of the Hebrew tribes and was also the first prophet of the Hebrew God Yahweh. It is said that he may have had a very close link to the conclave of Indo Aryans who lived in the town of his kinsmen, Harran.

Now the name of the Hebrew God, Yahwah is indicated to possibly come from the Sanskrit word Yahveh which means overflowing. There is also another possibility that Abraham's name related to the names of the Aryan priestly caste of India, known as Brahmins.

Cyrus Gordon says that the Hebrew people and Indo Aryans had a close relationship in terms of literature, linguistics and custom. It is through their book the bible that the Hebrewite priest reflected the laws and social attitudes of the land as they now perceived them. Like the Indo-Aryan invaders, whom they showed a close relationship with, everything is turned on its head in terms of the creation myth. At this stage all the symbols of the Goddess become turned around, put upside down, and shook of all positive meaning. The turning around started with the birth of humanity, and continued on its sullied journey.

A rib not the earth. That was what the creation myths began to look like. Gone was the ethereal dance of Prakruti from

Hindu mythology. Gone was the Sumerian myths where the Goddess created men and women from mud. In both Sumer and Babylon Man and women were created together. Gone, gone, gone. No longer did the ancient myths of the world emanate from the divine Mother Goddess. In the male dominated religion of the Hebrews creation was, according to Merlin Stone, to suddenly take on "an unnatural twist". Man in the Garden of Eden gives birth to woman from all places – his ribs!

How unnatural and unscientific can you get? At least mud represents the primordial elements of water and earth coming together to create life. We also know that mothers do give birth to both male and female children. But who gives birth from a rib! It was this one little act of bizarre creation which was to now justify the fact that women were "divinely" lower than men. No more are they Goddesses they are blamed for the Great Fall. According to Merlin Stone Eve represents the Goddess, and now she is placed below the male God. This one act, also marks the beginning of the justification of Divine Kingship amongst the Hebrews. This was important so that property could now pass through the male lineage and not the female.

His eyes stared transfixed to the apple upon the tree, and from the apple did he bite. With that bite Eve becomes viewed as the cause of the "original fall". The tree and its fruit that was her symbol became something to be hated. Now let's go back to the tree. Cultures all over the world believe in a cosmic tree which is said to be the pillar of the world. It is called by the various names: World Tree, Tree of Life and Trees of Knowledge. These trees are often the connection between this world and the other.

In Africa the baobab tree is of great significance. In some African villages, court is held under that tree which is said to be able to communicate great wisdom. It is quite an amazing tree which is also called the Tree of Life. For good reason too. It provides shelter, food, water for animals and humans alike. Its cork like bark is fire resistant and is used for making cloth and rope. The leaves are used for condiments and medicines and its fruit is rich in vitamin C. The tree also stores hundreds of liters of water which is tapped in the dry periods. Some Baobab trees are said to be over 2000 years old. For most of the year it is a leafless tree and looks like its roots are sticking in the air obtaining its nourishment from the heavens.

A tree with roots in the heaven is said to be one of the crucial signs of a world Cosmic tree. It is said the Cosmic tree was created with its roots growing upwards so that it could live for a very long time, as its nourishment is drawn from the heavens.

The Aztecs had a Cosmic Tree which is said to come up from the body of the Earth Goddess who lies on a row of crocodile spines, the symbol of the fertile earth. The trunk of the tree is said to rise from a disc containing water which is called the "all-encompassing sea". The two ears of maize which grow from the tree symbolizes the fruit bearing earth. The Gods Quetzalcoatl and Macuilxochitl can be found to the left and right of the tree drawing blood from themselves which they are said to fertilize the Earth Goddess with .

In India the Banyan tree is said to be the Tree of Life. It reaches over 100 feet into the sky. It has the features of a Tree of Life as it has magnificent aerial roots which grow down into the Earth from widely spreading branches. Like the Baobab tree it can live for thousands of years.

This tree derived its name from the Hindi word, Banya which means "Merchant". For merchants would always sit under the shade of the tree and trade. Europeans often went back home to Europe speaking about a Banyan tree – the tree that merchants traded under.

It is said that the Banyan protected the Lord Krishna when the world was flooded. It is also a species of the baobab tree, known as the Boddhi tree, that the Buddha found enlightenment under. The Banyan is said to be the tree of fertility, love, protection and healing. It is a tree that can according to ancient text grant the wishes of anyone who worships it.

In the Ackawoi culture of the Orinoco River basin the mythical Tree of Life created by their god, Makonaima, bore bountiful fruit which sprung from the earth. The tree is said to be the origin of all cultivated plants, the stump is filled with water which has all sorts of fish, while animated being were created from cutting of pieces of the tree with an ax and throwing them into the river.

While the Ainu people of Hokkaido and Sakhalin islands believed that the human backbone was originally fashioned from a tree. Namely the willow tree. I found it interesting that the Goddess Guanyin is often pictured holding a willow branch in one of her hands.

Now interestingly the Celtic alphabet is known as the Ogam alphabet. It is divided into five set of five letters, called aicme (meaning tribe or family). Each set bears a name derived from the first or "chief" letter, and the letters themselves are said to have the names of various trees. It is apparently this association that has led to Ogam being referred to as the "tree alphabet". The Ogam system was said to operate as a divination system. It is said that the Celts who comprise the major part of the Irish, Scottish and Welsh population were known to the Romans as Gauls. They apparently sent priests to a sacred festival for the Goddess Cybele in Pessinus, Anatolia in the second century B.C, and were said to be influenced by the Mother Culture of the place. Thus, it would make sense why the trees of the Ogam system had so many Goddess associations.

As I speak to Derrick about the connection of the Tree of Life to the Goddess. He notices I have the "Green Man Tree Oracle" book by John Mathews and Will Worthington on the brown hard wood coffee table I am working on. It details the Ogam divination system and has the meaning of each tree. He slowly picks up the pack of cards and holds it reverently between his palms, and ask a silent question. He draws a card from the pack. It is a Beech Tree.

"Imagine that, this tree is the very last tree of the book!" he exclaims

For some reason this feels very significant to him. He hands the book over to me so I could read the explanation for him. Before I read, I look at the picture of the Beech Tree. It is depicted as a He. Eyes stare out from an old ancient looking tree face. I stare at that face for quite a while. Then I read the words of the explanation that accompany it,

"crossing the thresholds is a way of moving from one state of being to another."…"being creatures of habit it is easier for us to stay with the known and familiar, yet if we refuse to confront what lies beyond the threshold we can remain in a stagnant condition."

I read on and discovered that the Beech tree was considered to be the "Queen of the Woods". It was associated with serpents, and has serpentine roots. It is believed that it reflects the idea of the wise serpent giving knowledge to those who ask for it. Several Celtic alters to the Beech tree were discovered in French Pyrenees which the author suggest signifies its importance to the Celtic tribes who lived there.

Slivers of Beech wood and leaves were once carried as talismans to bring good luck and increase creative energy. The thin leaves of the beech wood were bound together to form the first book which the authors revealed was in line with its association with writing, learning and the transmission of lore. They inform us that the Anglo Saxon word for "beech" was bok (which became book); in German Buche is "beech" and Buch is "book". While in the Swedish language bok means both "book" and "beech". The beech tree was associated with the Goddess Diana. Who is a virgin Goddess, Lady of the Hunt and was said to be popular amongst the lower class because in her sanctuary they could receive shelter. She is also associated with women who heal.

I close my eyes and thank the "Green Tree Oracle" for adding further light to my research. For there in the honorable and revered Beech tree was all the original markings of the ancient Goddess mythologies which connect her in her former glory to the symbolism of the tree. Here was not a disgraced Mother Goddess, but one who was still wise, and life giving to all life forms. I also made a small bow to the Goddess Diana for showing once again the Mother Goddess was "She Who Shelters All".

Where did the original Tree of Life come from? Now interestingly enough the Tree of Life symbolism is said to originate from ancient Egypt. The oldest depiction of the Goddess Hathor (the Goddess of love, wisdom, joy, fertility, grace, longevity, fortune and life) is said to be the Tree of Life.

Merlin Stone reveals that the Tree of Life was known as "the Living Body of Hathor on Earth". To eat of its fruit was to eat of the sustaining flesh and fluid of the Goddess. Some Egyptian murals apparently depicted the Goddess within this tree, passing out its sacred fruit to the dead as the food of eternity, immortality and continued life even after death.

If we look back on some of the Tree of Life of different cultures we will notice how closely they are related to the Hathor's symbolisms. You have the wisdom, wealth, and health giving symbols. Then there's the snake, the nourishing fruit, healing waters and so on. Even the story I open this chapter with has this tree of life symbolism from the ancient Yoruba's Wisdom tradition.

Merlin Stone further reveals that one of the most explanatory evidence of the symbolic meaning of the tree lies in the memorial rituals of the annual death of Osiris brother/husband of Isis. When Osiris was first buried he was placed in a mulberry coffin. The coffin was later placed inside a living sycamore tree, symbolic of Isis-Hathor as his mother/wife. In this way she was to provide him with the food of eternity. The custom was linked to the legend when Isis went to Canaan to retrieve the tree in which Osiris had been buried, cut the coffin of Osiris from the tree and left the remainder of it as a sacred relic in her temple at Byblos. Merlin Stone informs us that this was the Canaanite shrine at which Isis-Hathor and Balaal were sycamores.

The Tree of Life is said to be an axis mundi. It is a place that represents the center of the world where heaven and earth connects. Every culture has such a center where they think the whole world began. In Nigeria that center is called Ife which means "The Earth That Spreads". When I Flick through The Penguin Dictionary of Symbols it reveals the *axis mundi* image appears in every region of the world and takes many forms.

The image is both feminine (an umbilical providing nourishment) and masculine (a phallus providing insemination into a uterus). It may have the form of a natural object (a mountain, a tree, a vine, a stalk, a column of smoke or fire) or a product of human manufacture (a staff, a tower, a ladder, a staircase, a maypole, a cross, a steeple, a rope, a totem pole, a pillar, a spire).

According to Mircea Eliades in his book "Shamanism: Archaic Techniques of Ecstasy". The shamanic ladder found in many myths is one of the oldest representations of the axis mundis. It is found in numerous creation myths in the form of a tree.

As I read more about more about the Tree of Life, I discover in Budge's book "Egyptian Gods" that the sycamore tree (which I now knew represented the Goddess Hathor) was also seen as made of turquoise. For we are shown that in the Egyptian Book of the Dead there were "two sycamores of turquoise" between which the sun-god rose each morning.

Latter I was to discover something interesting buried in the 1st Dalai Lama's praise poem to the Goddess and Bodhisattva Tara. In it Tara is likened to the "heavenly Turquoise Tree". Once again I was left pondering on the similar symbols that Tara had with the Goddess Hathor. The two were obviously one.

First Dalai Lama (1391-1474) Praise Poem to Tara

On a lotus seat, standing for realization of voidness,
(You are) the emerald-colored, one-faced, two-armed Lady
In youth's full bloom, right leg out, left drawn in,
Showing the union of wisdom and art - homage to you!
Like the outstretched branch of the heavenly turquoise tree,

Your supple right hand makes the boon- granting gesture,
Inviting the wise to a feast of supreme accomplishments,
As if to an entertainment-homage to you!
Your left hand gives us refuge, showing the Three Jewels;
It says, "You people who see a hundred dangers,
Don't be frightened-I shall swiftly save you!"
Homage to you!
Both hands signal with blue utpala flowers,
"Samsaric beings! Cling not to worldly pleasures.
Enter the great city of liberation!"
Flower-goads prodding us to effort-homage to you!

Hathor as Sycamore Tree. Tomb of Panehsy, 18th Dynasty

Merlin Stone states that it was most probably the sycamore tree which was the tree in the Garden of Eden. Why? She reveals that ancient records often mention a tree that is called the Sycamore tree, which is sometimes called the Fig or Mulberry tree. This tree was apparently the Near Eastern Ficus Sicomorus, the Sycamore fig, which is sometimes called the Black Mulberry. It is distinctive from the common fig tree in that it has reddish colored fruit which grow in large clumps like a cluster of grapes.

According to Stone, Eve (The Goddess) gives Adam (who is symbolic of the male Hebrew God) the fruit from the Tree of Life to eat. Their eyes are opened up and they become ashamed of their nakedness. All in one fell swoop of the pen the symbols which had existed for thousands and thousands of years as ones of renewal and goodness become dirty and ruinous.

For in ancient times sex was not seen as dirty. In fact there was an ancient Egyptian custom where the Priestess engaged in sacred sexual rites. They did not see sex as we see it today. Our vision of sex is very Indo Aryan. In the ancient past when a selected man had sacred sex with a temple priestess then it was seen as a blessing. Now here is the interesting thing. The child was seen as the Mothers and not the mans. His paternity was not that important. For the property rights were through the woman. As a result the power was with the woman.

The sacred sexual rites were held to be very sanctified. The women who engaged in this act were highly honored. However, when the Hebrews invaded the Mother cultures they wanted to ensure the property rights and power rights were through the men. Sex was the only way they could root in their dominance. So they made sex to be dirty and shameful. Any woman partaking in the sacred sexual rights was now considered a harlot. In fact by virtue of Eve giving Adam the fruit of life, she had been turned from a Goddess to a sinner.

Just when I think my tired mind can rest. The Dancing Girl of Mohenjo – daro swirls in her Devadasi. They dance into my sphere of awareness in a moment of a mental break where I casually read a few news articles. I almost past over them. For my mind was so exhausted from the flood of information that had already presented itself to me. When exhausted like that, one is afraid to go down a rabbit hole. But, the Devadasi did not let me go. I groan for down the rabbit hole I must go.

The custom of the Devadasi still continues in India today. The name Devadasi translates into "servant of God (or goddess)." On one hand they are likened to Christian nuns, because they marry to the local temple. They were then free from the normal obligations that applied to married women. However, unlike Christian nuns, in ancient times these women were trained in all the ways of a temple priestess: classical arts of dance, music, poetry and sacred sex. Under the goddess religions sex is seen as a divine act which mirrors the creative and renewal powers of the Mother Goddess. It was highly elevated as being of great spiritual importance. Something our cultures do not understand today.

In pre-Islamic times the Devadasi was a respected member of the community. Just as her sister equivalent was in Egyptian times before the Indo Aryan invasion. It was considered auspicious to touch a Devadasi and she was paid well to offer her services as a dancer, musician, poet or consort. Just like her Egyptian counterpart, as the temple priestess, she had the absolute freedom to choose which men she would take as a lover. Famous Devadasis were often employed by the local Rani (queen) to entertain the court and her status was such that she could sit beside the Rani.

Over a period of time the Devadasis saw their status diminish. Today they are dumped at temples across the country where they get rudimentary training and are dedicated to the Goddess Yellamma. When they have their first period they are initiated by either the head Aryan priest (Brahmin priest) or sold to the highest bidder (usually a high caste landowner or a wealthy local businessman.) From that time on the Devadasis essentially works as a prostitute for the temple. The Devadasi is sold into prostitution when she is seen as too old (in her late teens), or after her first child. A survey suggested there were 20,000 registered Devadasi in the Indian Karnataka state alone.

My mind swiftly, like a ghost train, travels back and forth through the doorways of history. I cannot seem to help it but my heart is laden with sadness. For I feel as though I am on a ghost train watching the rise and fall of our relationship to the divine Feminine that balanced our lives with her compassion, love, joy and deep wisdom. But, in all the sadness, I had to admit there was a joy there too. The Dancing Girl of Mohenjo – Daro puts it there as she forces me to plow back and forth like a weaver of history gathering the threads of time.

I discover that each January, nearly half a million people visit the small town called Saundatti for a festival, to be blessed by Yellamma, the Hindu goddess of fertility. The streets leading to the temple are lined with shops selling sacred paraphernalia – glass bangles, garlands, coconuts and heaped red and yellow kunkuma, a dye that devotees smear on their foreheads. The older women are called *jogathis* and are said to be intermediaries between the goddess and the people. They all start their working lives as Devadasis and most of them would have been initiated at the temple.

It becomes apparent to me that the Devadasi system has been part of southern Indian life for many centuries. It also becomes obvious that no one seems to quite know how it originated. However, in my mind's eye the Devadasi culture seemed to originate from none other than ancient Egypt (as you can see from my comparisons to the priestess of that culture and their Egyptian equivalents).

One telling story which most people quote about the origins of the Devadasi goes something like this (it has slight variations according to which source you read it from)

Yellamma was the wife of the powerful rishi Jamadagni. The couple and their four sons lived in a simple wooden hermitage by the lake. Here the sage punished his body and performed great feats of austerity. After the birth of his fourth child, these included a vow of chastity. Every day, Yellamma served her husband, and fetched water from the river for her husband's rituals. She used a pot made of sand, and carried it home in the coils of a live snake.

One day, as Yellamma was fetching water, she saw a heavenly being, a gandharva, making love to his consort by the banks of the river. It was many years since Yellamma had enjoyed the pleasures of love, and the sight attracted her. Watching from behind a rock, and hearing the lovers' cries of pleasure, she found herself longing to take the place of the beloved.

This sudden rush of desire destroyed her composure. When she crept away to get water for her husband, she found, to her horror, that she could no longer create a pot from sand, and that her yogic powers of concentration had vanished. When she returned home without the water, Jamadagni guessed what had happened, and in his rage he cursed his wife. According to Rani and Kaveri, within seconds Yellamma had become sickly and ugly, covered with boils and festering sores. She was turned out of her home, cursed to wander the roads of the Deccan, begging for alms.

Now another version of the story I read goes something like this,

> *One day there was a woman called Renuka, who was the daughter of a Brahmin, married to sage Jamadagni and was the mother of five sons. She used to bring water from the river Malaprabha for the sage's worship and rituals. One day while she was at the river, she saw a group of youths engaging themselves in water sports and forgot to return home in time which made Jamadagni to suspect her chastity. He ordered his sons one by one to punish their mother but four of them refused on one pretext or the other. The sage cursed them to become eunuchs and got her beheaded by his fifth son, Parashuram. When the father offered Parashuram a boon he asked what he wanted. One of the things was for his mothers and brothers to be brought back to life. To everybody's astonishment, Renuka's spirit multiplied and moved to different regions. Renuka was back as a whole too. This miracle inspired her sons and others to become her followers.*

I found it interesting how Renuka as Yellamma rose from the waters to take her place in the Goddess lineage, and play her part in putting things right again. For there was the force and rush of the primordial waters telling our story again, this time through Renuka's water pot.

I trembled and allowed the electrical current to course through my body like lightening bolts. In Renuka/Yellamma I could clearly see the hall marks of Hathor, and therefore I could also see unfolding from her beingness the DNA of the gentle side of all the Mother Goddesses I had encountered along the way.

Then I see it, the trademark of Indo Aryan invasions. The turned symbols of the Mother Goddess turned on their head. For in the Renuka/Yellamma stories sex is a bad thing, the snake is present, the Goddess falls from grace, and becomes a banished, sickly sinner.

As the dots begin to join, the Dancing Girl of Mohenjo-Daro who smiles.

Picture of Devadasi from 1920, Tamilnadu
South India

I do a little more research on Yellamma and then jot some notes on paper comparing her symbols and stories to Hathors.

Image of Renuka/Yellamma

Yellamma

✓ *Yellamma's color is yellow. Hathor's color is yellow. Osun's color is yellow. Amma means Mother. So I am making a wild guest and figuring the Yell connects with the word yellow. Thus the word Yellamma means Yellow Mother.*

✓ *Goddess of fertility, healing, wisdom, joy, sexuality and compassion*

✓ *Yellamma is also seen as having a fierce protective side and is often seen as an incarnation of Kali*

✓ *Hathor is seen as the Goddess of fertility, sexuality, healing, joy, compassion and wisdom.*

✓ *Hathor is the fierce protectress in her form as Sekhmet/Bast (I have already connected these Mother Goddesses with Durga and Kali)*

✓ *Yellamma has the snake symbol*

405

- ✓ *Hathor is connected to the snake symbol of Uatchet, who represents royalty. In Egypt the Snake was seen as connected with special prophetic abilities and was associated with the priesthood.*
- ✓ *Yellamma is connected with the power of water, and with the river.*
- ✓ *Hathor is seen as Nut the primordial water Goddess. She is also the Sirius star which appears just when the Nile is going to inundate.*

I pause and look over all the similarities. The likeness of the symbols are surprisingly very close. I continued my notes, and analysis looking at the similarities of Yellamma's and the things that marked the fall of the ancient Mother Goddess in history.

- ✓ *At first Yellamma is powerful.*
- ✓ *Her sexuality and desire for pleasure causes her shame, her downfall, and all her powers are diminshed*
- ✓ *She becomes banished from her husband's house to live a life of hardship*
- ✓ *She becomes ugly*
- ✓ *Oh, the snake is present in this whole story as well. So the snake is connected to her powers. So that too by default becomes a bad thing*

One thing that becomes clear to me from the Yellamma story is that although the Goddess is killed of it seems hard to obliterate her. Yellamma reflects the primordial Mother Goddess's resilience throughout history. For Yellamma multiplies and spreads over the land.

As I think on all of this, and Yellamma's predicament, another story comes to mind that is very similar. It is involves another Goddess, who loves the color yellow, her fall from and rise back to grace – the beautiful graceful Osun.

One day after living sometime with the God Erinle, Osun falls into a predicament. Erinle falls tired and loses his desire of her. With a lack of desire in his heart Erinle boots Osun out of their marital home to face a life of poverty and dejection.

The beautiful Water Goddess travels in poverty. She travels far and wide, becoming poorer and poorer with each passing day. Eventually her exquisite white dress turns yellow.

As she nears a cross road, all tired and worn down, she comes across three brothers fighting. When she starts to run away she is told by one that he will give her their inheritance. He keeps his promise to the Goddess thus ending her poverty and hardship. Thereafter, Osun who only had one dress and only dejection to her name lives a life of great wealth.

It is a few months later, and I revisit the story of the Devadasi in William Dalrymple's article: "Letter to India: Serving the Goddess". My heart stops, as I dwell on a poignant exchange between the journalist and a Devadasi. One that seemed to sum up the fate of the Devadasi, and the Yellow Mother Goddess of the World.

She turned to face me.

"He drinks anything he can get," she said. "If someone told him his own urine had alcohol in it, he would drink that, too." She laughed, but harshly. "If I were to sit under a tree and tell you the

407

sadness we have to suffer, the leaves of that tree would fall like tears.
My brother is totally bedridden now. He has fevers and diarrhea."
She paused. "He used to be such a handsome man, with a fine face
and large eyes. Now those eyes are closed, and his face is covered
with boils and lesions."

"Yellamma never wanted it to be like this," Rani said.

"The goddess is sitting silently," Kaveri said. "We don't
know what feelings she has about us. Who really knows what she is
thinking?"

"No," Rani said, firmly shaking her head. "The goddess
looks after us. When we are in distress, she comes to us. Sometimes
in our dreams. Sometimes in the form of one of her children."

"It is not the goddess's doing."

"The world has made it like this."

"The world, and the disease."

"The goddess dries our tears," Rani said. "If you come to her
with a pure heart, she will take away your sadness and your sorrows.
What more can she do?"

As I read more of the article, that familiar tingle comes
back to me. I freeze when I read,

Some experts trace the institution to the ninth century;
others maintain that it is far older, and claim that what is arguably
one of the most ancient extant pieces of Indian art, a small bronze of
a naked dancing girl from Mohenjo-Daro, dating to around 2500
B.C., could depict a devadasi.

The Dancing Girl of Mohenjo-daro seemed please. She
rested from her dancing, and allowed me to tuck into a big
plate of Jamaican rice and peas.

I touch the smooth edges of the fossil looking stone with the cobra head embedded into it. As I do so I pick up Merlin Stones book, and return to the unfolding epic of the Goddess's story. Ironically, its threads pick up from another symbol of the Goddess turned on its head by the Indo Aryan invasions – the snake.

Merlin Stone reveals that on the Island of Crete there was a snake Goddess called "The Lady of Serpents". Whom ample evidence shows came from the pre-dynastic people of Egypt. Experts say she ended up in Crete about 3000 BC. This was about the same time that the first dynasty of Egypt was forming, and around the same time that the Egyptian people were fleeing from invasions and seemed to have ended up in Crete. I found these facts interesting, especially since I remembered that experts believed the statute of the Dancing Girl of Mohenjo – Daro dated back to 2500 BC.

According to Stone, the use of the cobra in the Goddess traditions of Egypt was so ancient that the sign of any Goddess was the sign of the cobra. A picture of a cobra was the hieroglyphic sign for the word of Goddess. Uachet was the cobra Goddess of Lower Egypt. This cobra Goddess is later seen worn on the foreheads of other deities and Egyptian royalty. She was known as the eye of Uachet and was a symbol of mystical insight and wisdom. Hathor and Maat were latter derivations of the cobra Goddess and were both known as the Eye. The eye itself is written in the feminine form. The Eye latter became associated with the male deities as a result of the Northern Invaders.

Merlin Stone reveals that there is an Egyptian text which says that Hathor had been the serpent who had existed before anything else had been created. She then made the heavens, earth and all life that existed on it. In this account she is angry. There is no real stated reason. As a result she threatens to destroy all of creation and once more resumes her original form as a serpent.

The connection of the Goddess in relation to wisdom was seen through the fact that the Priestess of the Goddess were often consulted as Prophetess who gave vital political, social, governmental and military advice. The Goddess Delphi of Greece was held as the sacred one who supplied divine revelations through her priestess.

The woman who brought forth the oracle of divine wisdom was known as Pythia. A snake was coiled about the tripod stool upon which she sat – Python. In the early days Python was seen as a female but in latter times it was known as a male. This wise Serpent Goddess of Delphi originated from Crete's Serpent Goddess who originated from Egypt. The female prophetess of Rome were known as Sibyls. They were identified with a prophetess of Anatolia known as Sybella who was it appears connected to the Cybele.

I later discovered in the book "Egypt: Land and Lives of the Pharaohs revealed" (yet another book that had been lined up for me to read by the grand masters of old) – that Crete was considered to be the first European civilization. Egyptian style pottery, scarab beetle amulets and other items had been found in Crete; and Cretan pottery had been found in Egypt, indicating that there had been early contact and direct trade links between the two countries.

It was in Dr. Jeremy Narby's book, "the Cosmic Serpent" that I discovered more about what the symbol of the snake meant to the ancients. It was yet another book that was virtually handed to me by my Book's Angel.

Dr. Jeremy Narby, a leading Anthropologist, wrote his ground breaking book about what the snake really meant in ancient cultures. Apparently, he had no intention to write a book about the snake, but that is how callings work. He was actually in the Amazon to help the Rainforest Indians keep the right to their lands by proving they are the best custodians of it.

He wanted to show that they knew the healing plants of the forest better than anyone else. So they needed to keep being the custodians of that land. He wanted to prove this by using empirical data. You know collecting plant species, and documenting the Rainforest Indian's knowledge about them. But a stumbling block appeared. When he went away for a little trip someone spread the nasty rumor that he was a doctor trying to steal their knowledge. On his return back to the Ashaninca Indians he ended up giving his plants to the local school to prove his good intents.

But what was he left with? Nothing, but the stories of the local people. Every time he asked where did their knowledge come from he was constantly told from Ayahuasca, a plant which induces a kind of trance like state allowing one to dream travel. Well, Dr. Narby thought it would be a good idea to experience this state. Good idea? Joseph Campbell would have called it not so much a good idea, but a "golden ball experience" where the golden ball of destiny is thrown high up into the air for the Hero to go find, catch, and be launched into his/her calling (for the ball always gets lost and as the Hero goes searching for it they are launched on the adventure of a lifetime).

Dr. Narby's Ayahuasca journey renders vivid a huge mesmerizing snake. He writes,

"Deep hallucinations submerged me. I suddenly found myself surrounded by two gigantic boa constrictors that seemed fifty feet long. I was terrified." "These enormous snakes start talking to me

411

without words. They explain that I am just a human being. I felt my mind crack and in the fissures, I see the bottomless arrogance of my presuppositions. It is profoundly true that I am just a human being and most of the time, I have the impression of understanding everything, whereas here I find myself in a more powerful reality that I do not understand at all and that I do not understand at all and that, in my arrogance, I did not even suspect existed. I feel like crying in view of the enormity of these revelations. Then it dawns on me that this self pity is part of my arrogance."

In this state he also seems to encounter the Mother figure. For as he has his dream like experience he sees "an Ashaninca woman dressed in traditional long cotton robe. She was standing about seven yards away from me, and she seemed to be levitating above the ground. I could see her staring at me in silent clear darkness."

Yes, Snakes and the World Mother did seem to go together. So what happened next? The snake and the golden ball have got him. He wants to find out the reason for seeing the snake. This is fuelled by the words of his Ashaninca Advisor and friend, who informs him the mother of Ayahuasca is a snake. He then goes on to explain how his grandfather was trained as a tobaquero. That is someone who can see and heal illness after ingesting specially prepared tobacco. Dr. Narby rightfully felt "I had the impression that the more I asked the questions, the less I understand his answers."

Well, this snake thing is now definitely on his head especially at the Rio Earth Summit that he attends. He says "impressionable numbers" are quoted about the number of remedies that come from the Amazonian basin and how much the Amazonian Indians know about these plants. There are plenty of oohs and ahs. However, something disturbs Dr.

412

Narby. Nobody addresses how the Rainforest Indians gain their knowledge. He understands why. "Colleagues might ask, you mean Indians claim they get molecular verifiable information from their hallucinations? You don't take them literally do you? What could you answer?"

Well, remember it is Dr. Jeremy's golden ball calling to find out, not theirs. So it is not surprising when he says,

"When I understood that the enigma of plant communication was a blind spot for science. I felt the call to conduct an in depth investigation of the subject."...."furthermore. I had been carrying the mystery of plant communication around since my story with the Ashaninca, and I knew that exploration of contradictions in science yielded some interesting results. Finally it seemed to me that the establishment of a serious dialogue with indigenous people on ecology and botany required that this question be addressed."

As an example of the impressive knowledge on the indigenous people about the earth he reveals that millenniums ago that a muscle paralyzing substance was developed as a slow poison. It kills tree born animals without poisoning the meat. In 1940 scientist realized that curare could help with surgery of the torso and of the vital organs, because it interrupts nerve impulses and relaxes all muscles including breathing muscles. Chemists synthesized derivatives of the plant mixture by modifying the molecular structure of one of its active ingredients currently anesthesiologists who curatize their patients use only synthetic compounds. In the entire process only the original developers have received no compensation for their work.

He further explains there are 40 types of curares in Amazon made from seventy plant species. The type used in

413

Western medicine comes from Western Amazon. He reveals that producing curare is quite complicated. Explaining,

"You have to combine several plants and boil them for seventy two hours, while avoiding the fragrant but mortal vapors emitted by the broth. The final product is a paste that is inactive unless injected under the skin. If swallowed, it has no effect. It is difficult to see how anybody stumbled on this recipe by chance experimentation."

He makes the interesting point, that when Rainforest people are asked how they got the knowledge they say "the creator gave it to them".

"most scientist don't believe "stone age" Indians could discover anything. They just "stumbled" on things." In the case of curarare this is highly unlikely. "

Dr. Narby continues bravely on his Hero's journey and oh what a very brave journey it is. I mean how do you begin to prove that a snake gives knowledge. After going to a friend's house he is shown a book. You know one of those ones where the pictures are in those little annoying dots and the image is meant to jump out at you if you look at the collage of dots in a kind of funny way. They call it de-focalizing your gaze. This has only worked with me once. It was a pretty awesome experience to realize there was a beautiful picture behind those crazy little confusing dots.

Dr. Narby de-focalized his gaze and saw a beautiful dolphin jumping through waves. Well that did it. He realized that is what he had to do with the search for the Mother of Ayahuasca. He had to de-focalize.

To cut a long story short Dr. Narby enters What Joseph Campbell calls The Belly of The Whale. Information begins to crop up in all sorts of strange ways. His eyes are opened and he begins to see snakes everywhere! And in everything. He reads an experience of Michael Harner an anthropologist who

414

went to the Peruvian Amazon in the 1960's to study the Conibo Indians.　　　After a year of making no head way he decides to drink Ayahuasca. He sees all sorts of things, namely dragon headed things. These reptilian creatures began to project things before him　which they said were reserved for the dying and dead. What he saw were (and these are his words)

"black specks dropped from the sky by the hundreds and landed in front of me on the barren landscape. I could see the "specks" were actually large, shiny black creatures with stubby prerodactyl like wings and huge whale like bodies...."

They told him they had created life on earth and hid within the multitude of forms. Then he saw creation taking place on a large scale. In his foot notes Michael Harner jotted down,

"in retrospective one could say they were almost like DNA, although at that time in 1961 I knew nothing of DNA"

After that Dr. Narby has that self-realization that happens when you are in the Belly of the Whale. He looks back over the Creation Stories of the　Rain Forest Indians He re-calls that the Desana Indians say that in the fissure of the brain is a snake which has at its head a hexagonal rock crystal. Then he noticed there was a drawing of two snakes intertwined.

Both serpents symbolize a female and male principle and the binary opposites which has to be overcome in order to achieve individual awareness and integration. The snakes are imagined as spiraling rhythmically in a swaying motion from one side to another.

He then looks at pictures from a fabulous artist called Pablo Amaringo who paints vivid pictures of his Ayahuasca Visions. He notices that the drawings look like DNA. He finds the same with Australian Aborigine pictures of their Rainbow Snake.

When he shows his scientist friend the pictures of Pablo Amaringo he excitedly points out the DNA connections,

"look there's collagen..and there, the axons embryonic network with its neuritis...Those are triple helixes...and that's DNA from afar looking like a telephone cord...This looks like chromosomes at a specific phase...there's the spread out form of DNA, and right next to it are   DNA   spools   in   their nucleosome structures."

Of course, Jeremy Narby is a true Hero. He has discovered something important that needs to be taken back to society. He is now really excited and looks at the traditional depictions through stories and pictures of the serpent and realizes the snake is described as small, large; single, double and both at the same time. He realizes that DNA has all those forms.

He notes that DNA can be like a long snake. When it is stretched out the DNA contained in the nucleus of a human cell, becomes a two yard long thread that is only ten atoms wide. He explains that this thread is "a billion times longer than its own width. Relatively speaking, it is as if your little finger stretched from Paris to Los Angeles."

We are then told that one thread of DNA is smaller than the visible light human's perceive. Like a snake DNA coils up endlessly on itself so that it can fit into the little pin head of the cell nucleus. Many of the cosmic snakes are said to exist in water. Like Vishnu residing on the large snake with Lakshmi massaging his feet. Well, all cells in the world contain DNA and they are filled with salt water, in which "the concentration of salt is very similar to that of the worldwide ocean."

416

Like the mythological ladders of the ancients Dr. Narby explains that,

"As DNA's four bases cadenine, guanine, cytosine, and thymine are insoluble in water, they tuck themselves into the center of the molecule where they associate in Paris, then they twist into a spiraled stack to avoid contact with the surrounding water molecules. DNA's twisted ladder shape is a direct consequence of the cells watery environment. DNA goes together with water, just like mythical serpents do."

As for DNA's double helix he says that Christopher Wills a Biologist shares, "the two chains of DNA resemble two snakes coiled around each other in some elaborate courtship ritual." This concept of a double helix is also contained within the creation stories where there are twins, we are told.

Dr. Narby helps us to understand that "DNA and its duplication mechanisms are the same for all living creatures. The only thing that changes from one species to another is the order of the letters." What order of what letters? Well he explains that the coded universal language of DNA is contained within the four letters A, G, C and T which are four chemical compounds contained in the DNA double Helix.

Dr. Narby concludes that the indigenous people were able to connect with the very source of life information DNA through their techniques of various forms of shamanism. He concludes that the language of DNA is not static. So it is not like there are these books of information and you just get to a page and read it. Oh no. All of life gives of bio photons and their emission is a "cellular language" or a form of "non substantial bio communication between cells and organisms."

"Over the years they have produced repeatable experiments to show cells use these waves to direct their own internal reactions, as well as to communicate amongst

417

themselves and even between organisms for instance, photon emission provides a communication mechanism that could explain how billions of individual plankton organisms cooperate in swarms behaving like "super – organisms"

Something that the very well-known environmentalist and scientist James Lovelock called the Gaia hypothesis, which postulates that the biosphere is a self-regulating entity with the capacity to keep our planet healthy by controlling the chemical and physical environment. Now Gaia by the way is the Greek Mother Goddess known as the Earth Goddess.

I pause. The revelations of primordial snakes is lengthy, but I know they are important, so I allow them to sink deeply into my consciousness. My mind goes back to the very first story that appeared in my journey about Osun saving the world. I ruminate over it. In that story Osun is plaiting hair. I remember how I had rolled my eyes up to the heavens when I first read that part of the story.   Why does the woman always have to be doing something subservient?

However, now thinking about it again a dawn of realization burst forth from inside of me. Of course, Osun was not doing something lowly, she was in fact showing her connection to the very strands and essence of life – DNA.

One thing bothered me about this revelation, however. Osun did not appear to be DNA. She appeared to be associated with DNA, putting its form together, just like actual water does with real DNA strands causing it to form a twisted ladder shape.

That electrical current of time and history seemed to be trying to get my mind somewhere. It seemed important, where ever the "it" I was being taken to was. I felt there was an answer waiting to spring forth. It came in the form of Derrick's words,

"What if water contains memory of all consciousness? DNA may be a subset of that consciousness. Remember that everything is born from water maybe DNA takes its sequencing from water's consciousness."

Bingo! Bingo! Bingo! Didn't God say he gave all the wisdom of the world to the woman (who happened to be Mother Goddess of primordial waters)? Was Derrick right? Something seemed absolutely right about what he was saying. The electrical current was dancing in my body like Prakruti gone wild.

My mind raced ahead...*if the ancients saw water as not only physical, but also as a Goddess itself. If God said he gave the wisdom of the world to the Mother, does that mean the ancients knew something about water that we don't know or understand? Is water truly the seat of all consciousness?*

I thought of our rice experiments and how every time I went to water the story of the Earth just seemed to open up. I had never understood how that could happen. Yet, it did. Water seemed to contain a wisdom to it that was beyond our understanding. Was it indeed the primordial Mother of Life? Nut arching over the universe?

I think about my dream again, where the Goddesses of the world fall into the waters. Was it the sign of the times? Were things so bad that they had to find a way to rise from the waters again? A way to come forth from an ancient world we no longer understood in order to warn and help us?

I thought of what Dr. Narby said, "DNA goes together with water, just like mythical serpents do". As I do so I thank Osun for acting, once again, as the Greek which detangles the language of the Rosetta Stone.

419

Wadjet (the Snake Goddess) as Wadjet-Bast, depicted as the body of a
woman with a lioness head, wearing the uraeus (snake symbol)

Sat Nam. Sat Nam. It is about the end of August. My head is buzzing and hurting from all the findings thrown my way. It begins to cool down as I sink deeper and deeper into my meditation. I AM. I AM. That is what Sat Nam means. As I sink deeper and deeper I see only darkness. It is comforting. I am alone but not alone. The darkness warms me. I feel as though I have entered the center of the world. In that center is me and the dark stillness. I think of atoms. Why atoms? Why am I thinking of atoms during my meditation? But I do, and suddenly I feel at one with the information that flung itself at my feet. They dance and swirl into a skirt of integrative awareness. The cosmos embraces me.

"That's why meditation is important," my inner self tells me as I continue sinking deeper and deeper into Sat Nam until I am sitting in the center of its heart beat. I am there. Just there and I understand the there. I sense the self, the creative awe inspiring self. There is the SELF. Then there is me the Self. We are one. We merge and I rest my head in its embrace. Just as I had Amma's.

I exhale, and when the meditation is just about finished the Mandala I had made earlier flashes in my mind's eye. Then my inner self smiles and says,

"you do know that the Mandala is nothing but the ancient atom. In the West the atom is a physical thing only. However, for the ancients it was very much made up of sacred life force just like the Mandala. The Mandala is like a golden atom"

When I finally open my eyes I open up Romio Shrestha's book "Celestial Gallery" again, and notice how at the center of many of the mandalas sits the Mother Goddess depicted in various forms, as the womb of life.

A few weeks later my book Masters send me to the university library. I go there to hand in books. Yet, when I go browsing its shelves my hand stops on a large book. Curiously I pull it off the shelf. I carefully wipe some of the dust from its vibrant red cover, and look at the title "The Mandala: Sacred Circles in Tibetan Buddhism" by Martin Brauen. I flick through a few pages and stop to read a section that catches my eyes,

"there is talk of the Mandala as a "magic circle", a round "ritual geometric" or "symbolic" diagram, or typically a circle which surrounds a square with a center symbol, which may be a numeral" or "alternatively mandalas are described as symbols of the cosmic elements used as an aid to meditation, models for certain visualizations, an aid to self discovery or to meditation on the transcendental'. All of these definitions have their own validity, but are not nearly as precise enough."

So what is a Mandala? He explains they are a visual replication of how the ancients saw the cosmos. Revealing that when we view a mandala on paper we are looking at a flattened 3D image of the cosmos. When not flattened out like this, the shape of a mandala can also be seen reflected in the structure of buildings, formations, and even the human.

At the center of this ancient depiction of the cosmos is not a materialistic nucleus but the divine creative force. Braun elucidates,

"unlike the cosmology of the European Middle Ages, the Buddhist conception of the world does not place the earth and human beings at the center. Rather here you find the gods, corporeal, subtle, spiritual and formless beings – and their worlds, that form the 'theocentric' axis of the universe, while human and other living beings eke out an existence on the margins of the center."

To help us de-code the essence and meaning of the mandala Brauen takes a deeper look at the Tibetan Kalacakra Tantra Mandala. I found it a little technical, but clarifying.

Mount Meru, fascinated me. It seemed to sum up the whole feel of having a spiritual cosmos as ones world view. For In the middle of Mount Meru resides the city of Sudarsana which means "Beautiful to see". There in that city was the palace of the Gods.

A few weeks latter I go back to the university library to return the Mandala book. The ancient masters and my Watery Mother Osun seem ready to complete the epic sweeping story of the Mother Goddess's rise and fall in history. I am made to take home two books which virtually fall on the floor as my fingers gently sweep across a row of books: "When the Women Were Drummers," by an author called Layne Redmond's and E.A Wallis Budge's "Osiris: The Egyptian Religion of Resurrection".

It is the voice of Layne Redmond who truly picks up the threads of the Mother Goddess's story. She explains, the destruction of the Goddess led society down "a narrow path leading to death and divine judgment. Time had become linear."

"When the Goddess and her consort consummated their marriage in the temple of ziggurat, they set the New Year in motion. Their union blessed the harvest and affirmed the eternal cycle of the seasons, of life and death and rebirth. Initiatory rites gave the individual a place in this cycle, and centered her (and him) in nature and in the cosmos."

Redmond takes up the fall of the Mother Goddess from Roman times. It's the third century and Rome is under Constantine's rule. According to Redmond, the struggle is on. That is the struggle between the old Gods and Goddesses; the peaceful ways of the Mother honoring cultures and the

423

aggressive and rather suppressive ones of the Aryan father worshipping culture.

Redmond says that the struggle is played out in many arenas, but especially through music. The church finds the pagan's (which by the way we are told means people of the land) ways near impossible. They just can't stand all that joyful singing and dancing. They hate when the locals go to their local festivals and have a darn good sacred time.

They particularly find it obnoxious because when the locals are of on these sacred jaunts they are normally honoring the Goddess and her wonderful music of life. Well what to do? Redmond helps us to understand the church's answer was to stop the music. Allowing worship now only in Christian Psalms a cappella.

But, oh what a protestation there was. The "People of the Land", who were the early Christians, pointed out that in the Old Testament there was "explicit reference" to the use of music in worship. Why the timbrel (frame drum) had been played by Jewish women in marriage rites and precession to honor the Lord of the Old Testament. "Your procession has come into view, O God, the musicians; with them are the maidens playing tambourines." (Psalms 68:24-25). "And Miriam the prophetess, the sister of Aaron, took timbrel in her hand, and all the women went out after her with timbrels and with dances." (Exodus 15:20).

But the church was not interested in all of that talk. They kept their ban on music being used for service. They also replaced local traditional festivals with Christian ones (which were normally traditional festivals dressed in a different skin). But what a battle they had on their hands. The locals still continued to see Easter, Christmas and the likes for what they were – sacred celebrations of their great Mother Goddess and Gods.

So what did the church do? Redmond divulges that in 300 they banned women from singing and dancing, and women who danced and sung at funerals were not allowed to attend church service. She explains the frame drum was very important to funeral rites. It was used to bring resurrection and rebirth of the individual spirit. But the church were far from interested in these deeper meanings of traditional music. By the third century they decided to take further extreme measures and ban women from funerals. Redmond tells us that in some parts of Spain women are still barred from them!

Well, things went from bad to worse. The power of the local way of worshipping was hard to shut down. Paul and Timothy preached that women should not even be allowed to speak in public. This was due to an in built Hebrew and Indo Aryan fear of the power of women. Remember in traditional cultures women were powerful prophetesses consulted for social, political and religious affairs.

By the thirteenth century we were well and truly in the dark ages. Women were murdered by the thousands and possibly millions. There were also men, and babies killed in an attempt to completely stamp out traditional ways.

Not only was the Mother Principle silenced through the music being stopped (oh by the way women were banned from singing in church). Redmond explains that it was also silenced by making the Mother, Father, Son trinity that had travelled from Egypt (Osiris was the male God concept, Horus became Jesus) and Isis was represented by Mary) to become now father and the son. The Mother was now to be merely the Holy Ghost.

She further reveals that as sexuality was considered to be the life giving gift of the Mother – it to was stripped of the Mother Goddess who was essentially Isis as Mary. Her conception of her child was now considered to be considered by the church as a "conception chastely conducted by the Holy Spirit". Now in the actual story of how Isis had become pregnant it is clearly stated that she re-pieced Osiris's body back together again, and through magic raised his phallus up and had sex with him.

Anyway, despite trying to strip the Mother Goddess of her full identity. Redmond divulges it was impossible to keep her down. Many of the symbols of the Great Mother Goddess remained with her. Devotees often drank Mary's milk and honey. I noted how these two foods were symbols of Hathor, as well as Goddesses Saraswati. Honey was a symbol of Osun, as well.

Redmond lets us know that in the early days she was even prayed to as the Moon Goddess and compared to the humming of the honey bees. She mentions the fascinating fact that the enormous rose window stained glass which is most often put opposite Christ's cross in the apse - symbolizes Mary's presence as the Holy Rose. The Rose was actually the Flower of Venus (also known as Aphrodite).

Mary's rosary, a string of rose beads is often seen hanging from the hands of the Goddesses of India. According to Redman the repetition of the rosary is definitely from traditional cultures because in the Mathew Gospels devotees are admonished by these words, "when ye pray, use not vain repetitions, as the heathens do". (Mathew 6.7)

Now E Wallis Budge, was an Egyptologist who worked in the British museum. His work and contributions to Egyptology were so impressive that in 1920 he received a Knighthood for his works. Budge wrote many books on Egyptology. In one book that jumped of the shelf into my hands, "Osiris, The Egyptian Religion of Resurrection" he shows extensively that the Egyptian religion travelled all over the world and took hold of the world's imagination. Isis is actually the Greek name for the Goddess Auset who was sister to Hathor and both Goddesses merged identities.

He states, "many shrines to Isis, both public and private seem to have been erected in many parts of Greece." Coins of Malta contain images of Osiris and Isis in the first and second century before Christ. In Southern Italy there were "many temples to Isis, and the remains of statutes". While in Rome "in the first century before Christ Isis was regarded as one of the principle goddesses of the city. Splendid buildings and temples were set up in her honor, filled with Egyptian objects, obelisks, alters, statues, lavers etc. which were brought from Egypt with the view of making the shrines of the Goddess to resemble those of her native country."

Budge goes on to tell us that Priestess of the Goddess lived in or near the temples and assisted "in performing services and ceremonies in which large congregations participated." Then "From Rome, the capital, the cult of Isis naturally spread to the provinces and thence, little by little, to Germany, Switzerland, Spain, Portugal, Gaul, and finally by way of Marseilles to Carthage and the countries of North Africa."

According to Budge it was part of the tradition in Egypt and amongst the Nubians to identify Isis and in fact Gods and Goddesses with many "purely local spirits and goddesses, and the facts now available prove that the custom of identifying her with foreign goddesses went on in Greece and in Italy, and nearly every place where her worship was introduced.

He says the cult of Osiris and Isis spread because,

"in the first place the new cult came from Egypt, the land of mystery par excellence, and the home of civilization which had lasted for thousands of years. The ascetics practices of the priests and priestess, their abstention from meats, their fasting and habits of self denial, and their continence appealed to all men. The ceremonies connected with the worship of Isis impressed the imagination of all beholders."

He continues, "moreover, it revived and increased the faith in God and in reality of spiritual things, which the teachings of the philosophers had well-nigh destroyed in their hearts. Above all, it gave men the hope of a resurrection, and preached the doctrine of a second birth, and of a new and pure existence in heaven, in the Kingdom of Osiris and Isis, the passport to which was the forsaking of sin, purity in word and deed, and reverent worship of these Gods."

In fact by the time the Osirian religion had travelled he states,

` "her (Isis) worship had wholly eclipsed that of her male counterpart."

Isis was known to be a great healer and was able to perform amazing healing feats such as bringing Osiris her husband back to life. Her name translates into "seat, throne, chamber, house, abode, place". Mary is also known as the Throne on which Jesus can be seen sitting. Also Isis was often depicted suckling Horus on one lap. Just as Mary is often depicted as suckling Jesus on one lap.

This is all to say it was hard for the Christian Fathers to keep the Mother Goddess down, or to take away this archetypal energy from the world.

All this talk of Mary reminded me of a dream I had months before where Myself and Derrick were driving pass the British museum and the statute of Mary was very far from us. It looked very very old, tired and neglected.

Redmond shows that despite the church's great suppression of the Mother Goddess many spiritual women in the church had experiences of the Mother energy such as German Hildegard of Bingen who had established an independent convent for nuns and was known as a prophetess. She was interestingly known as the "Sybil of Rome". This was an ancient term for the Prophetess Priestess of the Goddess. Then there was Saint Theresa of Avila who wrote books on mystical theology including one called "The Interior Castle". Which describes what is essentially a healing and enlightenment journey through the Chakras which she calls the seven mansions. She says it is at the seventh mansion where the soul reaches a place of complete transfiguration and communion with the divine. This is what happens at the seventh chakra which is the Crown Chakra at the top of the head. I found it interesting that there was Hathor's number seven again.

Now back to the question of the Mother and Rhythm. Why was the drums and rhythm so important in ancient societies? Redmond eloquently lets us in on a secret – when we are engaged in playing, indulging and listening to rhythmic vibrations we relax and our brain eases into Alpha waves. Now these waves are important because they correspond to the electromagnetic field of the earth. This is why all the ancient practices of the Goddess such as meditation, yoga, dancing, and music – all brought the individual into alignment with the alpha rhythm. In other words we were brought into full alignment with the Earth, ourselves and that inner sense of total wellbeing and peace.

With her infinite knowledge of music Layne Redmond helps us to know that the brain is divided into the left and right hemisphere. The left is connected to sequential and analytical thinking. It is associated with the masculine principle and dominates our present societies. The Right side of the brain is the seat of visual, oral and emotional memory. It processes information much more holistically and intuitively. It is said that when we engage this side of our brains we learn much quicker. It is the side that great leaders and groundbreaking scientist are good at using. The right side of the brain is connected to the feminine principle.

Layne Redmond educates us even further by informing us that both brains operate in different modes and in different rhythms. So the right brain may be generating an alpha rhythm while the left is generating something else. They can be generating the same type of rhythm and still be out of sync.

However, it has been proven that in intense states of mediation, creativity or with the influence of sound then both hemispheres of the brain begins to synchronize with the same rhythm. When things vibrate with the same rhythm they make a beautiful sound called resonance. When the two hemispheres of the brain generate the same rhythm we experience a state of clarity, heightened awareness, oneness and wellness. When this happens we are in sync with the earth's vibration of Alpha waves.

This is why Layne Redmond states, "by banning her drum, the patriarchal religions that suppressed the Goddess cut off our access to significant parts of our psyches. They destroyed psychological and spiritual techniques that had been used for many thousands of years."

As I paused in the sweet nectar of Redmond's revelations. All her talk of rhythms and the Alpha waves of Earth made me think of a book I had flicked through months ago called "Sacred Earth". Derrick had purchased it at Barnes and Nobles for a superb discount price. Now after months of not reading it, it now beckoned me "come". Written by Martin Gray the book documents his twenty years of travelling to sacred sites. A journey triggered of by a vision which compelled him to document as many of the sacred sites as possible before they disappeared.

Through his book Gray helps us to understand that the Earth has power which is more heightened at certain spots. Being tuned in with the Earth's rhythm and especially the vibration of those spots "actually stimulate experiences and feelings that dowsers and meditators are able to perceive consciously." Gray explains that many a temples and shrines were built in a way where we could experience these healing vibrations of the earth. So the Temple of Luxor in Egypt had various sections of the body which were incorporated into the proportions of the temple. He discovered that specific locations within the temple corresponded to the seven chakras of the body.

After many years of visiting sacred spots Gray reveals that he believes being in tune with the earth's vibration can really bring healing to the world,

"I believe it is highly beneficial for people to make pilgrimages to sacred sites because of the transformational powers available there. These legendary places have the mysterious capacity to awaken and catalyze within visitors the qualities of compassion, wisdom, peace of mind and respect for the earth. The development of these qualities in increasing numbers of the human species is of vital importance, considering the numerous ecological and social problems occurring in the world. At the root of all these problems is human ignorance."

One night as I edited this chapter Derrick decided to take our baby girl, Omo for a walk. It was often the only way to get her to sleep. He came back and shared this experience with me,

As I walked alongside the trees lining the estate, I could hear a noise in their depths. It was kind of strange but I kept on walking. The noise continued. I looked to see what was making the noise. It was too dark to see, but one thing I knew for sure was that it wasn't a deer. That worried me, because I couldn't figure out what else it could be. Part of me thought of turning back and going home. Just as I had that thought large drops of water fell on my head. Then the strange noise emerged from the darkness again. I looked up in the sky and thought it was about to pour down. I mean where else would a drop of water come from. But the sky was a peaceful deep clear night blue happily lit up by the full moon.

Truly puzzled I continue my walk and hear the noise again. I try to see into the woods. It is too dark so I see nothing. Just as I think about turning back home again, another large drop of water plops onto my head. I walk a few more paces then two more large drops do the same thing. It felt as though someone or something was deliberately putting water on my head as these drops were falling no where else but on my head.

I eventually stop walking altogether. I feel completely unnerved by these strange occurrences. Omo's almost asleep. I stand still and listen real hard to the noise in the dark. Then suddenly I realize the noise in the woods is the water the trees had gathered from the morning's rains. The water was falling from leaf to leaf. The water drops were no more than the water from those leaves. But I was still really puzzled by how the water just seemed to drop very carefully onto my head.

It was then I had what felt like a profound spiritual moment. I suddenly realized nature truly is an intelligent life force. It was almost as though the trees were deliberately dropping water on my

head. Like they were trying to catch my attention. I felt as though they were using those drops to re-connect my senses back to nature. How often do we walk past trees and nature and not notice them. I can't explain it but it was a deeply moving and profound experience. Somehow I felt re-connected back to Mother Earth. I felt healed.

OSE MEJI

Girl: Mother tell me about the Ose Meji.
Mother: Ose Meji shows us that abundance is secured when we follow divine wisdom and the divine plan. You know many of the stories of the Mejis speak to this point. Ose Meji shows that is only those who are true to their purpose and aligned with divine advise and destiny who achieve true prosperity.
Girl: Mother tell me a story from Ose Meji.
Mother: Girl, there are so many but I will tell you this one.

It is said that Ose Meji really did not do anything special in heaven, but he did do one important thing and that was to reveal how prosperity in the form of money came to earth from heaven. According to Ose Meji there was a heavenly priest by the rather long name of Orokunarokoosemunukun who divined for money when money was preparing to leave heaven for the earth. The same heavenly priest made a divination for the Gods on what to do to enjoy the benefits that money can give.

    Now before we continue this story you might be interested to know that the long name of the heavenly priest actually meant, "The knee of the cripple does not bend." In regards to enjoying the benefits of money each of the Gods was told to make an offering of was told to make an offering with 16 pigeons, 16 hens, 16 rats, 16 fishes, 16 bean buns. Instead of doing this offering individually they all decided to do one single one. After which money left heaven for earth in the form of cowries. As the money fell to the ground the divinities got together to decide how to get the money to their various homes.

Now Orunmila, the God of Wisdom always tried to do things in accordance with divine law. He told the other Gods that they should have a fresh divination done and discover what further offerings they needed to make before they took the money. The God of Iron, Ogun was not interested. He told Orunmila to go home and do his divination, but they the other Gods would go and get the money. Orunmila was not deterred from following the right way, and thus left them to it.

When Orunmila left Ogun was the first to dig into the money. He created a hoe and digger just for the purpose of digging deep into the money heap. As he extracted the money he placed it to the side of him. It fell on top of him and killed him. All the other divinities suffered the same fate. Well when Orunmila went back to the site of the money he saw all the divinities had died. So all the wealth passed into his hands.

The two Humanity4Water awards seemed to roll into each other. The dust of 2009 just sort of blew into that of 2010. In that period Goddesses rose from the waters, but so did the Humanity4Water Awards. They were the anchor that reminded myself and Derrick what the importance of all these findings really were. It was through the Humanity4Water awards that the issues seemed to be constantly brought back to home.

2009 Humanity4Water Awards

The Humanity4Water 2009 was to be our second award year. We actually had the chance and financial circumstances to put on a ceremony this time. We were pleased about this. We got planning, and decided to theme the day "thinking out of the bottle", and highlighted it with a quote by Gandhi, "my life is my message".

We held the award ceremony at the local university knowing that only three awardees would most probably attend: David Merryman, the Catawba River Keeper, Gary Fourstar and Debbie Fourstar from Many Horses. The others lived in far flung places such as India and Africa.

Yet the attendance of the awardees was not the most important thing to us (strange as it may sound for an award ceremony). What was the most important thing was positively highlighting the work of the awardee's in order to raise environmental issues, and inspire others to action. There is nothing like seeing someone else do it. We figured if we could be educated, made aware and inspired to action by the work of the awardees; Then others could be too.

Our list of 2009 awardees was long. I think it proved to be the longest one we would have for many years. It included an impressive group of people who had done impressive things. Some were known; others were quite unknown to the normal Joe Blogs. The list included the likes of: President Obama and the First Lady Michelle Obama, Ted Danson (actor and Board Member of Oceana), Susan Wenger (Post Humus. Austrian Artist and Re-Constructor of the World Heritage Site the Osun Grove), Her Holiness, Sri Amma (the Hugging Saint and Founder of Mata Amritanandamayi Math, Dr. Wangari Maathai (founder of Green Belt Movement and Noble Peace Prize Winner), David Merryman (Catawba River Keeper), John Francis (He had spent 17 years in silence for the environment), Andy Lipkis (founder of Tree People), Gary and Debbie Fourstar (Founders of Many Horses Foundation), Lindsey Pettus (President of Katawba Valley Land Trust), Paul Katzeff (Founder of Thanksgivingcoffee), Bruce Henderson (Environmental Journalist for the Charlotte Observer), Dan Huntley (former Charlotte Observer correspondent and Chef par excellent), and Dennis Nelson (Founder of Project Wet).

For 2009 we truly did not know what type of ceremony to put on. We wanted something that people would remember, that would help them to remember the issues, but where they didn't go home and say,

"boy that was boring".

Eventually we hit on a formula that included good food, a fantastic presentation, Native American Music, speeches from awardees who showed up, and a water tasting. Now it was the last thing that I was not sure about. It was Derrick's idea and he truly believed that people would find it interesting. Yet, I did not see how lining up five bottles of water with no labels and getting people to identify (through tasting) which was tap, which was store bought and which was natural spring water we got from the Healing Springs – could be anywhere near fun. I caved into the idea only because of logic. The whole evening was after all focusing on the tap versus bottled water issue as a way of discussing the broader facts about why we must look after our waterways.

Now despite the fact the attendees for the day was small, it was still an awesome day. The evening opened with Gary Four Star (whom we had never met, but who turned out to be one cool guy) pulling out a huge eagle's feather from the far reaches of his pockets, while Derrick walked by his side with an incense bowl. I thought there was no way the people from the deep South present were going to let an Indian's eagle feather pass smoke over them, but they did. So that was my first surprise for the evening. The second surprise was how much they enjoyed the presentation on all the awardees and seemed fascinated by the environmental issues at hand. The third surprise for the day was the water tasting event. Everyone thoroughly enjoyed it. Not just enjoyed it but got really into it. One friend, an Archivist friend from the university, even swished the water around in his glass as though it were wine. He stuck his nose right up in that glass to see if he could smell differences in the water. He swore he could.

The fourth surprise for the evening was when people had to place each bottle of water in preference order (without knowing what type of water was really in the bottle they had drunk from) on a piece of paper. They had to identify whether they thought the water they had tasted was store bought, tap or Healing Springs water. The Healing Springs Water made number one on the list, the tap water made number two, and all the store bought waters were placed at the bottom of everyone's list (with the most expensive one being placed last). Each person present had thought the store bought water was tap water, and the tap and Healing Springs water was actually store bought water. That small exercise had made a difference. A year later at the Humanity4Water ceremony we discovered that many people had given up buying bottled water, and instead drank filtered water.

I have to mention Gary Four Star's prayer here, because although simple it moved through our bones,

"my grandfathers did not pray to things they prayed through things. Meaning that it was to the creative force we always connected. My grandfathers also said that there are plenty of humans but not plenty of human beings. A human being is someone who cares about all things, all of the Creator's children."

David Merryman, the Catawaba River Keeper followed on from that prayer with quite an eye opening albeit depressing report of the mighty Catawba River. The long and short of it was that the Catawba had dangerously high levels of mercury in it, and was being used as a dumping ground for all sorts of harmful chemicals.

Here I think is the place where I would like to share the facts that were shared about water with those who attended. They were facts that opened mine and Derrick's eyes, along with all who attended the ceremony. These facts I see as part of the long journey with the Mother Waters, and how to treat her better. We can only treat her better when we grasp the issues that affect her and all our relations.

Water, Water Everywhere and Not a Drop to Drink

The amount of water we have in the world mirrors the amount of water we have in our bodies. We are 70% water and so is the world. We can only be sustained with fresh water. We cannot drink sea water (a lot of people did not realize this fact).

Out of all the water on Earth, about 97 percent of all water is in the oceans. The other 3% is fresh water. About 69 percent of that 3% is locked up in glaciers and icecaps, mainly in Greenland and Antarctica. The remaining freshwater, is almost all below our feet, as ground water. No matter where on Earth you are standing, chances are that, at some depth, the ground below you is saturated with water. Of all the freshwater on Earth, only about 0.3 percent is contained in rivers and lakes. About 40% of the water we use is from ground water the other percentage is from surface water (rivers and lakes).

Other than the location, one of the primary differences between surface and ground water is that ground water moves much slower than surface water. This is because ground water experiences far more friction as it moves through the pores in soil than surface water experiences as it flows over the earth's surface. Surface water is much more easily contaminated than ground water. Filtration through the soil helps clean ground water.

Water gets underground through precipitation (rain, hail, snow) that lands on the ground. This water from precipitation enters the soil. This process is called infiltration. Because of gravity, the filling or saturation of spaces between soil particles, and the pressure of the overlying water, water may continue to move down through the soil layer. As water moves past the root zone, the movement is referred to as percolation. Layers of soil and rock that are saturated with water are called aquifers.

Aquifers are able to transport water and supply water to wells, rivers, springs and marshes. A ground surface area that provides a water entry port for a confined aquifer is called a recharge area or zone.

1.1 billion people, about one-sixth of the world's population, lack access to safe drinking water. Aquifers under Beijing, Delhi, Bangkok, America and dozens of other rapidly growing urban areas are drying up. The rivers Ganges, Jordan, Nile, and Yangtze are all dwindling to a trickle for most of the year. In the former Soviet Union, the Aral Sea has shrunk to a quarter of its former size, leaving behind a salt-crusted waste.

The Ogallala aquifer is the world's largest underground water system, irrigating one-third of the united states corn crops and providing drinking water to Colorado, Kansas, Nebraska, New Mexico, Oklahoma, South Dakota, Texas and Wyoming. It contains enough water to cover the entire United States to a depth of one and one-half feet.

But because of heavy usage, some water experts have pronounced the Ogallala aquifer one of the fastest-disappearing aquifers in the world. Now, after generations in which water from the Ogallala was treated as if it were an inexhaustible resource, farmers, cities, states and the federal government are having to talk seriously about conservation.

The cost of Bottle water

Financial

- In the year 2003 alone, Americans spent 7 billion on bottle water at an average cost of more than $1 a bottle.
- Water cost more than gasoline at $2.50 per liter ($10 U.S a gallon)

- Bottled water produces 1.5 million tonnes of plastic waste a year
- According to the Container Recycling Institute in Washington, D.C - 86 percent of plastic water bottles in the U.S becomes garbage or litter
- Plastic in the environment takes between 400 and 1000 years to degrade
- Recent reports reveal - Plastic deteriorates faster in ocean water leaching chemicals Bisphenol A (BPA) and Styrene Monomer, a derivative of styrene trimer. The former interferes with reproduction; the latter is a carcinogen
- 44 percent of all Marine birds eat plastic by mistake
- A 2008 study in the journal Environmental Research by oceanographer and chemist Charles Moore, of the Algalite Marine Research Foundation revealed - 267 marine species are affected by plastic garbage often they mistake plastic for jelly fish in mid-ocean - Chemicals in plastic cause cancer in humans
- 10 percent of the 260 million tons of plastic produced annually ends up in the oceans trash vortices like the Pacific garbage patch which is twice the size of Texas.

Atmosphere & Crude oil

- Bottled water is expensive to the environment. More than a quarter of all bottled water crosses national borders to reach consumers – Emily Arnold, EPI

Public Water

1.5 million barrels of oil annually are used to meet America's demand for bottled water

Public Water vs. bottle water

- Bottled water undermines public water
- National Resource Defense Council who conducted a four year review of bottled water discovered - 25% of bottled water is "just tap water"
- Emily Arnold, researcher with the Earth Policy Institute (EPI) exposed the fact - "bottled water is often no healthier than tap water, but it can be 10,000 times more expensive"
- Chartered Institution of Water and Environmental Management (UK) stated bottled water was an unsustainable use of natural resources, "where there already exists a wholesome and safe supply of drinking water cannot be seen as sustainable use of natural resources," said Nick Reeves, the institution' executive director.
- Yale University School of Medicine's Dr. Stephen Edberg, the person whom the International Bottled Water Association told ABC's "20/20" to talk to, agreed that bottled water is no better for you. "No, I wouldn't argue it's safer or not safer."
- Big Corporate bottling companies are leading the way in privatization of our water in many countries such as South Africa privatization has left millions without water.
- South Africa's Bill of Rights states that every citizen has a right to water. Privatization poses a threat to that commitment because once privatized, water will no longer be provided on the basis of need but on the ability to pay. Many poor people in South Africa simply cannot afford to

pay for water – BBC News, 2003 "Water Privatization: The Case Against"

2010 Humanity4Water Awards

Every person can make a difference

Now the 2010 Humanity4Water Award ceremony was a high roller coaster event marked by Omo's 45 minute dramatic birth (which took place just a few months before it was due to occur). Whacked out by the whole thing, tired as a new nursing mother would be – the ceremony almost did not happen. That was until I had a dream.

I was in a strange place with a beautiful green hill. On top of the hill were statues that could talk. Somehow they seemed to be connected to the award ceremony. I started arranging the statutes. I took one and put it in the middle of the other two. The statute said,

"No. I don't want to go there. The last time I went there I fell right over."

So I moved the statute. When I was satisfied with the arrangements I started to leave the property. As I left I heard a woman's voice talking. I turned around and found at the bottom of the hill a small little body of water had formed and a woman sitting in the lotus position sat there. Her head was bigger than the rest of her body. Her skin was grey and very ancient looking and her hair was matted and down to her shoulders.

I looked at the woman and then went to turn away. Then I suddenly felt that this woman was the great Mother herself. So I decided to brave it and approach her. I went by the body of water and I started speaking to the woman. I said,

"Momma?"

She said, "yes," in somewhat of a stern voice.

444

I said, "you know all this work you keep on giving me?"

she said, "yes," Still in a stern voice.

I said, "well, Momma sometimes it seems a little too much and too overwhelming."

She replied, "I see," and pursed her lips.

"Yes Momma if you could just help out a little I would be grateful."

"Uhmm," the woman said again pursing her lips.

Then she said, "Consistency is what I reward you know. Consistency."

Then I leaned over, cupped some water in my hands and gave her some to drink. She seemed pretty thirsty, and that surprised me. Afterwards, I bade her goodbye and started walking away.

I woke up from the dream and knew the show had to go on! But what type of ceremony would we have? I had a strong sense that somehow we should not exclude children from the ceremony. I also wanted a day that was fun, because I knew that talking about the environment and the crisis we face could feel so overwhelming. Being a true Island girl I believed that laughter, food and music were important ingredients to any occasion. It was really Omo's birth that reminded myself and Derrick how important the children were, and how much we overlook their happiness. In the midst of all this contemplation on how the day should go I had a second dream.

I was in a house and I was fretting about the ceremony. The following day I woke up and went outside. There were ten white horses with gold reigns on. In the middle of the horses was a man on another white horse holding all the reigns. Then a man appeared at my side and said,

445

"Madam, the Prince sent these horses and carriages along so that the children could go to the ceremony and have a good time."

On each horse sat a child. I got up on a horse. The horses moved at a slow trot then suddenly they came to a halt outside the King's gates. The gates opened. I and the children were welcomed inside the courtyard where there were the most beautifully laid tables just for the children. There were people in a podium watching as we ate our award meal. The children were a little embarrassed because they had never been to such an event before. Then there was the fact of all the people watching them.

When I woke up from the dream I was completely convinced we had to do a ceremony that was about children as the future. Eventually myself and Derrick hit on the idea of having something called, "The Island Earth Party For Our Children".

It turned out to be a beautiful, vibrant day filled with all the things I loved: Music, laughter, children, dancing, and joy. Held in December everything flowed nicely. Our special guest entertainers were awesome: They were: Drummer and Music Educator, Nate Brown; and South Carolina's famous Slave Narrator Kitty Wilson. The kids had goodie bags and munched on their treats as they listened to a fun presentation of eco facts and messages (through recorded Skype interviews) we had collected from our Humanity4Water 2010 Awardees just for them.

They included messages from: *Archbishop Desmond Tutu, Captain Paul Watson (Co-Founder of Green Peace and Founder of The Sea Shepherds Conservation Society), Dr. Jeremy Narby and Baba Credo Mutwa (Keeper of the Zulu Treasures and Wisdom), Rebecca Fowler and Lisa Moore (Publisher and Editor of Natural Awakening publication, South Carolina).*

Each of the awardees shed light on the down and positive side of our environmental crisis. The down side was the fact we were heading the earth towards a sixth extinction, the up side was how our crisis had brought forward, in many, the brilliance of the human spirit of action and love.

Captain Watson spoke live from his Steve Irwin ship which was on a Southern Ocean campaign to save the whales. He told the children,

"Know that everything that you are told is impossible is actually possible. Impossibilities become possibilities." Adding, "imagine being on a space ship. There is the driver and the passenger. Well the trees, the water, and all these things are the drivers (of Mother Earth) and we are the passengers having a good time on the ride."

He gave several examples to illustrate his point, "The worm is more important than humans, because we cannot live without the earthworm but they can really live without us. Einstein once said that humans would only last four years without the honey bee. With this in mind we need to live harmoniously with all things in life."

Dr. Jeremy Narby, who worked conscientiously to help save the rain forest and the Amazonian Indians, spoke to the children in a fun yet serious tone from his home in Switzerland,

"It is possible for one organization or even one person to make a difference. It takes one step after another, 20,000 steps, no highlights, and no awards, just doing it. You can really make a difference if you go about it this way."

He added "Our ambition should not be about saying "Hey baby look at what I have got," but "look at what I know". He let the children know "knowledge" and not

447

"things" should be the measure of a good person. He also reminded them to "hold onto their natural curiosity, gifts, talents and ambitions". While always having "an appreciation for all things in life."

Baba Vusumazulu Credo Mutwa delivered his message to the children via a pre-recorded telephone conversation from South Africa,

"Children of the world study hard, be compassionate, and most of all – be loving. Know that you are the bright stars that shine in the darkness of tomorrow."

Archbishop Desmond Tutu's who was on a Cruise ship conference took the time out to deliver the following inspirational message via e-mail to the children:

"I am pleased to accept the 2010 Humanity4Water Award in the Compassion category and thank all of you for this special honor. For many years I have watched and been glad to support all who have worked towards a better planet that benefits all nations, all people and all children. I salute their efforts and congratulate them on their successes. It is my pleasure to know that the children are being honored today at this ceremony and are present to be part of this wonderful event. I believe, like so many others, that you are all our future. It is my deep wish that you all will realize that you are special, and powerful beyond measure. There are many great things that each of you can do to help us all live in a happy and peaceful world. "

Rebecca Fowler and Lisa Moore, Publisher and Editor of Natural Awakening Charlotte sent the following sentiments:

"My message to the children would be that anyone can make a difference. I don't have a special degree or training to do what I do. You all have unique gifts and talents, more than you know right ."

After the awards myself and Derrick spent time listening to the interviews with each of the awardees. Those interviews and messages deeply touched, transformed and deepened our walk. When you encounter other fellow travelers who sacrifice so much for humanity and Mother Earth, it cannot but touch one. Here are the issues and points that some of the awardees raised.

Vusamazulu Credo Mutwa On The Status of Women, Mother Earth and Children

Vusamazulu Credo Mutwa had brought up several interesting facts. I loved when he said in Africa children use to be viewed as royalty and in fact an African word for Child "mtoto" also meant Royal.

Then there was what he said about women. He said that there was a time when women were treated like royalty, along with children. Stating "they were worshipped". He revealed that there was an "abomination" going on in South African society where women and children were being raped and murdered because it was believed, by the individuals doing these heinous crimes, they brought them healing, power or luck.

He shared that there was a time when this was unheard of. His revelations reminded us of the issues of the worldwide inhumane treatment of women and children. Both ironically, seen in traditional African societies as symbols of the World Mother.

Soon after speaking to Vusamazulu Credo Mutwa, I received this insight from one of my daily meditations, *"people today shudder at the word sacred. They run from that word. They want nothing to do with that word. They even think the idea of thinking things as sacred is a strange concept. The idea of treating the trees, water and all of life as sacred is a ridiculous notion. But they don't shudder at the abuse and murder of women on their TV screens. They don't shudder at the idea of cutting down the very trees that give them their breath. They don't shudder at polluting the very waters that are their lifeline. What kind off back to front world is this where people shudder at the word and everything sacred but they kill the very things that sustain them?"*

I had always wanted to speak to a great prophet like Vusamazulu Credo Mutwa about 2012. So I used the rare moments we had with him to raise the matter. He was very frank in that African way,

"Many say 2012 will be a time of great light and enlightment. But I tell you that it won't. What I see is that 2012 will be an age of the beginning of great darkness turmoil and strife. We need to prepare for these time. The children are the ones whose wisdom will lead the way in these times. They will be our bright stars."

I remember how Baba Mutwa's idea of 2012 depressed myself and Derrick who asked him,

"Baba, why do you think this?"

He replied,

"let's put it this way imagine a ship that is going towards an iceberg. It means that everyone has to steer the ship to ensure it does not hit that iceberg. All hands have to be on deck. This is how the world is at the moment. It is like that ship heading towards the iceberg. Everyone has to steer in the same direction, but I don't see this happening. But that is the only way to save this world."

I was curious to know what he thought about the importance of honoring the energy of the mother. How could this help our world crisis?

"The mother is the beginning of all things. I am not a sexist but I must say that we must turn away from the angry aggressive footsteps of men and slowly slowly and gently start to move towards the soft gentle footsteps of the mother. This is the only true way the world will be saved from itself."

He also believed it was important that we started to honor the children.

"We must also honor the children. They are special and close to spirit."

As he spoke he made a deep appeal that "Africa be allowed to speak". He felt there were those who were trying to kill of indigenous cultures such as the African one. Once again in his rather frank way he said, "If the world kills of Africa it will go to hell in a basket."

Dr. Jeremy Narby and The Rainforest

"They are being destroyed and even killed of"

"why?" Derrick asked.

"So that loggers and other industrialist could have access to the rainforest."

This was the beginning of a conversation with the very impressive Dr. Jeremy Narby. Who informed us he was currently working on a project which brought the wisdom of the scientist and Peruvian people together in order to rebuild devastated areas of the rainforest.

"I am working with the Asanika Indians to reforest their lands which had been deforested by drug traffickers.

They know the rainforest well, but they have never had to reforest the forest. So their expertise about the trees and how the eco system behaves is now being combined with the knowledge of scientist with great results".

He also shared,

"to the Rainforest people the earth and water are not there to be plundered. All things are living. They believe that all living things should be treated with the utmost care and respect."

The more I contemplated the things he had spoken about, is the more I contemplated the Rainforest and how we were destroying them. The rainforest are described as "the lungs of the world". Because, they provide 50% of all the oxygen we breathe. They are also described as "the womb of the world" because 50 to 90 % of the world's species live there. Today, what covered 14% of the earth's land surface now only covers 6%.

Every year an area of rainforest the size of New Jersey is cut down and destroyed. The plants and animals that used to live in these forests either die or must find a new forest to call their home. As a result of the disappearing rainforest nearly half of the world's species of plants, animals and microorganisms will be destroyed or severely threatened over the next quarter century due to rainforest deforestation.

Humans are the main cause of rainforest destruction or deforestation. We are cutting down rainforests for many reasons, including: wood for both timber and wood for making fires; agriculture for both small and large farms; land for poor farmers who don't have anywhere else to live; grazing land for cattle; and road construction.

According to experts we are losing about 137 plant, animal and insect species every day as a result of the disappearance of rainforests. As a result we will also deprive

452

ourselves the access to potential cures for life-threatening diseases. Presently, there are 121 prescription drugs sold worldwide that come from plant-based sources. Furthermore, 25% of Western pharmaceuticals use rainforest ingredients and scientists have tested less than 1% of these tropical trees and plants.

The disappearance of the Rainforest also means the disappearance of indigenous peoples and their extensive knowledge of its medicinal plants. In his book "The Cosmic Serpent" Dr. Jeremy Narby speaks about the outstanding and precious knowledge that Native Americans have in regards to the rainforest.

Captain Paul Watson and the Economics of Extinction

The Blue Fin Tuna

"You know one of the greatest causes behind the disappearance of the big fish in the ocean are actually humans."

Captain Paul Watson said as Derrick and I interviewed him over Skype. All ears we asked him,

"How is that possible?"

His reply was quite disturbing. He gave an example of the Japanese overfishing Bluefin Tuna because they fetched a higher price when faced with scarcity. It was all about the old law of supply and demand. He explained a recent incident how one Bluefin Tuna sold for $173,000. Scientist are in total agreement that the Blue fin tuna is near extinction. It was an example of what Captain Paul Watson called *The Economics of Extinction*.

Following on from our talk with him I discovered A National Geographic article entitled, "Bluefin Tuna in Atlantic Nearing Extinction, Conservation Group Says". The article confirms that Bluefin Tuna is being driven into extinction. They quote the World Wild Life Fund who say some of the biggest culprits of overfishing the Bluefin Tuna include France, Libya and Turkey. They revealed that the majority of the Bluefin Tuna, up to 80%, goes to the Japanese market. They have asked the International Commission for the Conservation of Atlantic Tuna (ICCAT) to instigate an immediate recovery plan for the Bluefin tuna. Where they restrict tuna catches across the Mediterranean to 32,000 tons (29,000 metric tons).

Apparently Governments have proven to be incapable of putting a stop to this carnage due to the deep pockets of the fishing industry, and corruption is rampant.

The Bluefin Tuna is seen as quite an incredible fish which has swum the oceans for millions of years. It is the largest fish in the sea. Reaching more than six feet long and weighing up to 1,500 pounds. They are warm blooded and this allows them to inhabit areas of the ocean that are very cold. They are one of the top most predators of the seas and travel long distances and up to 55 miles per hour to find their prey. They take eight years to reach maturity and they can live up to 30 years.

It is said that the stock of Bluefin Tuna has fallen over 85% because the International Commission for the Conservation of Atlantic Tunas (ICCAT), have set their quotas too high. The World Wildlife Fund reveals that Bluefin Tuna are caught alive and kept in live Tuna farms. There they are fed and fattened for about three to six months before going to market. Much of the highly prized fish stock is exported to the sushi and sashimi market. At least 25,000 tons (23,000 metric tons), and perhaps more than 30,000 tons (27,000 metric tons), of tuna from the Mediterranean and eastern Atlantic go to Japan.

They say Tuna prices can reach as much as U.S. $15 a pound ($33 a kilogram) in Tokyo. A single large adult Bluefin tuna can sell for upward of $50,000.

While you may not care about the disappearance of the Bluefin Tuna and other big fish you should, because it means the disappearance of our Ocean eco system as we know it. Other large fish are disappearing at a crazy pace. It is estimated that 90% of our large fish are now extinct.

The Dolphins

Before we could catch our breaths a passionate Captain Paul Watson moved right on to the annual slaughter of thousands of Dolphins by the Japanese.

We had watched "The Cove" an Oscar Winner for Best Documentary and produced by one of our 2011 awardees Louie Psyios. The documentary was about the terrible frenzied killing of thousands of Dolphins in the Taiji Cove, Japan. The reason for the slaughter? – so that a few prized Dolphins could be sold to Aquariums. The documentary manages to secretly capture this slaughter which the Japanese have been denying for the longest of whiles.

As a result of seeing this harrowing documentary and Captain Paul Watson's input into it we asked him about his mission to help those beautiful sentient being.

"So we hear one of your missions is to help the dolphins. Tell us about what is going on with that?"

"Thousands of Dolphins are being slaughtered every year," Captain Watson replied.

"Why?" we enquired.

"Thousands of dolphins are driven into the Taiji Cove in Japan where just a couple are picked out. The ones considered to be the best are the ones that are sold to aquariums for a high price. The rest are speared, slashed and knifed to death and sold in Japan and given to the Japanese children to eat. The problem is that the Dolphins have dangerously high levels of mercury and this is causing problems with the Japanese children," explained Captain Paul Watson.

It was after the interview and through a little more research I later discovered it was the Sea Shepherd's 2003 world release of photographs of a sea of red as thousands of dolphins were being slaughtered in the Taiji Cove in Japan that inspired the film, "The Cove".

Captain Paul Watson and his team were a major part of helping to make the documentary happen. Along with the world famous Dolphin trainer of Flipper and now dolphin liberator, Ric O'Brien.

After the Sea Shepherds had released the pictures of dolphins being mindlessly slaughtered to the world the Japanese closed Taiji Cove to tourist and the media. Especially during the dolphin slaughter season which goes on for a couple of months for the year. From September to May. During this period over 20,000 are killed.

I have lived in the Island of Trinidad during various periods of my life. There I was use to seeing the ocean. I could not imagine a large portion of the ocean turning the color of blood, but that is what happens when the Dolphins are slaughtered in Taiji Cove.

In "The Cove" documentary Flipper's Trainer, Ric O' Brien reveals,

"the biggest deception in the world is the smile of the dolphin".

He eloquently explains, that dolphins are very self aware and that he still remembers to this day when Flipper died. He said that Flipper came up to him and lay in his arms. Then she went up in the air and took one gulp of air and refused to take another. She sunk to the bottom of the water and was dead. Mr. O'Brien believes that Flipper committed "suicide".

"When dolphins breathe it is a conscious decision. I believe that Flipper just refused to take that second gulp of air. She committed suicide"

But why would a dolphin commit suicide? In the documentary "The Cove" it is explained that that dolphins swim in pods of 10s and much more. They are playful, friendly, caring, protective (even towards other species), very gentle and extremely intelligent. They have been known to protect humans from shark attacks. In the documentary a surfer is interviewed over this latter point. He explains when he was surfing with friends and a pod of dolphins protected them from a shark who was circling them.

"The Cove" also reveals,

"Bottlenose dolphins, especially ones that look like Flipper, are pre-selected by trainers and sold off for upwards of $200,000 to marine mammal parks around the world, where they will remain in captivity performing as circus acts. After the trainers and spectators have left, the rest of the dolphins are inhumanely killed in what can only be described as a massacre."

We are also informed that the Japanese tradition of eating dolphin meat is part of the reason for the slaughter of these dolphins. But in fact, the more lucrative captive dolphin industry is the driving economic force behind the dolphin slaughter in Taiji. In the U.S. alone, dolphinariums represent an $8.4 billion industry, while a dead dolphin fetches a mere $600. International law provides no protections against the killing of dolphins, and other slaughters that occur in places outside of Japan. The International Whaling Commission (IWC) affords no protections for 71 (out of 80, known) cetacean species, including all dolphins and porpoises, which is why Japan and other countries can legally kill them by the tens of thousands.

Latter I came across this commentary by Captain Watson on the whole issue,

"It's time for Taiji to realize that this is the 21st Century and cultures that practice barbaric rituals have no place in the kinder and gentler new world we must create if we are going to protect diversity and guarantee a healthy eco-system for our children and our children's children. The extermination of the dodo, the passenger pigeon, the Caribbean monk seal, and a thousand other species now extinct was almost always preceded by the human justification that it was part of the "culture. In today's world however, the word "culture" has now replaced the words "manifest" or "divine" destiny. The Japanese fishermen at Taiji do not have the manifest right to slaughter dolphins and the film "The Cove" points out that sometimes "culture" must be sacrificed for the greater good of the planet and humanity."

The Sixth Extinction is the new talk. Speaking to our Humanity4Water awardees led us to an important fact – we are heading towards the sixth stage of extinction. Scientist say the planet has been through five extinctions before. The last one, which killed all the dinosaurs, was caused by a meteor striking the planet at 20 times the speed of a rifle bullet. However, this is the first one that has been caused by a single species – humans.

We all talk about global warming, and it is true that global warming is a serious issue for this planet, caused by the mere fact of greed and power. Derrick and I believe that we should also be paying attention to the Economics of Extinction. When we are aware of it, we can realize that our actions as consumers and citizens of the Earth really can make a big big difference.

Here are some extinction facts we should all be aware of.

- 90% of the big fish in the ocean are now extinct
- Lots of fish are dying because of overfishing, plastic waste, severe pollution in rivers, dams, and drying surface and ground water (as the latter is intricately tied to the former).
- Rainforest have now dwindled to only 6% of the world's surface. Annually we lose a piece of rainforest the size of New Jersey.
- In 2003 it was revealed there are now only 23,000 lions left in Africa. That compares with over 200,000 in the 1980's, and if the populations continue to fall, experts predict lions will soon become extinct. This dwindling has been caused by human beings shooting the animals to protect livestock or for poaching. However, experts say it just takes awareness to understand that humans and predators can live side by side peacefully.

- Conservationists warn that many birds are facing mass extinction due to human behavior. In a National Geographic 2003 article by James Owen entitled "Humans Are Driving Birds to Extinction, Group Warns "The culprit, they say, stares at us from the bathroom mirror every day".

  They mention a report published by the Worldwatch institute, a U.S.-based environmental research organization, which reveals that scientist fear that we are facing the biggest mass extinction of animals in 65 million years a fact which is "backed up by plummeting bird populations." The report claims that in the last two centuries over 100 bird species have disappeared. Another 1,200—12 percent of the planet's total—face extinction this century, according to BirdLife International, a worldwide conservation organization.

  Worldwatch researcher Howard Youth, author of the report, says human factors are central to declining bird life. These include human encroachment on bird habitat, invasions by alien plant and animal species introduced or transported unwittingly by humans, hunting, and climate change wrought by human activities. And like canaries down the coal mine, he says, birds act as a crucial early-warning system that should alert us to the vulnerability of other plants and animals.

  He further reveals that we are inspired by birds, they provide a critical service to the environment such as: distributing seed dispersal, insect and rodent control, scavenging and pollination. In addition many bird species are valuable environmental indicators, warning us of impending environmental problems. He claims that deforestation are putting 85 percent of the world's most threatened bird species at risk.

- The honey bees are said to be one of the last wild pollinators. Over 70% of them are gone. The last couple of summers I can count the honey bees on one finger.
- In terms of water the facts are quite shocking. Our rivers tell the story of our grim exploitation of nature and the price we have to end up paying for it. Climate change is resulting in ice caps across the world melting at a fast pace, leading to receding movement of glaciers and reducing water levels in the rivers.

The number of fresh water sources across the world is now reducing at a super speed. The World Wildlife Fund reveals that the world's top ten rivers are endangered. Five of them are in Asia and remaining are sited in various parts of the world. The rivers include: Salween (Asia), Danube (Europe), La Plata (South America), Rio Grande (North America), Ganges (Asia), Indus (Asia), Nile (Africa), Murray/Darling (Australia), Mekong (Asia), and Yangtze (Asia).

However, the majority of the rivers around the world are facing problems. In India alone a large portion of the Himalayan rivers which are used as water sources and sustenance are dying. One such river, the Ganges aka Ganga which is revered as the Goddess Ganga is said to be dying a slow death.

Phenomenal pollution, over-exploitation of water, reduced inflow from tributaries and climatic changes are dealing death blows to the mighty river, on whose fecund plains live over one twelfth of people of the earth's population.

The death of rivers like Ganga is not impacting human life alone, numerous species of life forms are in danger. Ganga's degeneration will wipe out several species of aquatic and terrestrial creatures. For the river hosts over 140 fish species, 90 amphibian species and the endangered Ganga river dolphin.

I remember once reading someone say, "when the Ganges dies, Ganga the Goddess dies too." The thought made me shudder.

- Ground water was mentioned earlier, but it is worth remembering it again. It provides 40% of our water and it is running out fast.
- Then there are our seeds. Vandana Shiva is a Food Activist and environmentalist. She has done much to publicize the real and growing concern of the take over of our food supplies. On her website you can find "The manifesto on the future of seeds", Produced by The International Commission on the Future of Food and Agriculture.

Some very disturbing facts are included in this manifesto including the fact that there are companies who are genetically engineering "suicide seeds". Seeds that produce plants that do not produce seeds. These same companies are genetically producing foods such as maize, soy beans. They plant their crop next to normal farms in places like India. Their crop seeds cross over and mix with the local crops. The local farmers are then prevented from using their crop by being taken to court for the infringement of patent rights. Imagine!

Crops are also being genetically engineered in a way where they produce a poison which kills of bugs. But these bugs are needed in the eco system. These poisons which ooze from the roots of these plants also affect the micro organisms in the soil.

That's just a little mention about the future of our seeds and food supply. Shiva Vandana's "Manifesto on the Future of Seeds" rightfully says,

"Seeds are a gift of nature, of past generations and diverse cultures. As such it is our inherent duty and responsibility to protect them and to pass them on to future generations. Seeds are the first link in the food chain, and the embodiment of biological and cultural diversity, and the repository of life's future evolution."

Blue Gold

As the facts about the Economics of Extinction rolled on we encountered the works of Maude Barlow, who was to become one of our 2011 Humanity4Water Awardees. She wrote an excellent book called "Blue Gold: The Battle against Corporate Theft of the World's Water". The book was rendered into an equally excellent documentary. Both myself and Derrick, stumbled upon this documentary (called by the same name as the book) one day, and discovered that it was made into a film by Sam Bozzo. Who is often described as "a normal citizen like you and me". His catching the golden ball experience happened after he watched the science film called, "The Man Who Fell to Earth" which starred David Bowie. The film portrayed an alien from a planet where water was running out. The alien left. Sam Bozzo realized that we on Earth cannot leave our planet. As he imagined a world without water he discovered (of course, because that is how spirit works) the book "Blue Gold."

The movie had myself and Derrick gripping the edges of our chairs in a disturbing white knuckle ride that portrayed the "grab" for our waterways. The scene that stuck out in my mind the most was one from South Africa – where private companies have been busy buying up the fresh water supplies and selling it back to communities. Individuals can only access their water with a token which most cannot afford.

The tokens are so precious, that in the movie a mother goes to work with hers. A fire starts in her home. Her children are inside and cannot put the fire out because there is no water. The neighbors stand by and cannot and will not help to put the fire out, because of their limited access to water. No one wants to use their tokens. They don't want to use the little water they have. So the heart wrenching results follow – the children are burned alive.

Then there is the scene where a US military station is put up near one of the biggest supplies of fresh water in the world. One that happens to be in Brazil. The film suggests that it seems as though the world's leading governments are beginning to secure the water supplies that are rightfully ours. They are expecting the day when there will be no real available fresh water. They want to basically be the ones to own it. Why? Well, water is suppose to be the new gold and oil.

Maude Barlow even suggests in the film that the pollution in our water supplies may be a deliberate method of the big boys buying up our water. What do you do when the waters are polluted? you call in a private corporation to fix the problem. Now they control the waters.

Watching Blue Gold led us to the documentary, "Thirst" produced by Alan Snitow and Deborah Kaufman who teamed up with author Michael Fox to write the movie. The three followed water privatization battles across the United States -- from California to Massachusetts and from Georgia to Wisconsin, documenting the rise of public opposition to corporate control of water resources.

They found that the issue of privatization ran deep.

"We came to see that the conflicts over water are really about fundamental questions of democracy itself: Who will make the decisions that affect our future, and who will be excluded?" they wrote in the book's preface. "And if citizens no longer control their most basic resource, their water, do they really control anything at all?"

According to the authors of "Thirst" water is controlled publicly by 90 percent of communities across the world and 85 percent in the United States. However in 1990, 50 million people worldwide got their water services from private companies but by 2002 it was 300 million with the number growing.

According to Ashley Schaeffer of Corporate Accountability International "Globally, corporations are promoting water privatization under the guise of efficiency, but the fact is that they are not paying the full cost of public infrastructure, environmental damage, or healthcare for those they hurt. Water is a human right and not a privilege."

Then we have to consider the environmental abuses of our natural precious resource of water that happens in the hands of private owners. According to Alan Snitow. "Water, we think, is the line in the sand -- when your water is actually a profit mechanism, people really react negatively to that."

The movie shows how in 2000 Bechtel privatized water in Cochabamba, Bolivia, with such miserable consequences that it was shortly driven out of the country in an incredible feat of cross-class organizing. But just a few years later, it was awarded a $680 million contract to "fix" Iraq's ruined water systems.

Before you gloat and think the problem does not affect you. Think again. It turns out the West is now a very attractive place to these companies who found out they were not making as much profit in developing countries as they would have liked to.

The authors of "Thirst" show the results have been disastrous: rates are increasing, quality is suffering, customer service is declining, profits are leaving communities and accountability has fallen by the wayside. An example, amongst many given, is In Felton, California, a small regional utility ran the water system until it was purchased in 2001 by California American Water, a subsidiary of American Water, which is a subsidiary of Thames Water in London, which has also become a subsidiary of German giant RWE. Residents in Felton saw their rates skyrocket, "Thirst" reports. A woman who runs a facility for people in need saw her water bill increase from $250 to $1,275 a month.

The Humanity4Water Award revelations had left Derrick and I panting for a breath that could save us, save our world, restore a future for our children. That breath was love. For everything from the committed action of the Planet Heroes we honored to the harrowing facts we discovered about the Earth pointed a quivering finger to love and compassion. It was either there or it wasn't, but it was still the issue of the day. In the heights of trying to grasp for a breath I found something interesting on eco warrior's Vandana Shiva's website. It was an article entitled, "Swaraj: A Deeper Freedom"

Gandhi's Hind Swaraj has for me, been the best teaching on real freedom. It teaches the gospel of love in place of hate. It replaces violence with self-sacrifice. It puts 'soul force' against brute force. For Gandhi, slavery and violence were not just a consequence of

imperialism: a deeper slavery and violence were intrinsic to
industrialism, which Gandhi called "modern civilization".
He identified modern civilization as the real cause of loss of freedom.
"Civilization seeks to increase bodily comforts and it fails miserably
even in doing so. This civilization is such that one has only to be
patient and it will be self-destroyed."
This, I believe, is at the heart of Gandhi's foresight. The ecological
crisis, which is a result of industrialization, is the most important
aspect of civilization. Industrialization is based on fossil fuels, and
fossil-fuel civilization. Fossil fuels have given us climate chaos, and it
is now threatens us with climate catastrophe.

As I near the end of editing this chapter I feel the deep need to meditate. I decide to open up a book I have bought recently. It is called "Dream Yoga", by Tenzin Wangyal Rinpoche, a custodian of the Bon Tradition. I am fascinated by the book. It talks about everything in the world being a dream state. We just have to realize that there is no difference between our night dreaming and our day dreaming. When we come into this awareness we can come into the realm of the true illumination of consciousness. No longer do we slumber when we are asleep. Instead we become fully awake.

I am curious to know more about the author of the book and the Bon tradition and it is with this curiosity that I come across yet another gracious manifestation of the great World Mother Goddess. Her name is Sherap Chamma. I am excited for I know from her symbols, her favorite color, and what is said about her that she is none other than the World Goddess who traveled from ancient Egypt in the Mut Composite of Goddesses.

It is Sherap Chamma's gentle yet protective compassionate presence that reinforces the fact to me – that all the world Goddesses today fall into the two energy aspects of the World Mother Goddess represented by her prototype in Hathor and Sekhmet. Each represents the Gentle loving and fierce compassionate Mother of the Universe.

It seems like each face of the great Mother Goddess that has appeared so far Sherap brings her own message and gift to us. Her key symbols are the mirror, and the color yellow. I make a note that these were amongst Osun and Hathor's primary symbols, along with other Mother Goddess I already encountered and decoded. There are more important symbols: the sun, moon and lotus flower. All echoing Sherap's ancient origin that goes back to the Nile Valley civilizations. I want to know what gift Sherap brings besides being another Mother Goddess who connects us all together. It was through what Rinpoche Tenzin Wangyal shares about her on his website that I discover what it is. He writes,

Sherap Chamma, Wisdom Loving Mother, yellow in color and youthful in appearance, is beautifully adorned with the 13 ornaments of a peaceful deity. She sits atop sun and moon disks on a lotus throne. In her right hand, at the level of the heart, she holds a vase filled with the nectar of compassion. Her left hand holds the stem of a lotus whose blossom supports the mirror of wisdom, which reveals all passing phenomena as empty of inherent existence. Sherap Chamma, also known as Gyalyum (Mother of all Conquerors), is an important emanation of Satrik Ersang from the group of the Four Transcendent Ones. Included among Sherap Chamma's many manifestations are the wrathful protector Sipé Gyalmo (Queen of Existence) and Yeshé Walmo (Magic Wisdom Goddess).

I smile and salute Sherap Chamma silently. I thank her for once again ensuring I had the Mother's song of oneness and compassion ringing in my ears. For, whatever we read about her it is always this song she seems to sing.

Children having fun at the Humanity4Water 2010 Awards

Humanity4Water 2009. Derrick, Humanity4Water
Gary FourStar and Me at ceremony

Results of Plastic bottle Waste at Lake Maracaibo

2010 Humanity4Water Awardee
Dr. Jeremy Narby

Derrick with Kitty Wilson-Evans,
South Carolina Slave
Historian, and children at the Humanity4Water 2010 Awards

The belated Wangari Maathai, founder of the
Green Belt Movement with
Humanity4Water Award

OFUN MEJI

Girl: Mother tell of Ofun Meji

Mother: Ofun Meji tells of humble beginnings can end up with prosperous endings. In Ofun Meji there is a strong message about how the humble spirit becomes the noble prosperous one. Now Ofun Meji also tells about how the seventh day of rest came about.

When Ogun, Olokun, and Orunmla went to the heavenly priest called "the difficult problem that was resolved peacefully". He told them that it was important for them to make an offering to their guardian angels over a period of six days. This would open the way for them to rest in peace and tranquility on the seventh day.

Orunmila, the God of Wisdom asked why should the offering last for this length of days. The priest said that God took six days to create the land, seas, atmosphere, plants, animals and humanity. All these living beings were created before man so that he could have all his needs provided for. In order to make his life on earth comfortable.

Jill Scott's voice floats like a fragrant flower straight out of the small speakers,

I am a voiceless river
I am a boisterous mountain
I am a fragrant flower
And If you don't recognize me.
I am still here.

I sway my body. Then the memories come floating back. The confusion that had bothered my mind, when more broken pieces of history turned up in need of my attention. Doesn't time fly, Omo is growing and it is spring 2011. I glance over at the mellow yellow mandala I had just finished painting awash in bright yellow and orange. In the middle sits Osun in a Buddha pose. I smile. Yes, life is a funny thing. The thought flows right into another Jill Scott verse of her song as it blasts more lyrics from those small speakers.

I am a source of power
I am excited journey
I am the rock of patience
I am a whisper singing
I am unbridled freedom
I am the thought from thinking
I am love unshattered
I am the great orgasm

And if you don't recognize my presence, I am Here
And If you don't recognize my presence, I am here.

475

My body sways like water. Like the water that wet my hands just a few weeks ago at the Healing Springs, North Carolina. It was a pretty warm April 2011 day when the family arrived at its cool banks with up to 50 empty containers. It was almost exactly one year to the date of the Water Blessing we had with our Little Horse Creek friends. We weren't the only ones who were thinking about filling up our containers with water till our heart's content. No, there seemed to be a milieu (so it seemed to me) of people with hands and mind ladened with the same intentions.

We stayed for at least an hour filling those containers. But the idea of having some cool healing waters to take home made the time fly. Then there was baby Omo. We believed the Healing Springs had done a lot to heal my fifteen year infertility issue. So it was an absolute joy when we could at last dip her wiggling toes into its waters. I was surprised, she barely flinched as the extremely cool waters touched and washed over the arch of her feet.

I should have known, after so many similar experiences, that water was going to open up another pandora's box full of secrets. But for some reason I didn't think this would happen. Not this time. I truly thought it had revealed as much as I needed to know for the moment. As much as it had hidden. I had been looking forward to wrapping the journey, at least this stage of the journey, up. However, water and the spirit that belonged to it had other ideas in mind.

My mother was right, "Omi you are writing your journey as it unfolds before you." Now that made writing this book a strange experience. For I never truly knew what was going to turn up next. Try writing under those conditions. It is quite a maddening experience. But those were the conditions I wrote under, and so I had to accept this book was not so much of my own making, but one of the Dreamtime of Mother Earth awakening.

Before leaving the Springs that day its waters moved me to write,

"I had forgotten all about water. My writing emerges from the dry paper of time and rises up wet, healed and dripping with its memory. Thank you Healing Springs for reminding me what it is all about. Clean, fresh, beautiful water."

When I finished writing my heart felt heavy. How could I have forgotten the power of these waters? How could I have forgotten the power within water? It was so easy to. I tucked my pen away and that night I dreamt that,

I went into a room dominated by a white porcelain bathtub. It was filled with very black water. I started ranting in the dream.

"Look how these people have left the water of this tub. All they had to do was keep this water clean."

I was quite angry.

Then I said,

"let me put my hand in this tub and see what is below this surface."

As I did so my mother rose from below the dirty water. She was covered in mud. The sight of her made me laugh. My mother was having a mud bath and that was why the water had been so dark.

Then I looked outside the window and I see everything submerged in water. Then I notice that people are trying to swim in the water like it was a normal day to go swimming. The water was crashing everywhere but they were trying to have a good time.

I then turned to my mother and said,

"have you seen the water outside there. It is all over the place."

477

My mother looked at me and replied,
"if I had known that I would not have been here relaxing in
this tub."

Derrick said that he believed the dream meant that people do not know how serious the water crisis is. I was inclined to agree with him. Months later, when I read the dream again I was more acutely aware of the symbolism of my mother being submerged in the dirty water. You know in all traditional cultures around the world the waters are the Mother. The Mother of life and nourishment. This is not just talk, but it is a real belief that water is sacred and not a commodity. It's spirit is the spirit of the Mother. So for my mother to be submerged in dirty water seemed to indicate the state of the waterways to me, and the fact that we are interfering with its sacredness and cleanliness.

I closed my eyes. Jill Scott is so cool. Never knew she sung this tune. I rewind it and the lyrics of what was to become my favorite verse belted out afresh. With my eyes closed it almost sounded like the lyrics were being sung by the most ethereal presence. No, that is not what it sounded like. It sounded as though the invisible voice of Mother Nature was singing herself,

I am a voiceless river
I am a boisterous mountain
I am a fragrance flower

And if you don't recognize me. I am still here.

I swayed. I couldn't help myself, I just had to. Then a beautiful thing happened, the further revelations our spiritual histories that had flung themselves before me in a jumbled mess, began to unravel and make sense.

Shiva came dancing back into my memory. I squeezed my eyelids shut tighter. I tried to remember how Shiva had appeared to me. Ahhh yes, it was after my Healing Springs visit. It was when the Dancing Girl of Mohenjo –daro had appeared before me again swirling and a dancing. She swirled me right to the location of the Shiva Seal. It too was a remnant of the past that had been found in the Indus Valley, right alongside the Dancing Girl of Mohenjo-Daro's statute.

Before the memory and stomping rhythm of the Shiva Seal could take root. Jill Scott's song made me have flash backs to three important dreams I had come to call simply "My Three Dreams". They occurred between the months of October and December 2010.

Dream 1: The Waters are Coming

I dreamt I was in this place and it was by the water front. I was with this woman and we were both admiring the waterfront and its waters. We weren't right up on the waterfront but were on a walkway which was set a little bit away from it.

As we admired the waterfront I noticed a huge ancient carving several feet high. It was of a deity. This deity had chakra deities coming out of it with arms in an offering position. All the deities were also carved and they came out from the area of his stomach all the way to his pubic area. The figure stood on top of a carved pyramid. It had been made in such a way that the moon could hit it at a certain angle. It was quite awesome. I excitedly pointed the deity out to the woman. As I was doing so I noticed that my feet were getting a little wet. I said to the woman,

479

"the water is coming up".

She said, "no it can't be. The river is way below".

I said, "It is coming up".

Then there was more water. Then we started running. I ran into the apartment where Derrick was and I told him that the waters were coming.

He said "no they are not."

I said "they are!".

As I said that the waters whoosed under the door. We put our backs to the door and outside the door we could really hear the waters. Then the wind started howling forcefully and I was so scared. I started saying,

"Momma, Momma, please subside. Don't be angry."

The voice said, "I am tired with humans. Look at everything they have done to the Earth."

"Give one more chance Momma. I know I have not delivered the messages Momma. I know. I promise I will. I promise Momma."

The voice said it did not believe humanity could change.

"It can. It can. It Can." I begged and pleaded with the voice.

The voice said, "one more chance."

Then the waters subsided. The next day in the dream I was telling Derrick the dream about the deity and the waters.

As I was talking a voice said,

"who called my name? who called my name? I am understaffed."

The deity seemed so terrifying to me. I ran and hid from it.

I woke up from this dream staring into the dark of the night, feeling scared and hopeless. I felt helpless in terms of the request that was made in the dream. I knew the gravity of the messages and revelations I had been shown, but deep down I had little confidence they would ever see the light of the day. Everyday after that dream I fretted and worried about my own ineptness to tell the world that our actions were taking us to the brink of destruction. Nature was wholly fed up of us. The more my ineptness washed over me, was the more the truth of how far we had come away from the bosom of Mother Earth filled me.

Dream 2: A Not so Gentle Reminder

The second dream was a month later, shorter and a slight repetition of the first. The waters were rising again. There was a tsunami that was hitting the world. Then in this dream I remembered the first dream and said,

"mama, I know, I know I have not told the world as yet. Please forgive me."

After the dream I woke up feeling guilty. The guilt stayed with me for weeks. The burden to tell the world about the Mother and the deep problems we were in for, if we chose to keep on disrespecting her weighed heavily on my heart. Yet I still could not see how to tell the world.

Dream 3: Pay Back

The third dream was around December 14th 2010. It was just before the third annual Humanity4Water Ceremony event myself and Derrick had planned. The one where we had thrown that huge party for the children. In my diary I entitled the dream "Pay Back". A few days after I had the dream I recorded it in my journal:

I dreamt I was in this mystical place and I was about to walk up this path and a man appeared. He said

> *"you have to payback on your promise."*
> *I said, "payback?"*
> *He said, "yes payback".*
> *Then I started walking away from him and up the path. Then all of a sudden nature dissolved into this huge tsunami like colorful ball of wind and began to head down the path in my direction. Then Kem Ra (my son), who was standing at the side of the path, shouted,*
> *"say it!.*
> *" Say what?" I shouted back.*
> *"the words "Pay back!"*
> *"why?!" I shouted back.*
> *"Mommy just say it. Just say it."*
> *Then I started shouting at the top of my voice,*
> *"payback! Payback! Payback!" and the wind stopped howling and nature went calm again.*

On awakening from that dream the word "Payback!" played on my mind and weighed it down for a long time. If I lived in ancient times I felt my responsibility to share all I had learned from the our Universal Mother would be easy. You know you would tell some high priest, they would check your message with the oracle, then an announcement would be made to the relevant quarters.

But I didn't live way back in the day. I was in the here and now. The more I thought about the dreams was the quicker I tried to work on the manuscript. I knew I needed to finish it. I knew it was not mine to hold back. Yet, I had one major issue and that was – a family to take care of. Included in that troupe was my beautiful new four month teething baby girl, Omololu. So the pace was slow. It dragged on each day, and with that so did my heart.

That was until the Tsunami in Australia and then Japan hit. They both reminded me of the dreams I had been having. I am not saying that these events are the things that I dreamt about but they reminded me sharply of my promise to "payback". So I picked up the speed, in the best way I could.

I am still here...The music booming out from my I Pod and Jill Scotts voice pulled me back into the memory of Shiva's appearance, again. When I had encountered Shiva he sat there crossed legged, in a meditative pose, hands resting on knees, surrounded by animals. He let me know that he was called "Pashupati", "Lord of the Animals". This Shiva was the pro-type of Shiva we know today. He is claimed to be of Pre-Aryan origin. Now as I said earlier he was found on the Shiva Seal, which had been found near to the statute of the Dancing Girl of Mohenjo-Daro.

The largest animal next to this Shiva on the seal is a tiger. It is on his right hand side. Now, besides this seal, there is a smaller one of the same proto-type Shiva. I remember how I had stared at Shiva for some time, and how he had smiled and urged me to find out more. I quickly grabbed my notes from that period and read,

Shiva is known as the "auspicious one". He is part of the Hindu trinity of Gods which includes himself, Vishnu and Brahma. In that trinity it is Shiva who is said to be the Destroyer and Transformer. Brahma is the Creator, while Vishnu is the Preserver.

Now it seems that Shiva is usually worshipped in the abstract form of the Shiva lingam. (Penis, in English!) It is said to

represent the male creative energy, and is often represented with the Yoni, a symbol of the Mother Goddess or of Shakti. The female creative energy. The two together are said to represent the unification and oneness of the masculine and feminine principle.

The wives of Shiva are said to be Kali, Durga and Parvati. His son is Ganesh, the God who opens the way. Upon Shiva's forehead is the crescent moon. His body is often seen smeared in ashes. This seems to be part of the pre - Aryan tradition of cremation-ground asceticism that was practiced by some groups who were outside the fold of Brahmanic orthodoxy. These practices associated with cremation grounds are also mentioned in the Pali canon of Theravada Buddhism. One of the epithet for Shiva is "inhabitant of the cremation ground".

Now what I find interesting is that Shiva's hair is very distinctive and he is described as "the one with matted hair." His hair is often fashioned into a shell. Through his matted hair the Ganges river is said to make her abode.

Around Shiva's neck is often a garland of snakes. Oh Shiva has another epithet (he has quite a few), and that is Nandi. It is the name of the bull that serves as his mount. He also has the epithet Pasupati, or Pashupati which can mean "lord of cattle" or "Lord of the Animals"

Ps. Remember that Parvati and Durga are Shiva's wives (now Durga is Shiva's wife because Parvati is her incarnation).

The Shiva Seal Found at Mohenjo-Daro

There was much about Shiva that reminded me of Osiris from Egypt. I had wondered how much they had in common and if they were one of the same. I had reminded myself that I had already correlated Shiva's wives to the Mut Goddess Composite. That trembling feeling filled my bones again every time I thought about Shiva. It had been the book "The Osirian Religion" by E.A Wallis Budge, that helped me wade through the threads of connections I was making in my mind and spirit. I made copious notes from the book. With Jill Scot playing in the background I re-read them again.

Osiris, whose proper Egyptian name is Ausar, was a divine African King who ruled Egypt. He was apparently very benevolent and kind. He taught his subjects how to live in an even more civilized way. Once he felt he had accomplished his mission, he left Egypt and travelled around the world teaching various nations the things he had shown his own subjects. He did not force anyone to practice the things he was showing them.

485

It is said that during his absence his wife Isis (known properly as Auset. Isis was the Greek version of her name) administered to all the Kingdom's needs. She ruled with great vigilance and wisdom. While Osiris was away her wicked brother in-law Set (Set was sometimes said to be her brother) decided he was going to get rid of Osiris.

On Osiris's return he decided to throw a party. However the party was a trick. A beautiful box was prepared for Osiris. As the party got rocking Set declared he would give the box to anyone who could fit in it comfortably. Seventy two of his conspirators tried to get in the box, but of course they couldn't fit. Then like a good sport Osiris said he would give it a try.

Well, that was it. As soon as he did, that Set and his men sealed the box and whisked Osiris away. Well, of course he suffocated to death. The box was cast into the river which carried it Northward.

Now Isis was in a city called Coptos. When the news of Osiris death met her she began to wail and dramatically cut of one of the locks of her hair. Then she immediately went looking for the body of her husband. Some children said they had seen the box which contained the body floating down the Nile. The waves had carried the box up the coast of Syria and cast it up at a place called Byblos, as soon as it rested on the ground a large tree sprang up and grew all around the box enclosing it in.

The King of Byblos found the tree and thought it was beautiful. He cut the tree down and took it to his palace. Isis eventually discovered what had happened and headed to Byblos. When she arrived she was eventually invited in by the Queen to look after her baby. Isis suckled the child from her finger. Every night she also put the child in the fire to give him the gift of immortality. However, one night the Queen spoilt the whole thing. When she saw her child in the fire she of course shrieked. Therefore the child did not gain immortality.

It was then that Isis explained who she was and why she was there. The King and Queen gave her back the pillar and she cut the box out from it. She gave the pillar back to the King and Queen who sent it to the temple of Byblos upon which the pillar became an object of worship.

Isis threw herself upon the box and lamented so hard that it is said that the King's son was frightened into convulsions and died in shock. Some say he did not die.

After mourning Isis arrived back in Egypt with the box. Set discovers that Isis has returned Osiris body back and goes and discovers the box. When he does so it is said that he chopped the body up into about fourteen pieces and scattered it throughout the country. Once again Isis is on a mission. She goes searching for all the limbs of her dear husband's body and is successful. She finds all but his phallus which is said to have been thrown into the region of the Delta which is full of marshes and canals.

Wherever Isis found a piece of Osiris body it is said that she buried it and built a sepulcher over it. They say this explains why there are so many tombs to Osiris all over Egypt. Some say that actually what happened is that Isis only buried figurines of Osiris in Egypt . Eventually after Isis found all the members of his body but his phallus which had been eaten by a fish. She pieced it back together. She reconstructed his phallus and created an obelisk which was worshipped in commemorative festivals

Through medicine she conceived a child with Osiris's spirit through Immaculate Conception. That child was Horus who it was foretold would avenge his father's death and defeat the evil Set.

Now there is much more to the story and there are slightly different versions of the story, as well. However, all agree that eventually Orisis descends to the underworld where he becomes Lord of Eternity, Ruler of the Dead and Lord of the Underworld. While Horus, his son, becomes "King on earth". Osiris becomes the ultimate judge of souls of the departed. It is his ultimate decision that determines the ability of a soul to live in eternity or not. The seat of the individual's soul was said to be the heart and that is why the heart was weighted on the scales of Maat.

My notes break and then continue as I start to make the connections between Osiris and Shiva.

- *The missing phallus of Osiris and its reconstruction, and worship – are major themes. Shiva is associated with the symbol of the Lingam (which is the image of the lingam and yoni together). This symbol is worshipped throughout India. Wherever, Shiva is worshipped there is the Shiva Lingam. Just as with Osiris.*
- *The Tet is one of the oldest symbols of Osiris. The Tet represented him and it was nearly always set up next to Hathor's sycamore fig tree which was strongly associated with the Tet. Which is said to be his backbone and it looks very much like a phallus.*
- *The epithets for Osiris are many and they like Shiva depict his many roles. Budge explains that he absorbed the characteristics of many local Gods.*

I remembered how the phallus symbol had made an impression on me. For both Shiva and Osiris were connected to that symbol. I had made further notes which compared the two gods in more detail. The similarities were striking. In my mind, not just striking, but almost totally identical. After a short while it had become obvious to me that we were definitely talking about the same God.

- *One of the translations of Osiris's names means "he who takes seat". The Pre – Aryan Shiva appears to be sitting on a seat.*

488

- Osiris is also said to have been associated with ancestral worship and according to Budge "took the place of the tutelary ancestor-god who was honored and worshipped in every village of the Sudan of any size from time immemorial." As a result he was associated with the honoring of the dead. His connection with the dead was also seen in terms of his role as the Judge of the Dead. This brings to mind the pre-Aryan practice of Shiva being associated with crematoriums. Which in other words associates him with the dead and the ancestors.

- Osiris is connected like Shiva with extreme purity of the self and behavior. This can be seen from his symbols he wears and holds: A white crown (the crown of upper Egypt) a scepter, an ankh (which represents life), a flail (which represents discipline). He is also dressed in white (which represents purity.

- Osiris was also fused with the identities of one of the oldest grain gods of Egypt Nepra who is often personified as wheat, barley, dhura, and corn etc. He was also known as Osiris-Aah which means Osiris, the Moon God. In his book Budge shows a depiction of him with a crescent moon and full moon on his head as he holds all his symbols which represent: stability, life, serenity, power and dominion over the self. Shiva too is depicted with a crescent moon on his head. It is actually placed on his forehead.

- In the form of his name Osiris-Har-Machis-Temu Osiris is said to be a triad which represents the evening sun, the night sun and the morning sun. Shiva is also part of a triad which is Brahma (The Creator) whom like Osiris has a beard which represents wisdom or eternal processes of creation. He too like many depiction of Osiris wears a crown which indicates supreme authority. Vishnu is known as "Preserver of the Universe". Osiris is also known as the "Lord of Eternity" Osiris. In this form he is called Osiris-Neb-Heh and appears in the form of a mummy with the head of a Bennu Bird or phoenix.

- When we look at the Shiva Seal we see that Shiva has a bull as his mount. One of the most important forms of Osiris was said to be from about 600 B.C to the Roman period and it *was the form as Asar-Hep or Sarapis. This form was made by the fusion of the attributes of the bull God Hep. Osiris was also connected with the ram.*

- *Shiva is often depicted as "The Lord of Dance". Budge quotes Greek Diodorus who says, "Osiris was a man given to mirth and jollity, and took great pleasure in music and dancing". Budge says that dance was very important to the cult of Osiris.*

- *Now it is interesting to note that Shiva is often depicted with Parvati. Their relationship is one of great devotion and dedication. Like Shiva, Parvati also performs austerities. She is the gentle face of Durga and Kali. Now this is of great interest for Budge claims that "one thing is for sure her fortunes were bound up with Osiris". This he says in reference to Isis and Osiris. He further states, "Those who took the view that Osiris was a mere tribal chief would regard Isis as a tribal chief's wife; those who worshipped Osiris under the form of a bull would naturally think of Isis as a cow; those who revered Osiris as a great, might and terrible ancestral spirit would consider Isis as his spirit counterpart.*

- *Isis was seen to be quite mighty and powerful on her own accord and as Osiris fame grew her own presence eventually "eclipsed his". She, according to Budge, "became the personification of the great feminine, creative power which conceived and brought forth every living creature and thing, from the Gods in heaven to man on the earth and the insect on the ground. What she brought forth she protected, and cared for, and fed, and nourished and she employed her life in using her power graciously and successfully, not only in creating new beings, but in restoring life those that were dead."*

- *Like Shiva and Parvati. Osiris and Isis had a child by Immaculate Conception. Horus spent most his time trying to remove Set (the personification of the negative ego) out of the way. Ganesh is the "Remover of Obstacles".*

As I re-read the notes I re-remembered when the discovery had been made how a bolt of electricity had shot through my stomach. I remembered because those bolts were doing it again lighting me up like a bulb. The discovery that Shiva and Osiris was beyond a doubt one of the same had made me jump with joy. Shiva had felt like the obscure dot in the middle of the Goddess's mandala I had painted. Now he was showing with his wife Parvati, Durga and Kali how completly our ancient traditions were connected. He was a man, but he (as one who protects order and balance) was speaking up with his wives.

"The waters have to be mended," he stomped wildly, as the lyrics of Jill Scott's song "I Am Still Here" continued to play on.

A question had formed on my mind when reading on Shiva and that was - how on earth could the teachings of Osiris have ended up in India? Now Budge had answered that question earlier when he said Egyptian tradition had gone from Rome onwards. But the question was still on my mind. I realized that today our historical outlook was much more limited than our ancestors. Was it that difficult to truly imagine how much, and far our ancestors traveled around the world in those days.

Now it was obvious to me that with Osiris and Isis would have travelled a whole pantheon of Goddesses and Gods with them. I reminded myself that it was important to remember that Hathor and Isis albeit separate were also considered to be one when this collection of Goddesses and Gods travelled. Most of the time Isis is seen holding only the ankh sign and a simple staff in her hand, but in later images she is said to sometimes have the items usually associated only with

Hathor, the sacred sistrum rattle and the fertility-bearing menat necklace.

The relationship of Hathor and Isis was further illustrated by the fact that Horus, the son of Isis was housed within Hathor's body. Sometimes she is depicted as the actual mother of Horus. In fact, Hathor's original name Het Heru meant House of Horus.

I remember how I had delved into the *Oxford Guide to Egyptian Mythology* in an attempt to learn more about the relationship with Hathor and Isis. It stated that in the cult of Osiris eternal life was promised to those deemed morally worthy. Originally the justified dead, male or female, became an Osiris but by early Roman times females became identified with Hathor and men with Osiris. I had found this tit bit of information interesting as Tara was the feminine aspect of the Buddha energy, and she claimed she would be birthed as a woman so all women could realize their Buddha nature. Understanding Hathor and Isis relationship had been important to me as it seemed that Hathor dominated the Mut composite where all the Goddesses seemed to be separate in their own right, but also faces of Hathor. In other words Hathor seemed to be "she who ruled as Mother Universe". In my mind's eye Shiva's wife Parvati seemed to be very much a Hathor/Sekhmet-Isis combination; and the whole Durga family reflected the Mut composite of Goddesses whom Hathor seemed to rule.

All of this was important because if Parvati was Shiva's wife, and Parvati was a mirror of the Hathor/Sekhmet-Isis combination. These Mother figures further showed the connection between Osiris, Shiva, and the ocean of history.

Just as Jill Scott's words floated and rose within my heart I re-read some more notes I had on Shiva. I smiled as I re-read the words that had made me leap of my chair.

That the precise placement of both heels under the scrotum is an advanced Tantric Yoga technique called Bandha, meaning knot or "lock". It is usually done to sublimate and re- direct the sexual energy and can endow the practitioner with spiritual powers. Many say he is sitting in a cross legged Lotus Position of Hathor Yoga.

I can't remember how it happened. How I noticed it. But I remember how it leapt out at me like a fire goddess. *"Hatha Yoga, Hathor, Hatha Yoga, Hathor"*......The name had looped around in my head. I researched the word Hatha further . *Ha* was the sun and tha the moon.

My limited knowledge had reminded me that that both the sun and the moon were both Hathor's symbols. The cow horns on her head are said to represent the crescent moon. Right in the middle of that moon sat the sun. Like a flash it became clear to me that Hatha Yoga was connected to Hathor the Goddess. How could it not. The spellings were only slightly different. The meaning of Hatha Yoga reflected the symbols the Goddess wore proudly as her crown.

What had been of further interest to me was how Hatha Yoga was said to be first taught by Shiva to Parvati (whom I had already identified very intimately with Hathor). The pieces of history had fallen together in jumbled but somehow clear heaps. It was really up to the beholder, in this case me, to accept what was placed right before one's field of vision.

In fact Hatha Yoga was one of the four branches of Tantra which is about the expansion of one's consciousness.

Jill Scott's voice kept on taking me deeper and deeper into the jumbled memories of my journey compiling them now into understandable data.

"I am still here".

I closed my eyes and continued to sway through the broken threads of history coming together. I remembered how a question had formed itself on my mind over and over again. Over the days, months and years.

"What is the importance of knowing Mother Consciousness, anyway?"

Then I remembered something the Dalai Lama had said in a documentary,

"we are talking about a peace for Humanity. A peaceful world. This is not from prayer, not from technology, not from money, not from religion but from the Mother."

As if using this as a cue I remembered how two more Goddesses took their place amongst the compassionate song of the gathering Mothers of the World. How they both came with their own jigsaw pieces, and gifts. Their names were Amaterasu of Japan, and Bramari Devi the Bee Goddess of India.

Amaterasu emerged from the dust of the "Records of Ancient Matters" and from the pages of Joseph Campbell's "The Hero with a Thousand Faces". I was fascinated by her tale which went something like this,

One day Susannowo, the Storm God, the brother of Amaterasu, is behaving very badly. Not just for one day but he was being a pain in the behind for quite some time. She tried to be patient with him, even tried to forgive him for some of the things he was doing. Yet, he

wouldn't stop his nonsense. He destroyed her rice fields and begun to pollute her institutions. Finally he broke a hole in the top of her weaving hall and threw a horse through the roof which he had killed. The ladies of the Goddess who were busy weaving the August garments of the deities were so shocked they died on the spot.

Amaterasu was also terrified. She retired to her heavenly cave, closed the door behind her and secured it tightly. Her permanent disappearance as the sun would have meant the end of the whole universe before it had even begun. Without her presence everything in the world and beyond went dark. The evil spirits ran riot through the world. So many problems on the earth began to occur. Things were so bad that the eight million Gods assembled in the bed of the tranquil river of heaven and asked one of the deities named Thought-Includer, to devise a plan. As a result. A plan was hatched. A mirror, a sword and cloth offerings were made. A great tree was put up and decorated with jewels; Cocks were brought that might keep up a perpetual crowing; bonfires were lit; elaborate prayers were recited. The mirror which was eight feet long was tied to the middle branches of the tree and noisy dance was performed by a young Goddess called Uzume. The eight million divinities were so amused that they laughed so hard making their voices fill up the whole air.

The racket outside made the Goddess peak out of her cave. As she did so she asked everyone what were they so happy about? The deities told her there was one even more wonderful than her. Astonished by the behavior of the Gods she came out of her cave and she beheld a radiant image in the mirror that was now held up before her. As she gazed a powerful God took hold of her hand and drew her out more. Another stretched a rope of straw, called the Shimenawo, behind her and across the entrance of the cave. She was told she was not allowed to go beyond the Shimenawo.

As a result the sun now rests a little but never disappears completely.

I had been moved by Amaterasu's story for within it seemed to be the whole history of the Goddess and her journey with humanity. I was astonished at how many of her symbols echoed those of other Mother Goddesses, and specifically Hathor's from ancient Egypt. Amaterasu stood proudly with history in her weaving loom. She was a proud partaker in the jigsaw pieces that seemed to be leading to a renewal of our Earth. I had decided to do some further research on the Goddess and made notes making references to her similarities to Hathor.

Similarities of Amaterasu and Hathor Notes

- *The Birth From the Eye - Amaterasu is birthed from her father's eye. Hathor is birthed from Ra's eye when the world is said to be conspiring against him. The Goddess Tara is also birthed from the left eye of Avalokiteshvara. Eyes are strongly associated with Hathor. In Egypt the left and right eye are associated with her. Layne Redmond points out that the right eye is associated with the sun and the left with the moon. She also quotes Egyptologist R.T. Rundall Clark when he says, "complex meshes of eye symbolism are woven all around the Egyptian Goddess," and the eye is "always a symbol for the Great Goddess".*

- *The sun: Amaterasu is a powerful sun Goddess of royal persuasion. Hathor wears the sun disc on her head and was associated with royalty, as well.*

- *The mirror: Amaterasu is tempted out with a mirror. Hathor's symbol is also the mirror.*

- *The Sword: It is one of the offerings made to the Goddess along with the mirror and cloth. The sword Is one of Hathor's symbol when she is in the form of her compassionate warrior self, Sekhmet.*

496

- *Dance and joy: A dance is performed, and lots of joy generated by the Gods in order to draw Amaterasu out. Hathor is associated with dance and joy. Dance and joyful activities were said to help us reach the illuminated soul.*
- *The tree: a great tree is erected and decorated with jewels. Hathor is associated with trees and jewels. In fact Hathor is the original tree of life which we see in many of the ancient mythologies.*
- *Weaving: Hathor is associated with the creation of beautiful things. Osun her Nigerian name is connected to weaving and dying cloth. She also plaits hair which is a symbolic weaving gesture.*
- *Caves: After the Goddesses die Amaterasu hides and retreats into a cave and the world enters darkness. Hathor is associated with caves and death. In "When the Women Were Drummers" Layne Redmond reveals that the Mother Goddess "stood at the threshold of the door to the Mountain of the Dead, beckoning arriving souls, whom she took into her womb for rebirth. Her vulva was the gateway between two worlds". That vulva was symbolized by the cave. Apparently her caves were often carved into cliff sides to represent entrance to the other world.*
- *Saving the world: Amaterasu comes out and her illuminating presence saves the world. Hathor helps save the world through her form Sekhmet who is also known as "The Lady of Flames".*

I then made a small side note on Amaterasu and the Indo _- Aryan Battle with the Goddess.

- Amaterasu's brother Susannowo is called the Storm God. He destroys everything that belonged to the Goddess, and eventually he frightens all the Goddess's to death. This is story has all the hall marks of the Indo –Aryan battle with the Goddess honoring cultures.

So what was Amaterasu's gift?

"I am still here," Jill Scott's voice penetrated through my thoughts.

Was it the message that only the illumination of the Universal Mother Consciousness could save the day. That we must entreat her out of her cave and pull tight the Shimenawo rope across her threshold?

From my notes appeared a dream I had written down. I read it.

I went over to a house. Which house? whose house? I do not know. When I knocked on the door, a beautiful very dark woman opened it. She welcomed me in. I seemed to know her and not know her, but she seemed to know me fully. I went into the house and she had a sister living there to. She was equally as beautiful. They both invited me to stay for dinner. Before dinner they threw their Western clothes of and started to walk around the house proudly naked. The only thing they wore was a small cover over their pubic area. They seemed so relieved that they could walk around like this. It was obvious that they walked around like that all the time, anytime they got a chance to. I remember saying to myself, "okay then". The whole scene seemed kind of strange and for some reason I wanted to giggle. Then I turned to the sister whom I had met in the house and said,

"it is a shame your children will not learn how to dance because of the school they are in."

The sister who was obviously a very proficient dance teacher sat on the floor in a cross legged position. She replied,

"I always teach my children how to dance".

498

Yes. Yes. I thought. The Mother always teaches us to dance in rhythm with the earth. It is that dance we need to remember again.

Bhramari Devi, the Honey Bee Goddess of India turned up as I casually looked on the internet for nothing in particular. For some strange reason I found myself thinking of honey bees and she turned up on the back of their saucy dances. I was intrigued to find her, or that she found me. For Osun was connected to the honey bee, and according to Layne Redmond author of "When the Women Were Drummers" so was the Goddess Melissa of Greece, an ancient Anatolian Goddess from Asia Minor in Turkey, and the prophetess Deborah from the bible who was apparently known as the "Queen Bee". Bhramari Devi had a story to tell,

One day there once lived a demon called Arun. He wanted to establish his kingdom by driving out the devas (nature spirits). The devas gathered together to decide how to defeat their enemy, but mean while, Aruna, surrounded by his army, invaded the heavens and dislodged the devas from their stations. The devas left their city, families and wives to seek advice from Lord Shiva. As a result Aruna entered heaven with no resistance. He summoned his fellow demons and angrily told them to summon the wives of the devas. The devis were brought before Arun. In utter fear they closed their eyes and prayed to Parmeshi Devi to save them.

Parmeswari Devi transformed herself into a large bee and with a swarm of bees which emerged out from her form, surrounded the wives of the devas and set out numerous lines of black bees, which lined and joined with those emerging from her hands, covering the whole Earth. The sky was completely overcast with the swarm of bees and the Earth was cast into darkness. The sky, mountain, peaks,

499

trees, forests, all became filled with bees and the spectacle presented a terrifying sight.

Then the black bees began to tear asunder the breasts of the demons, as bees sting those who disturb their hives. The powerful demons could not fight or communicate with each other, and began to perish rapidly. The Goddess in her form as the divine bee approached Aruna and said, "O asura! Meet your end!" and she stung him to death. The devis thanked Parmeshwari Devi. That is how she got the name of Bramari Devi, as protector.

Did she come to remind us that the Honey Bees were the symbol and messengers of our Mother Universe? Straight after reading her story I came across an article that surprised me. For there was Bramari Devi and her message – that the Universal Mother is the only one that can save the world. Found in the British The Mail newspaper, and written by a David Derbyshire. The heading and article read,

British hives for British workers:
Hardy native black honeybee poised for comeback

Derbyshire informs us that a scheme to reintroduce black bees was unveiled by the Bee Improvement and Bee Breeders' Association (Bibba) and the Co-op Group. Paul Monaghan, of the Co-op said: 'The hardy native black honeybee has had a bad press over the years but it may hold the key to reversing the decline in the UK's honeybee population.

Jill Scott's voice trailed off...*I am a voiceless river, I am a boisterous mountain, I am a fragrant flower, And If you don't recognize me, I am still here.*

Bhramari Devi, The Honey Bee Goddess of India

BOOK 4

WHERE THE RIVERS END

THE SONG BEGINS

ASE

At the end of every prayer is an Amen or in the case of the Yoruba's an Ase. As I bowed my head to the floor I thanked the Divine Mother Goddess, the ancestors and all those relations who had made my journey possible I reflected on how much it had changed me. I started of wanting to be "normal". Not wanting to live in the realm of the supernormal - the place where spirits dwell. The outstanding source of our wealth, wisdom, abundance, and renewal.

Then I realized one could not escape from the existence of the indwelling universal soul. Within us lay a tiny bit of its spark. Even though part of me still wanted to deny its fullness, another part of me just couldn't. Not after my extraordinary experiences, profound dreams, explicit revelations, channeling of privileged historical information. Not after it, the primordial waters, had risen and enfolded me into its embrace. Taken me around like Ebenezer and shown me the horrors, sorrows, joys, oneness and love of the world. The world within and the world without.

With my head bowed I remembered fragments of a dream. Where I saw myself saving myself by carrying my dead body down to a river. I lovingly lay it in the still waters, then slowly but surely I came back alive, again.

There with my head bowed without a shadow of a doubt I understood that the Feminine Grace of the Mother was here to save us. Whether I could fully accept it in all its breadth, depth and marvelousness was a whole other question. But I could not deny the waters that flowed before me.

Mother. We call her by so many different names. We see her in different ways, but her essence is always the same. She is simply really Mother. Her story leads us to the truth of who we are, and the heart of our universal oneness. What better gift could we hope for in this time - the truth of what she means to us, the truth of what this earth means to us and what we mean to each other. She shows us the source of our cultures, histories, spirituality and heart.

Ase! Little did I know that in that Ase that the final banks were still to burst. That it would be such a ferocious breaking of waters. Such a current that would sweep me through the final destinations of history. Little did I know that there was more weaving for the Mother to do. Her needle had not finished mending our broken world.

The spirits didn't warn me, nor my watery Guardian Osun, but I Ebenezer of the world of those wanting to be "normal" was soon to be whisked off again towards the dizzying heights of some grand finale.

Ase! As I said those words I should have remembered that in the Yoruba tradition that Ase is said in threes. Some add a fourth one on for good luck. I lift my head from the ground and thought about how to finish the editing of this book, and how to put together the bits and pieces of information that still lay somewhat broken on the ground. Little did I know that the story was not quite over. I was to become carried away along gentle rivulets of water that would become the rushing torrents of destiny. There was no way to tame the waters, but to swim with them, dive underneath and pick up the gifts.

As I happily conclude my manuscript, my computer crashes.
Nu Wa stands with her arms crossed waiting for me on the
brinks of mythological time, and technological crisis. The
spirits land me at her mighty feet and I look up. She taps her
foot impatiently. It is early August 2011, and she knows time is
running out. She knows I will soon return back to the Dream
World where I only see with my eyes open. Before I do so, she
has things to show me. As Derrick attempts to fix my
computer she ensures that I meet her, as Kem Ra bounces
down the stairs with "the Land of the Dragon" book tucked
securely under his arms. She waits for me to flick the book
open to kill some time. As I do she looks out through its
pages, grabs me by the hands and pulls me in. Of course when
I see there is a Mother Goddess called Nu Wa, my interest is
whetted. Instinctively, even before I know anything about her
I know she is yet another Mother Goddess who has come to
close the gap in our wounded humanity, and to bear the gifts
of wholeness.

**Nu Wa revealed to me that she was the Chinese grand
Mother Goddess.** I go back and forth between the book in my
hand and another computer in the house following her story.
Nu Wa begins her story at the great Yellow River and takes me
across its rolling landscapes.

"China's Sorrow," that's what they call it, she
whispers.

"Sometimes it will nurture you, sometimes it will
destroy you. Just like the mighty Nile River"

As I watch her talk her eyebrows furrow, a sadness
clouds her radiant ancient beauty and her head bows. The
Yellow River is dying. It was soon to join the water graveyard
of the world. Dammed by man's greed, chocked by his

pollution her vast mighty waters were dwindling to a lifeless trickle. So much so that the Chinese government was now playing God and trying to make rain clouds by bombarding clouds above the river with silver iodide crystals, around which moisture collects and becomes heavy enough in order to fall with rain.

The Tibetan people in whose land the mighty Yellow River begins, as a small spring shooting up from the ground, say that the thunderous noise of the planes were only making the Gods angrier.

"Traditionally people had respect for my waters," Nu Wa tells me.

She takes me by the hand and shows me the words of a Chinese Blogger who makes a pilgrimage to the Yellow River's source. He writes about the thoughts that fill him, like a blossoming lotus, as he stands at its small trickling source,

"After crossing mountains and rivers, eventually we got to the headstream of Yellow River. There was no torrent, marsh, glacier, only a spring flowing from the earth. People who hadn't come here would never imagine that it was the source of Yellow River, the Mother River."…"It constantly and slowly flows to the distant place. It silently and deeply narrates the historic stories. Some people respect her and not dare to move close to her; some people love her, weeping besides her; Some people appreciate her, exciting her."

I am moved. Hadn't I too stood near the source of a great river? I thought about when I had stood at a small stream that eventually joined others to become the great body of the sacred Osun River, in Nigeria. As I bowed my head in reverence for the Yellow River, I prayed a prayer that I frequently said for all the rivers – that her beautiful waters would never leave us.

Nu Wa The Great Mother Creatrix , The Great Mother Protector

Once my bowed head raised Nu Wa was ready to give me a few history lessons. Ones that placed her in the great lineage of ancient Mother Goddesses, and their grand work for humanity. She showed herself to be not only she who created all things in life, but also as she who had saved the world from the brink of total devastation. She led me to her creation story in the pages of "the Land of the Dragon" which I have adapted.

As I read it I think: Hathor and Sekhmet saved the world; Osun saved the world, Durga and her many manifestations saved the world; Tara helped to save the world, Guan Yin too, and now Nu Wa. Same story, different Goddesses from different cultures. In each story mankind is dying from sickness, water crisis, world chaos, and from severe ecological imbalances caused by a refusal to go along with the divine play, and the innate balance that lies within all things.

One day Nu Wa created the first human beings. It is said that a long time ago, after Earth had come into being Nu Wa roamed the land. The sky was filled with stars, the waters with fish, and the fertile countryside was teeming with animals, but Nu Wa felt very lonely.

Her feelings of loneliness was made worse when one day she gazed briefly into a pond and saw only her own reflection.

"How nice it would be to have a companion," she thought wistfully.

In this moment of wistful thinking she came up with an idea. She could use her divine powers to make people in her own likeness. Those people could be her companions.

So with this in mind Nu Wa got to work. She stooped down low, and took a handful of mud from the water's edge and began to mould it into shape. She made a tiny body with two arms and two legs. As soon as she set it down, it became filled with life and moved around on the grass before her. She was very pleased with the being she had created and she went about to make more. These beings were the first people of the Earth.

Nu Wa worked hard and toiled until the sun disappeared and the night sky took over. Tired she rested her head on a rock. In the morning she carried on as before. The Goddess made many little people, but it was slow work. When she looked around the vast plains of the Earth and the mountains she knew it would be hard to fill the whole Earth up using her current method. What was she to do?

She hit on another fabulous idea. Why, she would use a rope or builder's cord and dip it in mud, swing it about her and allow the drops to fall to the ground. These drops of mud would form more people for the Earth. She immediately put her new plan into action and countless humans were created, enough to populate the Earth.

It is said that she taught these Earth Beings the gift of procreation and marriage. So that when one died they could re-create themselves.

Now life went on sweetly on Earth until one day there was an almighty fight amongst the male Gods. Now in some accounts the argument was between Gong Gong, Spirit of the Water, and Jurong, Spirit of Fire. They fought in the far north of the country at the foot of Buzhou Mountain, a mythical peak that, according to the tales lay northwest of Kunlun Mountains and was one of the pillars that held the sky in position. Gong Gong sent floodwaters but they were driven back by Jurong's ravenous fires. This defeat was said to drive Gong Gong beyond crazy with rage. So much so that he ran into Buzhou Mountain like a maddened boar, reducing it to nothing more than a rubble.

Without the mountain peak to support it, the northern sky tilted towards the ground. Half the sky caved in, and great openings appeared in the Earth; the sun, moon, and stars fell into the path that is familiar today. Waters poured out of the great chasms in the ground, and covering the plains; on higher land, flames raveished the forests.

Now as a result of the great impact, the north west lifted up which resulted in rivers and streams running away to the southeast where they gathered to form the seas, found there to this day.

If that was not all bad enough we then had the wild beasts who were driven by fear. They attacked and devoured the fleeing people, while sharp – beaked birds desperate for food swept down from the skies to peck the last flesh off the bones of corpses. The seasons fell out of their proper order.

Nu Wa acted quickly to repair the damage by Gong Gong. She took boulders from a river swollen with floodwaters and set a fire so fierce it melted the stones to a thick liquid. She used this as a paste to patch the pieces of ravaged sky back together. Next the goddess looked around for something to support the heavens and stop them falling in again. She took a tortoise, sliced off its four legs and used them as pillars to support the sky at the four corners of the Earth. She drove back the fierce beast that had been preying on people, especially the black skinned dragon that patrolled the Yellow River valley, whipping up floods. She controlled the floodwaters by building dykes made from ashes of burned reeds.

When Nu Wa's work was done, order returned to the universe. This order ushered in a new era of comfort. Sweetly Nu Wa rewarded the survivors with the first musical instrument, a thirteen piped instrument named shenguang.

510

NU Wa, Pan Gu & the Yoruba God Obatala

Nu Wa warned me that I was to pay close attention to the things she wanted to show me. She wanted me to notice that there was another version of her creation story in "the Land of the Dragon". However, not where she was creating the world but where the God Pan Gu was. As I read the story, like a good student, I noticed several things: 1. That Nu Wa's creation story showed the two phases of the Mother Goddess in history. The first is where she is the all-powerful universal force from which all things are birthed; the second is where she is taken over by the Indo Aryan version of creation which puts a male God in her exact role. I remembered Joseph Campbell explaining this switching up in the creation story was important as ancient cultures were on the whole matrilineal and power passed through the line of the females. 2. How the creation story of Pan Gu and the Yoruba God Obatala where virtually the same.

Now in terms of the first observation the editors of "Land of the Dragon" have this to say,

"Some scholars identify Nu Wa as an ancient mother deity; certainly her myth predates that of Pan Gu by several centuries. She is mentioned in texts of the fourth century BC, some 700 years before Pan Gu made his first appearance"

They further reveal,

"in later myths Nu Wa's role as great Mother was modified to allow for a masculine contribution to the origin of people."

Explaining this is when Fu Xi becomes her companion. They are sometimes depicted as brother and sister and were said to be peasant children who married to produce a new race of humans. It was sometime afterwards that I discovered that

511

Nu Wa shared the same creation myth as the Sumerian Mother Goddess Inanna, who made humans out of clay.

In terms of my second observation I have to first share with you the creation story of Pan Gu creating the world (I have adapted it from "The Land of the Dragons")

Once upon a time the the Creator Pan Gu did the grand task of separating Heaven and Earth. He created plants and animals, but he and then brought plants and animals into being. But he was not quite happy with his handiwork. The reason? because none of the birds and beasts had the power of reason. He decided there ought to be one creature with the ability to care for and make use of other living beings.

He skillfully began to mould the first people from mud, and as he finished each figure he set it to dry in the sunshine. Now some of the creatures he filled with the female qualities of yin and fashioned them into women, others he endowed with the male qualities yang and fashioned them into men. It was quite laborious work, especially under the blaze of the hot sun. As he toiled he piled his completed creation of people up against a rock outcrop.

As the sun began to go down he decided to take a little lie down. When he looked up he saw some dark storm clouds brewing. Worried he realized that some of the clay people had not dried the storm would obliterate his handiwork.

Quickly he rose up and hurriedly moved the clay people he had created to the shelter of a nearby cave, but as he did so the storm broke, the rains poured down and damaged some of the clay figurines. Those damaged were said to be the ancestors of people with unusually shaped bodies or disabilities.

Like Pan Gu, the Yoruba God, Obatala creates people from water and earth mixed together to form a clay substance. As he is making the people from clay he starts to get very tired from the hot sun. To help keep himself going he takes some Palm Wine, yet the palm wine makes him fall asleep. That would have been okay, if it was not for the fact that in his sleep he keeps on making men and women from clay. When he wakes up he notices that the men and women he made while sleeping were malformed. Feeling great sorrow at what he had done, he vows to protect all those who are disabled in life.

As I compared the two stories a tingling ran through my body. It was that same tingle again. The one I got when a discovery had been made. Right before my eyes was a story from China and a story from the Yoruba people of Nigeria which was exactly the same. How did that end up being the case? Just like the story of Osun saving the world and Durga saving the world? Then I thought of another significant thing and that was the fact that the Yoruba oracle system is divined with something called the Ikin and the Chinese oracle system is called the I Ching. Still pondering how stories from Africa could be the same as the stories in Asia. I thought about how the Mother Goddess had shown that many of these river cultures had flown and crossed from ancient Nile Valley Civilizations. So where there any clues that connected Nu Wa to these ancient roots. If Guan Yin, who was from China had been connected to Egypt could Nu Wa?

As if my questions pleased her Nu Wa's knotted eyebrows now lifted. Her sad ancient looking face was now lit up by a mischievous smile. A kind off "come let me show you something to look at". She stretched out her hand. I took it trembling. She presented to me three stories from "The Land of the Dragon", which I have adapted for this book. I waded through them not knowing what I would find. As I did so I couldn't help noticing how Nu Wa shared virtually the same name as the Egyptian Goddess Nu (another form of Hathor).

Story 1: The Cow herder and the Goddesses of the Milky Way

One day there was a beautiful Girl Weaver. She was said to be a Goddess of great and luminous beauty, who had woven the clouds that covered the nakedness of the sky. She is also the granddaughter of Xi Wang Mu, Queen Mother of the West.

It is said, that in those times the Milky Way was a sparkling celestial river whose clear shallow waters flowed over multi colored pebbles and stones. On one side lived the gods and goddesses; on the other the land of mortal men and women lived.

The cowherd lived on the banks of the river. Although he grew enough food for his needs, he felt an overwhelming sense of loneliness. He had an ox as company, but that was it. It also was not enough. He really wanted a companion.

One day, the Ox was so saddened by the Cowherd's loneliness that he spoke to him. He told him about a beautiful Girl Weaver who loved to bathe in the river. The next day the cowherd hid himself on the bank and watched the Goddess and her six sisters undress and plunge into the stream. It is said the clear waters grew opaque and hid their nakedness.

As the Goddesses bathed the Cowherd stole the Girl Weavers clothes. He agreed to return them only if she married him. She did. Apparently she fancied him, anyway. After a while the two had a beautiful boy and girl.

All was going well until big grandmother of the Girl Weaver discovers she is married to a mortal. Furious she sends messengers to take her away. Carrying the children the cowherd pursues her thinking he could cross over the Milky Way, but things change swiftly before his eyes. Where the river should have been it was no longer there. The girl's grandmother, Xi Wang Mu had lifted the river from the Earth and set it in the night sky.

The Cowherd was really distraught. He went home. When he did his Oxen told him he was about to die, but his hide had magical qualities. When he died he could take it, and it would allow him to reach heaven.

In heaven he reached the banks of the Milky Way and could see the Girl Weaver on the far side, however the grandmother spotted him and transformed the river into a raging torrent. The cowherd spent long hard days emptying it with a ladle. It was this devotion that led grandmother Xi Wang Mu to announce that on one night each year – the seventh day of the seventh month – a flock of magpies would form a bridge across the Milky Way, permitting the two lovers to meet.

I re-read the story and noticed unmistakable symbolisms that belonged to the Egyptian Mother Goddess Hathor. I jotted my findings onto paper:

Cows: *Hathor is associated with cows. The Cow herder is a primary figure who is connected to the Weaver Girl. (Latter I was to find out that the Hathor also took the form of the Goddess Neith – The Weaver, who wore a simple headdress made in the form of the weaving shuttle).*
Milky Way: *Hathor is perceived to be the Milky Way. The Girl in the story is connected heavily to it, along with her Grandmother.*
Seven: *the girl has six sisters; she makes seven. Now Hathor had the seven Hathors who often appeared together.*

Exhilarated Nu Wa led me to Story two about *Xi Wang Mu and the Peaches of Immortality*

Xi Wang Mu, the Queen of the West, has in her care a garden filled with peaches of immortality. Her palace was made of pure gold and set on the summit of the mountain Kunlun. She lived there with a heavenly entourage that included five jade fairy maids. Whenever, she ventured from her paradise she travelled on white crane and used a flock of bluebirds as her messengers.

The mystical fruit of immortality which grew in her palace gardens took 3,000 years to grow and a further 3000 years to ripen. Whenever one of the fruit matured, the goddess served it as a centerpiece of a feast whose other courses included monkey's lips, dragon's liver and phoenix marrow. Guests were entertained by music from the invisible instruments and songs from her tongues.

Interesting, I thought and made more observational notes:

Fruit of Immortality: *Hathor is the tree of life. In the Egyptian Book of the Dead she is seen feeding the deceased with fruits of immortality from her sycamore tree. Xi Wang Mu like Hathor feeds the fruit of Immortality to guest. I have already discovered that the original tree of life symbolism is from ancient Egypt.*
Music: *Music plays an important theme just as it does with Hathor who is associated with the all important sistrum and the Menit.*
Phoenix: *This bird is originally from ancient Egypt and is originally called the Bennu Bird.*

Pleased with my findings Nu Wa led me to story number

three which I called - The Kingdom of the Birds

One day Shao Hao's mother, a beautiful fairy named Huange, worked on the heavenly looms. She loved go on the gentle Milky Way and visit the wonderful mulberry tree named Quiongsang that stood near the Western Sea. Beneath the tree's branches a good – looking young man would wait for her; he was the morning star.

They would sometimes go on the river together, sing and play a zither. From precious jade they made a model of a dove and set They eventually became lovers and from their union Shao Hao was birthed. He grew into a very handsome young man, he was so capable that his great uncle named, Huang Di named him God of the Western Heavens.

When he got older Shao Hao travelled to the five mountains of the Eastern Paradise and established a kingdom populated by birds. As its ruler he took the form of a vulture. And oversaw a vast feathered beaurocracy with the phoenix as his Lord Chancellor. He put the hawk in charge of the law, and the pigeon was in charge of education. He placed the four seasons in the charge of the pheasant, the quail, the shrike and the swallow.

Eventually he went back to the west and left his son Chong in charge of the birds, with another of his sons Ru Shou he settled on Changliu Mountain and ruled over the Western Heavens. Father and son together were responsible for the sunset.

My excitement was reaching its zenith. My fingers trembled as I made a note of the symbolisms in the story,

Mulberry Tree: *As said earlier Hathor is the Tree of Life, which is known as the sycamore, which also goes by the name of the Mulberry tree.*

517

Milky Way and the Mulberry Tree: *The symbol of the Milky Way and Mulberry tree are closely connected together. Both these symbols are Hathor's symbols.*

The Morning Star: *In the Egyptian Book of the Dead the deceased can rise from the dead and become like the Morning Star. The Morning Star is actually seen as Hathor. It is interesting that the Milky Way, Mulberry tree and Morning star are all linked together.*

The Phoenix and Eagle: *The phoenix is one of Egypt's important great symbols of resurrection. The phoenix was often depicted as an Eagle, which symbolizes royalty.*

The Vulture: *This is a symbol of the Goddess Nekhebet and Mut. All royalty wore this symbol on the front of their crowns with Uatchet, the Snake Goddess (Nekhebet's twin sister). It is interesting that in the story the ruler takes the form of a vulture.*

The Swallow: *was a symbol of the Egyptian Goddess Isis.*

I re-read all three stories and my notes several times. Between all of the stories a tapestry of history had been woven. Nu Wa had placed herself amongst the Great Mother Goddess lineage. She stood proud and tall snuggly fitting herself into the forever forming jigsaw puzzle picture. The song of her compassion rang out. For even as her almighty Yellow River died she cared enough about us – to make us whole again.

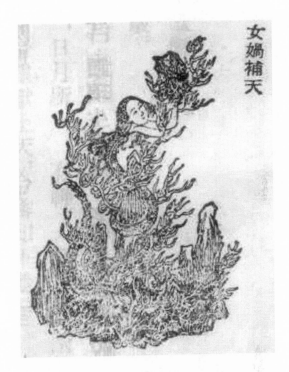

Nu Wa Repairing the hole in the sky

Nu Wa and the Peacock

I thought Nu Wa had finished with me, but she hadn't. There was something more that she wanted me to show me. We both stood at the banks of her Yellow River. Together we admired its gushing waters. A sadness filled us both, I think at the same time, as we thought about the fact that this mighty river was actually dying.

"Please don't die," I begged her.

She smiled gently at me, "I am trying not to. We are trying not to."

We both smiled because I knew that the "we" referred to her many sisters that made up the one Mother Goddess.

But Nu Wa did not want me to focus on my sadness. No. She still had important business to take care of. There was an urgency to how she grabbed my hand and drew my attention to the name of the Yellow River. For the Tibetans called it the Peacock River.

I don't know why the name Peacock River took hold of my imagination, but like an electrical bolt it did. I think Nu Wa knew that it would. I think she knew that I would initially think "how romantic" then my mind would make me think of Osun's symbol the peacock, and how I had tried to chase one (in an attempt to get a picture with it) at her famous Palace and shrine house when I stayed in Osogbo, Nigeria.

I also think Nu Wa knew that it would also make me think of that dream I had about a month ago in July. The one where an extraordinarily beautiful woman sat on the banks of a clear blue river singing the song "Beautiful Waters". Its words bounced mesmerizingly along a dazzling sparkling extremely long blue river, upon which deep indigo blue peacocks swam.

On waking up from that dream I knew that the title of this book was to be "Beautiful Waters" and the extraordinarily beautiful woman who had sung the song was none other than the Mother herself. I knew that she was letting me know what she wanted the book to be called.

I wished I could remember the lyrics of the song, as they had been so detailed. They seemed to recount the entire history of mankind, our moving away from the divine, and the results. Calling for us to move back to all that was balance.

In that dream I didn't understand why deep indigo blue peacocks were swimming on the water, except for the fact they were a symbol of the Mother Goddess and represented all that was beauty, love, joy, fertility, wisdom and happiness. I had been suspicious that the peacocks were trying to tell me something more than that when I had another dream just a few days after the first. One where I stood by a beautiful aqua blue lake. When I peered into its waters I noticed a peacock sitting right at the bottom. As I looked on it fanned the most glorious tail feathers out to form a circle. The forming of the circle with the feathers seemed significant. I just didn't know what the significance was. Not then anyway.

Nu Wa obviously knew me well. She knew that peacocks would stay on my mind until I figured out their significance to this stage of the journey. She also knew she would lead me to their meaning.

I was frustrated. I knew the peacock was trying to tell me something about this whole big history of ours. But what? What? What? Okay, so Osun has the peacock symbolism, I reasoned. Okay, but where did that symbolism come from?

Hathor? I had not noticed any of the Egyptian Goddesses connected to the peacock. Dead end. More frustration.

Just as I was about to give up the ghost I found something on the internet, Alexander the Great loved peacocks. I didn't know how true that was, and I didn't know anything about Alexander the Great really. Yet, somehow the find felt significant.

I decided to follow the ball of wool to see where it would lead me. I quickly found out Alexander the Great had actually ruled Egypt. He had taken over Egypt from the Persians in 334 BCE. I found this fact out in a lovely book I had in my library called, "Egypt: Land and Lives of the Pharaoh". Apparently the Persian rule was harsh and not so respectful to the Egyptian ways. The result - dissent. Alexander on the other hand decided to take on a different strategy to the Persians, altogether. His goal was to become a man of the people by not rejecting but embracing the Egyptian traditions.

As I read on I was not sure what all of this had to do with peacocks, but I decided to continue trudging through the rocky grounds of history.

On taking over power Alexander immediately set about making himself agreeable to the Egyptian people. First he made sacrifice to the Apis Bull, which was seen as a most holy creature, an incarnation of the popular and revered God Osiris. He also built the great city of Alexander where he had statutes of Greek and Egyptian Gods erected. He not only venerated the most holy God Amun (whom became aligned with the Greek God Zeus; while Amun's wife Mut became aligned with Hera), but became declared by the Amun oracle to be the son of Amun. After that Alexander was most definitely part of the in club. He was now a legitimate ruler of Egypt not through force but through claiming a place in the countries divine spiritual ancestry.

Now it was shortly after finding this information that my brother Jeff and his girlfriend visited from London. Serendipity had us going to a Greek Festival in Charlotte. The most interesting thing about the festival was the rare and valuable collection of Egyptian and Greek artifacts on display. Luckily, the owner of the collection happened to be present. What a privilege as I was able to ask him the question that was burning a hole in my mind for that day- why did he have Egyptian and Greek artifacts? He explained that Greece was heavily influenced by Egypt.

We got talking some more and I told him about how my strange journey with the waterways had led me to connecting the Asian Goddess and Gods to those in Egypt. I also shared with him my current frustration about the peacock symbolism. How it seemed to be connected to the whole story but I didn't know how.

"Did Alexander love peacocks?"

"You know I know a lot about Greek and Egyptian history but peacocks I had never thought about. I really don't know."

Oh well, that's it I thought. My heart fell. One of those dead end pieces of information.

"But you could check out Alexander in India. You know he conquered parts of India?" The owner of the collection suddenly informed.

"No I didn't," I said excitement raced through my veins.

"Yes, I think it was around 300 and something BC. Check it out," the owner of the collection encouraged me.

"I will do," I assured him.

That night I discovered that Alexander had indeed conquered large parts of India, including the Indus Valley where the Dancing Girl of Mohenjo – daro was from. It was around 327 BC. In 530 BC it was the Persians. They ruled until Alexander took over. Apparently history has it that the Greeks had a good stint in India exchanging philosophical and spiritual ideas. Even the name India is supposed to be a Greek.

I read and re-read these facts over and over again for a few days. As I did so it dawned on me that the peacock had lead me to a connective bridge of history. Deep instincts told me the bridge had something to do with how the Egyptian Goddesses and Gods ended up in India. I put on my thinking cap, and jotted my thoughts down onto paper. As I did so a light began to fill my mind.

Now I have already seen a strong correlation between the Egyptian deities and the Indian ones. Now I am not sure how the Egyptian deities got to India, but now I am adding up these facts. The Dancing Girl of Mohenjo-Daro was from around 2000 and something BC; while Alexander the Great was in India around 327 BC. Since I have connected the Dancing Girl of Mohenjo Daro to Africa, Egypt in particular through looking at the customs of the Devadasi; and since Alexander turned up in India much later. It seems to me...

I pause as I wrote, weighing the gravity of my thoughts. Then continued,

that there seemed to be two waves of migration from Egypt and Egyptian thought into India. The first being around 2000 and something BC and before; the other being when Alexander went into India. It seems that when Alexander went into India he could have renewed and strengthened the Mother Goddess culture and the Osirian tradition.

I did a little more research. I was curious to find out the dates of some of the Goddesses I had encountered. I was very opened minded. Even though it certainly appeared from all the evidence I had encountered that the Indian Goddesses came from ancient Egypt. How they had done so especially from the first wave of influence I was not sure. Who knows history is a funny thing. That my journey had taught me.

However, what I discovered firmly placed the waters of history as flowing from ancient Egypt. For many of the Egyptian Goddesses and Gods I had connected to Indian ones were said to be Pre – Dynastic. A period that began back around 6000 BC. They were also recorded in one of Egypt's oldest written religious text, the Pyramid Text which was a funerary text that dated back to about 2400 BC. Most of the key Goddesses of India such as Durga, Kali and Parvati, I had been looking into were pre-Aryan (in other words Dravidian). They were documented in one of India's earliest religious text, the Rig Veda. It dates back to about 1700 BC.

An important bridge of history seemed to have closed itself. I was pleased. Well, almost because even though all the evidence pointed to the fact that the Egyptians, and or their thoughts, travelled into India. The pre-Aryan Dravidian Gods seemed to be forming the important old link between India and Egypt. However, if that was the case then that meant the Dravidians were African. That my dears is where the sticking point was. For although the Mother Goddesses seemed to be pointing their holy water pots in that direction; historians preferred to remain confused about the matter.

I began to strongly suspect that this confusion was causing a broken circle in humanity that needed mending. Wholeness cannot be seen in a broken looking glass. I groaned as I felt the Goddesses and the river of history had not quite finished with me.

Nu Wa stood patiently by, allowing me to be lost in my jumbled thoughts for awhile. She was however, pleased enough to take me next to the point of discovery. She kept the

525

peacock symbol on my mind, and made me still hanker to know more. For my restless mind still wanted to know how comes so many of the Goddesses I had connected to Egypt had peacocks but the Egyptian Goddesses had none.

I think this is when Nu Wa must have said,

"rise Phoenix rise."

For out of my computer screen jumped the Phoenix. Which caused me to jump out of my chair and shout to Derrick in the next room,

"Sweetie! I found it! I found it! I found the peacock connection!"

I read and eat all the information up with a ferocious appetite. The Egyptians called the Phoenix the Bennu bird. It was associated with the eagle or the Egyptian purple Heron. The Greeks depicted the Phoenix more like a peacock or as an eagle. They identified the Bennu Bird to their own word for Phoenix, Phoinos. I paused, re-read and savored that sentence before plowing on.

In the Comprehensive Etymological Dictionary it is said that the Phoenix is related to the Greek word for Phoenix, which is phoinos which means, "blood red". They used this word because the Bennu Bird was associated with fire and the sun.

It was said that the Bennu/Phoenix was a bird that had very colorful plumage with a tail of gold and scarlet. Its life spanned 500 to 1000 years. Near the end of its cycle it was known to build itself a nest of twigs and then ignite it. Both the nest and bird burnt until they were reduced to ashes. From those ashes a new phoenix arose. In some stories the phoenix would embalm the ashes of its old self in an egg of myrrh and deposit it in one of the oldest Egyptian cities, Heliopolis. Which in Greek meant "Sun City".

In his book, "The Gods of the Egyptians," Sir E.A. Wallis Budge explains that that so many cultures had fabulous stories about the Phoenix but these stories were essentially, "a result of misunderstandings of the Egyptian myth which declared that the morning sun rose in the form of the Bennu, and of the belief that declared that this bird was the soul of Ra and also the living symbol of Osiris and that it came from the very heart of the god of Osiris." In fact, he shared that the Goddess Nut and the God Seb produced the Great Cosmic Egg. From this egg sprung the Sun God in the form of the Bennu (phoenix).

The more I read about the Bennu/Phoenix was the more I felt that the peacock symbol had not only come to bridge our historical gap but had come to bring a message of renewal of the soul, mind and spirit. That message seemed to be engraved in its fanned out feathers, and the flapping wings of the.

"I go in like the Hawk, and I come forth like the Bennu, the Morning Star (i.e. the planet Venus) of Ra; "I am the Bennu which is Heliopolis,".

This is a passage Budge shared from the Egyptian Book of the Dead. Explaining not only was the Bennu bird seen as Osiris (the enlightened soul of man) it also "in the earliest period of dynastic history it became a symbol for the resurrection of mankind.

I re-read the passage again and saw that the Bennu bird was not only Osiris and Ra but was also Venus herself. The Mother of all things beautiful, refined, intelligent and balanced. It was the divine Mother with the divine masculine principle who brought this message of renewal together in ancient flight across the celestial skies. It was right there in the wing and flight of the Bennu bird.

Tired with all the discoveries, awed by the magnitude of history that was unfolding the currents of its waters constantly before my weary eyes, I began to pack up my folder for the night. My head was throbbing and I needed to sleep. As I lifted my folder from the table a piece of paper fell out. My bones ached as I attempted to pick it up. With the smooth white sheet stuck firmly between my fingers I noticed something. On it was a drawing. It was a beautiful picture of the Ghanaian Sankofa bird. I stepped back in surprise.

It was a picture I had drawn a year or two ago when Derrick's brother Michael had died. I had made a copy of it onto card stock, and beaded it. It became a beautiful family bereavement card that Derrick's family signed and gave to Michael's wife.

I couldn't take my eyes of that picture. How that picture had turned up in the folder I didn't know, but it had, and I was staring at it intently. As I stood in the dark of the room with a small light shining from a side table something made me turn my head. I looked straight towards the three drums that stood by our fire place. One had the Sankofa bird beautifully and expertly carved onto it. The drum belonged to Derrick and it was the first time I had noticed that the carving on the drum was of the Sankofa bird. I had never really bothered to look at it before.

Now I stared at it intently. There was a message. I knew the signs when a message was trying to rare its head. Then as I slowly looked from the picture to the drum, from the drum back to the picture a thought began to form in the depths of my mind and rise. Was the Sankofa bird the phoenix? Didn't Budge say the Earth God Seb and Nu gave birth to the egg from which the Bennu arose? Didn't he also say Seb was called the "Great Cackler", and was therefore associated with ducks? With these thoughts I looked at the

528

picture of the Sankofa again. Drawn as a duck, the Sankofa had an egg in its mouth, and its head looked backward. The duck and egg where symbolisms from the God Seb. I thought about the symbolism of the Sankofa bird looking back. Doesn't the Phoenix return home to renew itself? Yes, it does. I answered my own question, and made the dynamic connection - the Sankofa bird is the Phoenix. I was now certain about that.

Electrical bolts ran all through my body. Another symbol that connected cultures. As my excitement died down I was aware that the Sankofa bird seemed to want me to focus on something, the message it was trying to deliver. What was that message? I thought. I decided to Google the Sankofa bird. I found this definition from good old Wikipedia,

Sankofa can mean either the word in the Akan language of Ghana that translates in English to "go back and get it" (san - to return; ko - to go; fa - to look, to seek and take) or the Asante Adinkra symbols of a bird with its head turned backwards taking an egg off its back, or of a stylized heart shape. It is often associated with the proverb, "Se wo were fi na wosankofa a yenkyi," which translates "It is not wrong to go back for that which you have forgotten.

Then I understood. Don't ask me how, but I did. The message was one of renewal through connection. The Mother Goddess comes to help us rise from the ashes of our own demise to re-birth ourselves anew. I bathed in some kind of spiritual awe. Bowed my head to the mighty Nu Wa for bringing her gift to humanity.

That night I remembered a dream I had a few weeks ago.

I dreamt that this amazing human like bird glided into the house with the most extraordinary long and beautiful feathers. I was astonished. I said to Derrick,
"Derrick Look!"
He was in the other room and shouted back,
"catch it!"
I was too afraid to catch this magical extraordinary looking creature. It then glided into Derrick's room and stood on the floor. Derrick took one feather from the crown of its head. He said,
"do you know how long I have been waiting to see this baby."
The bird we saw was a very rare bird.

I realized the rare bird I had dreamt was none other than the phoenix. For some reason I could feel my eyes becoming wet. Some inexplicable force was moving me emotionally, and in that moving I felt like scattered fragments of myself were binding themselves together. Healing me in the dew of history. I felt that I like the phoenix was rising from my very own ashes. I saluted Nu Wa for bringing this mighty healing.

Sankofa Bird of Ghana

Fenghuang the Chinese Phoenix at the Longshan Temple. Notice How the bird looks like a cross between an eagle and peacock just like how the Greeks depicted the phoenix sometimes as an eagle or sometimes as a peacock.

Nu Wa Gathers the Royal Peacock Family

In the morning I saluted Nu Wa. I was ready to pack my Nu Wa notes up, but the grand matriarch and her running gushing waters had not quite finished with me. She wanted me to take a closer look at her source, the Peacock River. I didn't know why, but I did. I discovered that it flowed down from the sacred hills of Mount Kailesh. It was not alone for there were three more rivers that flowed from its mouth. They were named like the peacock river after animals: Horse River, Lion River, and the Elephant River. It was said that if one bathed in any of these rivers you would obtain the auspicious qualities of the animal it was related to. Bathing in the Peacock River made you look as beautiful as a peacock.

Something caught my attention about Mount Kailesh, and that was how many Eastern traditions tied their origins to that place. In Buddhism it is referred to as the Sumeri Mountain, a magical hill that forms the center square of the traditional mandala. The Jains believe their very first prophet obtained enlightenment there. While In Hinduism it is said that Shiva and Parvati sat there. The people of these traditions and others walk around the mountain in a holy act of remembrance and respect.

The lake close to the mountain is referred to as *Everlasting Jade Lake*. It's actually called Lake Mana Sarovar. The Hindus say if you drink from its waters you return to the everlasting land of Shiva. While the Buddhist say that it is the lake where Queen Maya conceived Buddha.

Coming into this knowing led to one simple question that lingered like hot air on my mind: *Since I had discovered that the Asian holy couple Parvati and Shiva had the same attributes of the old Egyptian trinity Osiris, Isis/Hathor, Horus – was Mount Kailesh the very Mountain where it had all started?*

Truthfully, I didn't expect an answer to such a far-fetched question. However, a response did come. Not quite the one that I expected, but one that helped to close more gaps in the history of our spiritual lineage. Once again the peacock symbol led the way. For as I studied Parvati and Shiva a little closer I noticed something I hadn't paid attention to before – they had another son besides Ganesh, called Murugan.

When I discovered Murugan or more like when he decided to show himself to me – he was quite splendid on top of his peacock mount with a divine spear and sword in his hand. A warrior God who defeats evil, his peacock mount is said to represent his victory over the ego. The more I look at his picture is the more it looked as though the peacock was actually part of his body. Unbeknownst to me, Murugan was about to solve a mystery that had long been plaguing my mind. The mystery went something like this. Even though I had associated Hathor and Isis son Horus with Ganesh, they did not seem a comfortable match. That always puzzled me since Hathor and Isis were obviously connected to Parvati, whose son was Ganesh. However, I thought *well Ganesh opens the way and Horus fights evil so he opens the way. They must be the same.* But, that thought never quite sat well with me.

Murugan sat patiently on his peacock mount waiting for me to unravel the muddle in my head. He had a gift and he wanted me reach out and take it.

"Research me," his glorious presence commanded. So I did.

I decided to see if Hathor had any more sons besides Horus. Bingo, my research paid of. What I discovered was sweet natured Khonsu. He was waiting for me in the passageways of history with the sign of the moon on his head, and the symbol of life, the ankh, in his hand. A pre-dynastic God he was said to be associated with the moon. His name meant "Traveler" and may have related to the nightly travel of the moon across the sky. He was a god that opened the way between dimensions. His mother was the great Mother Goddess Mut and his father the great father God Amun. He was also seen as the son as Hathor and Sebek.

I carefully followed the threads of thought that pulled on my mind. Firstly Ganesh was a God, like Khonsu, who opened the way. So I paired the two together. They were a perfect match. Once I matched them both, there was Horus and Murugan left. These two warrior Gods matched perfectly too. I smiled. Awesome. All the children connected to their parents: Hathor/Isis and Osiris – Khonsu, Horus; Parvati and Shiva – Ganesh, Murugan.

Pleased, I continued to follow the threads of history in front of me carefully. I turned my attention next to thing, the symbol of the moon. I noticed once again how Khonsu had the moon on his head. So did Shiva. It was interesting to note that one of Shiva's epithets was in fact *Chandraśekhara* which is Sanskrit for, "Having the Moon as His Crest". Parvati, Shiva's mate was also often depicted with the crescent moon bound between her locks. While A distinct form of Ganesha is called Bhalachandra which means "Moon on the Forehead. At this point I remembered how Osiris, Hathor and Isis were all connected to the Moon symbolism. A royal moon family?

The God Murugan

Was Nu Wa and the peacock symbol finished with me as yet. Not quite. There were still a few more unfinished historical tears she wanted to mend. Just how she had mended the sky that was fallen in.

I was game. For the peacock was truly living up to its meaning of joy. It was joyful being part of such great discoveries. I was curious to know more. I allowed myself to be pulled forward by that familiar tug of the ancient past. The further finds came on the back of Murugan's peacock feathers, and through their beauty I was to discover his step mothers, the Matrikas who were also known as "The Mothers". They were gathered together, all seven of them. As seven they are also called Saptamatrikas which means the "Seven Mothers".

They were considered to be, amongst other things, the assistants who helped Durga/Kali, defeat the evil demons who were wreaking havoc on the world. Considered to be dark skinned Pre-Aryan Dravidian Goddesses, one story reveals that Durga created them from herself and they helped slaughter the demon army. In another story Shiva is said to have created them to combat a demon called Andhaka. It was interesting to note that there were seven females depicted on the Indus Valley seals of Mohenjo – daro, many say it could have been the Seven Mothers.

Authors Jagdish Narain Tiwari who wrote "Studies in Goddess Cults in Northern India", and Dilip Chakravati, who is mentioned in "Archaeology and World Religion" by Timothy Insoll both say that the figures of seven females, whom are found on coins from the Indus Valley Civilization which dates back to about 2600 BC, are believed to be the Seven Mothers.

In terms of the pre-Aryan origin of the Seven Mothers David Kingsley, author of "Hindu Goddesses" writes,

"It is hard to resist the conclusion that the groups of goddess called Matrikas in the Mahabharata represent the many village goddesses throughout India who are widely worshipped by the common people and who are often associated with disease or the prevention of diseases, especially those that afflict children. Such deities are not found in the Vedic pantheon but are probably indigenous to a non – Brahmanic, if not pre-Aryan, religious universe."

It is said the epic text the Mahabharata dates back to most probably 400 BC. Kingsley says, the first written mention of "The Mothers" seemed to date from 1 AD. As the mention of them in the Mahabharata does not belong to the earliest layer of the epic.

Now I was excited for Hathor also came in a group known as the Seven Mothers. Budge in his book "The Gods of the Egyptians" said that Hathor represented so many of the Mother Goddesses in ancient times, that eventually there came to be a group known as the Seven Hathors. Sometimes this group numbered ten or more. The Seven Hathors are well known for their appearance when a child is born to predict his or her destiny. I found it highly interesting that the Seven Mothers of India were also connected to the conception of children. Worshipped by pregnant women and nursing mothers it was not a good idea to get them angry. For the consequence would be infertility and a child with disease. However, honor and appease them and they would assure the long life and good health of your child.

Throughout India there are carvings and temples in honor of the Seven Mothers. Their association with Shiva is strengthened by the fact they are often depicted on the main door of Shiva temples. Their shrines are often located in the wilderness, usually near lakes and rivers. Their connection to the Shiva shrines was of great interest to me, as well as their connection to Murugan. For I had already connected Shiva and Parvati to Osiris and Hathor/Isis. The Seven Mothers, stood proudly long with all the other evidence, to consolidate this royal spiritual lineage connection.

The Seven Mothers of India were not finished with me. They wanted me to know that they were also associated with the seven star cluster known as Pleiades, which is also called "The Seven Sisters". This one they showed me for good measure knowing that later down the road I was to discover Hathor was related to the important star of Sirius, and also the seven star cluster in her form as the Egyptian Goddess Sefkhet – Aabut. In this form she was known as "Great one, lady of letters, Mistress of the House of Books." She wore Hathor's inverted horns which are inverted over a seven rayed star or flower with seven petals.

As the Seven Mothers slowly released their grip on me I encounter several beautiful songs entitled, "Beautiful Hymn of the Seven Hathors". The hymns are translated by Barbara Ann Richter, and found on the 5th Crypt at the Temple of

Dendera (one of the best preserved temples of Egypt and Hathor). The main temple in the complex is actually Hathor's.

The ancient songs seemed to silently chant history back into its rightful order. Their unheard notes reached to the zenith and the rivers in the sky. For the first praised Hathor as Sekhmet "the Lady of Unending Drunkenness". As Durga and Kali were also associated with drinking wine as they fought their battles against evil, I saw this hymn as a praise song to the Great Mother in her many forms, across all the waters, who conquered all negativities with her fierce motherly compassion.

The second hymn praised Hathor as the "Great Perceiver". As Guan Yin and her male counterpart, the Buddha Avalokiteshvara names translated into the "Sound Perceiver" or "he or she who looks down upon sound"; and since I connected Guan Yin with Durga and Durga with Hathor/Sekhmet I saw this praise song as one which celebrated the Mother as the great perceiver of the mysteries of life.

The Mothers were singing.

First Hymn

We play the tambourine for your ka,
We dance for your majesty
We exalt you – to the height of heaven.
You are the Mistress of Sekhem, the menat and the sistrum
The Mistress of Music for whose ka one lays
We praise your majesty every day
From dusk until the Earth grows light,
We rejoice in your countenance, O Mistress of Dendera.
We praise you with song.
You are the lady of Jubilation, the Mistress of the Iba dance,

539

The Lady of Music, the Mistress of Harp playing,
The Lady of Dancing, the Mistress of Tying on Garlands,
The Lady of Myrrh and the Mistress of Leaping.
We glorify your majesty – we give praise before your face.
We exalt your power over the Gods and Goddesses.
You are the Lady of Hymns,
The Mistress of the Library – the Great Seshat.
At the head of the Mansion of Records,
We propitiate your majesty every day.
Your heart rejoices at hearing our songs.
We rejoice when we see you, day by day.
Our hearts are jubilant when we see your majesty,
You are the Lady of Garlands, the Mistress of Dance
The Lady of Unending Drunkenness.
We rejoice before your face, we play for your ka.
Your heart rejoices over our performance.

Second Hymn

The Great Het-Hert, Mistress of Iunet, Eye of Ra, Mistress of
Heaven, Sovereign of all the Netjeru.
The Beautiful Lady to Whom the Foremost of the Powerful Ones
address beseechingly.
They cry out to Her Majesty every day.
The Beautiful Perceiver for those who follow Her Path;
The One who gives sight to the blind.
The excellent Guardian who protects the one who invokes Her on the
day when he faces life or death.
Ma'at the Great, Mistress of Sentences for the supplicants, who does
what is right for the one who is zealous.
The Marvelous One whose rites are glorious when they are

performed.
The Supreme Lords of the open shrines are carried to the exterior of
Your sanctuary.

I feel the energy of history loosening its grips on me some more. I sigh, I can rest for a while. As I pack all my notes up, tidy my books, away, turn the computer of I notice one last thing. I know that I am supposed to notice him, and that is the forceful presence of the God Garuda. He announces himself as Shiva's mount. He is depicted as having a golden body of a strong man with a white face, red wings, an eagle's beak and a crown on his head. He is a deity that is large enough to block the sun. Right there in his iconography it is clear to me that he is a depiction of the mighty Egyptian Phoenix. I smiled - the deities had a sense of grand humor. Shiva was sitting on top of his Egyptian mount.

Garuda, the mount of Shiva

2ND ASE

Nu Wa's waters had led me from the Yellow River, peacocks, and right into the bosom of the ocean. I suppose if I had thought more about the connection of the rivers to the oceans then this should not have surprised me. But everything was a surprise to me on this journey. I had come to accept myself as being no more than a child in Mother Earth's grand plan. It was Friday 12th August 2011 when myself and the family found ourselves on Myrtle Beach, South Carolina and discovering the beauty of Kahil Gibran's statement, "in one drop of water contains all the secrets of the ocean".

By the time we got there and settled down the dark had fallen. The ocean was roaring. Lots of bodies were still glistening in the water as they splashed about under the moon's radiant light. The darkness did not discourage us. We just wanted to feel that water run over our bodies. We ambled down to the beach with baby Omo in hand, and right there in the darkness our feet touched the soft cool sand. Near the waters front I sat with Omo, and together we felt the sand and water beneath our bodies. There and then I decided to give her a first baptism of ocean water. I cupped my hands, scooped up some water and then allowed it to fall over her shoulders and onto her body. She laughed in surprise. I also do the same ritual for myself. I smile as we both watch Kem Ra and Olu splash away in an abandoned world of their own. I looked around, my smile deepens as I watch couples walking hand in hand slowly across the sand. Then I wash the waters over my face.

That night Derrick could not sleep. He wants to leave the door of the balcony wide open. The purpose? to hear the ocean crashing and singing. I appreciate its majesty, but I am cold.

Kem Ra is cold and plus we all wanted to sleep. There is no fun trying when your shivering. Derrick obliged our moans and closes the door.

He seemed agitated. It is almost as though he wants to become totally one with the ocean. It is haunting his soul. Calling him. I could tell. He sits on the balcony and I sink into the beginnings of a deep sleep. I am almost there and then something tugs on my toes. I open my heavy eyelids and peer through. Its Derrick. He urges me onto the balcony. Won't hear no for an answer until I follow him groggily there.

Secretly inside I am rumbling like an old bear. I sit down and eventually I feel my shoulders relax. The ocean's roaring engulfs me.

"Look," he says pointing to the full moon.

Then he points to what we believed might have been Venus. We weren't sure.

"The moon and Venus are the only two lights in the sky. Osun is blessing us," he smiles looking up.

I agree. It definitely felt that way. I close my eyes. *This is the river's end. This is the water's end. It is the end.* These are the words I say to myself. The sea air brushes against my skin. I think of how a river starts high up on some snowy hill as just a few drops of rain that gather and converge into streams which get larger and larger. Then finally the river empties into the ocean. Sometimes a river like the Catawba River, Osun River in Nigeria, and the Yellow River in China will emerge from a spring.

I think of how a river is flowing even when we can't see it. It flows deep beneath the bottom of the river and it flows underneath the ground on both sides of it. If we stand on the bank of a river, often without knowing it the river will be flowing right under the feet.

I sink into the awesomeness of water that can flow underground and reach even the tiniest insects such as Mayflies, other insects and crustaceans. They all can move far underground and hide between the rocks which protect them from predators, yet the water still flows to them, and brings them nourishment.

I think about the area of the river that is flowing deep under the ground. How it often extends way beyond the river we can see. Sometimes into flood plains. Then I think about how a river will ensure it obtains nutrients by changing its course. The change is so slow that we often cannot see it with our eyes. But change its course it does, as the force of its water erodes away banks as the river moves unpredictably one way and then another. I think how rivers have to meander because that is how they renew themselves.

Then I think of the journey how much like the rivers journey this has been. I think of the river of humanity's consciousness and how much it is mirrored in the actions of water and its rivers. How much our personal and collective rivers flow, meander, and gather nourishment along the way. I think of how the celestial river of the Nile meets, joins and sings with all the other celestial rivers of the sky and land. We are all so much part of the unseen waters that flow deep at the bottom of the river we visibly see. Part of its width and breadth.

I think of how each of the Goddesses from around the world appeared as separate drops of water along the way, then became the streams that make up the flowing river of the one Mother Goddess. How each one held a nourishing clue in their hands. Gifts to humanity.

I think of how the water falls onto the ground and sinks into Mother Earth who acts like a sponge. The water below is called an aquifer. It is this water that also feeds our river's waters. But when we drill the wells and take out more than we need the aquifers run dry and they take with them the streams and the rivers that they feed. The way we build our cities does not allow for our underground water to be refreshed, instead when the rain falls it runs of the concrete and not into the ground.

The aquifers are like the Mother. The water shows us if we keep on laying concrete over our hearts, culture and humanity how can the nurturing waters of life touch and nourish our way forward.

I think about how water lets us know we need to take down the dams. The dams in our hearts, the dams on the heart of the earth, and let life flow again. The young salmon rely on the currents of the river to flush them down stream so that they can make it to the ocean. The dams stop them from making it. They stop the river from flowing. They stop the consciousness from flowing. The damns are dwindling life down to a final drop. The final drop can represent death or rebirth. A spring that becomes a stream that becomes a river, that becomes the sea.

I think of the important clue that appeared from the doings of Mother Nu Wa's guidance. How just before we had arrived to the sandy beaches of Myrtle Beach the clue stood on a discounted bookshelf of Barnes and Nobles. It answered the question I had been carrying in my mind for days, "Is the Tibetan Book of the Dead and the Egyptian Book of the Dead more connected than in their titles?" Answering this question seemed important to the whole. The question had arisen from the flowing waters of Nu Wa's The Peacock River which flowed from the sacred Kailesh Mountain in Tibet. When I had learned that it was from this very mountain that Shiva and Parvati had sat, and the very mountain where the teachings of the Tibetan Bon tradition had its beginnings. For some reason the "Tibetan Book of the Dead" and the "Egyptian Book of the Dead" flew to my mind. I knew that both books were important to their respective cultures. I also had always wondered if they were the same book. Now due to this journey I felt compelled to find out. A spirit force moved within me, pushing me once again forward. It did not seem as though I was answering a personal question any longer, but one that could help connect the spiritual history and odyssey of humanity together.

They say the dead talk. Maybe that is why these two books turned up, because I sincerely don't know what really made them come into my mind, except for the fact the dead were ready to state their case.

I hear the oceans roaring from deep within my thoughts. The ancestors, the custodians of this land, understand the Dreamtime. That place and space of waking consciousness. Their collective energy still exist. It is in every blade of grass, every swaying tree, every drop of water, every grain of dirt, every cell of our bodies.

The "Tibetan Book of the Dead" at Barnes and Nobles was a big orange book with the peaceful figure of Buddha sitting in a ray of light. Written by W.Y Evans – Wentz, it had a beautiful forward by Gregory Hillis. I remember how I had run my hands along its smooth pages. How excited I was to have the chance to read it, especially on the back of just finishing reading E.A Wallis Budges "Egyptian Book of the Dead". I wondered what the pages of this ancient book would reveal. What I found I will share with you now. Wentz reveals that the "Tibetan Book of the Dead" is called in its own language, "Bardo Thodol" which means "Liberation by Healing on the After – Death Plane". It is according to him,

"Among the sacred books of the world, unique. As an epitomized exposition of the cardinal doctrines of the

548

Mahayana School of Buddhism, it is of very great importance, religiously, philosophically and historically".

He reveals that it is essentially a treaty based upon Yoga Philosophy which were fundamental to the curriculum of the great Buddhist University of Nalanda and is "one of the most remarkable works the West has ever received from the East".

He goes on to disclose,

"As a mystic manual for guidance through the Otherworld of many illusions and realms, whose frontiers are death and birth, it resembles the "Egyptian Book of the Dead" sufficiently to suggest some ultimate cultural relationship between the two."

Many of the things that Wentz describes in terms of the ancient funerary rites of Tibet I noticed when I read Budge's "Egyptian Book of the Dead". Which is properly called "The Book of Coming Forth from the Light of Day". Wentz confirms my observations when he declares,

"Having begun my Tibetan research fresh from three years of research in the ancient funeral lore of the Nile Valley, I realized as soon as I gained knowledge of the Tibetan funeral rites – which are very largely pre-Buddhistic – that the effigy of the dead, as now used in Tibet and Sikhism, is so definitely akin to the effigy of the deceased called "the statute of Osiris (or deceased one)," as used in the funeral rites of ancient Egypt, as to suggest a common origin.

Further more the spyange-pu taken by itself alone, as the head – piece for the effigy, has its Egyptian parallel in the images made for the Ka or spirit. These sometimes were merely heads, complete in themselves, to replace or duplicate the head of the mummy and to furnish additional assistance to the Ka when seeking – as the Knower in the *Bardo* seeks – a body to rest in, or that which our text calls a prop for the body.

549

And even as to "the statue of the Osiris" the ancient priests of Egypt read their "Book of the Dead", so to the Tibetan effigy the Lamas now read the *Bardo Thodol* – both treatise alike being nothing more than a guide – book for the traveler in the realm beyond death."

He continues,

"Again the rituals of the Egyptian funeral were designed to confer upon the deceased the magic power of rising up in the ghost body or Ka possessed of all sense of faculties, the service having consisted of "the opening of the mouth and eyes" and the restoration of the use of all other parts of the body. Likewise the Lama's aim, at the outset, is to restore complete consciousness to the deceased after the swoon – state immediately following death, and to accustom him to the unfamiliar environment of the Otherworld, assuming that he be like the multitude, one of the enlightened and thus incapable of immediate emancipation."

According to Wentz he had a total belief that the parts of the Tibetan funeral rites he was talking about came most definitely from pre – Buddhist doctrines, and were from very ancient sources . His conviction being backed he believed by Dr. I. A Waddell who states,

"This is essentially a Bon rite, and is referred to as such in the histories of Guru Padmasambhava, as being practiced by the Bon. (i.e, the religion prevalent in Tibet before the advent of Buddhism, and in its transcendentalism, much like Taoism), and as having incurred the displeasure of the Guru Padmasambhava, the founder of Lamaism."

Wentz mentions that even how the Tibetans dispose of the corpses of the Dalai Lama, the Tashi Lam and some other great man or saint is by embalming the corpse, "in a way

550

somewhat resembling the ancient Egyptian embalming process."

The corpse is placed in a box of marsh salt for about three months or until all the water has been absorbed from it. It goes through some other processes, "a very Egyptian looking mummy is produced".

The rites for the deceased in both Egyptian, and Tibetan culture showed a deep belief in the ultimate journey of the soul being spiritual liberation. Such an attitude breeds and bred a culture that had a deep respect for the order of the universe and to live life, as far as possible, according to the natural law of balance.

Furthermore, when Wentz states that the "Tibetan Book of the Dead" is based on Yoga philosophy. It reminded me of the discovery that linked Hathor to the seeding of Yoga in India.

As I listen to the oceans roaring I review all the pieces of the jigsaw puzzle that had pieced themselves together. I am duly and humbly impressed. So much, so vast, just like this ocean.

Before closing my eyes for sleep I say to Derrick,

"You know sweetie, this is all Shakti. This is all the powerful compassionate, giving creative force. You know what I learned when I was swimming in the ocean tonight. You have to respect that force. It is powerful and all giving, but it will take you down. Drag you down from under your feet. Yes, you got to respect it."

I nodded my head up and down.

"You are right, you have to respect it you know. There's no choice but to respect it," Derrick replied back.

"You know the other thing I learned. Is that the ocean never ceases its activity, even when we are sleeping. That the universe never stops nourishing us. The energy of the Mother, of Shakti is everywhere all around us. If we don't realize that, it means we have become disconnected form nature, because when you are by the ocean you just can't help but feel connected,"

We both nodded together falling into a deep ocean of sleep.

Two days later on reaching home I have a dream. This woman takes me to her church. It is a church flanked by houses on either side. I am impressed by how passionately they worship. The following day I go back to the church and start having a look around. I notice a fair sized statute of a white woman, curvaceous and serene. She is holding a baby to her breast. Her lush hair is piled high. She has a bread basket at her feet. The statues begins to talk to me without moving its lips,

"I am Sophia. I am the Wisdom. Christ is of me, but not I of him."

Then the lady who had taken me to the church came back. I said to her,

"you honor the Mother?"

She said, "yes, of course we do. She gave birth to everything."

On waking I remember the dream vividly. I felt, I had heard that name before, a long time ago. I discuss the dream with Derrick. As I do so I remember I had a book about the early Christian tradition in my book case. I had read its intro two years ago. I tried to remember if I had come across the name Sophia there.

"I'm going to get the book," I told Derrick and darted up stairs.

It was there on the shelf sitting crammed amongst the other books. I flicked through its pages (it being "The Essential Gnostic Gospels"). I tried to see if I could see a name Sophia. Then I found a whole section entitled, "The Sophia of Jesus Christ". It was a sweet feeling. The opening to the section stated,

"This complex revelation discourse given by the Resurrected Christ describes invisible celestial regions. Christ is the Incarnation of the Gnostic Savior and Sophia is the personification of Divine Wisdom, an archetype of the Great Mother."

There was the Wisdom. The Sophia of my dreams had spoken about. I read on,

"After the resurrection from the dead, Christ's twelve disciples, with the seven women, went to the Mountain of Divination and Joy."

Now I was dumbfounded. There were the seven Hathors as the seven women. Joy and divination were all part of Hathor's remit.

I continue to read. Bartholomew asked Christ,

"Why are you called Son of Man. Who is Father to this Son?"

The reply he receives is,

"Primordial Archetypal Man is creative, Self Perfected Wisdom. He mediated with his bride Sophia and his first offspring was born, an androgyny. His male part is named the son of God. His female part, the Sophia, Mother of the Universe. Her name is Love, and the son is Christ since he derived power from his Father who created angels from spirit and light."

A familiar surge of electricity went through me. For in the mirror of that passage I could see the same story of Parvati and Shiva who once sat upon the sacred mountain Kailesh and meditated a baby boy into existence. Through meditation Osiris and Isis gave birth to Horus. Osun and Orunmila of the Yoruba system gave birth through immaculate conception to Esu, the God who Opens the Way. All these couples had the same thing in common – giving birth immaculately to a child whose birth had a connection to saving and protecting the world from its imbalances. Coincidence?

Christ then has a long discourse about the importance of unity. Summed up in his words,

"that is why I've come! So spirit and breath might be united and two become one."

I closed my eyes. That was beautiful. Unification instead of separation. Love instead of hate. Awakening through breath instead of the slumber of ignorance. This was the direct essence of Christ coming through instead of the dogma of the ages.

I knew there was something else the Sophia from my dreams wanted me to get. Then a white light of illumination lit up inside of me. That spirit force moved me again, and I quickly searched for my copy of Joseph Campbell's "A Hero With a Thousand Faces". I flick through its chapters and stop on the chapter "Atonement with The Father". I realized there and then that no aspect of the Hero's journey as detailed by Campbell seemed to be inaccurate. I swear he had inside knowledge beyond what he let on. For after meeting the Mother, Joseph Campbell tells us we have to meet the father, where we discover the "father and mother reflect each other and are in essence the same."

Its then that I think of the Buddha Avalokiteshvara, who is also Chenrizig the Tibetan Buddha of Compassion (whom the Dalai Lama is a reincarnation of). I think of how he embodies the fact that compassion, Karuna, lies within every aspect of the human both the masculine and feminine. How it lies in every aspect of nature. He is the father figure, and within the father figure he is also the feminine wisdom and way of compassion. He represents the balanced Earth. As I read more of Campbell's "Atonement With the Father" I see that he to thinks of the male/female Buddha and states,

"peace is at the heart of all because of Avalokiteshvara – Kwannon, the mighty Bodhisattva, Boundless Love, includes, regards, and dwells within (without exception) every sentient being."

I close my eyes and think of how much I had not fully embraced the idea of our perfect balance, as also being the perfect balance of the masculine and feminine principle. Derrick had mentioned it earlier, but I now realized how important it was. This part of my own Hero's journey had now caught up with me. The knowledge and embracing that we are all co-creators of this Earth. We all have a stake in it. The Mother energy shows us that we are all one. For in her womb is born either the male or female who goes forth to co – create the world. In her essence all gender is transcended. We are all one life force, which springs from the same river's source.

Latter, and in relation to this point, I discovered something interesting Joseph Campbell said in his "Pathways to Bliss (another book that fell mystically into my hands). He states the issue of sexuality of the deity only happened when the occidental traditions of the West wanted to establish the masculine over feminine. But in the Orient, "they don't have this problem." For "the notion is that the ultimate mystery of the universe, the ultimate being – if we can call it that – is beyond human thought and beyond human knowledge. It is beyond even the categories of human thought."

555

He continues managing to squeeze a giggle out of me,

"In that mythology of the cosmic order, the whole sphere of the universe is the womb of the Mother Goddess, whose children we are. And the deities who make her fertile are usually represented in animal forms. These consorts are secondary to her. She is the primary divinity. The first object anybody experiences is Mother. Daddy is second. He can't put in claims. Who wants Abraham's bosom?"

In my mind's eye I revisit an image that had haunted me, in a beautiful way, of Osun and Orunmila, both the Yoruba Goddess and God of Perfect Wisdom sitting in total peace, harmony and balance together. As they divine for their community. Their union and partnership is one of equals, ignited by the passion of divine love which stems from a place of spiritual balance. I give a special thank you to the Sophia of my dreams for ensuring that this message of the Mother was ignited, inflamed and shared. For all to also realize – Jesus like all the others was connected to the compassionate stream of consciousness which fed the message of unity and love.

As I close this chapter I decide to take a break and give my brother in London a call. It's late, but he kindly obliges me. We chit chat, then he suddenly comes out and says,

"Sis you know things are really kicking of this year. There's riots in London, all over the world in fact. The economies are crashing, tsunamis, birds are dropping out the sky and thousands of fish are being washed up on shore."

It was the bit about the fish and birds that caught my attention.

"What do you mean birds are dropping out of the sky?" I asked startled.

"Sis where have you been?" he replies truly surprised I did not know.

"I'm normally up to date with things but I ain't heard of no birds dropping from no sky."

"Well, they have been and by the hundreds. It's been all over the news."

My heart falls.

"What's the cause?"

"They say they don't know. They think it has something to do with the ozone layer getting thinner and the birds are being affected by the weakened magnetic field of the Earth."

"Wow, this is bad stuff. I am going to look this up."

As soon as we get of the phone. I Immediately look for and find articles on the incident. MSNBC News had the dramatic long title in January 2011 "No poison found in birds that fell on town: First tests suggest midair collision, but why? still isn't certain; number raised to at least 4,000".

I discover that particular incident happened in Arkansas. While the Times News Feed had this heading, dated January 2011, "Why Did Thousands of Birds Drop Dead in Arkansas Sky?". In a smaller related article they comment how 100,000 drum fish died along a 20-mile stretch of the river. In Arkansas. "Disease—not fireworks or stress—appears to be the culprit," they state.

The incident of birds dropping out of the sky also seemed to have happened in Sweden, as well. I didn't bother to read on anymore. It was all too depressing. Too much like the River Eulogy. The one thing I was thankful for was the reminder that this is what the whole journey was all about, securing a better future for the Earth and our children. I silently thanked all the Mothers for the wonderful gifts they had brought forward, and Mother Sophia (as the latest Mother who had appeared) for her presence and message. Finally I close my eyes and pray,

Dear Mother,
help the world to get it, the fact that we are killing ourselves, and
everything else. The fact that you and the father gave us all this
abundance and we are not taking care of it. The fact that we just have
to get it before it is too late. Mother, I pray from the bottom of my
heart that there is always clear cool water for the world, that the clear
cool water of the world never runs out.
Ase.

3rd Ase

I am back home from Myrtle Beech. I move like water to the flutes and ocean music of Kweku Covington's "Mommy Waters" track. My body undulates, bends and flexes until I am the giving oceans. My arms flow to one side then another, as though I am giving life to all around me. I am lost in the energy of the water. I slow my movements right down and become one with my breath and allow the breath to become one with me. I open my eyes and I feel healed.

The Peacock and Sati

The Mother's peacock symbol had not finished with me. This time it was to turn up at Jeff's workplace and would eventually lead me to Parvati's previous incarnation Sati. It decided to turn up as I spoke to Jeff about the latest discoveries that had been spearheaded by Nu Wa and the peacock trail of clues.

"Interesting, interesting," Jeff responded and continued "You know suddenly this peacock is just hanging around the entrance of my office. For over three weeks now. Imagine for ten years I have been working here and I have never seen the peacocks. I mean it's a lot of land you know. Don't laugh, but every time I see the peacock I look at it and wonder – if it could speak would I believe it?!"

We both laughed.

"No sis, I am serious I kept on thinking that peacock had a message. Now here you are telling me of all this strange stuff that has been happening with you and peacocks."

"strange stuff," I agreed.

"I will e-mail you some pics of the peacock as soon as I get off the phone," he promised.

Just as we were about to hang up I noticed a new e-mail had popped up in my e-mail from Derrick.

"Hold on let me just check my this e-mail," I said to him

I opened it. Out jumped a big beautiful picture of a alluring smiling Greek Goddess with a large emboldened title above her head, "PEACOCK FEATHERS: THE EYE OF ARGUES".

"Jeff you're not going to believe this!" I shouted down the phone.

"Is everything okay?" he replied back anxiously.

"You're not going to believe this...it's the peacock again!"

After our oohing and aahing I settled down to read the story below the picture of the smiling Goddess. She turned out to be Hera, the Greek Goddess. The tale was about Hera, Zeus, Argos and Zeus's mistress, Lo. Apparently Hera was fed up of Zeus's philandering ways and sent Argus, who had one hundred eyes, to watch over Zeus's mistress, Lo, whom the God had transformed into a cow so that his wife would not recognize her. Well, Hera was obviously no one's fool and saw through the trick. She got round to getting hold of that cow tied her up. It was Argus's job to keep all his eyes on her.

When Zeus found out what was going on he hatched a plan, and decided to send his son the God Hermes to sing and tell boring stories to Argus. The aim was to put him to sleep. He succeeded, killed the poor fellow and set Lo free. There's nothing like a woman's scorn. Hera was furious. Poor old Lo got taken care of with the sting of a vicious gadfly. Grieved, Hera honored Argus by putting his hundred eyes on the tail of her favorite bird the peacock. It is said that those eyes could not see any more but beautifully decorated the tail of the peacock.

After reading and contemplating the story I bowed to Hera for she was obviously not being left out of the Goddess Water Songline

Jeffrey's Picture of the Peacock at Kew Garden

As the iridescent green tail of Argus's peacock closed my two volumes of Budge's "The God's of Egypt" arrived with the post man's knock. I thank him profusely; and hold those two volumes in my hands like they are precious china. Not sure where to start reading I allow the spirits to guide me. I chose to casually flick open the pages of Volume II first.

They offer up their pearls as I curl up on my ruffled bed tucking the pillow beneath me. A slim beautiful woman peers out wide eyed and curiously at me. She is wearing a close fitting dress, holding the symbol of power and dominion in one hand, and the ankh of life in the other. Her head dress symbol the vulture identifying her with the Goddess Nekhebet and Motherhood. While its cow horns aligns her to Hathor. Below her image she is identified by the simple words Sati.

I read her name several times over. Something in my brain stirs like a sleeping coiled snake. Hadn't I seen that name somewhere before? I wrack my brain, but nothing seems to come up but the vague memory that Parvati had a previous incarnation of herself that I faintly remembered may have been called Sati. I shrug the thought of and begin to flick randomly through some more pages. But slowly the thought that had begun begins to uncoil itself and gather strength. As it springs to full life I jump of the bed. Desperately I scramble through pages of faded notes until I find the section on Parvati. Then a sentence catches my eyes *"Sati's, Parvati's previous incarnation"*.

The air squeezes right out of my body, electric shocks tingle my fingers. Could it be possible? I gasp for air as if I am wading under water. I dare not even think a profound discovery could have been made. But there they were – Sati in Egypt and Sati in India. I had already clearly aligned Parvati (Sati's other name) with Hathor.

A deep breath tries to control me, and the rising excitement. I decide to be cautious, and read more about the Egyptian Sati.

According to Budge, the beautiful Egyptian Sati is the wife of the first creator God Khenemu who created the divine Cosmic Egg from which sprang the sun. He also fashioned the ancient Gods of Egypt on a potter's wheel. Often depicted with four heads which represent the four Gods whom he embodies: Ra, Osiris, Shu and Seb – he is known as "The Guardian of the

Doors that Kept the Flood In". His role as a Water God was absorbed by the God of primordial waters Nu (Nut's husband).

His female counterpart was Her – Shefit. Latter she became known as Sati. Sati's name means "to shoot, to eject, to pour out, and scattering seeds from abroad". She was considered to be non-other than Hathor and Isis combined.

I pause trembling. "scattering seeds abroad"…."Hathor and Isis combined"….the meaning of Sati's name seemed to smile out at me, and yes I had identified Parvati with Hathor and had always found that she had some of Isis attributes, as well. For didn't they share the same husbands? I had already identified Shiva with Osiris. The force of history moves me. Tears begin to stream down my face. I want to jump of the bed and declare Sati to the whole world in my Living Room – Derrick's watching television. But, first I read on.

Budge reveals more about Sati, like a master in all his glory,

"she must have been regarded as the goddess of the inundation, who poured out and spread over the land the life-giving waters of the Nile, and as the goddess of fertility. She sometimes carries in her hands a bow and arrows, a fact which suggest in her earliest form she was a goddess of the chase; according to Dr. Brugsch, she was identified by the Greeks with their Goddess Hera."

I freeze. Hera. Oh Hera this is the gift you came to give me. You came to bring me Sati. I shout with electrifying joy that shouts through the air. I calm down long enough to notice Sati's arrows. I wonder, does Parvati have one too? Do they share this as a symbol? I check my old notes, again. I finger through them delicately, and I find them - Parvati's five arrows and a sugar bow.

I can no longer contain myself. The electrical jolts throw me of the bed and I run into the living room, jump up and down shouting wildly,

"Derrick, Derrick I found Parvati! I found Parvati! I found Parvati! She's right here in the pages of Budge's book. right here!"

I point and gesticulate wildly at the flapping book in my hand. I begin to dance and pounce like a wild mad cat around the house. Before Derrick can say a "but" or "what?" I am on the phone to my mom in London,

"Mum, I found Parvati! I found Parvati mum! I found Parvati! In her previous incarnation as Sati!!!! Do you understand what this means?!"

Mum could not get a word in edge ways. She manages to squeeze out,

"Wow that is quite interesting."

"Mum, this is not interesting. It is awesome! It is phenomenal! Awesome! Awesome! She still has her Egyptian name!"

I jump high into the air until I am exhausted. I jump up and down, up and down, until I cannot speak. Spent I hand the phone over to Derrick. The tide of emotions burst forth from me like the Nile breaking its banks.

"I found Parvati, I found Parvati."

I say in the tiniest smallest whispers.

Hathor, Her Majesty Arrives

Hathor rose from the pages of "The Gods of Egypt". Proud, tall, dignified, serious yet joyful,

"so you found me," her gaze across the oceans of time seemed to tease.

She stood there holding the Papyrus Scepter in her left hand, and the ankh of life in her right. The royal snake Goddess Wadjet of Northern Egypt protected her third eye, and her famous cow horns curved gently inward on top of her head upon which the sun firmly sat.

She commands and draws my eyes to another picture of her. This time she has the headdress of the Vulture Goddess of Southern Egypt, which is surmounted by a tiara formed of Uraei (snakes) and above these is a pylon (an erect standing rectangular shaped object) set amongst a massive fan of lotus flowers and buds. Curiously they look like the fanned out tail of a beautiful peacock.

It seemed as though Hathor stood there to answer and put straight a few of the questions that had been twirling on the skirts of my mind. One was a conundrum I so badly wanted to solve. I had noticed that the Mother Goddess images from around the world were definitely a composite of Egyptian Goddesses who seemed to have traveled to different parts of the world as part of the Osirian doctrine and teachings. I had nick named this group of Goddesses, the Mut Composite.

However, I had also noticed over and over again that the Mut composite seemed to be dominated by Hathor and Sekhmet with Isis in third runnings. This dominate coupling of Hathor and Sekhmet seemed to be the Feminine Divines that dominated all the Goddesses that had come forward. Such as the combinations of Durga-Parvati, Green Tara-White Tara (although Tara has many forms her two most popular forms is that of the Green and White Tara), Osun-Oya-Isis (Osun also has within her what seems to be the whole Mut Composite. For she is the grand Universal Mother of the Yoruba. She even has Mut's Vulture Symbol).

At last Hathor was here with the final answers. She had waited all this time, and was now fully present, with pieces of the Goddess jigsaw puzzle of our historical ancient past piled high on top of her crown. The Grand Lady who had spread her wisdom abroad, was here to give a personal account of a few things I needed to know about her. So she proceeded to let me know what was what, with a discourse from the pages of Budge's "Gods of Egypt" book.

The more I read about Hathor was the more I could see her reflection within all the Mother Goddesses around the world. Above all it became easy to see and understand how all the Mother Goddess scattered through time and history was She Who Was the Universe, the Law of Balance, the Carrier of Wisdom, the Dancer of Grace, the Mother of Compassion, the Queen and the Bringer of the Good Life.

According to the records of history, Hathor is amongst the oldest known deities of ancient Egypt. She was worshipped in ancient times under the form of the cow. A flint model of the head and horns of the cow, which was her type and symbol, was found among the early archaic or late pre-dynastic flints in Egypt. This symbol and form of Hathor was her oldest form. It was preserved in the "Book of the Dead" until the beginning of the Roman period. The Heavenly cow fed the whole of life with her nourishing milk, which was considered to be the Milky Way (which Hathor was also seen as a personification of). I reminded myself that this symbol of Hathor connects her to the Goddess Nu, the Mother of Primordial Time.

The pre-historic origins of Hathor is also confirmed by her presence on the ancient Narmer Palette of Ancient Egypt. King Narmer was amongst the first of the pre-dynastic rulers who ruled at the end of the pre-dynastic and the beginning of the early dynastic period.

567

Hathor also appears as the lioness in her Sekhmet form and is often depicted with the symbols of joy and pleasure, the sistrum and the menat. They were also used to create the rhythmic foundation of temple rituals.

She was very important in the Egyptian rituals of the dead which involved the deceased evolving to the next stage of their journey, eternal life. In the judgment scene of the "Book of the Dead" she is the One Who Watches the Weighing of the Heart and who "afterwards decree joy and felicity for the heart which has been weighed and found just," says Budge.

She forms the eyes of the deceased and it is from her sycamore tree, which is also known as the Tree of Life, from which the deceased receives the nourishing waters and fruits of eternal life. This tree of life I had already identified as the proto-type of the World Tree of Life found in most cultures. In fact, Hathor is seen as the sycamore tree itself.

Another form of Hathor is depicted as holding the notched palm branch in one hand. In this form she is the Egyptian Goddess Sefekh – aabut, the "Lady of Books, Learning, and Chronographer". Sefekh-aabut is also seen as the wife of the Wisdom God Toth (known as Tehuti by the Egyptians.) In this association Hathor connects the rivers of wisdom that runs through all the Great Mother Goddesses.

As a Creatrix Hathor was closely connected with women, fertility and birthing of the macro universe and the micro universe. She is often depicted on birthing stools that Egyptian women used while in labor. These stools were said to invoke the birthing power of Hathor.

Omi's painting of Hathor as the
Tree of Life giving nourishment of water to the soul

Hathor Birthing Stool

Hathor as the owner of the Sistrum and Menit. Symbols of joy, love, life and protection. She is the "Mistress of Life" itself. The embodiment of all that was good in life. It is her rhythms that helped to sustain the balance of the universal rhythms that exist within and without us.

According to Budge the worship of Hathor was universal from "the earliest period, and dynastic shrines which were specially consecrated to her worship were common throughout the country. Her shrines were even more numerous than those of Horus.

He goes on to explain,

"She was the great Mother of the World, and the old cosmic Hathor was the personification of nature which was perpetually conceiving, and creating, and bringing forth, and rearing and maintaining all things both great and small." Her Creatrix proportions were expressed in the fact she was seen

570

as "The Mother of Her Father", and the "Daughter of Her Son" and heaven, earth, and the Underworld were under her rule and she was the mother of every god and goddess."

At last Hathor addresses the question that has been on my mind – why did it seem that she dominated the Mut Composite? She gives her answer through the mouth of Budge,

"In all the important shrines of the local Goddesses she was honored with them, and she always became the chief female counterpart of the head of the company or triad in which she had been allowed to enter."

Budge elaborates that clear proof had been given by a Dr. Brugsch who had compiled a list of various forms she took in all the large cities in upper and lower Egypt, and from this it is seen that she was connected to all the Goddesses and was the head of all the Goddesses.

Hathor on a column of Dendera Temple, Egypt

The Two Satis Meet Again, and Gather All the Pieces Into One

The two Satis are determined to keep on revealing their shared identities. Hathor leads the way she has me contemplating, once more, her form as the Seven Hathors, in more detail. According to Budge there were so many forms of Hathor that from a very very early period of pre – dynastic Egyptian history she was formed into a company of Seven Hathors. The forms did not always include the same Hathors, but whichever forms they were they covered her major characteristics.   The Seven Hathors are sometimes more in number. Just like the Seven Mothers of India.

A few weeks later I was to find out that the Seven Mothers of India were also, like the Seven Hathors, grouped in ten or more Mothers. In curiosity to find out more about the Mothers I decide to go through the pages of my David Kingsley book, "Hindu Goddesses" in more detail. I was even more surprised when the Indian Goddess Sati rose from those pages smiling to reveal more connections between herself and her Egyptian sister self. According to Kingsley the,

"Ten Mothers were birthed when Sati's father Daksa decided to perform a great sacrifice and invited all of the heavenly sphere to it. All but Shiva and Sati. He apparently, did not like Shiva and considered him "uncivilized" and "disheveled". Shiva did not care about not being invited to the party, but Sati does. She tells Shiva she is going to the party to disrupt it. Shiva tells her not to. When he is unable to change her mind she multiplies herself into ten forms as the Mahavidyas (great revelations or manifestations): Kali, Tara, Chinnamasti, Bhuvanesvari, Bala, Dhumavati, Kamala, Matangi, Sodasi and Bhairavi."

In fact he reveals that Sati who is normally seen as willingly submitting herself to her husband – changes all of that when she brings herself forth as the Ten Mothers. In this powerful form she changes from "Submissive to the assertive feminine principle".

Further revealing,

"Sati announces that she has appeared in these dreadful forms so that her devotees not only may achieve ultimate release (Moksha) but may achieve desires and invoke magical powers over others. She actually frightens Shiva in her dreadful form into giving her mantras and instructions for worshipping the Mahavidyas."

Kingsley explains that the ten forms that Sati takes are not always the same figures, and "some forms like Kali and Tara have several manifestations". However, each form represents, just like the Seven Hathors, the gentle and fierce side of the Goddess.

The Goddesses of the Mahavidyas are obviously pre-Aryan. Most of the time they are described as very black. There are some who are said to be red or fair colored. These two skin colors seemed to still have all the hall marks of Hathor. For Budge says in the Egyptian sacred text Hathor is "brought forth by the goddess Nut in the form of a black-skinned, or blackish – red skinned child and received as her name that of the last hour of the day, Khenemet – ankh".

I find myself gripped by the extended version of the Sati story. According to Kingsley when she goes to the party her father has organized, she kills herself. Shiva hears the news and proceeds to where her father's house is. When he arrives in his grief stricken state he picks up Sati's body and begins to wonder around the whole cosmos. His crying, sobbing and grief threatens to knock the whole universe from its balance. It is Vishnu who remedies the situation. He apparently enters Sati's body by Yoga or slices bits of her body of little by little until it is completely gone. When Shiva discovers that his beautiful Sati is literally gone he recovers from his grief. Wherever her body fell sacred places called Pithas (which means, "seat") were established. These places are marked by various Goddess shrines. Their number in the tales varies from 4 to 110.

These Pitha's and the shrines established at them are said to be scattered all over the land of India, and unifies India into the living body of the Mother Goddess, Devi (also known as Shakti). For don't matter which Goddess the shrines are dedicated to, they are all said to represent the one Mother Goddess.

I pause, as I see that even now Sati's body was reuniting the Mother back into one again. I read on. Kingsley puts it this way,

"according to the myth, then, the Indian subcontinent has been sacralized by the remains of Sati. India is in affect her burial ground. The subcontinent is sown with the pieces of Sati's body, which make the land especially sacred. The myth also stresses that the numerous and varied Pithas and goddesses worshipped at them are part of a larger unified whole."

I am riveted for right there in Sati's story I see the Egyptian Osirian story but in reverse. How bizarre. In the Osirian tale it is Osiris's body that is chopped up and scattered. While it is Isis who is in deep grief. She is the one who searches for the pieces of his body, and brings them together again. It is said that she buried the body pieces in various parts of the land of Egypt. Wherever these parts were buried the land became holy. I pause...different continents, same royal spiritual couple, same story just reverse.

On a final note, Kingsley helps me to understand once again how much the Mother Goddess wants us to understand she is many but one form. He reveals,

"an important point in Mahadevi theology is the Devi's (World Mother) tendency is to display or manifest herself in a great many forms. Many myths about the Devi describe her as producing goddesses from different parts of her body, and she often announces to her petitioners that she assumes different forms at different times in order to maintain cosmic stability."

Shiva Carrying Corpse of Sati on his Trident,

Sati being worshiped by the pharaoh
Sobekhotep III of the thirteenth dynasty-
Brooklyn Museum

The River that Crosses

On awaking from a small nap I get back to Sati, the Indian Sati. This time her waters pour all over me, literally. For as I re-visit Kingsley's book "Hindu Goddesses" Sati begins a deep dialogue about the waters of life. One that is opened up by the portals of her Pithas, the sacred sites where her parts are buried. Her Pithas are also called Tirthas. A term which means a place where one fords a river. A river ford is somewhere you cross over from one place to another. It also signifies a place where you cross from one reality to another.

I thought on this for a while. For surely hadn't both the Satis of both India and Egypt opened the way for the waters of history to be crossed and mended. Through Kingsley I discover that Sati helps us to cross "from the limited human sphere to the unconditional divine sphere".

Suddenly, as if to deepen the point about the celestial restoring properties of the waters Ganga, Sati's, sister turns up. She explains through the pages of Kingsley's book that it is her holy waters that restores the health of the sick, makes the earth abundant, and bestows blessings on the world. It is on her waters that the body of the deceased are floated in order to cross over to a renewed life. Her waters are so potent that according to Kingsley,

"A strong and widespread belief is that to die in the Ganges, or to have a few drops of the Ganges water poured on ones lips just prior to death, is to gain liberation."

Gange's waters _flow between three worlds: Heaven, earth, and the ancestral realm, She is, according to Kingsley,

"a liquid axis mundis, a pathway connecting all spheres of reality, a present at which or in which one may cross over to another sphere of the cosmos, ascend to heavenly worlds, or transcend human limitations."

Then he quotes something that takes my breath way. For it seems in the words of this simple paragraph he sums up the power of water to heal the world. What he quotes is from Diana Eck, and I make a note to cherish it in my mind forever.

"For the Ganga's significance as a symbol is not exhaustively narrative. First, she is a river that flows with waters of life in a vibrant universe. Narrative myths come and go in history. They may shape the cosmos and convey meaning for many generations, and then they may gradually lose their hold upon the imagination and may finally be forgotten. But the river remains, even when the stories are no longer repeated. The river flows on, bringing life and conveying the living tradition, even to those of this age for whom everything else is de-mythologized."

I bow deeply to Ganga for her messages from the waters.

The Peacock Gloriously Fans Her Feathers

After a few nights of those discoveries it seemed that the Mother and ancestors were in a celebratory mood. For they took us to the coolest little party in Lancaster, a place where it is nigh impossible to find anything cool. Me, Derrick, Kem Ra and the baby bopped our heads to the soul music, eat cheese, strolled and viewed the lovely art pieces on display. I stopped by a large midnight sky blue carefully hand crafted vase. I admired it in all its details. Then I noticed the peacock feathers and jumped! There seemed to be dozens of them fanning themselves out in exuberant celebration.

578

Feeling dizzy. I went and found Derrick and dragged him to the peacock feathered spot. He too was surprised that once again there was the peacock symbol.

As the party drew to an end we decided to take a walk and explore the small Arts Festival taking place outside. It to was almost over. Even so the area was still lit up by dozens of warmly glowing lamps hanging elegantly from the still branches of the trees. I browsed the vendor stores until Kem Ra came and dragged me by the hand to a stall whose owner's business it was to educate the world about the history of ancient languages.

I was fascinated by the exhibitor's extensive array of Egyptian letters, ink, and special paper onto which one could print one's name in hieroglyphs. What a great idea. Of course I wanted to see what my name would look like in hieroglyphs. The exhibitor seemed pleased that someone had taken an interest in his stand, for we were the only ones there. I carefully stamped my name in hieroglyphics onto the cream paper. When I finished I held it up to the lamp light on the table. I giggled with excitement, my name looked so cool in hieroglyphs. Feeling like a small child in a candy store I decided to get the names of Derrick, baby Omo, and Mom stamped onto the paper too.

As I inked each of their names into their Egyptian equivalents it felt somewhat wild that after being steeped in so much history which had traced its headwater to ancient Egypt - that here I was standing at a stall in little ole Lancaster printing my families names in hieroglyphics. How likely was that? As I thanked the man for giving us the opportunity, and just as I was getting ready to leave the table I had a thought.

"Sir, do you mind if I print one more name?"

The man seemed genuinely pleased by my display of enthusiasm,

"No go ahead."

Very carefully I printed O S U N onto the special paper given. I felt a tingle as each letter translated into its ancient Egyptian equivalent. I couldn't stop staring at the paper when the full name was printed onto it. I felt all strange inside. Osun was the ultimate peacock Goddess. She was also the one who had opened the flood waters for all this history to flow forth, and here I was printing her name in hieroglyphics. Was she giving the confirmation loud and clear that yes it was she who was the Water Rosetta Stone?

Osun's name in hieroglyphics

The next day I found myself inspired and painting in Indian Inks. It was Omo's birthday and I painted three pictures. The first was a warm collage of purple warmed yellow and oranges. The whole piece looked just like what I decided to name it, "The Womb of Creation". The second was a wilder, and more layered creation with vibrant reds, greens and yellows. I painted a gold leaf which emerged from the middle of the carnival of colors. I called it "Osun Leaves: Out of Primordial Essence Arises Life".

The third piece was a stylized lotus flower coming out of a pond of red, gold and green. I called that one, "Emergence". Painting that one reminded me of a book I had encountered a few days ago - "The Journey to Sarah" by the former Duchess of York. The first page it opened up on was a chapter titled "Lotus Flower.

On Omo's birthday a fourth picture jumped out at me. It was not one I had painted. It was the ariel view of a river that showed how much like a tree the waterways looked. As I looked and looked and looked at that picture it dawned on me that Hathor's tree of life was none other than a depiction of the celestial and physical river systems.

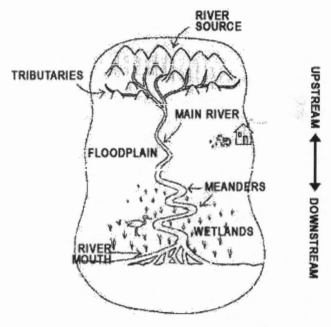

From Canadian Council of Geographic Education

When I shared my thoughts and findings with Derrick he sat and listened quietly. Then it was as though he spoke from another place, somewhere other worldly. What he said felt important so I picked up a pen and scribbled as he spoke. Somehow, I knew if I didn't write his words down they would be lost in the waters of time forever.

"Omi this is not about the Mother, per say. The ultimate message of your book is about treating everything as sacred. This is the message that the Mother comes to bring. For she represents the sacrality of the whole Earth. Yes, the Earth really is her body. In Sankofa it is about going back. The egg is humanity. The bird is the mother. Picking humanity up in her beak and carefully redirecting its energy so that it can be reborn. Out of the ashes comes the phoenix. Humanity is in a complete state of destructions, like the phoenix's ashes. It is about taking the egg back so that it can be re-born, and renewed again. The phoenix goes back to its origin to renew itself. Every species goes back to renew itself, like Salmon. They kill themselves to get back. If you break the flow they will die out, because their main thing is to go back to their origin. That's when they experience a revitalization.

The Symbols of the cultures never changed. They were brought forward. Its just a matter of interpretation. The Goddess bears the symbols the people just don't know what they mean anymore. The Egyptian language is one of symbols. They knew symbols transcend time. We have forgotten to read symbols. It was a common language. We lost an appreciation and regard for them and what they want. Because we are in crisis, we have to take serious measures to avoid this crisis. Credo Mutwa said "all hands on deck turning the wheel in the same direction." We are in a crisis. Who is the captain that will tell the people what to do and will they listen? Credo said, "nope". Well, the head is the Mother. Every culture has a mother. She needs to be resurrected. We need to go back to the source to resurrect and revitalize ourselves like the Phoenix. That is what will save us in these times. What is the downside to being sacred. There is no downside to treating everything as sacred, and discovering the meaning behind our symbols. That is what will save us.

Every person is called on to take this journey. In the Egyptian tradition every heart got weighed. This is about every heart. Every heart has a chance to renew itself. You do this by saying that everything is sacred and must be treated as such. "

I totally understood him and once again some words of Joseph Campbell's floated hauntingly back to me, "the symbols lay broken beneath our feet"......"we are free falling into the future"..... "We need to awaken".

FOURTH ASE – FOR GOOD LUCK

Joseph Campbell in his "Hero with a Thousand Faces" says that "when the hero quest has been accomplished, through penetration to the source, or through the grace of some male or female human or animal personification, the adventurer still must return with his life transforming trophy." He must begin the task of going back over the threshold. According to Campbell many have refused to go back over the threshold, including the Buddha who "after his triumph doubted whether the message of realization could be communicated".

You see the problem is that the hero has been in the land of the gods, a "forgotten dimension of the world that we know". The gifts of wisdom he brings back has "from the standpoint of waking consciousness, a certain baffling inconsistency between the wisdom brought forth from the deep, and the prudence usually found effective in the light world,"

So now the hero has the issue of how do you teach "what has been taught correctly and incorrectly learned a thousand times, throughout the millenniums of mankind's prudent folly?" Basically, how do you truly "render back into light world language the speech defying pronouncements of the dark? How to represent on a two dimensional surface a three dimensional form, or in a three dimensional image a multi – dimensional meaning?" How on earth do you communicate with people who "insist on the exclusive evidence of their senses the message of the all generating void"

Now the Hero has a major problem for he or she has to accept that what they experienced in that world of the Gods is real, for it is as said earlier, a dimension of the world we already know. The second problem is that they have to convince themselves to re-enter a world where they know

585

people are entrenched in the world of passion rather than "transcendental bliss". For deep within they know in this world, "dreams that were momentous by night may seem simply silly in the light of day". The third problem is that the task of going back often cannot be avoided. For as Campbell puts it,

"The easy thing is to commit the whole community to the devil and retire again into the heavenly rock dwelling, close the door, and make it fast. But if some spiritual obstetrician has meanwhile drawn the shimenawo across the retreat, then the work of representing the eternity in time, and perceiving in time eternity, cannot be avoided."

Now the good news is that apparently if the hero has the blessing of the goddess or god and is then commissioned to return to the world with "some elixir for the restoration of society" the final stage – the stage of return back over the threshold, "is supported by all the powers of his supernatural patron". On the other hand if he has taken this elixir and trophy without the permission of the Gods he will be chased by them as they aim to prevent him from his crossing over.

Buddha's Breath

It was January 2012, and I thought about those words and much more as I looked out at the light house which stood in the distance of the ocean water. The day was fading hard and just the illumination of the light house lit the way. I touched what our Native American friends called the Grandfathers. They were smooth and solid large stones standing like guards on the ocean front. Myself and Derrick were on a work trip to Charleston with his boss and another colleague. The history of the place weighed heavily on my heart. I could feel the ancestral sorrow in the land. I tried not to, but I could. I felt pain as I had walked through the market place where they had been sold, with nothing hanging there that remembered their names or pain. That walk made me think of the importance of honoring the source of a thing. Without doing so something seemed to be inextricably missing.

My feet sunk in the cold sand, Derrick held the boots that had stopped me from navigating my way down to the ocean on this surprise jaunt organized by his boss. Omo nestled her head on my shoulder. We all just let the sound of the ocean engulf us. We kept on staring at the light house as if it was the most astonishing attraction we had ever seen. The noise of the ocean filled me up and I thought about the 2000 year old tree we had just hugged before driving onto this historic part of the ocean front. I hugged it, The Angel Oak Tree, so hard as if I was hoping to pull a message out of it. I didn't care how stupid I looked hugging onto that old bit of history. I was aware we had arrived late, had only 5 minutes to go, and the warden was about to kick us out – so I was determined to get every last squeeze out of the tree I latter discovered the locals called fondly, "the Angel Oak tree". I noticed its branches were so old and heavy that some rested regally onto the ground. I read that some even dropped underground a few feet and came right back up looking like little trees.

As I hugged it I remembered how much like a tree the body of a river looked. From the one river were many branches which belonged to the same body. All those branches went back to a source, a surprising little trickle of water. The funny thing if that little trickle died then so did the whole tree. One of my main conflicts on this journey was thinking about who cares about all the stuff that had been discovered, especially when the overwhelming evidence pointed to the fact we had one spiritual inheritance, one source, one Mother who just happened to go by several names. It was all fascinating stuff, and even though the phoenix went back to renew itself from the source of its birth, why should humanity feel that it needed to do the same? Why should it care? As the journey went on this conflict waged inside of me. Joseph Campbell was definitely right when he said the hero would have weighed on his heart the thought could he or she "render back into light world language the speech defying pronouncements of the dark?"

I knew what I had experienced, I knew what I had written onto these pages, but I was doubtful on how to truly express it all to the outside world. Did I even want to? Just like the Buddha I did not feel as though I wanted to return back over the threshold. I had reached my bliss. I remember just before getting to "here" I had a strange experience where I was meditating and suddenly I could see the Buddha large and magnificent sitting on the edge of the world. He was just sitting there, not male, not female, with no color of any nation. He seemed to be everyone and everything.

He just sat there breathing and as he breathed I could see the whole world in his breath. In that world some people were still, some were rushing, some were ailing, some were happy and some were hungry, some were dying and some were living it up. Whatever each person was doing one thing that became obvious was that it was all being done within the remit of the Buddha's breath. It was then that I realized there was no good, bad, wrong or right (so to speak). It was all part of the experience of life. I also realized how caught up we become in small tiny worlds, without fully knowing it. We run around in small circles without knowing there is something so much more and enlightened waiting for us, and it's right there within our grasp, because we are in it, and it holds us already.

As I sat there in the enlightenment of the Buddha's breath I felt my wounded self being healed. My own discontentment with my life being mended. I felt grateful for the journey that had forced me to touch on the truth of unseen reality. The true reality that sustains the all. I was awed by the gracious presence of our World Mother. Mystified by her magnificence. I was cool with this feeling, and surely did not feel as though I needed to bother the world with it. But, as Joseph Campbell said you have to cross back over the threshold from whence you came. I had a deep sneaking suspicion that when we attended the Sweat organized by our friends Gary and Debbie Fourstar in Atlanta that happened to fall on Derrick's birthday – some inextricable force had already decided that back across the threshold into the world I was to go.

For on that day we did the sweat I was keenly aware of the symbolism of going over the threshold into the Mother's womb. Once inside you had to experience the belly of the whale and find your strength. Then it was time to return to the world a new person. It was obvious to me the whole sweat was a living metaphor and preparation for the heroes' journey.

Meditating on the Source

The ocean breeze brought my mind back to the lighthouse, the darkness that had now descended upon us and the growing feeling that I was standing on hallowed ground. I wondered how many lives had that lighthouse guided on their way for good and for bad. As I stared into its source of refuge glaring against the roar of the ocean I remembered a documentary I had seen a few weeks ago called "The Lost

Treasures of Tibet", where a whole community was falling apart and dying in the old Tibetan Kingdom of Mustang. As the temples, sacred statutes and paintings fell apart so too did Mustang. The locals believed that if the temples and sacred objects could be restored then their culture would spring back to life.

Lucky for them a Western conservation team, led by British conservationist John Sanday took an interest. They took on the great task of restoring the royal monastery in Mustang's capital of Lo Monthang. When they first arrive at the temple they are confronted with the poignant image of a ray of sunshine coming in from the roof and in that ray there was a little old lady covered in black, sitting.

John Sanday asked, "Who's she?"

The teams guide replies, "Oh, she's the woman responsible for lighting the butter lamp."   And he said, "Is there nobody else?"

And they said, "No, it's pretty dead."

That woman reminded me so much of the presence of the World Mother who watches over us even when everything is dying along with the hope that all will be restored again. She also reminded me of the day when I had a dream that revealed that this book should be divided into the 16 lamps of wisdom that light the way at the famous Osun Festival in Nigeria. Each lamp lit at that festival represented one of the original wisdoms that came to earth during the First Times what the Aboriginals call the Dreamtime to lay the laws down. As each chapter was a lamp they each would be lit until all 16 were made ablaze again.

All is going well for the restoration team until a point of contention happens. They want to stay true to the Western style of restoring paintings which means not filling in what you cannot detect. However the King of Mustang insist, "you should try to paint the remaining part as it was before. We need the assistance of the experts to help us restore the art as it was in the past. Then it will be good. But if the restoration does not complete the art then it will do more harm than good. We have to worship what is there."

For the King explains, any crack in the paintings means that the Gods have a scar in them. All the pieces must be fixed and connected back together again. The paintings must be restored to total wholeness. With much back in and forthing the issue finally gets resolved. The West and the Old World eventually meet eye to eye, and the paintings get restored fully. Then a miraculous thing happens life returns back to this holy land. Not just a little, but a lot. Where only the old lady occupied the temple keeping the God's company, hundreds of bodies now jostled for a sitting position in it. In honor of the restoration ten thousand butter lamps were now lit. As the viewer watches on the lights flicker, and the narrator says, "the old ways burn bright in the face of great change." It was then I had the thought – the restoration arriving in Mustang may have not been a stroke of luck after all, maybe just that one old lady, her prayers, and actions of lighting the butter lamps everyday were responsible. Then of course, the restoration of what was, also played a crucial role.

After the holiday, and despite all I had been shown on the journey I was still burning with the question as to why the importance of returning to the spring well of our traditions. It was during a morning meditation that some kind of answer seemed to come through a dialogue between myself and spirit.

Spirit: What are you doing now?
Me: Breathing.

Spirit: How does it make you feel?

Me: Good, refreshed, calm and whole. Back to my source. Gives me a feeling like no one can take this away from me.

Spirit: Now take that on a broader level. Imagine you are Humanity. That is what returning to the source does for it. It brings it back to a place of wholeness, refreshment, makes it realize the enlightenment that dwells within it. When they get to this place they feel whole. Don't matter what teaching they practice they know the underlying source behind it is enlightenment. No one can tell them anything else or different. Now do that other meditation. You know where you go through the various colors of consciousness.

Me: I knew the meditation spirit was talking about. It was the Tantra meditation I did where I went through five colors associated with the Dakini, the universal Goddess. I normally didn't get past the first color yellow, because I always fell asleep. This time I managed all the colors.

Spirit: Notice how you went through the colors: yellow, blue, red, green and then white. Each color was a luminous light on a lotus petal, and as you went through each of those colored petals you experienced a certain state of consciousness. Now the Dakini (World Mother) sits in the middle of all of this as a fully illuminated being. She sits as the white light in the middle of the lotus flower. It is her presence in the middle that now makes you realize you have experienced a whole lotus flower. It is that center that holds together the beauty and experience of the whole flower. When you stay in that white light you are fully whole. You see each dot is but a level of consciousness of the Dakini. By the time you reach the middle, the source, you experience her full luminosity. You experience the fullness of the whole. You can sit and be healed from that experience. When you go back to the source you are going back home to be healed, but you can only go back home

592

through each state of consciousness being acknowledged, experienced

Me: I think I get it.

Maat's Feather

Then as I began to open my eyes from the meditation, I remembered a dream. One where a Native American woman wanted me to help her find a feather so that she could help the nation of men from dying. Initially I found many beautiful feathers, but not the one she truly wanted. That one was small and red. After hunting high and low I gave up and sat on a comfortable sofa, and for no reason put my hand down a small gap between the cushion and the arm rest. My hand came back up with something. It was a small red feather

The woman smiled broadly, held the feather high above her head, and began to walk with it. She insisted I walk behind her. So I did. Excitedly she rejoiced,

"now the nation of men will be healed!"

Now that dream had been some time ago, it was around the time I had discovered the Egyptian Goddess Maat, as a form of one of Hathor's Wisdom Selves. The female counterpart to Toth the God of wisdom. Her name meant "that which is straight". It also meant the rule, law or canon by which the lives of men and their actions were kept straight and governed.

The more I read about Maat, was that I realized the keeping of Maat was the same as keeping the Dharma. The Goddess herself was the personification of the physical and moral law, and order and truth. Maat was "the Lady of the Judgment Hall". The heart of each person had to weigh as light as her feather

I wondered if the feather in the dream, held high above the elderly Native American woman's head was symbolic of the feather of Maat, and her universal law, order and balance. The dream seemed to indicate that we would find it again, when we least expected. But we had to make the effort to begin the search for it. Curiously, I remembered being in Nigeria and seeing the Osun Priestess wearing the prettiest red parrot feather in their heads as a symbol of divine power and royalty.

Maat

The Sea of Lotus Buds

We take our final gazes at the light house. Derrick does a prayer just between the two of us – giving thanks to the waters, ancestors and Mother. He also prays for the soul of those who have gone before to rest in peace. We turn our backs on the dim lights, and trundle back up the path from whence we came. My feet sink deeply into the sand. I don't bother to put my boots back on even when the sand becomes stony ground. My feet somehow feel tougher. I walk on the stones confidently, as if they were sand.

When we get back to the hotel, I take full notice this time of all overwhelming lotus buds present. The restaurant area of the hotel is plush decorated with the most beautiful orange glowy lotus bud lights. There are pictures on the walls of more lotus buds and some open lotus flowers. I get back to our room and the pink picture in the bathroom resembles a lotus flower blossoming, and there are lotus buds on our bed head too. We were swimming in a sea of lotus buds, and flowers and I hadn't even really noticed.

The lotus was to establish itself as the next symbol messenger. A few days after arriving home I casually browsed the internet and my notes on the Goddesses, and up came Durga smiling at me. She emerged with a gift in her hand – the blue lotus flower, half opened. I was soon to discover that in this state it represented the budding potentiality yet to still bloom. Once I got it, she re-emerged in her form as Parvati this time holding a fully bloomed blue lotus to symbolize that which had completely awakened.

She then led me to a lovely little story found in the ancient Indian epic the Ramayana. One that epitomized the deep importance of the blue lotus flower to her. One day Lord Rama was going to battle to defeat the demon who was destroying the place. To give himself the edge he decided to perform an offering ceremony, Chandi Pooja, to Durga. This blessing involved him having to find 108 blue lotus flowers to honor her with. However, he could manage to gather only 107 of the fragrant flowers. At a total loss where to find the final blue lotus flower, he hit upon an idea. Why not give one of his own lotus shaped blue eyes to the Goddess? Okay it's not a solution most of us would want to take up, but Rama obviously thought it was a good idea for give that blue eye of his he did. Durga was completely satisfied with his display of devotion, and proceeded to bless him. Backed by the blessings of the Goddess, Rama fought and won his battle.

Of course my brain got ticking. That familiar electrical jolt ran through my veins, as it did so a question began to form in my mind. Where did the blue lotus flower originate from? Some quick research led me to an unexpected find-Egypt. The blue lotus known scientifically Nymphaea caerule was originally found along the banks of the Nile and other parts of East Africa. I was also to discover that the blue lotus was actually a symbol of Upper Egypt. The home of Durga's Egyptian counterpart Sekhmet (the fierce Mother side of Hathor).

The electrical currents of my body jumped up and down. My head spun. Yet, another connection to Egypt between the same Goddesses. I inhaled deeply and felt a little calm settle over me. As it did so I decided to take a little break from my research to contemplate the findings that were unraveling themselves like gold dust before me. Holding her blue lotus up high, Durga knew this was a victory for herself and her origins. I rested in the glorious moment of the findings, just as Rama most probably had rested and basked in the warmth of his victory.

But the blue lotus symbol was not finished with me, its delightful fragrance filled the air, and grabbed me so that I could have a vantage look at Sekhmet and her twin warrior Egyptian sister Goddess Bast. When I saw Bast she was proudly showing of their son Neter Tem. It was as though he was ensuring that I really got the message for he was none other than - the Lotus and Blue Lotus God himself. He was the very world lotus flower that had arisen from the primordial waters of time, Nu. In fact, the ancient Egyptian "Book of the Dead" urges us all to,

"Rise like Nefertem from the blue water lily, to the nostrils of Ra (the creator and sun god), and come forth upon the horizon each day."

As I read these lines, I cannot help but see the vision of Nefertem rising higher and higher up to gloriously taking his place under the world sun. I see us taking our place under the sun with him. That is when I truly notice his mother Bast a little more. She is a woman of two forms. One that is connected to the cooling fertile energy of the moon. Here she is connected to fertility, children, nurturing of women and families. She is the quaint essential moon mother, who is closely aligned with the Moon God Khensu. In her second form Bast is closely connected to the heat of the sun where she is seen as the fierce warrioress.

Then as suddenly as the warm sunlight that falls on the scented petals of the blue lotus flower I see Kali, Durga's twin warrior sister, rise up strongly. Now her mystery seems solved. She shows me how her image of the fierce loving mother comes from none other than the mighty Bast herself in combination with Sekhmet.

598

Singing the Songlines

After the heady scent of the blue lotus filling the gaps in this long travelled journey I get my head down to finish the editing of this book. Derrick will laugh because this book has been finishing for the last few years. How do you finish something whose footsteps are the very journey you are travelling? I truly don't know, but as I bury my head into the editing something floats up and sings to the surface-. The Songline of the ancient Mothers. It is filled with movement, rhythm, form and the vibration of the universe swirling in on itself. Moved by the vision I see I am launched back in time to a dream I had where the Goddess was singing "Beautiful Waters". The memory moves me and begins to fill me up with the joy of its song. The words begin to spill over into actual existence. I need to share them with someone, and so I find Derrick in the lounge watching TV. The overflowing song blurts out,

"I have something to share with you."

Derrick switches the TV off, then I share what seems like an endless river that flows right from the center of my heart. I admit what came out was more like a monologue than a dialogue, but Derrick patiently listens,

"You know as I was editing the manuscript I realized something. That this book, this journey has traced the whole of human history and consciousness through the Mother's songs, symbologies and even dances. They became like the markers that made the connections. Like the beautiful voice of the Mother singing "Beautiful Waters" in my dream state. You know the one where she is singing those words. In that dream I could see the words floating down this glistening crystal clear river. They just bounced right down the waterways. My eyes followed the words, but I could not see to where they were going. In terms of history you know dates can get confusing, they can be off. But I have discovered that the ancient symbologies are there carved into the vibrating stone of existence. They are always there, even when we deny them. In them they hold our hidden story. I suppose it has dawned on me that this whole journey, this whole book that documents it follows the Mother's Songline. That's it, this is a Songline. I think I have heard that term in relation to the Aboriginal dreamtime, but I am not sure"

Derrick listens patiently, letting my words have the grace of tumbling over each other as they run ahead of my mind,and my spirit ahead of both. I begin to fumble with his ipad. I have the sudden urge to look up what Songline really means. Even if there was such a word. Then I find it. The word, and a perfect definition in good old Wikipedia. It made for fascinating reading. I read it out aloud,

Songlines, also called Dreaming tracks by Indigenous Australians within the animist indigenous belief system, are paths across the land (or, sometimes the sky) which mark the route followed by localised 'creator-beings' during the Dreaming. The paths of the songlines are recorded in traditional songs, stories, dance, and painting.

A knowledgeable person is able to navigate across the land by repeating the words of the song, which describe the location of landmarks, waterholes, and other natural phenomena. In some cases, the paths of the creator-beings are said to be evident from their marks, or petrosomatoglyphs, on the land, such as large depressions in the land which are said to be their footprints.

By singing the songs in the appropriate sequence, Indigenous people could navigate vast distances, often travelling through the deserts of Australia's interior. The continent of Australia contains an extensive system of songlines, some of which are of a few kilometres, whilst others traverse hundreds of kilometres through lands of many

different Indigenous peoples — peoples who may speak markedly
different languages and have different cultural traditions.

Since a Songline can span the lands of several different language
groups, different parts of the song are said to be in those different
languages. Languages are not a barrier because the melodic contour
of the song describes the nature of the land over which the song
passes. The rhythm is what is crucial to understanding the song.
Listening to the song of the land is the same as walking on this
Songline and observing the land.

I put the i pad down and say to Derrick, "You see that is what the Mother has done she has journeyed us through her Songline, helping us to navigate through difficult territory, across desert lands of history and consciousness, to awaken and enliven our earth,"

Fascinating stuff," he says.

"You should tell Ann about what has been revealed to you. You know because of the thing we are planning. That human chain around the waterways seems to actually be a Songline."

Now Ann Rosencranz is a beautiful spirit who recently entered our lives and this phase of the journey. One of the founders of the International Council of Thirteen Indigenous Grandmothers. A group of indigenous grandmothers from around the world who offer prayers and healing to the earth, whilst sharing their profound wisdom.

How we met Ann was a pretty astounding Dreamtime experience itself, but needless to say we met along the modern drumbeat of the internet, Skype, and through the will of the Mother. Spirit always knows best. Our initial meeting was suppose to be between her, one of the Grandmothers, myself and Derrick. The chat was to be about our ecological and earth healing journeys.

However, it didn't happen that way. Instead only Ann was available for a chat. We all came to realize that was exactly how it was suppose to be. For something very wonderful began to birth from our conversations. We didn't know what it was, however Ann and her lovely husband Bob showed us how to pray it into existence, the Native American way. Together, during the new moon, in different locations (us in South Carolina, them in California) we breathed in some tobacco smoke and held it in our mouths. Then we prayed for whatever was trying to birth itself to be revealed. With that the wispy body of the smoke was released into the cool night of the new moon. It was approximately one month later that the prayer seemed to work, and clarity began appearing through the fog, and the spirit of what was birthing made herself known.

She revealed what she was, just as Bob said it would. It was to be an international collaborative effort of offering prayers, and sacred dance to the earth, water, and humanity along the waterways of the world. With the sharing of the thoughts that had come to me about the Aborigine Songlines the spirit of what had birthed itself revealed that she wanted to be called WaterSongline. Our directive was to launch WaterSongline on an auspicious date, but what was that auspicious date to be?

Let's back track just a little bit. That night I spoke to Derrick about the Songline I remember deciding to paint something that would use the Aboriginal style of dot painting I had recently discovered. As soon as the baby was asleep I took out all my paints, got out the old battered blue folding table we

602

had, fetched my water and turned on the computer. I studied the ancient Aboriginal symbols in more depth. In their simplicity, I realized they weren't so simple after all. They told a complicated story about the land, its people, their relationship to it, and each other. Each symbol had a depth and richness to it like the acrylic paints I had sitting on my table.

As I studied the symbols some more, two of them struck me as looking familiar. I felt I had seen them somewhere before. One was a spiral of circles – the iconography for the waterhole around which people met, and the other was the symbol for a campfire – a kind of squiggly looking fella. Suddenly I felt I had seen those same images in the Adinkra family of images belonging to the Akan in Ghana. I decided to do some further research and there they were – the Adinkra symbols that resembled them. I had been guided well once again.

Aboriginal Symbols for waterhole and camp side

Ghanaian symbol for greatness (this is the chief of symbols), and supremacy

603

I decided to look at some other symbols and found a few more in common, although the meanings were different.

STAR

Ghana Moon and the Star symbol; Aboriginal star symbol

Aboriginal women's ceremony picture reminded me of the Ghanaian moon and star picture, but this symbol is upside down.

These similarities surprised me, and intuitively I felt as though I was looking at the same language, same symbols and same people. What was more when I was drawn to an aboriginal symbol which depicted the milky way I found a little surprise waiting for me when I read the website jintaart.com details about it.

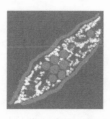

Aboriginal Milky Way symbol

The white patterning is the Milky Way.
The seven circles are the Seven Sisters and the one on its own is the
Jakamarra.

This icon tells about the Milky Way. The story is about the seven
sisters and the Jakamarra. Where ever the sisters went the Jakamarra
would always be with them. One day the sisters wanted to get rid of
the Jakamarra so they came down from the sky. They all walked
together from place to place and the Jakamarra was always with them
in the sky.

In winter, summer you could easily see the stars moving across along
the milky way traveling west. You could only see the stars in the
evening as they move along the Milky way.

Goose pimples erupted all over me like dreamtime hills - there was no mistaking that within the story of Milky Way was Hathor as the seven sisters. She was there as the Seven Sisters in association with herself as the Milky way. Riding the crest of my excitement I began my painting. Now on a You Tube video I learned that before doing an Aboriginal dot painting it was a good idea to write a simple story. So I did. I just let the thoughts flow on paper.

One day there were many people on Earth. Times started becoming very bad. No one knew what to do. So the people around the world decided to gather around the waterways. There the nations of all people began to sing. The water brought all the people together. The cosmic stars shone bright when they heard the singing. The heavenly waters danced and all the people on earth were happy again.

After writing the story my canvas began to fill up with ocean blues, sunflower yellows, and celestial white dots spiraling and cascading across the land and into the heavens. The orchestra of colors took about forty minutes to shape itself up. Finished I felt spent and tired and overcome by a strange feeling that the picture was painting me awake. As I held the it away from me I was struck at how much it looked like a blossoming cosmic mandala exploding its sweet nectar into the heavens. I got a nice thumbs up from Kem Ra and Derrick. It was Derrick who suggested that it should take its home above the TV. The logic being it would always remind us of the Dreamtime whenever we were at risk of forgetting about it.

As if my Book's Angel knew I was ready for the next thing, a couple of days latter Kem Ra was watching a documentary on TV which showed how mankind's history could be traced all the way back to Africa through his genes. It was part of a National Geographic project. I didn't get to see it all but what I did see was fascinating. To think that one could swab someone's cheek and trace their lineage back over thousands, and thousands and thousands of years. Led by synchronicity, as I lay on my hotel bed on our Charleston trip, I decided to idly Google African's in India as a dream floated in and out of my mind. I had it about two years ago. In it a young Indian girl showed me a copy of a very ancient book. I flicked through it noticing it had stories about the beginning of creation and all the laws of the universe.

I asked her, "what is this book?".

She replied, "this is the book they give us to study so we can know about the whole of creation."

I asked her the name of the book.

She replied, "The Book of the Gond".

I asked her if I could have a copy. She refused explaining there were only a few copies of the book left. When I woke up from the dream I decided to Google the word Gond, and low and behold there were a people in India called the Gond. On further research I discovered these people were supposed to be amongst the original indigenous inhabitants of India. Where they lived was apparently named after Gondwanaland. In one of the stories of their origins they are driven out of their home land by Indo – Aryans who overthrew the Gond Kings, whom they considered to be dirty and savage.

In Gond stories, the Gonds are Dravidians whom it is said that when their gods were born their mother abandoned them. The goddess Parvati rescued them, but her consort Sri Shambhu Mahadeo (Shiva) kept them captive in a cave. Pahandi Kapar Lingal, a Gond hero, who received help from the goddess Jangu Bai, rescued them from the cave. They came out of it in four groups, thus laying the foundations of the basic fourfold division of Gond society.

At that time I was truly surprised to find the royal spiritual couple Parvati and Shiva in that story. With those strong instincts that had guided me for five years I knew their appearance acted as a marker which connected the Gonds along mankind's spiritual lineage which seemed to stretch from Africa/Egypt, to India, Asia and Europe.

607

As this dream played on my mind in the hotel room, up came indigenous Africans from deep within cyber space. It was the Jawara people and others from India's Andaman Islands who apparently have been there for thousands of years. The Jawara, number 200 to 400 members now and have lived in the Andaman islands largely untouched by modern society. In my eyes I felt as though I was looking at some of the original inhabitants of India and Asia. For they resembled the bushmen and pygmies of Africa. Peter Bellwood, an Anthropologist at the Australian National University believes that these groups were the pre-Mongoloid of South East dating back some 6000 years back.

As I paused to contemplate these findings I thought – maybe here are those who helped to bring the first wave of ancient Egypt and Africa into the land of India. How much coincidence was it that they were connected to Parvati, who I had clearly shown was connected to the Goddess Hathor.

In the midst of my internet browsing and research the name of a Spencer Wells, is thrown up. He is the author of a book "The Journey of Man". After looking into the write up I thought it would be a good one to order. A few days after getting home from the trip I order the book and it promptly arrives. That is when I discovered "The Journey of Man" had been the name of the National Geographic documentary I had partially seen a few days back.

Not only was it the name of the documentary, the whole documentary was based on Spencer Well's work into the DNA of mankind. Once again the cosmos had managed to surprise me, and now I couldn't wait to dive right into the book in all its totality. It had me from its introductory opening,

"This is not a book on human origins. Rather, it is about the journey we have taken as a species, from our birthplace in Africa to the far corners of the earth".…."I would hope that this book might be a small step towards changing the field into what it really is – a collaborative effort between people around the world who are interested in their shared history."

I paused. Beautiful...beautiful.... As I read on I noticed that Wells said he had traced the human family tree through the male Y chromosome. I found this interesting for my own journey had traced the human family tree through the footsteps of the mother not the father, and therefore through the celestial X chromosome. But what I saw were the similarities not the differences. Both stories mirrored the journey of mankind.

Venus Transit – a cosmic birthday surprise

I sink down into my chair after reading Spencer Wells introduction and decide to idle my way through You Tube. As I do so I come across a sensational video by Dr. Wayne Dyer. It is about living an inspired life. The video is called "Inspiration". I am riveted all the way by his finely crafted presentation. He has me at every turn of word, especially when he decides to tell the story about himself and a Monarch butterfly that appears for a few brief hours in his life, just when he is finishing the last chapter of his book near his birthday. Dyer sees the appearance of the Monarch as a confirmation from the divine that his book is right on track, as these butterflies are indeed special renowned for their migratory and life cycle habits I too see it as a divine sign.

As I go to bed their flapping wings have me down on my knees in prayer.

"Momma could you send me something like that, you know an auspicious sign."

I shrugged my shoulders knowing that I would be so lucky. In the morning I wake up and check my e-mails. There's one by my brother Jeff. It is entitled: "Cosmic Birthday". Curiously I open and read it.

Sis it looks like you are going to have a Cosmic Birthday. Happy cosmic birthday in advance ☺

The rest of the words read,

On June 5th-6th 2012, a transit of Venus across the disk of the Sun takes place. Venus transits are very rare events which can be observed from much of the world, however since they involve viewing the Sun, extreme caution must be taken when attempting to observe them.

During a transit, Venus is seen as a small, black dot moving slowly in an East-to-West direction across the Sun. The transit commences on June 5th at 22:10 UT and ends on June 6th at 04:50 UT, with mid-transit taking place on June 6th at 01:29 UT. The total duration is about 6 hours 40 minutes, however because of the effect of parallax, the exact duration varies by ± 7 minutes depending upon the observer's location on Earth. The 2012 transit lasts 27 minutes longer than the previous one (June 8th 2004) because on this occasion Venus passed closer to the Sun's centre. In 2004 the planet transited the Southern hemisphere of the Sun; in 2012 it transits the Northern hemisphere of the Sun (see illustration below right).

I latter discovered that the Venus transits happen in pairs about 8 years apart. The last pair of Venus transits were 1631 and 1639, then 1761 and 1769, followed by 1874 and 1882 and then finally 2004 which was the opener to a pair which would occur in June 2012. The next event would appear in the next 150 years. Wow Jeff was right I was going to have an auspicious event for my birthday!

I ran back into the bedroom and jumped on top of Derrick who was lying on the living room floor.

"Sweetie guess what? Momma answered my prayers. She has given me a sign. I am going to have a cosmic birthday-the Venus Transit!!!!!!!!!!!!!!"

I explained to a puzzled Derrick how I had prayed for an auspicious sign that everything was on the right track. Just like Dr. Wayne Dyer had the Monarch butterfly come to him (I shared the story with him).

After we spoke we immediately spoke to Ann about the Venus Transit. The excitement grew and we all decided this would become the auspicious launch date for the WaterSongline and its first global prayer. Latter myself and Derrick discovered from an excellent astrologer Steven Nelson that this Venus Transit actually heralded in what astrologers were calling a new Super Venus, and feminine divine power. It was also bringing to a close the end of the Mayan fourth sun era which was to finally end on December 21st 2012.

Medicines to the Waters

Every night leading up to the Venus Transit, Venus actually shines through the diamond shaped window of our bed room. Every night her light virtually falls on our bed. She is the brightest planet resting on the celestial waters. It's hard not to feel blessed by her presence. Every day we feel more and more filled by her energy.

As her light fills our lives, I think about the overwhelming response to the global call to prayer we had.

The homemade trailer I did for the event received almost six thousand hits in just a few days. Individuals and groups began to send in their prayer ceremonies from all over the world. They deeply believed these ceremonies could help to ignite Mother Earth's Water Songlines.

Excitement filled me up, but so did sadness. For we strangely enough had no where to hold our ceremony in which I had been called to bring out Osun's Sacred Calabash for the first time since receiving it. Ironically our ceremony was seen as the central holding one for all the world prayers, Yet, we bizarrely had no idea where to hold it. We had initially thought that we could hold the ceremony at the Catawba Reservation, as we had done so in the past, but on this occasion that was not a possibility.

It was during one of my meditations that Osun had channeled to us how the global ceremony should go. We were to have everyone hold ceremony and pray with a sacred light by a body of water such as a glass, ocean etc. There were to be sixteen wisdom keepers from different locations of the world who would light sacred holding fires for the prayers. These sixteen sacred fires were to be represented in the form of sixteen candles that were to be placed at the central holding ceremony. These sixteen sacred fires were to represent the sixteen Wisdoms who first came and gave the Earth its laws. The honoring and of these primordial sixteen Wisdoms also happens at Osun's sacred annual river festival when sixteen lamps are lit for these Wisdoms.

I was to prepare medicines for the Sacred Calabash and then pour them into a waterways as an offering to the Mother for healing of the world's waters, and Mama Earth. So this is why I was sad. Osun needed a waterways for me to do such an important ceremony. Yet, Osun seemed to be an orphan

612

who could not find his/her parents. She had no waterways and that was a travesty.

In tears I sit at my Osun shrine where the Sacred Calabash rest.

"Mama I have no home for you I am so sorry. Mama how is this ceremony to happen when you have no home. I have no waters to put your medicines into. All these years you have said that we humanity have to propitiate you in mass. Now here is the opportunity to, and I have nowhere for your offerings. Mama you have to help me. I don't know what to do. Show me Mama where you want to go. Where you want your ceremony to be."

Filled with anguish I crawl into bed and fall asleep with Venus's light on my face. I wake up disappointed. I thought I would dream of something in relation to my appeal, but nothing. I drag myself to sit at Mama's shrine again. I sit in stillness allowing myself to sink deep into prayer, and meditation. Then I hear a voice say ever so softly,

"look for the Sacred Grove. Look in your copy of Natural Awakening."

I jumped out of my meditation. The Sacred Grove. The only Sacred Grove was the Sacred Grove I stayed at in Nigeria. The Sacred Grove that was re-built by her honorable Susan Wenger. The Sacred Grove where the Sacred Calabash came from. No there was no Sacred Grove to my knowledge anywhere near where we were.

However, on automatic and with a sense of urgency running through my body I quickly and obediently dig out my copy of Natural Awakening. I thumb through it. My heart falls. I cannot see any Sacred Grove. Then just as I am about to

613

close the magazine, I see something in a tiny box, in tiny letters that read, Sacred Grove Retreat.

I jump out of my skin, and jump up and down joyfully. Derrick's amusement. I explain in breathless excitement

"Sweetie, there is a Sacred Grove Retreat. Osun told me to look in Natural Awakening for a Sacred Grove. There is actually a Sacred Grove baby. What chance of that?"

Before he can answer my fingers tremble as they did the number I see, I am not sure what I am going to say to whomever picked up the phone. Doubting the person would even be receptive.

A sweet beautiful voice answers. The rest is history. Ellen Whiteside, the owner of Sacred Grove Retreat, fascinated by the story, said "yes" without any hesitation to hosting the ceremony. There was one catch. She had no river on her large property. Or let's put it this way-she had a creek that ran dry for most of the summer. She sincerely doubted there would be any water in the Creek for the ceremony. At first my heart fell, until she told me we could go to the Yadkin River nearby. A few hours it was settled. The ceremony would be held at the Sacred Grove Retreat.

June 5ᵗʰ, it's my birthday, and the famous Venus Transit. We all peered into the celestial waters of the sky. As we did so I remembered again how the ancient Egyptians called the waters of heaven the Heavenly Nile River, and also epitomized it as the Goddess Nut, whose whole body was often depicted as wrapped protectively around the world birthing the celestial bodies during the day and by night.

Now here we were staring into the sky waiting for Nut to reveal her daughter Venus transiting across her holy body, and the face of the awaiting glory of the Sun. We peered hard into the sky even though we knew already that from the vantage point of the Sacred Grove Retreat we would not be able to physically see Venus. Yet, there was something about just peering in divine reverence that made us almost feel as though we could see her. If not with our physical eye, but our Dreamtime eyes.

The energy was high as fifty or more of us gathered at the Sacred Grove to collectively bring our hearts, minds and powerful intentions for a healed future together. It was obvious that we were all acutely aware that we were making history. For thousands of people all around the world had decided that they would ignite the WaterSongline and send their prayers up to the divine sky.

As we stared with utter reverence into the sky, Robbie, the Fire Keeper, with big luscious red curls, stood by the flickering fire protectively tending it. Silence reigned as Derrick kept an eye on his watch waiting for 6 pm exactly. That was when he would give the signal, when the drums would boom, and our voices would collectively transcend cultural barriers and send prayers of all kinds to the milky river of the sky, Venus herself. Our feet would dance and massage Mother Earth. Once we were exhausted from giving praise we would light the sixteen candles around the big sacred fire Robbie had lit. Each one would be lit by a different person. Then we would throw cornmeal and tobacco into the big flickering of Robbie's fire just as she had directed us to do. With this gesture we would be throwing away our problems and calling in the positive outcomes of good intentions held.

All during that time Mama Osun would descend and settle her energy into the Sacred Calabash which sat in the small log cabin Ellen had allowed the family to stay in. The following day Mama Osun would then migrate into my body, as I carried her Sacred Calabash full of medicines and offerings for healing the waters, the Earth and Humanity – to the chosen river. As I did so, I was to remember the words of our sacred advisor in Nigeria,

"do not let your toes hit a stone, do not walk backwards on yourself, do not get angry."

If any of these things happened the ceremony and all the offerings given to the waters would be non and void. As we continued to peer into the dark celestial river, I prayed for Osun and the ancestors to keep on guiding the hearts, minds, and feet of humanity so that we would move together in the right direction. I thought of Vusamazulu Credo Mutwa, the Zulu Wisdom Keeper and Shaman whom I had spoken to many years ago, and then I thought of our most recent conversation where he agreed that he would join us in our global prayer.

I tried to visualize himself and his faithful wife and fellow Shaman Virginia praying around the nine candles they said they would send their intentions from. Nine because it represented birth.

"You know in times of crisis my people believe you must go as a collective to the Beautiful Mother. We see ourselves as her children, and we believe that when we pray she hears our cries. She squeezes her milk of peace upon our heads. This is how she answers our prayers. We visualize her as a bed of peace with a rainbow over it."

I asked the question,

"Baba do you really think that this global prayer can really make a difference?"

He replied, "Yes of course. I have seen in my lifetime these kinds of prayers answered."

"5, 4, 3, 2, 1," Derrick's counting interrupted my thoughts. Venus was ready to begin her most holiest of dances. The drums thudded awake, the singing and prayers began.

The following day after the fire ceremony, it was raining hard outside. I was all alone in the cabin, on my knees praying to Mama. Derrick, and the rest of the family had left me to be with Osun, and to allow her to be with me.

The floor was slightly chilly beneath me, but I persevered with my prayers and offerings. I paused for a while and listened to the torrential down pour of the rain. A deep despair and dichotomy filled me. I knew that rain was a blessing from the Mother so I was happy for it. She was present and giving her seal of approval. Yet, I also knew it would be hard for the water ceremony and offering to go ahead. For no one liked to stand in rain, especially a thunderous down pouring.

I saw a vision of me, the Sacred Calabash, and Derrick standing in the pouring rain, by the river all alone. The scene seemed so lonely. That was not how I wanted this historic event to go down. My heart fell. Maybe, that is how the ancient spirits wanted it to be. Who was I to question how they arranged things, I always found out their arrangement was always for the best anyway. Yet, even so I still wanted the event to be a full on lively offering. I mean we were not going to see another Venus Transit for a long time.

I finished my prayers poured a small amount of the water onto the floor, drank some and said Ashe. I arose of my knees and looked down at the clear glass of water astonished at how lively it looked. I gazed steadfastly at the Sacred Calabash. She too looked alive dressed in a lush deep purple

617

embroidered peacock cloth. The feathers of the peacock seemed to jump out and dance in iridescent yet tasteful glory.

Despite the dancing energy filling the room up, I was still disappointed. It was still raining cats and dogs. Strange there had been no rain forecast for that day, and the last few days had been hot. I began to pace the small space of the room in hesitant steps. I was not sure what else to do. I briefly looked at the yellow dress I had made especially for the occasion. Yellow was Mama's special healing color. My attention soon focused back on the rain beating down above my head. The heaviness of my heart grew with each rain drop. Then just as I was about to fall into the pit of despair I heard a clear voice say,

"pray for the rain to stop. Isn't that the gift that was given to you? Why don't you use it now?"

"that's silly," I said back loudly knowing no one could hear me but the rain.

"Why is it silly, why don't you just try?" the voice said.

I resisted for a moment and then shrugged my shoulders. A try was worth better than nothing. I had made the rain stop once in Africa when it had been pouring down like this and I had to get home. I had made it stop and start on many other occasions. Despite this, I still doubted the gift but it had worked each and every time. I doubted it would work this time if I prayed to Mama. Even through this disbelief I got back down on my knees and prayed,

"Mama you know all these people have come to receive your blessings. Mama you know we have to put the medicines into the waters to help your waters, the world and all the living things on Earth. Mama this is the right time to do it. Mama I know the rain is a blessing from you, but Mama can you please let it stop now so that the ceremony can go on. Mama if the rain doesn't stop then the ceremony won't be able

618

to go on in the same way. I will have to, with Derrick, walk and be soaked by the rain. I don't want to drop the Sacred Calabash Mama. That would be disastrous. Then all the ceremonies all over the world and their offerings won't be accepted Mama. Please Mama, let the rain stop."

I truly didn't expect anything to happen, but as I sat on the bed feeling forlorned I noticed that the rain seemed to start falling lighter. Half an hour later the rain completely stopped. It was exactly three or so hours before the ceremony was due to start.

At first I thought it was my imagination, so I strained my ears. I could hear no rain. I continued to listen expecting to hear something, but there really was nothing. The rain had stopped. Mama had stopped the rain.

I began to jump up and down, the floor boards creaked under the strain. A knock stopped me mid-stream in my jumping.

"sweetie can you come to the door for a second," Derrick said.

I opened the door for him and beckoned him in.

"I don't know what happened but the rain stopped, so that is good news. Also Ellen has asked if the ceremony can be done at the Creek on her property. You know the Creek was bone dry yesterday, and that she said it is normally bone dry throughout the whole summer. Well, guess what? the rains have filled that Creek right up. It is running just like a river."

"Wow!" was all I could manage. Explaining to him that I had prayed to Mama for the rain to stop.

"Thought so," he said not surprised at all. Not much did surprise him.

"Do you think we can do the ceremony by the creek, instead of going to the actual Yadkin river? The Creek actually empties into that river."

619

"I don't know. Remember we had been told that Osun will be waiting for us at whatever river we chose. We are not just going to the river, we have actually made a date with her. She will be there for the date and time specified."

"Well can you just pray on it and then check with the divination tools?" Derrick insisted.

I didn't really want to, but eventually I caved in. After praying I checked the oracle, and the answer was yes it was good fortune to move the ceremony to the property. We both hugged tightly. I actually felt relieved. The rain had stopped and I did not have to walk for a long distance with the weight of the Calabash filled with offerings and medicines on my head.

Osun had descended. I sat swathed in yellow with the Sacred Calabash on the bed besides me wrapped in its indigo finery. Derrick knocked on the door. I rose, and gingerly placed Osun on my head (as traditionally it is said she sits in the Sacred Calabash, as well as the person). Derrick gently took me by the elbow, and we began to walk towards the Labyrinth where everyone was waiting, including a peace pole in its center, and doves for releasing.

I walked carefully on the grass being sure not hit my toe on anything, as specified by the rules. I held the Sacred Calabash tightly so that she would not fall. As we walked into the blazing sunlight that had arisen from the previous rains, I could hear the drums rolling ahead of me, accompanied by the haunting sound of Native American flutes. I could only see the swishing of the hem of my dress and my toes moving forward. The weight of the Sacred Calabash kept my eyes lowered. I relied solely on Derrick for guidance on where to place my next steps. As we entered the labyrinth I could only see shoes of many different types. I was placed near the peace pole. Once stationery I allowed my head to raise a little, and was moved by the intense reverence of the many faces present. My neck felt as though it would break, as the weight of the Sacred Calabash began to crush me. Despite this I stood as serenely as I could through all the prayers and glorious releasing of the white doves who circled gracefully high in the sky in circles above our heads.

I did not buck my toes on the way to the creek which was a good thing, as there were big big stones everywhere. I did not drop any contents of the Sacred Calabash which was also a good thing. Once at the creek's boisterous waters the drumming and singing began again. The group seemed to enjoy the song Ashe Osun. It was one that Osun loved too. The repetitive lyrics of the song that praised the mother as Queen of the universe and waters allows one to build emotional momentum. As we did so the air filled with charged zeal. Whoooooooohhhhhhh. A large conch shell horn punctuated the air with this eerie sound. As the singing continued I began to propitiate the waters, carefully placing the offerings and medicines in.

I was touched as one woman poured a 10 gallon bottle of water in the creek, containing waters she had gathered from sacred rivers from all over the world gathered from a ten year journey.

The singing reached a crescendo. Whoooooohhhhh, the large conch shell horn continued to awaken the air. Then a pain began deep in my abdomen, ceasing me as it released a terrible wailing into the air. I could not stop it even if I had wanted to. It curled and unfurled itself doubling me over, almost toppling me into the moving waters of the Creek.

Derrick caught me in time. Osun was more fully in me now. She had met us at the Creek, as she had promised she would do. The blessings of water that flowed from the now empty Sacred Calabash seemed endless onto the heads of queues of awaiting people.

I was moved by how Mama Osun, as the great Mother Mother, in all her other worldly wonders had weaved so many cultures, people, and ways together into one global prayer. As I went on to bless the next person, Robbie, the Fire Keeper, I marveled once again at how powerful the Dreamtime was in its ability to merge in and out of our material existences.

It was when Robbie, the Fire Keeper, arrived for her blessing, and I bent to scoop water into the Sacred Calabash that I noticed we had company. A white baby poisonous moccasin snake which rested cozily next to the side of my stomping dancing feet. I froze. Looked up at Robbie and managed to squeeze out the word,

"snake."

My eyes travelled back down to where the snake lay. Her eyes followed mine. We both looked back up at the same time and said in hoarse unison,

"snake!"

I had to make a decision. Was I to run the hell out of those healing waters or stay? I sensed if I ran then the magic of the moment would be broken. I decided to stay. If Mama was with me then I would be fine. Everyone would be fine. The snake would not bite me, or anyone else. I stayed for another half an hour in the waters, and the snake stayed cozily at the side of my foot for the whole duration.

Post event Derrick freaked out when I told him the story of the snake.

"If I had known about it I would have dragged you the hell out!" he exclaimed horrified.

622

"I know," I said quietly. "But you know I thought that the snake is a symbol of the Mother. So it must be a good sign. It did test my faith though. I mean I was like, well Mama if you are not really here then I am in TROUBLE!"

We both laughed loudly.

If June 5th and 6th was loud and spiritually boisterous then June 10th was quieter, as Venus rose at sunrise to join her husband the Sun in the East of the heavenly river, as the Morning Star. We would no longer see her beaming light shining through our bedroom window which faced the West. As we prayed this thought saddened me. Yet, her move was important for soon in December 21st she would rise as the Bennu Bird, the feathered serpent to usher in the Age of the Water Bearer, Aquarius, and the Mayan fifth sun era. According to Mythic Astrologer Steve Nelson in June 10th she brought in a whole New Earth Plan. One that would be fully revealed in the new dawning of civilization.

It was the night after Venus rose to take her place in the watery regions of the Eastern horizon that I had this dream.

A spiritual teacher appeared in a classroom before myself, Derrick and a few others. He said,

"You have all received the messages of the Mother but people are still not listening. You all have done this much work,"

He pointed on a chart to visually indicate a shaded part that showed how much work we had accomplished.

"However, you all still have this much work to do to awaken the lotus flower."

He pointed to the unshaded part of the chart which was much larger in proportion to the shaded part. Then flipped the page on his presentation board and pointed to reveal a spectacular picture of a deep blue lotus flower in full bloom

16 sacred lights for the WaterSongLine
Lighting of the Lights Ceremony

Me praying and about to pour medicines
for healing world waters from Sacred Calabash. Picture copyright,
Episode XI Studio

*Me with Chief Holy Eagle, Derrick
and other participants of Venus Transit Ceremony*

*The lady with the glasses on is looking at ten year
of sacred water she collected from rivers all over the world
being poured into Creek
For Venus Transit Ceremony*

WEAVING IN THE LOSE ENDS

One month after the big Venus Transit Celebration and WaterSongline Water Ceremony I was tired. All I wanted to do was finish of the neglected weaving in my loom. It looked at me from the crooked angle I held it at. I was examining my unfinished piece of weaving which I had started but not completed. There were rows of warm yellows, sunset oranges, and rejuvenating greens climbing up the wefts, but they stopped just half way through the journey. They needed completion, I could see that; and in their completion I felt I would find some peace.

So I began weaving again. Albeit hesitantly it had been some time since I had picked up the loom. Beth, a master Navajo weaver, I had recently met, had taught me to weave the Navajo way over the island curry, pasta, and garlic bread I had prepared for her.

Restarting the weaving was not as bad as I thought it was going to be. The threads joined and bound tightly together easily. My fingers moved in and out of the wefts. My shoulders relaxed, and I leaned back to enjoy the experience of colors becoming patterns, becoming something beautiful.

I thought about Changing Woman, a lot as I weaved and the many conversations Beth had shared with me about her. I suppose that was natural, as Changing Woman was the one who had gifted the beauty of weaving to the Navajo. The more I thought about her was the more I realized that Changing Woman had come to help me weave together the loose ends of history. That was her gift to me and humanity, and I was forever grateful to her.

I was soon to discover that weaving in the loose threads was an art in itself. If not done correctly what seemed beautiful could be totally ruined. I knew from the few loose threads that attempted to poke themselves out of my work.

The more Beth told me about Changing Woman, and the more I researched her, was the more I realized one of the gifts she came with was to weave the circle of the Mothers and therefore humanity in tighter. For I began to realize very quickly that Changing Woman was none other than the Egyptian Goddess Hathor and the composite that she travelled with from her lands.

In fact Changing Woman's name seemed to smile down at me teasingly. Speaking to the truths of the great Mother's ability to revive herself in our times, actually in any time that she needs to. Asdzaa Nadleehe "She Who Rejuvenates Herself" was her very traditional name.

According to Navajo legend Changing Woman is seen as the Great Mother that appeared before the First People from the Fifth World disappeared. In these first times she was called Asdzaa Nadleehe "She Who Rejuvenates Herself". She created the Native American, Dine (Navajo). They became the heirs to the spiritual legacy of the first people.

To help the world Changing Woman also created a sacred medicine bundle which was based on the prototype that had been made by her guardian step parents, First Man and First Woman. This medicine bundle was like a sacred tool kit that would help the Dine (Navajo) keep the world in Beauty. Now this last thing is very important for the Navajo live their whole life by the laws of Hozho "Walking in Beauty" that Changing Woman lay down. Even their government and judicial system are laid on the foundation of these laws.

Right there in Hozho "Walking in Beauty" I could clearly see the laws of the ancient Egyptian laws of Maat, which later became translated as Dharma in India. For these laws in Egypt governed the very breath you took. Every King,

628

Queen, God, Goddess and normal civilian followed those laws.

Changing Woman had many forms which represented the various seasons, cycles and energies of Mother Earth. These forms also spoke very clearly to the many selves of the Goddess Hathor. I could see Hathor in Changing Woman's form as White Shell Woman, who symbolizes the full power of the noon day sun and the early aspects of our lives; Turquoise Woman who shares with us the full bloom of summertime of life and womanhood; Abalone Shell Woman, who talks to us about the autumn of life; Black Jet Woman who represents the wintery nighttime.

The more of herself she revealed to me, is the more I also saw a very well-known version of Hathor in Changing Woman - Net/Neith. Net was the Mother Goddess who wore the weaving shuttle on her head. Her epithets aptly referred to her as "Opener of the Way" and "One Who Weaves".

One day I decided to do one of my comparative analyses between Changing Woman and Hathor.

✓ **Hathor, Changing Woman and Turquoise:** One of Changing Woman's names is Turquois Woman. Hathor was associated turquoise. Her Sycamore Tree in the Land of the deceased is constructed from Turquoise. Her Menit, a protective amulet worn by God, Goddess, King's and Queens alike was also made from Turquoise

✓ **Various Forms:** Changing Woman is connected to weaving, Hathor is also associated with weaving through her personification as Net. As White Shell Woman, Changing Woman was seen as the Light of dawn in this role she governed the beginning of life, and the fertile stages of womanhood. In one of Hathor's epithets she is called the "Goddess of Light". She, like Black Jet Woman, governs the power of woman hood, fertility, child bearing. Changing Woman governed the Winter of the seasons of life. The last hours of life. This role of Hathors is seen through her name Khnemet-ankh which means, "last hour of the night."

✓ **Changing Woman Walking in Beauty:** Changing Woman gave to the Navajo the laws of balance and walking in beauty. So too did Hathor through her form Maat give to the Egyptians the ancient law of Maat.

✓ **Married to the Sun:** Changing Woman was Married to the Sun God; so too was Hathor, who was married to Ra.

I decided to share my findings with Beth, for I had a question for her.

"Beth you know that you mentioned that you read a book that connected the Navajo and Tibetan cultures, did that book say who Changing Woman was connected to?"

I asked this question for a reason. For I had already connected Hathor to the Tara of Tibet. I wondered if Changing Woman had any connection to Tara. If that was the case then the circle was closed. The Native American Mother would have helped to close the circle by placing her people in the hoop of nations.

"Oh you mean the book I read, "Circle of the Spirit" by Peter Gold. That's a good book," she enthused as I held my breath for the answer. "He connected Changing Woman to Tara," she revealed.

Was it by coincidence of cosmic design that a few days after Changing Woman had revealed her gift that the Goddess Tara floats up from the pages of an Exotic India essay smiling with a blue lotus in her hand.

Green Tara Holding Blue Lotus Flower
Nepal, fourteenth century.

Goddess Net/Neith with weaving shuttle on head

CHANGING WOMAN STILL WEAVING THE LOOSE ENDS

It was a few months after the Venus Transit, and the sea air was getting cool. The waters of Myrtle Beach once again lapped gently over my feet. I felt happy that we had been able to visit the oceans more than once for the year. Refreshed I headed back to the hotel room as I followed the urge to quickly delve back into Spencer Well's "Journey of Man".

Once again I was impressed by Well's research. I wondered what had inspired him to take on such a monumental task. To catch the Golden Ball so to speak. He shows how the journey of mankind is really one of water, that saw us migrate from the bosom of Africa to other lands. We came from ancestors who according to Wells "would have been fully modern in every respect-technologically, culturally, and artistically".

The water journey he traces through the Y Chromosome sees our ancestors travelling along coastal routes from Sudan, Ethiopia, and Southern Africa into the Middle East, India, SE Asia, Australia and Europe. This water route was, he explains, like a "pre-historic superhighway, allowing a high degree of mobility without requiring the complex adaptations to a new environment that would be necessary on an inland journey."

The fact that water was constantly talking to us, mirroring our history and connecting us back together could not fail to have me always fascinated.

I leapt of my chair in joy when my deepest intuition and findings were confirmed by Wells, that Africans had been the first inhabitants of India, in the form of the Dravidians of South India. For hadn't the journey revealed to me that the

633

Indian Goddesses and Gods who retraced our footsteps were Dravidian?

Well's explains that from North Eastern Africa a group of people travelled South and into India. The first wave of these peoples travelled from this region some 30,000 years ago. Their genetic marker is found at an extremely high frequency of over 50% in India's Southern population, the Dravidians - who also have a language that is completely unrelated to the Indo-European language family. This particular marker is not found much outside of India.

In an article I latter discover, "We are All Africans Under the Skin". Wells is interviewed by an India publication, Rediff. The article begins with an open paragraph,

"On a recent visit to Madurai and New Delhi to find out more about the origins of Indian ancestors, Dr. Wells said he found genetic evidence to show that the Dravidians were the first settlers in India from Africa and the Aryans followed later."

In that interview Well's says,

"The experiments were regarding the early coastal migration of human beings to Australia. Because according to our theory, the first time man migrated from Africa was to Australia. India proved a critical turning point for us as genetic testing of isolated Indian populations produces a key genetic marker (one of the genetic changes) linking India as a crossroads for the journey of man to both Australia and Central Asia. So we were looking in the south of India because most Indian scientists said that the oldest population in India stayed in south India. And we found in our experiments that these people were Dravidians."

The interviewer asks,

"But some people claim that the Aryans were the original inhabitants of India. What do you have to say about this?"

Wells replies,

"I don't agree with them. The Aryans came later, after the Dravidians"..."We are much closely related than we ever expected. Racism is not only socially divisive, but also scientifically incorrect. We are all descendants of people who lived in Africa recently. We are all African under the skin".

Well's backs up his claims by reconfirming that the great Dravidian cities of places such as Mohenjo-Daro were striving around 3500 BC. Then around 1500 BC they entered into a period of decline which many archeologists say seem to be the result of an Indo Aryan invasion. The evidence of this invading force is found in the Rig Veda.

He divulges that through DNA evidence it appears that there was indeed a second wave of movement into India from not North Eastern Africans who had settled in the Middle East, but Indo Aryans who came from Southern Russia. The Indo Aryan marker found in India (which he says is consistent with a marker which shows European origin) is highest amongst Hindi speaking populations such as New Delhi, and other Indo-European speaking groups from the South. However, the Indo-Aryan marker is lowest amongst Dravidian speakers. Which leads Well's to claim,

"this strongly suggests that M17 is an Indo European marker, and shows that there was a massive genetic influx into India from the steppes within the past 10,000 years. Taken with the archeological data, we can say that the old hypothesis of an invasion of people not merely their language-from the steppe appears to be true."

As I read his findings I could almost see the Dancing Girl of Mohenjo-Daro teasing me with her smile, laughing, and

635

saying, "see I told you so". As she did so I closed the book to rest my eyes. I could hear the ocean roaring. As I drifted asleep I thought of the Adinkra symbols of Ghana again, and how much like the Australian Aborigine ones they were. It all made sense to me now. I wrapped the blanket tighter around my body, as the chill began to creep into my bones. I wondered if the Goddesses were pleased with what they had accomplished – mending the river of our humanity. I thanked Mama Osun, an African celestial Eve for being the Rosette Stone that had actually allowed for all the rivers to be joined back together. I thanked all the Goddesses, and Changing Woman for weaving in the many loose ends.

Sleep engulfed and pulled me in deeper, as too did the memory of reading once that Parvati said she would not rest until her children the Gond (who are a nation of Dravidians) were remembered again. I wondered if she too was pleased that the gaping seeping wound in history had been closed once and for all, and our waters could flow undammed again.

It seemed as though Changing Woman was still busy weaving in those loose ends. For when I got home I just could not rest until I looked at an old map of Africa. I think I was triggered to do so after reading about the journey of man. Suddenly some key symbols from Ancient Egypt such as the Lotus and vulture began to float around in my head. I began to even think about the Tibetan celestial city Meru and the Hindu Kush mountains. Then I thought of Sati, and the Lion Goddess Sekhmet. I could not help but realize all of these reoccurring symbols came from Southern Egypt.

Derrick managed to help me locate an old map of Ancient Egypt. Immediately I noticed that the Egypt we think of today is not quite the Egypt of the past. Egypt then included Upper (Southern) and Lower (Northern) Egypt. Southern Egyptian territory was seen as todays Nubia Land which includes present day Sudan. It was considered to be the Kushite Empire. Ethiopia was also part of this empire. Egypt had many powerful Nubian rulers.

I found the city Meroe to be of great interest. It was a very important Kushite city with over forty Kings and Queens buried there. Meroe, was known as The City of the Gods. It had become internationally powerful as a result of knowledge of iron smelting and manufacturing. As a result it had extensive trade with India, East Asia and the rest of the world.

Now I began to do some mental spiritual arithmetic. It couldn't be a coincidence that the Meroe of Southern Egypt was called "The City of the Gods", and the Meru of the Tibetan cosmological system was also known as the "City of the Gods". The place where the Gods dwelt. Also history showed that Meroe had a lot of contact and trade with India. Plus, the two cities were pronounced the same.

I did some more spiritual calculations. The Kushite Empire of Nubia Land had actually ruled Egypt from 760 BC and 660 BC. They were the last of the indigenous Egyptian Kings to rule Egypt. Their rule was followed by that of the Persians and Greeks. Both these cultures travelled into India which is when I believe a second cultural renaissance of Egyptian spirituality happened there. Also it could not be a coincidence that India had a place called the Hindu Kush, and Southern Egypt had a Kingdom called the Kushite Empire. Or that the word and concept Naga existed in Hinduism and Tibetan cultures while also being the name for the ancient Ethiopian people. It was also their word for "King". I discovered that in Tibetan culture Naga was the name for water snake beings and also for a mysterious royal person.

637

The ball of wool now would not stop unraveling. The rivers flowed rapidly and carried me on the wave of their head waters. For my mind now went back to an earlier fact I had discovered. It involved a man from 522 BC. His name was Guamata. He had been responsible for getting rid of Cambyses, the Persian conqueror of Egypt. Herodotus claimed that Guamata was a Nubian King. They say that Guamata was killed. However, had he been killed? For I had one of my bingo moments and remembered part of the Buddha's name was Gautama. It was virtually impossible not to notice the spellings of the two names were more or less the same (the only difference being the endings seemed switched around).

When I had checked out the Buddha's birthdate I discovered that the Cambridge and Oxford histories of India accept 483 B.C as the date of Buddha's nirvana. He was 80 years old when he died, so his birth year was placed at 563 BCE. So in my mind's eye it was highly likely that these two men were the same. At the time I could not help but think of Buddha's elongated earlobes and discovered that these elongated earlobes were traditionally found in the Ethiopian Mursi and Kenyan Masai peoples.

Then there was the fact that the Tibetans say that their first ancestors came from a union with a monkey God and Tara. The Monkey God is seen as non-other than the Buddha Chenrezig. I had come across this information midway through my journey and had found it interesting that Hathor had been seen as the wife of Ra and Toth (in her form as Maat, and Mehurt, the Wisdom Goddesses). Toth was actually personified as either an Ibis or a baboon. I had connected Tara, Hathor, and their male counterparts (Ra, Osiris, Chenrezig) together. Now I could clearly see that Toth was in the mix too. He was seen as the author of many spiritual books including the famous "Egyptian Book of the Dead". I had shown a clear correlation between this book and the "Tibetan Book of the Dead". Toth was also closely associated with Ra. Budge says,

"Toth was regarded as a god who self-begotten and self-produced, that he was One, that he made the calculations concerning the establishing of the heavens, and the stars, and the earth, that he was the heart of Ra."

Therefore it had become clear to me that the first spiritual ancestors of the Tibetans have identified themselves for themselves, from their own mythological origins, as having their origins in Egypt and their revered deities Hathor/Isis and Toth/Osiris. What I had found of further interest as I thought of this connection was that the Dalai Lama states that the beautiful Kalachakra ceremony he conducts for world peace and harmony originated from the Ra lineage.

His Holiness the fourteenth Dalai Lama explains on his website the founding of the Kalachakra,

The Kalachakra continued to be transmitted through the succession of kalkis ("chieftains") of Shambhala, and eventually it was reintroduced into India. There are two main stories of how this came about, the story told by the Ra tradition and the story of the Dro tradition. (The Ra tradition and the Dro tradition will be discussed below).

According to the Ra tradition, the Kalachakra and related commentaries famed as the Bodhisattvas Corpus appeared in India during the simultaneous reigns of three kings. Taking Bodh Gaya as the center, the three kings were: Dehopala, the Master of Elephants, in the East; Jauganga, the Master of Men, in the South; and Kanauj, the Master of Horses, in the West. At that time the great pandit Cilu, who mastered all aspects of the Buddhadharma, was born in Orissa, one of the five countries of eastern India. Cilu studied all the Buddhist texts at the Ratnagiri Vihara, Vikramashila, and Nalanda.

In particular, he studied at the Ratnagiri Vihara that was undamaged by the Turks.

Cilu realized that, in general, in order to achieve buddhahood in a single lifetime he would need the Mantrayana, and in particular, that he would need the clarifications of these doctrines contained in the Bodhisattva commentaries. Knowing that these teachings were extant in Shambhala, and depending on the instruction of his deity, he joined up with traders who sought jewels in the ocean. Having agreed with the traders, who were setting out across the sea, to meet up after six months, they went separate The

These are not discoveries that I had gone hunting for. They are ones that had made their way to my doorstep. As such, I wondered if the River of Dharma was trying to desperately rush towards the fountain of its original spring. They say when the source of a river dies the entire river dies don't matter how mighty it is. I figured maybe the dharma did not want to die. Its waters needed to be honored, renewed, and refreshed.

Elated and exhausted with my nights findings. I wanted to quickly have a peak at Hathor's beautiful lotus headdress again. The one I had seen in Budge's "Gods of Egypt. I love the way it reminded me of the blossoming of a New Dawn and how we were fast approaching with December 21st 2012.

Instead what I found was something to do with the Apis Bull. The section of the Apis Bull was very short. Short enough for me to skip over it. But I didn't. I discovered that the Apis Bull was seen as an embodiment of Osiris, and was considered to be a God.

Suddenly a deep curiosity filled me. I was sure I was going out on the limb of a wild thought, but what was new? I wanted to know if Shiva had such a sacred animal connected to him. If I had connected Shiva and Osiris together, it could be possible that the bull did too. I was quite surprised that right there in the iconography of Shiva, there was a bull, Nandi the bull, the Shiva's mount. Nandi's stories clearly showed him to be a sacred embodiment of Shiva. Wow. What a beautiful find. A deep joy fanned its peacocked feathers over me filling my cup till it runneth over.

I did not miss the fact that the Apis bull was identified by a white mark the shape of the crescent moon; and his Indian twin, the Nandi bull, was an embodiment of Shiva, the God with the Crescent moon on his forehead. It was also very noticeable in a somewhat poetic way that both these sacred bulls from different continents and cultures were both seen as the guardians of the abodes of peace and enlightenment.

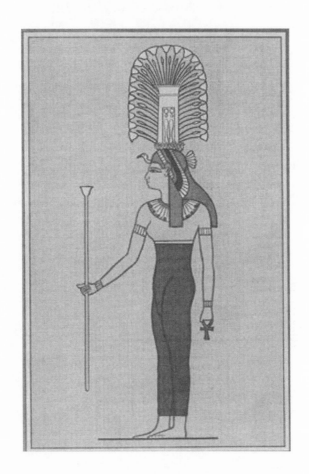

Hathor with Lotus Headdress

Nandi

Apis, the Sacred Bull of Osiris

Does the face of Buddha have the last symbolic say? Smiling Buddha face, Bayon Temple, Angkor Wat Temple Complex, Cambodia. Amongst oldest statutes of Buddha

The Last Dreams, the Book Inspector Signs Off

That night I dreamt I had two dreams. The first is a short one of an old beautiful Chinese woman, who owns an exquisite hotel where myself and Derrick are staying. After making polite conversation with her we head to our hotel room. As we say our goodbyes. She smiles and says sweetly,

"We all meet together, eventually, always."

In the second dream,

I was at home and this man came to visit me. A middle aged white man. He seemed to be some kind of Book Inspector. He had come to check my book notes and findings. He carefully went through my folder that was bulging at the seams. And he kept on saying
"Uh Huh, Uh Huh, Uh Huh."
Then after quite some time he turned to me and said,
"Everything is in order. That's good, very good, very good You've done a very very good job."
I smiled the biggest smile, thanked him and replied,
"Oh I am glad because that was hard work!"
Then he left and soon after he left a younger more plump white man arrived. He seemed to be someone I had seen before. He said he was here to actually do the final signing off on my work - if he found everything to be in order.
I told him,
"the other guy just came, carefully went through all my notes and said everything is in good order."
The guy then replied,
"that is good, very good."
Then he seemed kind of agitated and said,

"Omi I want you to know that I am the one who during this whole time had helped you get your notes and stuff together in the right order."

I genuinely didn't know, and thanked him profusely.

He then went to a part of my house where there was a hidden piece of paper on the wall. It was divided into about ten grids. Each one, but one, had a signature on it. It seemed that he had been signing the grid over a period of time. Each box seemed to represent different stages of completion for my book.

He went to sign the final box. As he did so he said,

"Once I sign this paper you won't be seeing me again. This signature means everything is finished and I do not need to come around anymore. You will no longer need my help again"

With that he signed the last box.

"Oh, thank you!" I said, so pleased that everything was done and over with.

As soon as I opened my eyes in the morning, I said to Derrick with a big smile,

"Sweetie, it's finished. I just got signed of in my dreams. "

FINALLY

THE AFTER FOREWORD

December 21st 2012, we watch the sun rise in the East. We know Venus just rose before it. For some reason the orange glow of the sun fills the sky up more gloriously than ever before. I hold my breath as we stare out of the window, it is the breaking of a new dawn, and new era.

Derrick wraps me tight in his embrace. It is hard to imagine that we are living in the midst of history. The end of a 5000 year Mayan Calendar and Earth astrological cycle. Some people believe it is the end of the world. Yet, it is clear from what the ancients said that it is not so much the end of the world in a drastic way. It is more the end of one age and the beginning of another. What marks our destiny is the road we choose to follow. It is for us to choose the world we wish to create. If we do so correctly the ancient prophecies say we will enter one thousand years of peace.

But, what is there to choose from? If we think there are only two true motivating emotions - hate or love. Then the choice is really between the two. Choosing the road of love is what I suppose the Hopi would call the long road for humanity. The good road.

As I watched the sun rise, I thought about the thousands of people all over the world who would be engaged in prayers for a better humanity. This was a good feeling. I also thought about the medicines I would once again put in the waters from the Sacred Calabash on behalf of the waters and Earth for the WaterSongline's Lighting of the Lights Ceremony: The Return of the Light.

Then I thought of the words in a recent discussion with Vusamazulu Credo Mutwa who said he would pray with the global WaterSongline,

"man was not made for war he was made for peace. We need to focus on the things that unite us, rather than the things that divide us."

I felt moved by our conversation especially since he strengthened my conviction that global prayers were important and necessary in these times.

"Myself and the Shamans of South Africa see a terrible terrible thing coming for humanity. Only a global prayer will avert it."

The terrible thing he, and they saw was a war. One that would cover the whole of Africa, some of South America and it would affect the entire world. Vusamazulu Credo Mutwa was so distressed by this vision that he wanted the conversation we had to somehow be shared with the Dalai Lama. I promised him I would, and I did. At least I managed to send the message to his office. Whether he ever received it or not was yet still to be seen.

The sun filled the sky more fully now, which now looked as though God had painted it bright dusty orange. As I watched it reach its zenith I truly wondered what was going to happen to us. I wondered if we were going to hear the messages from the waters. Its plea for a more compassionate oneness of heart.

"I remember when the Dalai Lama came to South Africa, and he told me we are all one. Those are words that ring in my ears and heart still. I will take them to my dying bed," Baba Mutwa had said adding, "we need to pray to the Great Mother to fill our hearts with love. We need to give sincere apologies to her. We need to look in each other's eyes and forgive each other. This is the only way forward".

Yes, we are all one, I thought. Hadn't this incredible journey shown us that what we see as many streams are all in fact one Mother River. I thought once more about the incredible ability of water to hold consciousness, and to tell the story of our sacred journey from the beginnings of time. The First Times. How water had such celestial and mysterious properties I did not know. How my one prayer at its banks had turned into five, into twenty, into thousands all over the world. I still did not understand how a simple command and act for me to go to the waters to help humanity had resulted in such an unfolding, such a blossoming that had affected not only me, but my entire family. It was all beyond the reach of my normal comprehension and I sincerely believed even our normal modern science. This journey belonged to the high science of our ancient fore fathers, and mothers. That I was convinced of. Wasn't it they who had codified the power that lay within watery spiritual DNA of the ancient Goddesses and Gods?

I wondered, truly wondered how I would explain such a journey as this to the world, its miraculous findings and powerful message to walk softly on our Earth, to honor her as a living sentient being as our fore parents had.

Derrick held me tighter as the skies were now completely washed with the energy of the sun. He loved the sun. As I watched it more intently greeting in our New Dawn I thought of another discussion we had recently had, this time with Linda Tucker, author of "Mystery of the White Lions". We interviewed her for the WaterSongline Round Table discussions held to help people prepare for and understand these times.

It was a fascinating conversation that was constantly interrupted by the challenges of technology, but we managed to get through it.

649

"I strongly resonate with the work you are doing with the waters. Us connecting makes total sense to me. The White Lions of South Africa are said to be celestial star beings that come to Earth in times when humanity is in need of remembering the cosmic balance of things again.

The Land they are born in Timbavati means in Zulu "The Place where the Starlions came down". This land is on the Golden Nile Meridian, and is in alignment with the Great Sphinx of Egypt. The Golden Nile Meridian is actually the central axis of the Earth. The White Lions and the Great Sphinx (which is the Lion energy) protects this meridian. It is important for this Meridian to always have balance, so that the world can have balance. It is said that there is an underground waterway and golden seam which runs the course of the whole continent of Africa. The river is called "The River of the Stars". It is the river that the White Lions protect. The Nile River is very sacred."

She continued,

"now this is very interesting. The prophecies of South Africa say that the Lion Queen and the Rain Queen had worked together to protect this central meridian and its celestial waters. The times we are moving into with this December 21st 2012 is the time of Zep Tepi. What the ancient Egyptian's called the First Times. We move into both the Age of Aquarius, but also the Age of Leo. It is a double age, although most people only mention Aquarius."

As she spoke I found this information resounding in the depth of an ancient memory in my cells. Something in me was stirred. The image of the Water Bearer and the White Lion keeping cosmic balance together filled me powerfully. So it is above, and so it is below, was all I could hear my spirit say. Yes, it was true for the Water Bearer and Lion Age were drawing in together to merge their energies again as protectors of the world.

I understood, I truly understood Linda's words not in my head, but deep in the stirrings of my soul. For had not the waters led me right there to Zep Tepi. The First Times, the well spring from which we all originated. The Golden Age. A time when we lived in balance with all things, when we knew our oneness with all things near, far and wide. I knew about Zep Tepi because of a book that had fallen in my lap just a few weeks ago about the Great Sphinx. Now I realized that it had, because it wanted me to be prepared for this conversation with Linda.

As Linda spoke with warmth and great enthusiasm, I could literally feel the White Lions at my side. At first I ignored the feeling but it would not go away. Yes, the thin skin between our time and the time we had closed our eyes to was definitely breaking. What the result of that breaking and merging of those waters would be I had no clue. In much the same way I had no clue as to how I had ended up being an avatar for the Mother energy.

I thought of my given titles, "Yeye Olomitutu-Mother Who Heals With Cool Waters", "Yeye Tayese, Mother Who Mends the World", and how my life over the last few years had been stranger than fiction. I thought of the man by my side, and how he had embraced his own spiritual walk and calling so that we could walk this brave path together.

I thought of my family and how all our footsteps had echoed along this great walk. The walk to the First Times, the First River. Then I thought about something that had been shared with us in another discussion with another beautiful soul who had made such great contributions to our humanity, Layne Redmond, author of "When the Women Were Drummers".

I remember how much her book had been a part of my journey, and how much I had admired her works. I felt awed at how serendipity had arranged for me to speak to her. I appreciated her sharing her thoughts about the importance of rhythm and how the women had been really the first custodians of the drums. I also appreciated her sharing with me how the first instruction I had "go to water" was not that strange after all.

"You know in Greek Mythology, the muses who give the arts, science and wisdom to the world live in the waters. In order to hear their song you have to go to the waters."

Latter I looked up the Greek Muses and discovered they numbered between seven and nine. It was clear to me that once again here we had the Seven Hathors. Yes, the story of the Mother, and the footsteps of our Humanity was right there in the waters, and somehow it had sung our song back to us. All we needed to do was listen. I suppose the way the women had listened to Osun's drum when the world was falling apart during a time when the women and men had become divided.

The King of the village so desperately wanted balance restored that he begged some of the highest most powerful individuals to end the war between the men and women. Each tried, and each failed.

Eventually Osun with a small drum went to the village of women and began to beat it. It was her drum beat that finally ended the division in the world as she led the women swaying back to the village of men. My conversation with Layne Redmond helped me to re-visit this story. Now I understood it not from my head, but with my heart.

Yes, we must return back to the primordial beat of the Mother's drum. The original waters of the wisdom of compassion. It seems to be the only way, and the only song that we should embrace. It is the song of Zep Tepi, the First Times. It is the river from whence the entire river of humanity came from.

As I thought of all these things, and as I thought of this incredibly exhausting journey I could not help but bow deeply to the Water Mothers who worked hard to dream us all awake, again.

This is a beautiful picture Linda Tucker e-mailed to me.
She revealed, "here are two powerful images of the Akeru,
the two White Lion brothers who guard the east-west
axis of the Nile Meridian. Their name refers to the
back-to-back Egyptian lion god, who guards
the sun rising on the east
and setting on the west, and may be seen depicted
beneath on the stone Stella beneath the paws
of the Sphinx."

Goddess Family Tree

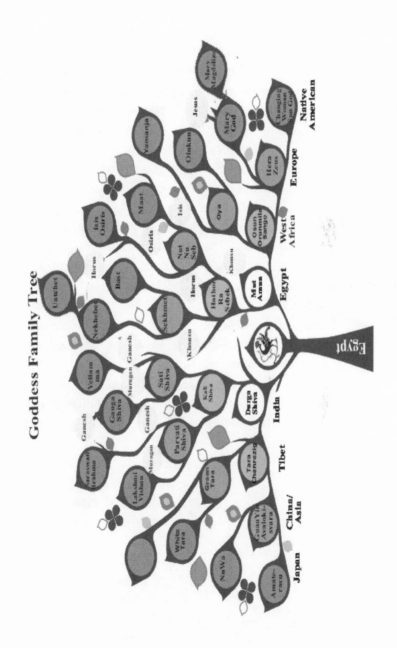

The Goddess Family Tree

Amongst the Aborigine it is said that the Songline traverses across landscapes, cultures, traditions and languages. It stretches and crisscrosses over the entire earth. Containing the traditional songs, stories, and symbols of the Dreamtime, it is said when the Songline is song then the land continues to live (the opposite is true if it is not).

As I travelled across the Mythological and real waterways the symbols, stories, mythologies of Mother Goddesses from different cultures began to connect. In doing so they began to awaken the long forgotten Songline of our humanity. One that needs to be song to the zenith right now.

Following the watery footprints of the Mothers and joining them together was no small task (often quite head banging actually). Now five years latter I can truly say it was a soul quenching journey. (I hope my husband thinks so too!)

I have produced a Goddess Family Tree that allows you to visually connect with the names you meet in the book. They are names that come up often. Using a tree to display their names seemed like the most logical choice. For the Goddess is the tree from which she nourishes us with her waters (this iconography is seen with Hathor the grand Egyptian Mother Goddess). Also the rivers form a tree, and each Mother Goddess that bowed and made her appearance was often connected to water. The story of our humanity formed a connective tree from which we can nourish ourselves again.

How to Read the Tree

So how does one read the tree? That's a good question. Throughout my journey I began to realize that each culture had a Mother Goddess composite (essentially a group of

Goddesses whom are all connected to each other). I also noticed that these composites were intricately connected to each other, and essentially constituted one Mother Goddess.

The lower branch of the tree contains the names of the Goddesses that helped to lead each composite. So there is the Mut Composite from Egypt (which is really headed up by Hathor), Durga Composite from India, Tara Composite from Tibet, Guan Yin Composite from Japan, and so forth. When you look above each of the Goddess's names on the lower branch, you will see their relatives on the connecting branches which spread upward.

Who's Related to Who?

I discovered the Mother Goddess essentially has two sides: 1. The destructive compassionate side which protects universal balance. 2. The soft, joyful, creative, life giving side which reflects our true nature once the inner demons have been conquered. So without further delay here's who is who on the tree, and according to what I found in my research.

Mut Composite - Egypt

Mut: She is the Egyptian Mother Goddess who was married to Amun. This composite is named after her because she from many eons ago fused with all the Mother Goddesses mentioned in her grouping. However, it is Hathor who really leads the pact.

Hathor: She is the leader of the pact and she absorbed all aspects of the Mother Goddesses over time.

The Seven Hathors: Often numbered seven or more Goddesses whom represented aspects of Hathor.

Sekhmet and Bast: They are the fierce compassionate sides of Hathor.

Sati: is another aspect of Hathor. In fact she is a Hathor/Isis combination. Her name means amongst many things, "she who scatters her seeds abroad".

Nut: She is the primordial watery mass, and she is also an aspect of Hathor. They both share the sacred cow iconography.

Net/Neith: She is the Goddess of the hunt and weaving who wears a weaving shuttle on her head. She is another aspect of Hathor.

Maat: She is like all the Goddesses, a Goddess in her own right, but she is also the Wisdom aspect of Hathor. Hathor has other Wisdom aspects including the Goddess Mehurt. Maat is the Mother who embodies the dharma, the way of balance.

Horus and Khonsu: They are both the children of Hathor. Horus is also the child of Isis.

Osiris: is the husband of Isis. By association, through Horus, he is also the husband of Hathor.

Ra: is the husband and father of Hathor.

Osiris/Ra: It is this divine male combination which travelled and was also spreading the wisdom of the Maat/dharma across the waters.

Osun Composite – West Africa

Osun: She is the ultimate Mother of all. She embodies many of the aspects of Hathor/Isis/ - Sekhmet

Oya: She is the compassionate fierce side of the Mother Goddess, and aligns herself with Sekhmet of Egypt.

Yemanja: Is closely associated with Isis, and the gentle life giving energy aspect of the Mother Goddess.

Olukun: Relates to the primordial waters of Nu and Nut. Olukun has a feminine and masculine aspect and is the God/Goddess of wealth that comes from the deep oceans.

Orunmila: Is the Wisdom God, who closely relates to Osiris. He is Osun's husband.

Esu: The son of Osun and Orunmila, closely relates to Khonsu, and even has aspects of Tehuti/Toth in him. The latter was the God of words.

Durga Composite - India

Durga and Kali: Are the grandmothers of this composite. Both Durga and Kali are manifestations of each other. They are the compassionate de-constructive aspect of the Goddess. Who deconstructs in order to re-build. She is aligned with the Egyptian Mother Goddesses Sekhmet and Bast. They by the way share the same iconographies and stories.

Parvati: Is the gentle side of Durga and Kali. She is aligned with the Egyptian Goddess Hathor/Isis. Her previous incarnation is Sati, who is aligned with the Hathor/Isis manifestation - Sati.

Lakshmi and Saraswati: Are the daughters of Parvati, and Durga. They both are aligned quite perfectly with Hathor's Wisdom and life giving aspects.

The Seven/Ten Mothers: are Goddesses who are represented as a group face of the Mother Goddess. They came forth from Durga (the Mothers/Seven Mothers), and Sati (the Ten Mothers). They are closely associated with the Seven Hathors.

Trimurti (Three Forms). These are the Gods who make up a trinity: *Shiva*: is the husband of Durga, Parvati, and Kali which connects these three Goddesses together. He is the God of Transformation and Destruction. He is aligned with Osiris. *Vishnu* is the God of Perseveration whose incarnations are said to preserve and protect the dharma. He is associated with Ra. *Brahma* is the Creator God, and he is associated with Ra. In this journey it became very clear that the Trimurti was a Ra/Osiris composite that travelled with the Mother Goddess from Egypt. The stories and symbols match quite well.

Ganesh and Murugan: are the children of Parvati, Durga, and Ganga. They align perfectly with Hathor and Isis Children Khensu and Horus.

Tara Composite, Tibet

Tara: She has many aspects but her Green and White Tara manifestations are the most popular. The Green Tara represents the protective and re-constructive energy aspect of the Mother Goddess. While the White Tara is aligned with the Mother Goddesses energy and life giving aspects. Tara is closely aligned through stories and symbols with Durga, and Hathor/Sekhmet.

Chenrenzig: Tara was birthed from a tear from Chenrenzig's eye. He is another name for Avalokishavra, and is the Buddha of Compassion (whom His Holiness the Dalai Lama is an incarnation of). Chenrenzig is closely aligned with the Ra/Osiris combination.

Guan Yin Composite, China

Guan Yin: Is the Mother Goddess who was birthed from the tear of Avalokishavra. Guan Yin is non-other than Tara. Guan Yin is actually honored not just in China but also in many areas of Asia.

Nu Wa: She is the Chinese Mother Goddess who helps to mend and save the world. The stories and iconography of several Chinese Mother Goddess or figures connect them with Hathor, Nu, and Mut.

Avalokishavra: Gave birth to Tara from a teardrop from his eye. He is closely aligned with the Ra/Osiris combination. He is also Chenrezig (Buddha of Compassion).

Amaterasu Composite, Japan

Amaterasu: She is the Japanese ancestress. The great Mother of the Japanese people and royal house. She helps to save the world with her radiant brilliance, her iconography associates her with weaving and closely aligns her to Hathor.

Changing Woman, Native American

Changing Woman: is the ancestress of the Navajo. There are a few other Native American Goddesses. However, changing woman is the one who appeared to close the circle.

Dates of the Goddesses

The stories and symbols of the Mother Goddess across continents, cultures and languages were the footprints that helped me to connect our humanity and humanitarian world spiritual tradition together. It was later down the road I decided to research their dates. They confirmed the findings, and thank goodness. The dates can look rather confusing on their own.

Essentially what is revealed through the Goddess iconographies, stories and dates is a story of Dharma (Maat). The river of dharma seemed to have two flows. One that took a route straight out of Ancient Egypt/Africa into the rest of the world; and one that took the route out of Ancient Egypt/Africa, through Greece/Rome and into the rest of the world. The dates below help to place the Mother Goddesses in their respective orders.

Egypt/Africa
Hathor - 6000 BC

Hathor is mentioned in pyramid text 3100 BC. She said to be a pre-dynastic Goddess. Pre-dynastic Egypt dates back to 6000 BC

Osun

She is the spiritual Queen of Osogbo Nigeria. The Yoruba say she is the World Mother to all. The first King of Osogbo dates back to 1760. However, it is said Osun was there long before the place now known as Osogbo was even established.

India
Durga/Kali– 2900 BC-1900 BC (Dravidian Goddesses, Pre-Aryan)

Durga/Kali are said to be pre-Aryan, Dravidian. The Dravidian Indus civilizations dated from around 2900 BC to 1900 BC so it is most certain that Durga too dated from this period. The image of her famous slaying of the demon became popular in written text in 400 A.D. By 600 AD she became very popular. In terms of Kali, she is first mentioned in written sacred text around 600 AD

The Seven Mothers whom Durga manifested for battle against the Demons are mentioned in written text in latter Hinduism. However, they appear on coins in the Indus Valley which are dated back to that period 2900 BC – 1900 BC. The Ten Mothers whom Sati – Parvati brought forth from herself which include Kali and Tara became popular in latter Hindu period

Saraswati – 2900 BC-1900 BC (Dravidian Goddess, Pre-Aryan)

Saraswati is first mentioned in the Vedic Text Rig Veda which date to 1500 – 1000 BC. Scholars say she is Aryan, although it is obvious that she is not when one sees her family tree connections and her similarities to the Egyptian Goddess Hathor.

Tibet
Tara – 617 AD

Tara is often closely associated with Kali and she is a manifestation of Durga/Kali. She is identified as wife of one of first Tibetan Kings, Songsten gampo who dates back from 617 AD to 650 AD. David Kingsley states the earliest written reference to Tara is in Subandhu's Vasavadatta which was written in 700 AD. Tara is also the same as Guan Yin

China
Guan Yin

Could not get an exact date for Guan Yin. However, she is the female aspect of Avalokiteshvara, and it is said that she was introduced into China about 100 AD. She was said to be introduced into Japan about mid-7th century.

Europe
Hera, and Greek Goddesses, 400 BC

Hera's earliest temple constructed to her was about 450 BC. Athena was identified by Greek Plato with Goddess Neith about 429 BC-347 BC. Many of the Greek Gods and Goddess are known to be aligned with Egyptian Gods and Goddesses.

Mary, 100 Or 200 AD

Appears first in Gnostic text such as the Nag Hammadi which dates back to 100 or 200 AD. Mary Magdalene is also dated to about 100 or 200 AD. Interesting that in the Gnostic text Jesus was said to go to the mountain of joy to preach with seven women. This seems to most probably refer to the group of Seven Hathors.

Native American
Changing Woman

Could not locate exact date.

Symbolism of the Goddess

Altogether the Symbols and iconography of the Archetypal image of the Mother leads us back to wholeness.

Mirror

Held by Goddesses such as: Osun, Hathor, Sherap Chamma, and Aphrodite, the mirror helps us to illuminate the truth of existence. It helps us to see beyond the physical self and into life's deeper truths.

Peacock

Is a symbol that unifies many Goddesses: such as: Osun, Saraswati, Guan Yin, Hera (Hathor is often depicted with peacock feathers in modern iconography, however she wasn't in Egyptian sacred drawings. The peacock is in fact a symbol from latter history). It represents glory, vision, royalty, spirituality, awakening, immortality, refinement, incorruptibility, and protection.

Water and the Water Vase

Hathor, Durga, Saraswati, Ganga, Nu Wa, Osun, Isis, Nu, Kuan Yin, Tara and others – have water, the Water Vase or Vase of Elixir associated with them. Water represents that which nurtures, fertilizes, and replenishes life. It is often seen as the body of the Goddess. The water or elixir from this vase is seen to have healing powers over all ailments.

Feather

Was associated with such Goddesses as Maat, Osun, and Guan Yin. It represents the laws of Maat/Dharma, and the ability to live life according to universal truth and balance.

Weaving & Plaiting

Associated with Goddesses such as Hathor, Osun, Changing Woman, Amaterasu. It highlights her role as she joins the fabric of life and existence together.

Sacred Wisdom

The Goddess in her forms such as Maat, Osun, Hathor, Osun, Saraswati – is associated with being the gatekeeper and holder of wisdom.

The Wadjet, Third Eye

The Wadjet was the Snake Goddess of Lower Egypt. Her symbol the eye also came to be associated with the God Horus, Hathor and others. It symbolizes protection, royal power, and protection. Guan Yin, Tara, and Amaterasu are all connected with this symbol.

Bell & Musical Instruments

Goddesses such as Hathor, Osun, and Saraswati have the bell, Sistrum, and other musical instruments associated with them. They remind us to tune our mind and intellect in order to live in harmony with the world.

Lotus

Is held by many Goddesses across the world. The Lotus grows in mud, rises above the water and opens to the sunlight. It represents the blossoming of spirituality, and the fragrant enlightened mind. Hathor, Durga, Parvati, Tara, Lakshmi, Saraswati and others are all associated with Lotus.

The Sword &Weapons

The Goddess's weapons signify the need to cut through the ego in order to liberate the higher self dedicated to living with true abundance and life balance.

Celestial Cow, Tree, Honey Bee

From her sacred udders the world below was nourished. Goddesses such as Hathor, Nut, Saraswati appear as the sacred Cow. The tree and the honey bee is also a form of the Goddess from which she nourishes mankind. The original tree was Hathor, who was the sycamore tree which in land of dead is said to be turquoise. Tara is also associated with turquois sycamore tree.

Map of Egypt 1450 BC From The Historical Atlas by William R. Shepherd, 1923.
Which shows the location of Upper Egypt, the Kingdom of Kush (Nubia) and Ethiopia (which was seen as Nubia)

THE BOOK OF GOING FORTH BY DAY
(THE BOOK OF THE DEAD)

42nd negative confession
I have not polluted the water

BIBLIOGRAPHY

Achikeobi-Lewis, Omileye. Dreamtime Awakening. Naked Truth Press, 2010

Badejo, Deidre. Osunseegesi. African World Press, 1996

Bohm, David. Wholeness and Implicate Order. Routlege, 2002

Brauen Martin, Mandala. Arnoldsche Verlagsanstaff, 2009

Budge, Wallis. The Egyptian Book of the Dead. Barnes & Noble, 2005

Budge, Wallis. The Gods of Egypt Vol I. Dover Publications, Inc, 1996

Budge, Wallis. The Gods of Egypt Vol II. Dover Publications, 1996

Campbell, Joseph. The Hero With a Thousand Faces. Princeton University Press, 1968

Campbell, Joseph. The Power of Myth. Anchor Books, 1991

Campbell, Joseph. Pathways to Bliss. New World Library, 2004

Cook, Francis. Hua Yen Buddhism. The Jewel Net of Indra. Pennsylvania State University Press, 1973

Dalai Lama; Vreelan Nicholas. An Open Heart. Back Bay Books, 2002

Dalai Lama. The Heart of Compassion. Lotus Press, 2002

Evans-Wentz, W.Y. Tibetan Book of the Dead. Metro Books, 2008

Conzo, Edward. Buddhism. One World, 2007

Gold, Peter. Navajo & Tibetan Sacred Wisdom. The Circle of the Spirit. Inner Traditions, 1994

Gore, Al. Earth in Balance. Rodale, 2006

Gray, Martin. Sacred Earth. Sterling, 2007

Iyengar, B.K.S. Light on Life. Rodale, 2005

Jacobs, Alan. The Essential Gnostic Gospels. Watkins Publishing, 2009

Kingsley, R.David. Hindu Goddesses. University of California Press, 1998

Murphey, Joseph; Sanford Mei Mei. Osun Across the Waters. Indiana University Press, 2001

Narby, Jeremy. Cosmic Serpent. Penguin, 1998

Perry, Cheryl. Egypt: Land and Lives of the Pharaohs Revealed. Global Book, 2006

Redmond, Layne. When the Women Were Drummers. Three Rivers Press, 1997

Ritcher, Barbara. Beautiful Hymn of the Seven Hathors (translation of sacred verses)

Shrestha Romia. Buddhas of the Celestial Gallery. Mandala Publishing, 2012

Singh, Karan. Essays on Hinduism. South Asia Books, 1998

Staff member. Land of the Dragon. Duncan Baird Publishers, 2005

Stone, Merlin. When God Was a Woman. Paradise Papers, 1976

ILLUSTRATION CREDITS

Unless otherwise stated picture credits belong to Omileye Achikeobi-Lewis or Derrick Lewis

Page 55, photo by Derrick & Omi

Page 56, photo by Derrick & Omi

Page 96, photo by Unknown

Page 97, picture by Kartapranata

Page 121, photo by Derrick & Omi

Page 123, photo by Andrew Hancock

Page 126, photo by Mkeranat

Page 141, photo , Wiki Media Common

Page 172, photo by Rotate the Globe

Page 180, photo by Derrick & Omi

Page 181, photo by Derrick & Omi

Page 182, photo by Derrick & Omi

Page183, photo by Derrick & Omi

Page 184, photo by Derrick & Omi

Page 207, photo by Derrick & Omi

Page 208, photo by Derrick & Omi

Page 235, photo by European Southern Observatory

Page 236, photo by Golden Meadows

Page 270, photo by Derrick & Omi

Page 271, photo by Derrick & Omi

Page 272, photo by Derrick & Omi

Page 313, photo by Derrick and Omi

Page 349, photo by Joe Ravi

Page 349, photo by Mcleod

Page 350, photo by Raji Ravi

Page 351, photo by Wiki Media Common

Page 369, photo by Anizotropia

Page 373, photo by Mathias Kabel

Page 397, photo by unknown author

Page 404, photo by PD India

Page 405, photo by Vishal Piakash

Page 420, photo by Rama

Index

676

677

681